Structure, Culture and Agency

Professor Margaret Archer is a leading critical realist and major contemporary social theorist. This edited collection seeks to celebrate the scope and accomplishments of her work, distilling her theoretical and empirical contributions into four sections which capture the essence and trajectory of her research over almost four decades. Long fascinated with the problem of structure and agency, Archer's work has constituted a decade-long engagement with this perennial issue of social thought. However, in spite of the deep interconnections that unify her body of work, it is rarely treated as a coherent whole. This is doubtless in part due to the unforgiving rigour of her arguments and prose, but is also a byproduct of sociology's ongoing compartmentalisation.

This edited collection seeks to address this relative neglect by collating a selection of papers, spanning Archer's career, which collectively elucidate both the development of her thought and the value that can be found in it as a systematic whole. This book illustrates the empirical origins of her social ontology in her early work on the sociology of education, as well as foregrounding the diverse range of influences that have conditioned her intellectual trajectory: the systems theory of Walter Buckley, the neo-Weberian analysis of Lockwood, the critical realist philosophy of Roy Bhaskar and, more recently, her engagement with American pragmatism and the Italian school of relational sociology. What emerges is a series of important contributions to our understanding of the relationship between structure, culture and agency. Acting to introduce and guide readers through these contributions, this book carries the potential to inform exciting and innovative sociological research.

Tom Brock is Lecturer in the department of Sociology at Manchester Metropolitan University, UK.

Mark Carrigan is Research Fellow in the Centre for Social Ontology at the University of Warwick, UK.

Graham Scambler is Emeritus Professor of Sociology at UCL, UK, and Visiting Professor of Sociology at Surrey University, UK.

Ontological Explorations

Other titles in this series

The Politics of Childhoods Real and Imagined
Volume 2: practical application of critical realism and childhood studies
Priscilla Alderson

Critical Realism, Environmental Learning and Social-Ecological Change
Edited by Leigh Price and Heila Lotz-Sisitka

Metatheory for the Twenty-First Century
Critical realism and integral theory in dialogue
Edited by Roy Bhaskar, Sean Esbjörn-Hargens, Nicholas Hedlund and Mervyn Hartwig

The Post-Mobile Society
From the smart/mobile to second offline
Edited by Hidenori Tomita

Enlightened Common Sense
The philosophy of critical realism
Roy Bhaskar

A Complex Integral Realist Perspective
Towards a new axial vision
Paul Marshall

Crisis System
A critical realist and environmental critique of economics and the economy
Edited by Petter Næss and Leigh Price

Structure, Culture and Agency
Selected Papers of Margaret Archer
Edited by Tom Brock, Mark Carrigan and Graham Scambler

Structure, Culture and Agency
Selected Papers of Margaret Archer

Edited by Tom Brock, Mark Carrigan and Graham Scambler

LONDON AND NEW YORK

First published 2017
by Routledge
2 Park Square, Milton Park, Abingdon, Oxon OX14 4RN

and by Routledge
711 Third Avenue, New York, NY 10017

Routledge is an imprint of the Taylor & Francis Group, an informa business

© 2017 selection and editorial matter, Tom Brock, Mark Carrigan and Graham Scambler; individual chapters, the contributors.

The right of Tom Brock, Mark Carrigan and Graham Scambler to be identified as the authors of the editorial material, and of the authors for their individual chapters, has been asserted in accordance with sections 77 and 78 of the Copyright, Designs and Patents Act 1988.

All rights reserved. No part of this book may be reprinted or reproduced or utilised in any form or by any electronic, mechanical, or other means, now known or hereafter invented, including photocopying and recording, or in any information storage or retrieval system, without permission in writing from the publishers.

Trademark notice: Product or corporate names may be trademarks or registered trademarks, and are used only for identification and explanation without intent to infringe.

British Library Cataloguing in Publication Data
A catalogue record for this book is available from the British Library

Library of Congress Cataloging in Publication Data
A catalog record for this book has been requested

ISBN: 978-1-138-93294-4 (hbk)
ISBN: 978-1-315-67887-0 (ebk)

Typeset in Times New Roman
by Sunrise Setting Ltd., Brixham, UK

Printed and bound by CPI Group (UK) Ltd, Croydon, CR0 4YY

Contents

Foreword		vii
Acknowledgements		x
Introduction		xiii
	Morphogenesis: realism's explanatory framework	1
1	Thinking and theorizing about educational systems	36
2	On predicting the behaviour of the educational system	50
3	The myth of cultural integration	59
4	The vexatious fact of society	77
5	Morphogenesis versus structuration: on combining structure and action	102
6	For structure: its reality, properties and powers: a reply to Anthony King	128
7	The private life of the social agent: what difference does it make?	138
8	The ontological status of subjectivity: the missing link between structure and agency	151
9	Reflexivity as the unacknowledged condition of social life	165
10	A brief history of how reflexivity becomes imperative	184

11	Morphogenic society: self-government and self-organization as misleading metaphors	215
12	The generative mechanism reconfiguring Late Modernity	235
13	How agency is transformed in the course of social transformation: don't forget the double morphogenesis	259
	The trajectory of the morphogenetic approach: an account in the first person	282
	Interview with Maggie	293
	Structure, Culture and Agency: selected papers of Margaret Archer: annotated bibliography	306
	Index	314

Foreword

It is my honor and great pleasure to have been invited to write this Foreword to the collected work of Margaret (or Maggie, as she prefers) Archer. In one sense, of course, the collection is a deserved tribute that expresses how the collectors feel about her. The collection, however, is primarily meant as a service to the field. The fact is that, although critical realists span multiple disciplines – philosophy, theology, education, business organization and more – among sociologists, Maggie Archer stands first. Her work, most well-known and most drawn-upon, represents what I have elsewhere called the canonical positions of critical realism in sociology. It thus is a service to scholars concerned with critical realism that encapsulated here in this collection are Archer's most seminal statements.

In this brief Foreword, I want to identify what I consider the crux of Archer's work. But first I would like to take the opportunity to say something about her as a person. In his *Sacred Project of American Sociology*, Christian Smith describes meetings of the American Sociology Association (ASA) as "tediously stratified," where "the 'best' sociologists largely circulate and talk with their own kind ... In fact, most of everyone's eye movements at the ASA meetings involve checking out other people's name tags, hung unceremoniously from lanyards around their necks, to see if their names are recognizable and at what college or university they work."[1]

All I can say is that, both as a person and as a sociologist, Maggie Archer displays no such status-orientation. As the biblical passage puts it, she is no "respecter of persons," meaning that she is not one to differentiate by social class. Instead, Archer always, in my experience, distinguishes rather by cogency of thought, finding it, if anything, more among the obscure than among the prominent. In comparison, then, with what characterizes ASA meetings, Archer's personal and professional openness is very refreshing.

But let me turn to the work. Clearly, Archer's work spans decades and develops over time. The present collection marks that development. Clearly, I cannot comment on it all. What I can do is identify what I believe is key to it all, namely two related positions: Analytical Dualism and the Morphogenetic/Morphostatic (MM) approach. As the latter depends on the former, I will begin with that.

Contemporary sociology is largely uncomfortable with binary distinctions. It is uncomfortable with the realist distinction between subject and object; it is uncomfortable with the distinction between culture and agency; equally uncomfortable with the distinction between structure and agency; and uncomfortable even with the distinction between culture and structure.

That discomfort has led to all kinds of collapse or, in Archer's word, conflation. For pragmatist and Bourdieusean perspectives, both widespread, the distinction between subject and object and other such putatively Cartesian oppositions are to be overcome either by some sort of non-realist dialectic or by the concept of habitus. With the so-called *cultural turn*, social or organizational structure was swallowed by culture (i.e., reduced to rules or schema), and, then, with the so-called *practice turn*, culture (and with it now structure) has been conflated with practice (agency). The end is Hegel's "night in which all cows are black." Lost, that is, are the distinct concepts through which to unravel different kinds of social causality.

Against this conflationist tendency stands Archer's analytical dualism. The designation may now be somewhat misleading as there are several dualisms Archer seeks to preserve. In *Culture and Agency* Archer sought to defend an analytical distinction between culture and agency. In *Realist Social Theory* she similarly argued for an analytical distinction between structure and agency. And, certainly, Archer affirms a distinction between culture and social structure. Thus, after Archer's (2013) "Social Morphogenesis and the Prospects of Morphogenetic Society," the more encompassing statement of position may be what Archer calls SAC, the defense of structure, agency, and culture as three distinct ontological features of social reality, which, however intertwined empirically, need to be sorted out analytically in social explanation.

How the three get sorted out leads to the MM approach. The words morphogenesis and morphostasis look more imposing than they actually are. They refer to change or constancy of social form, and that change or constancy involve dialectical (i.e., interactive) relationships over time between social form (structure and culture) and agency. I personally relate the point to Marx's dictum that people make their own history but not under circumstances of their own making. The analytical dualism here distinguishes both the original and resulting circumstances or conditions from the agential making or doing people perform in between.

The circumstances in which people find themselves – and which they either reproduce or change – are both cultural and structural. Thus, there are distinct cultural and structural MM cycles that themselves intertwine, complicating the empirical analysis of actual processes. But unless the analytical distinctions associated with SAC are maintained, explanation will lapse, as it often does in sociology, into subjectivism, interactionism, or positivistic sociological holism. Together, SAC and the MM approach are the more abstract, meta-theoretical principles that ward against such adverse analytical tendencies.

I call Archer's SAC, the MM approach, and the associated conceptions of structure and culture the canonical positions among critical realist sociologists mainly to register their lack of universal embrace among us. There are critical realist sociologists who disagree with some elements. But it was Archer who convinced Roy Bhaskar that his original *Transformational Model of Social Action* (TMSA) was too beholden to the conflations of Giddens's *structuration theory*; and it is

Archer whose views remain dominant among critical realist sociologists. And, together, SAC and the MM approach are key to Archer's views.

Doug Porpora

Note

1 Christian Smith, *The Sacred Project of American Sociology* (Oxford, New York: Oxford University Press, 2014), pp. 136–7.

Reference

1 Archer, M.S. (2013) "Social Morphogenesis and the Prospects of Morphogenetic Society," in Archer, M.S. (ed.), *Social Morphogenesis*. New York: Springer, pp. 1–22.

Acknowledgements

The work in this collection has been published previously in a variety of different forms. We would like to thank the publishers for granting permission to use the following copyright material:

Realism's explanatory framework was first published as Margaret S. Archer, 'Morphogenesis: realism's explanatory framework', in A. Maccarini, E. Morandi and R. Prandini (eds), *Sociological Realism* (Abingdon: Routledge, 2011). Published by Taylor & Francis Ltd. Reprinted by permission of the publisher.

Chapter One was first published as Margaret S. Archer, 'Thinking and theorizing about educational systems', in M.S. Archer, *Social Origins of Educational Systems* (Abingdon: Routledge, 2013 [1979]), pp. 1–53. Published by Taylor & Francis Ltd. Reprinted by permission of the publisher.

Chapter Two was first published as Margaret S. Archer, 'Review: on predicting the behaviour of the educational system', *British Journal of Sociology of Education*, 2/2 (1981), pp. 211–19. Published by Taylor & Francis Ltd. Reprinted by permission of the publisher.

Chapter Three was first published as Margaret S. Archer, 'The myth of cultural integration', *The British Journal of Sociology*, 36/3 (1985), pp. 333–53. Published by Wiley on behalf of London School of Economics and Political Science. Reprinted by permission of the publisher.

Chapter Four was first published as Margaret S. Archer, 'The vexatious fact of society', in M.S. Archer, *Realist Social Theory: The Morphogenetic Approach* (Cambridge: Cambridge University Press, 1995), pp. 1–30. Reprinted by permission of the publisher.

Chapter Five was first published as Margaret S. Archer, 'Morphogenesis versus structuration: on combining structure and action', *The British Journal of Sociology*, 33/4 (1982), pp. 455–83. © London School of Economics and Political Science 2010. Published by Wiley on behalf of The London School of Economics and Political Science. Reprinted by permission of the publisher.

Chapter Six was first published as Margaret S. Archer, 'For structure: its reality, properties and powers: a reply to Anthony King', *The Sociological Review*, 48/3 (2000), pp. 464–72. Published by Wiley. Reprinted by permission of the publisher.

Chapter Seven was first published as Margaret S. Archer, 'The private life of the social agent: what difference does it make?', in J. Cruickshank (ed.), *Critical Realism: The Difference it Makes* (Abingdon: Routledge, 2003), pp. 17–29. Published by Taylor & Francis, Ltd. Reprinted by permission of the publisher.

Chapter Eight was first published as Margaret S. Archer, 'The ontological status of subjectivity: the missing link between structure and agency', in Clive Lawson, John Latsis and Nuno Martins (eds), *Contributions to Social Ontology* (Abingdon: Routledge, 2007), pp. 17–31. Published by Taylor & Francis, Ltd. Reprinted by permission of the publisher.

Chapter Nine was first published as Margaret S. Archer, 'Introduction: reflexivity as the unacknowledged condition of social life', in M.S. Archer, *Making our Way through the World: Human Reflexivity and Social Mobility* (Cambridge: Cambridge University Press, 2007), pp. 1–22. Reprinted by permission of the publisher.

Chapter Ten was first published as Margaret S. Archer, 'A brief history of how reflexivity becomes imperative', in M.S. Archer, *The Reflexive Imperative in Late Modernity* (Cambridge: Cambridge University Press, 2012), pp. 10–46. Reprinted by permission of the publisher.

Chapter Eleven was first published as Margaret S. Archer, 'Morphogenic society: self-government and self-organization as misleading metaphors', in M.S. Archer, *Social Morphogenesis* (Dordrecht: Springer, 2013), pp. 145–64. © Springer Science +Business Media Dordrecht 2013. Reprinted by permission of Springer.

Chapter Twelve was first published as Margaret S. Archer, 'The generative mechanism re-configuring late modernity', in M.S. Archer, *The Reflexive Imperative in Late Modernity* (Cambridge: Cambridge University Press, 2012), pp. 93–117. © Springer International Publishing Switzerland 2014. Reprinted with kind permission of Springer Science+Business Media.

Chapter Thirteen was first published as Margaret S. Archer, 'How agency is transformed in the course of social transformation: don't forget the double morphogenesis', in M.S. Archer, *Generative Mechanisms Transforming the Social Order* (Cham: Springer, 2015), pp. 135–57. © Springer International Publishing Switzerland 2015. Reprinted with kind permission of Springer Science+Business Media.

Trajectory of the Morphogenetic Approach was originally published as Margaret S. Archer, 'The trajectory of the morphogenetic approach: an account in the first-person', *Sociologia problemas e práticas*, 54 (2007), pp. 35–47. Reprinted with permission of the publisher.

Every effort has been made to contact copyright holders for their permission to reprint material in this book. The publishers would be grateful to hear from any copyright holder who is not here acknowledged and will undertake to rectify any errors or omissions in future editions of this book.

Introduction

Tom Brock, Mark Carrigan and Graham Scambler

The editors' rationale for accumulating and making more accessible some of the key writings of Margaret Archer is straightforward enough. We see her as a major contemporary sociological theorist whose work has yet to receive the attention and dissemination it so richly deserves. This is doubtless in part due to the unforgiving rigour of her arguments and prose, but maybe it is a byproduct too of sociology's ongoing compartmentalization. Its mainstream theory and multiple substantive areas of research and application have tended to become detached. Archer's contributions carry the potential to bridge theory and research.

We are stuck with theory, like it or not, Archer has argued ('people in the street are social theorists'). In a recent interview she gives an example she has long deployed in first-year undergraduate teaching (Cale and Roll 2015, 159–60). She shows them a PowerPoint slide of a couple, perhaps in their mid-80s, or maybe their mid-70s if they have endured a harder than average life. They are talking to each other, possibly pondering plans for the future. There are objective considerations: they have some savings, a monthly income from the state, an occupational pension perhaps, and they enjoy a measure of intermittent financial support from family members. 'So, that's their objective base.'

And then came the financial crisis of 2008, leading to austerity and all but the 1 per cent being worse off. Our couple cannot afford to live as they did, but what do they spend less on? For many a social theorist the answer is obvious, even 'logical': it is luxuries that are cut first, then heating is traded off against eating, and so on. But what constitutes a 'luxury'? One British survey found that a luxury for some was the 'expensive' landline phone. To return to Archer's couple: they have kids, and these progeny want to move away, a common step in an increasingly mobile society. The landline would be a lifeline, what in her *Being Human* Archer (2000) calls a *primary concern*, for this ageing duo wanting to stay in touch with their kids and their grandchildren. It is not a luxury for them. Their 'personal subjectivity' becomes salient, 'but it's not free and unconstrained'. They must live within reduced means. Within these constraints, however, 'they do have degrees of agential freedom'. What they care about most will become their priority. Theory has a foothold here.

Now consider whether or not gender is pertinent. Do women want to keep in touch with their kids and grandkids more than men? If so, this is likely just a convention, so how did this convention arise? Is it an essentially British convention, or maybe one associated with particular ethnic groups? 'Once you start theorizing you can go on forever because one question and the answer to it leads on to the next one ... So, we just can't stop being theorists. It's not an option in life. All that's optional is which kind of theory you advance and on what grounds are you selecting one kind of theoretical position over another' (Cale and Roll 2015, 161–2).

Educational systems

The nub of Archer's sociology is in this telling excursion. It reflects and announces her career-long interest in the relations between *structure* and *agency*. It is an interest that can be traced back to her time as a post-doctoral student at the Sorbonne, which coincided with the explosive events of 1968. Part of Pierre Bourdieu's team, her research focused on a comparative study of national education systems. It struck her that the centralized structure of the French educational system was equally central to any credible account of the political outburst that nearly brought down the Fifth Republic. Her *Social Origins of Educational Systems*, published in 1979, broke new ground and has been a catalyst for subsequent macro-analyses. Her core claim was that centralization was crucial in accounting for what happened in French education, and decentralization no less crucial in accounting for what happened in British education. How did the former come to be centralized, she asked, and the latter decentralized?

In a nutshell she argued that, prior to the emergence of state systems of education, the church played a pivotal and dominant role in terms of both resources and curricula. Education was in this sense 'mono-integrated' with the church. In the event of increasing state intervention, however, this mono-integration was displaced by 'multi-integration' with a plurality of institutions. State intervention and its concomitant multi-integration have characterized the (less constrained) British education system far more than its (more constrained) French counterpart.

Archer presented each of centralization and decentralization as 'emergent properties', highlighting the ways the different parts of each system are linked together. Significantly, her thesis not only featured an early contribution to the macro-sociology of educational systems and the structure–agency debate but also introduced her 'morphogenetic approach'. The transition prompted by state intervention in education comprised a 'morphogenetic cycle'. Structural conditioning (which is temporally prior, relatively autonomous yet possessive of causal powers), she maintained, conditions social interaction, which in its turn generates structural elaboration. This scheme – structural conditioning underlying/leading to social interaction underlying/leading to structural elaboration – has underpinned all her subsequent writings. It made its embryonic presence known in *Social origins of Education Systems*.

Archer (2007a, 38) later reflected further on where state education systems came from and what novel causal powers they exerted after their elaboration, writing:

> these powers work as underlying generative mechanisms, producing empirical tendencies in relation to 'who' gained access to education, 'what' constituted

the definition of instruction, 'which' processes became responsible for subsequent educational change, and 'how' those ensuing changes were patterned. Crucially, the answers to all these questions differed according to the 'centralised' or 'decentralised' structuring of the new educational systems. This raised a major philosophical problem. It was being claimed that educational systems possessed properties emergent from the relations between their parts – summarized as centralization and decentralisation – that exercised causal powers. However, these two properties could not be attributes of people, who cannot be centralized or decentralized, just as no system can possess the reflexivity, intentionality and commitment of the agents whose actions first produced and then continuously sustained these forms of state education.

Her agenda was set.

The morphogenetic approach

The two volumes that succeeded *Social Origins of Educational Systems* sought to consolidate and advance sociology's grasp of the structuring of culture and of social institutions. In *Culture and Agency: The Place of Culture in Social Theory*, Archer (1988) conceptualized 'culture' as an objective phenomenon (akin to Popper's 'World Three'). In this way she distinguished between the ontological status of culture and what people and/or groups make of it epistemologically. Culture, for her, is therefore not a 'community of shared meanings'; rather, there exists a 'cultural system' ('replete with complementarities and contradictions'). There is also 'socio-cultural interaction', according to which groups draw and elaborate upon components of the cultural system in line with their interests and projects.

Significantly, Archer had digested Bhaskar's (1987) *The Possibility of Naturalism* before publishing her *Realist Social Theory: The Morphogenetic Approach* in 1995. It would be quite wrong, however, to infer that her work thereafter was somehow entirely subsumed by 'critical realist' philosophy or within what Lakatos would have termed its research programme: Archer's work has always shown an independent thrust and legitimacy. But the accent on ontology shifted. Her goal in *Realist Social Theory* was to set out a credible and 'useable' framework for conducting substantive sociological research. In the process she noted that social theory – including critical realism – had committed far more energy to articulating how structural and cultural properties are transmitted to agents and shape their thoughts, beliefs, values and actions than to how these properties are accommodated and dealt with, sometimes innovatively, by agents. Much of the work that followed addressed and sought to correct this disparity.

Archer observed that causal efficacy has tended (a) to be granted *either* to structure *or* to agency, and (b) to be granted more often to structure than to agency. She deployed and critiqued the notion of 'conflation'. She maintained that the denial of autonomy to agency (or 'downwards conflation') has far exceeded the denial of autonomy to structure (or 'upwards conflation'). An alternative account to be found in the sociological literature, in, for example, the work of Giddens, holds that structure and agency are 'co-constitutive': that is, structure is reproduced through agency but is simultaneously constrained and enabled by structure ('central conflation'). Archer rejects not only downwards and upwards but also central conflation. Conflationary approaches, she contends, preclude sociological investigation of the relative influence of each of structure and agency.

The approach associated with both her early and later labours on the relationship between structure and agency is epitomized in the term 'analytic dualism'. Bhaskar (1987, 129) famously wrote of this relationship:

> people do not create society. For it always pre-exists them and is a necessary condition for their activity. Rather society must be regarded as an ensemble of structures, practices and conventions which individuals reproduce and transform, but which would not exist unless they did so. Society does not exist independently of human activity (the error of reification). But it is not the product of it (the error of voluntarism).

Archer reinforces this interdependence between structure and agency. At any given time antecedently existing structures constrain and enable agents, whose actions produce intended and unintended consequences, which reproduce (*morphostasis*) or transform (*morphogenesis*) these structures.

What Archer adds is a timeline, as in the formula rehearsed above: structural conditioning underlying/*leading to* social interaction underlying/*leading to* structural elaboration. She refers to *morphogenetic sequences*. It is important to spell out what this amounts to given its centrality to Archer's theory. At any given moment in time, antecedently existing structures constrain and enable agents, whose actions deliver intended and unintended consequences, which lead in turn to structural elaboration and the reproduction or transformation of the existing structures. In the same vein, the initially antecedent structures were themselves the product of structural elaboration resulting from the actions of prior agents. Archer argues that this scheme – of morphogenetic sequences – permits, via the isolation of those structural and/or cultural factors that afford a context of action for agents, the investigation of how those factors mould the subsequent interactions of agents and how those interactions in turn reproduce or transform the initial context. Social processes are of course comprised of many such sequences. However, their temporal ordering allows for an examination of the internal causal dynamics of each sequence. In this way, it is possible to give *empirical* (as opposed to purely theoretical) accounts of how structural and agential phenomena interlink over time.

Archer has described her next volume, *Being Human* (published in 2000), as 'polemical'. In it she contested sociological imperialism in all of its many guises (most recently, social constructionist). The 'person', she insisted, cannot be portrayed 'as society's gift'. *Being Human* did not turn its back on structure and culture; rather, it offered a re-conceptualisation of human beings:

> each and every one of us has to develop a (working) relationship with every order of natural reality: nature, practice and the social. Distinctions between the

natural, practical and social orders are real, although it is usually the case that they can only be grasped analytically because they are subject to considerable empirical superimposition. Nevertheless, that does not preclude the fact that human subjects confront dilemmas, which are different in kind, when encountering each of the three orders. Neither does it diminish the fact that it is imperative for human survival to establish sustainable and sustaining relations with each.

(Archer 2007a, 39)

Sociology cannot wrap everything up.

Archer pinpoints *Being Human* as 'pivotal'. In it she conceptualizes 'unique human persons'. No society or social organization possesses self-awareness; but each and every human being does. What difference, then, does this self-awareness make to the nature of the social? Archer's analytic dualism comes into play here. Only if the distinction between structure and agency (and indeed between objectivity and subjectivity) is upheld can it be acknowledged that humans can and do reflexively examine their personal concerns in the light of their social circumstances; and that they can and do evaluate their social circumstances in the light of their concerns (Archer 2007a, 41).

The internal conversation

Structure, Agency and the Internal Conversation, published in 2003, moved this analysis of human reflexivity on. In it Archer maintains that personal reflexivity mediates the effects of objective social forms on us. It helps us understand *how* structure influences agency. With typical clarity, Archer (2007a, 42; see also Archer 2007b) writes:

reflexivity performs this mediatory role by virtue of the fact that we deliberate about ourselves in relation to the social situations that we confront, certainly fallibly, certainly incompletely and necessarily under our own descriptions, because that is the only way we can know anything. To consider human reflexivity play that role of mediation also means entertaining the fact that we are dealing with two ontologies: the objective pertaining to social emergent properties and the subjective pertaining to agential emergent properties. What is entailed by the above is that subjectivity is not only (a) real, but (b) irreducible, and (c) that it possesses causal efficacy.

It is the 'internal conversation' that denotes the manner in which humans reflexively make their way in the world. This inner dialogue about self-in-society, and *vice versa*, is what makes most of us 'active', as opposed to 'passive', agents. Being an active agent involves defining, refining and prioritizing concerns and elaborating projects out of them. In so far as these projects are successful, constellations of concerns translate into a set of practices. This set of practices constitutes a personal *modus vivendi*. So, *concerns lead to projects lead to practices*. Decrying any form of idealism, Archer adds that concerns can be ignoble, projects illegal and practices illegitimate! What people are doing in the course of their internal conversations is shaping themselves and contributing to the reshaping of the social world.

Reflexivity does not reduce to one homogeneous mode of deliberation. Rather, it is exercised through different modalities. Archer discerns three 'dominant modalities': *Communicative, Autonomous* and *Meta-Reflexivity*. The dominance of any one of these derives from their relationship to their natal context in conjunction with their personal concerns.

This analysis is deepened in Archer's (2007c) next volume, *Making Our Way Through the World: Human Reflexivity and Social Mobility*. She offers the following definitions of her three principal modes of reflexivity:

- The communicative reflexives are those whose internal conversations require completion and confirmation by others before resulting in course of action.
- The autonomous reflexives are those who sustain self-contained internal conversations, leading directly to action.
- The meta-reflexives are those who are critically reflexive about their own internal conversations and critical too about effective action in society.

Considered as generative mechanisms, these different dominant modes of reflexivity have what Archer calls 'internal consequences' for their practitioners as well as 'external consequences for society'. Internally, Archer found from a small-scale study oriented to social mobility that communicative reflexivity is associated with social immobility; autonomous reflexivity with upward social mobility; and meta-reflexivity with social volatility. Externally, communicative reflexives contribute to social stability and integration through their 'evasion' of constraints and enablements, their endorsing of their natal contexts and their active forging of a dense micro-world that reconstitutes their 'contextual continuity' and projects it into the future. By contrast, the autonomous reflexives act strategically, in Archer's words, by 'avoiding society's snakes to ride up its ladders' (Archer 2007a, 43). They represent 'contextual discontinuity'. The meta-reflexives are society's 'subversive agents', immune alike from the rewards and blandishments linked to enablements and the forfeits associated with constraints. They act out Weber's 'value rationality' amidst the 'contextual incongruity' that shaped their lives. They are a source of counter-cultural values, inclined to context both oppressive moves on the part of the state and exploitation arising from the economy.

The themes addressed here are picked up in Archer's (2012) *Reflexive Imperative*. She argues that society is currently being rapidly reshaped and distanced from modernity; she highlights in particular a new global realm of 'opportunities', as well as enhanced migration, increased education and a proliferation of novel skills, not to mention the changing nature of reflexivity itself. All this suggests a move away from communicative reflexivity, which is associated with traditionalism, towards autonomous reflexivity, which is apt and ripe for global opportunities, with meta-reflexivity producing 'patrons of a new civil society expressive of humanistic values'.

This move towards what Archer calls *morphogenetic society* jettisons some citizens. The logic and global reach of opportunity require the continuous revision of personal projects and serve as obstacles to any settled *modus vivendi*. The reflexivity of some, maybe many, becomes 'fractured' as a consequence. The fractured reflexives are those whose internal conversations intensify their distress and disorientation rather than leading to purposeful courses of action. It is the communicative reflexives who are most fragile and vulnerable to displacement into the category of fractured reflexive (the majority of fractured reflexives in Archer's own investigation started out as communicative reflexives).

Reflexivity and social change: the morphogenetic society

Archer's current work is focused around the notion of morphogenetic society. Partial morphostasis has yielded to untrammeled morphogenesis. This does not mean that she signs up – with Beck, Bauman and others – to the displacement or circumvention of social structure: there is never a non-structured social world. But it does mean that she detects a considerable social shift. Such shifts – for agents and social structures alike – occur, she avers, in interlocking and temporally complex ways. Agents are formed in contexts set by social structural parameters (embracing language-games, norms, communities, power relations and so on). On an altogether different time-scale, the structures themselves change as a result of the choices and activities of historically situated agents. The result is a series of cycles with different timelines. Back to a familiar 'formula': structural conditioning > social interaction > structural elaboration.

So what generative mechanisms are at work? This is the question that Archer broaches and attempts to answer in her current writings, as well as in a collaborative enterprise with close and like-minded colleagues in the critical realist camp. Social morphogenesis, she admits, is an umbrella concept, 'whereas any generative mechanism is a particular that needs identifying, describing and explaining – by its own analytical history of emergence' (Archer 2014, 95). She specifies three orders of emergent properties. Thus:

> the three coincide with what are conventionally known as the micro-, meso- and macro-levels: dealing respectively with the situated action of persons or small groups, because there is no such thing as contextless action; with 'social institutions', the conventional label for organizations with a particular remit, such as government, health, education etc at the meso-level; and with the relation between structure and culture at the most macroscopic level.
> (Archer 2014, 95)

Archer's argument starts at the macro-level, but with the important rider that each – macro-, meso- and micro-level – stratum is 'activity-dependent' on that or those beneath it; and that both 'downwards' and 'upwards' causation are continuous and intertwined.

Society for Archer comprises the relations between 'structure' and 'culture'. Society is the consequence of *relations between relations*, all of which are ever activity-dependent. Structures are primarily materially based, cultures primarily ideational. In a nutshell, Archer contends that in what she terms 'late modernity' the interplay between economic competition and technological diffusion has fuelled intensified morphogenesis across the whole array of social institutions. At the same time it has rapidly augmented the cultural system. Thus, the two – structural and cultural – constituents of the generative mechanism have (a) themselves undergone morphogenesis and (b) their synergy has extended this to the rest of the social order via knock-on effects (Archer 2014).

Archer is too cautious to precipitously announce the arrival of morphogenetic society. Nor does she put forward a 'manifesto for morphogenetic society' (Archer 2013). Although both structure and culture in late modernity can be said to promote morphogenesis, they nevertheless issue in different and contrasting 'situational logics of action'. The for-profit market sector would extend the *logic of competition* throughout the social order, embracing schools, universities, hospitals and so on. But scientific and technological 'diffusionists' are committed to a *logic of opportunity* and so are hostile to bureaucratic regulation and restricted access; outcomes are not assessed according to the criterion of profitability. This tension between structure and culture – discordance between logics – has given rise to a 'relationally contested order'. The generative mechanism of 'competition-diffusion' is extremely morphogenetic, but no social transformation is imminent. We may, Archer avers, have to live with gradualism for a while. Ending on a marginally more optimistic note, Archer (2014, 115) suggests that diffusionist agencies might yet become the research and development department for a future civil society and civil economy.

> Their interim task is to make the 'logic of opportunity' more wide-reaching within economic activity and to demonstrate that incremental increases in socially useful value and augmentation of the commons are contributions to the common good that are genuinely beneficial to all – thus illustrating that win-win outcomes are realistic goals for the social order. That alone grounds optimism about gradualism leading to the transformation of global society.

Criteria for selecting writings

It was no easy task to put this selection of Margaret Archer's writings together. It was what to omit that troubled us as editors rather than what to include: there are gems beyond these covers. We stand by our selection, however. In our judgement it (a) gives a fair indication of how Archer's theories – most notably around the interrelations of structure, culture and agency – have evolved over a long, distinguished and ongoing career; (b) gives a flavour at least of her inputs into substantive areas of sociological enquiry and concern, from education to reflexivity to social change; and (c) offers a summary of how her work provides a theoretical frame for much-needed, indeed urgent, sociological analyses of an ever-changing present that is an admix of past, present and future.

The headings we have used match those in this summary introduction, so we can be brief. Thus, following a general introduction on 'Morphogenesis: Realism's explanatory framework' from Archer, the first two selected papers focus on her early but embryonic work on educational systems. The seeds of her full-blown theory of social change and transformation were sown here. The next four items provide an overview of her morphogenetic approach. It is here that her analytic dualism is presented and defended against historic and contemporary criticism. The third selection comprises a representative trio of writings on the internal conversation. Privileging the concept of reflexivity, these contributions ground and explore just how structure and culture come together to shape, but *not* determine, human choices. The fourth and final assemblage consists of three items that focus on the accelerated change of what Archer calls late modernity, and for a potentially transformational shift to the morphogenetic society.

As editors we are united in our conviction that Margaret Archer is a premier sociologist and social theorist for the twenty-first century. Her eminence is in fact personal and institutional as well as theoretical. She was the first female president of the International Sociological Association, for example, and was appointed by Pope Francis to chair the Pontifical Academy of Social Sciences. She has been a catalyst for change within the discipline as well as a pioneer. It is our intention and hope that this volume of her writings will encourage our colleagues to learn of and from, appreciate and, above all, utilize her labours to their own ends.

References

Archer, M. (1979) *Social Origins of Educational Systems*. London: Sage.
Archer, M. (1988) *Culture and Agency: The Place of Culture in Social Theory*. Cambridge: Cambridge University Press.
Archer, M. (1995) *Realist Social Theory: The Morphogenetic Approach*. Cambridge: Cambridge University Press.
Archer, M. (2000) *Being Human: The Problem of Agency*. Cambridge: Cambridge University Press.
Archer, M. (2003) *Structure, Agency and the Internal Conversation*. Cambridge: Cambridge University Press.
Archer, M. (2007a) 'The trajectory of the morphogenetic approach: an account in the first person', *Sociologica, Problemas e Praticas*, 54, pp. 35–47.
Archer, M. (2007b) 'The ontological status of subjectivity: the missing link between structure and agency', in C. Lawson, J. Latsis and N. Martins (eds), *Contributions to Social Ontology*. Abingdon: Routledge, pp. 17–31.
Archer, M. (2007c) *Making Our Way Through the World*. Cambridge: Cambridge University Press.
Archer, M. (2012) *The Reflexive Imperative*. Cambridge: Cambridge University Press.
Archer, M. (2013) 'Social morphogenesis and the project of morphogenetic society', in M. Archer (ed.), *Social Morphogenesis*. New York: Springer, pp. 1–22.
Archer, M. (2014) 'The generative mechanism re-configuring late modernity', in M. Archer (ed.), *Late Modernity: Trajectories Towards Morphogenetic Society*. New York: Springer, pp. 92–118.
Bhaskar, R. (1987) *The Possibility of Naturalism: A Philosophical Critique of Contemporary Human Sciences*, 2nd edn. London: Harvester Wheatsheaf.
Cale, G. and Roll, L.S. (2015) 'Social theorizing: an interview with Professor Margaret Archer', *disClosure: A Journal of Social Theory* 24, Article 13.

Morphogenesis
Realism's explanatory framework

Introduction

Philosophers of science or of the social sciences incline to one of two roles, although the dividing line is not strict. First, there are 'commentators', who largely restrict themselves to analysing the doings of others: be they scientists or investigators. Such commentaries – critical, clarificatory, cautionary, diagnostic, evaluative and sometimes hortative – may indeed prove useful to the worker-bees they study. Second, there are (a smaller number) of philosophers of science who explicitly define their role as 'under-labouring' for a given discipline(s), by supplying an explanatory programme, a toolkit of concepts and, very occasionally, an illustrative model to guide practitioners.

The latter has been the case with Roy Bhaskar, who has described his own role as under-labouring for the social sciences. His has been a generous contribution, consisting of three main elements: a realist social ontology, vindicating the propriety of attributing emergent properties and powers to the social world; a fallibilist epistemology, insisting upon the limitations of our perspectival knowledge and thus the invalidity of substituting what we (think we) know for the way things really are (even if that eludes us); and a judgemental rationality, advocating a constructive (though *pro tem*) method of arbitrating upon theoretical disputes.[1] In social theorising, this generous under-labouring has gone even further and Bhaskar advanced the illustrative Transformational Model of Social Action (TMSA).[2] Nevertheless, none of the above does the sociologist's (or any other social scientist's) job for them. In a nutshell, the Weberian task of explaining why, in any given case, social matters are 'so, rather than otherwise' remains to be undertaken.

In practice, this means that specific accounts are required to explain *how* particular parts of the social order originated and came to stand in a given relationship to one another, *whose* actions were responsible for this, through *which* interactions, *when* and *where* and with *what* consequences. In all of this, the practising sociologist has to know a great deal about the historical origins and current operations of 'x'. Such practitioners may feel drawn towards realism but, even with its under-labouring, realist philosophy of science cannot give them guidelines about how to examine the questions listed above. This is what the 'morphogenetic approach' seeks to provide. It is an *explanatory framework*, which complements the realist philosophy of science and furnishes specialised practitioners with guidelines for explaining the problems they have in hand. Far from making such specialists (in the sociology of health, education, migration etc.) redundant, it is they alone who are qualified to *specify* the relevant parts, relationships and mechanisms pertinent to problems in their areas of expertise. What the *explanatory framework* offers are guidelines for *how* to undertake morphogenetic and morphostatic analysis, whatever the problem may be. A hallmark of realist philosophy and social theory alike is that both are meant to be of practical use.

Structure

One way to introduce this *explanatory framework* ('the morphogenetic approach') and to bring out its close connections with practical social analysis is briefly to glance back at its own genesis. It is noteworthy that besides Pierpaolo Donati only two social theorists – John Parker[3] and Frédéric Vandenberghe[4] – have recognised that I developed this approach (during the 1970s) in the course of confronting a substantive problem about social structure. The problem was the difference between the educational systems of England and France, in both of which I had studied. These, I maintained, were so different in their organisation as to engender completely different processes of educational interaction and patterns of change in the two countries.

At that time, the realist explication of emergent causal powers was lacking in the philosophy of social science.[5] Nevertheless, thanks to David Lockwood's seminal distinction between 'system' and 'social' integration,[6] it was possible to conceive of the two (taken to refer to 'structure' and 'agency') as exerting different kinds of causal powers – ones that varied independently of one another and were factually distinguishable over time – despite the lack of a well-articulated social ontology. Thanks to Walter Buckley, my attention was drawn to 'morphogenesis': that is, 'to those processes which tend to elaborate or change a system's given form, structure or state'[7] in contrast to 'morphostasis', which refers to those processes in a complex system that tend to preserve the above unchanged. However, Buckley himself regarded 'structure' as 'an abstract construct, not something distinct from the ongoing interactive process but rather a temporary, accommodative representation of it at any one time',[8] thus tending to 'dodge questions of social ontology'.[9]

All the same, when taken together, these two theorists enabled the 'morphogenetic approach' to be advanced in 1979, as it were, as a temporary, accommodative representation of realist social theory. What it gradually aimed to do was to set out a framework for giving an account of the *existence* of particular structures (social institutions in this instance) at particular times and in particular places. In the concrete case in question, the phenomenon to explain was the existence of a *decentralised* educational system in England and a *centralised* one in France. Further research revealed that a more general structural phenomenon called for explanation, namely the existence of State educational systems at all. But that is precisely what practical social analysis does. It leads us to detect relations between component parts that appear to have irreducible, relational properties, which realism calls emergent and whose influence it regards as the exercise of emergent causal powers. Such was my definition of State educational systems.[10] What the 'morphogenetic approach' first set out to do was to explain where such forms of social organisation came from: that is, how emergent entities in fact emerged.

Retrospectively, it is clear why the confluence with what came to be known as Critical Realism – advancing a social ontology of emergence – and the 'morphogenetic approach' – analysing the source of such relational properties – gelled well together. This is because, as Elder-Vass puts it, 'any account of a specific case of emergence will include a temporal element, an explanation of how the entity concerned has come to exist'.[11] In short, this was no marriage of convenience. If causal powers were to be attributed to any aspect of social structure, such a claim needed to be grounded in a social ontology that was earthed against reification. Equally, if emergent (social) entities were held to exist, whether or not their properties were exercised as powers, then an explanatory methodology was required to account for their social origins.

It has been argued – albeit quite sympathetically – that this is as far as the morphogenetic approach goes. According to Elder-Vass:

> However, morphogenesis does *not* explain how an entity can possess emergent properties. Such an explanation always depends on the existence of a specific set of *synchronic* relations between the parts: morphogenesis explains the development of such a set of relations over time, but the operation of a causal power at any given moment depends upon the presence of those relations *at that specific moment in time*. Thus the temporal element in the explanation of emergence must always be complemented by a synchronic relational element.[12]

He is entirely correct in this statement, but not, I believe, in maintaining that the morphogenetic approach does not or cannot (it is not clear which he asserts) also furnish guidelines for *synchronic* analysis. That is, I believe him to be incorrect *unless* he insists that a 'complete causal analysis' of the real powers or emergent properties of any emergent entity must proceed in the order he itemises. That would be to start from a list of its characteristic parts and an explanation of how these must be related to each other to form a whole, prior to a morphogenetic account of how this state of affairs comes about and a morphostatic account of how it is sustained and thus proves relatively enduring. Sociology is much messier than that; it begins from hunches, not from the naming of parts, and probably would not get anywhere if it were to start from there. However, I do not see that the adequacy of any causal analysis depends upon the order of its completion – nor do I think this is his argument, because it makes far too much ride on the nature of the context of discovery.

By briefly revisiting the morphogenesis of State educational systems and their distinctive forms of structuring, I hope to show that this framework can account for both the *diachronic* development of such systems and also the *synchronic* presence of those parts in those relations at those specific moments over which they endured – with the bonus of being able to say something[13] about the conditions under which such relations may cease to hold.

4 Realism's explanatory framework

Although all structural properties found in any society are continuously activity-dependent, it is possible through analytical dualism to separate 'structure' and 'agency' and to examine their interplay in order to account for the structuring and restructuring of the social order. Fundamentally, this is possible for two reasons. Firstly, 'structure' and 'agency' are *different kinds of emergent entities*,[14] as is shown by the differences in their properties and powers, *despite* the fact that they are crucial for each other's formation, continuation and development. Thus, an educational system can be 'centralised', whilst a person cannot, and humans are 'emotional', which cannot be the case for structures. Secondly, and fundamental to the workability of this explanatory methodology, 'structure' and 'agency' operate diachronically over different time periods because (i) structure necessarily pre-dates the action(s) that transform it and (ii) structural elaboration necessarily post-dates those actions, as represented in Figure M.1.

Full significance is accorded to the timescale through which structure and agency themselves *emerge, intertwine and redefine* one another, since this is the bedrock of the explanatory format employed in accounting for any substantive change in social structure. These three phases will be worked through, in standard fashion, in the next section on culture. However, allow me to revert to studying the structuring of educational systems in order to illustrate how a sociologist working on a substantive problem from a realist perspective would utilise analytical dualism to delineate the phases of the sequence, thus explaining the problem in hand. This will also provide the opportunity for clarifying certain misconceptions about the morphogenetic approach.

Usually, our thinking, though generally not our writing, begins at T^4 (the fact that it also returns there will be dealt with when considering the synchronic aspect). In other words, we note some relational property in the social order (or a sector of it) that seems to exert irreducible causal powers of its own kind – as detected through their tendential effects – even though its components can be fully described. The implication is that generative mechanisms, which exist largely unexercised will not usually attract the attention of social scientists. Although emergent causal powers are *judged* to be such according to the causal criterion, social science does rely upon (something of) empiricism's perceptual criterion for their *detection*. Although the social scientist is not reliant upon (or expectant of finding) Humean 'constant conjunctions', nevertheless, an established correlation coefficient is not a gift horse

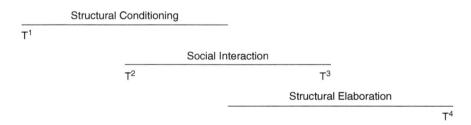

Figure M.1 The basic morphogenetic sequence.

to reject but rather an impetus to causal investigation. After all, our hunches usually derive from our observations.

This was the case for the English and French educational systems as I encountered them in the 1960s. They were made up of the same components – schools, universities, teachers, students, texts etc. – but the organisation of these parts represented 'decentralisation' in the former and 'centralisation' in the latter. 'Centralisation' and 'decentralisation' were not mere labels but ways of summarising how the organisation of these two kinds of system generated distinctive constraints and enablements as well as different processes of change (facilitating 'internal initiation' by teachers and 'external transactions' by outside parties in England, whilst constraining most educational change in France to be centrally and 'politically negotiated'). Equally, vested interests in reproduction versus transformation were entirely differently distributed to the elites of other institutions because of the high level of educational standardisation in France compared with the much greater differentiation of English education. Finally, the patterns of change were (then) 'incremental' in England, but governed by legislative 'stop–go' and punctuated by outbursts of direct action in France.

The fundamental question was 'Why this difference?' – accompanied by its subsidiaries: Who was responsible? What interactions brought it about? When did matters become this way? To answer questions such as these I suggest that *in practice* the social theorist generally moves *backwards* to the T^2–T^3 period in quest of answers that take the form of 'Who did what, with or against whom, with such an outcome?' Note several points here. To begin with, although the quest may be for *les responsables*, usually it is impossible to pin responsibility on any particular group. This is because what emerges is the result of compromise and concession amongst those involved and does not conform closely to what anybody wanted. Indeed, such general dissatisfaction is what keeps morphogenesis going.[15] Incidentally, this does mean that emergent properties can indeed be unintended consequences and, in society, they generally are. The reverse is clearly not the case because many unintended consequences lack emergent properties and powers. Nevertheless, this means that, in defining social structure(s), no strict demarcation can be made between the two, with all unintended consequences being classified as 'resultants', even though many of them are just that.

Next, examination of the interaction taking place between T^2 and T^3 is pointed and focused; we are explicitly searching for what led to those relational features at T^4 that are important because of the causal powers they can exercise. It would seem obvious that many things which develop over time (it is unfortunate that in English the verb 'to emerge' can be substituted grammatically for the verb 'to develop') may have nothing whatsoever to do with structural (or cultural or agential) emergence. Neither, it should go without saying, does the *historicity* of anything – social or otherwise – mean that it is an emergent entity. If it did, I would have to endow my tea set, inherited from a long-dead great-aunt, with causal powers because it has become an antique. Nevertheless, every current emergent structural property does have a history and an important part of giving a complete causal account of it is to explain where it came from.

However, Sawyer has recently produced the misleading comment that: 'Archer argued that it is emergence over time – morphogenesis – that *makes* emergent properties real and *allows them* to constrain individuals.'[16] Of course, if something did not exist it could be neither real nor constraining – accounting for existence is crucial – but *it is not* what accounts for the causal properties and powers in the italicised verbs above. What does will be discussed next when we come to examine the activity-dependence of emergent entities, such as educational systems, in the present tense. Past actions, importantly including those of the long dead, are indispensable to explaining how structures came to be organised the way they are (at any momentary T^4), but *not* to the fact that they have relatively enduring properties possessing causal powers.

Before that, let us first finish outlining the phases of the morphogenetic cycle. If the relevant chains of interaction are followed backwards from T^3 to T^2, it becomes clear that one or more of the parties involved devotes its time, energy and resources to the attempt to increase its influence over education because it seeks changes in that part of the social order. It pursues educational transformation and, if we are to understand its motivation, we need to know what it is this group sought to transform, how and why. This could be and, indeed, at one time was the desire to replace an absence by a presence (no provision for education by educational provisions). But, in that case, were the active group to have been unopposed, one would want to know why instruction was a matter of indifference to other parties in society. However, especially after social institutions became progressively more interdependent and interlinked in the course of modernity, initiatives for educational transformation were increasingly likely to meet with opposition from parties defending the institutional status quo in education. Having backtracked to this point (wherever it was in history) and established the key agents, it could be tempting to believe one had gone back far enough. The process would then be reversed and, having identified the key agents, a detailed account would be given of their interactions, culminating in the development at T^4 of educational change, such as the establishment of a State system. This would be the procedure typical of Methodological Individualist approaches such as 'conflict theory'.

Such accounts may be rich and detailed about the cut and thrust between protagonists, about alliances and counter-mobilisation, and about the compromises and concessions which brought about a particular instance of morphogenesis, such as the advent of a given State educational system. However, none of these can give a complete account. Neither the participants, nor the form, nor the content of the interaction will have been fully explained. They remain accounts of 'what happened', without a suggestion about 'why?'

Conversely, the 'morphogenetic approach' maintains that completeness requires the *structural contextualisation* of the interaction initiated at T^2. In short, it is necessary to broaden the temporal frame and return to the state of (educational) affairs at T^1. This further backtracking alone yields the source of motives, of *positions prises*, of ideological commitments, of strategies adopted but, above all, of precisely what was wanted (and, often more importantly, not wanted) sufficiently to move agents to engage in (educational) interaction. None of that can be understood without introducing the prior structural context that *conditioned* interaction between T^1 and T^2.

Substantively, the prior form of education (at T^1) was privately owned by the Church (Anglican in England) and by the religious orders (Catholic in France); its various components – often unconnected with one another – were designed, funded and staffed to service religious requirements alone. Certain other parts of society found themselves (meaning the institutional operations with which they were proximately involved as role incumbents) as 'adventitious beneficiaries' of the religious definition of instruction – they could make use of the educational outputs supplied, at no cost to themselves. Others were in a situation such that their operations were impeded, both positively (the educated had acquired inappropriate values) and negatively (they had not gained the requisite skills). Yet other institutional sectors of society remained indifferent because their operations (such as agriculture) stood in a relationship neither of complementarity nor of contraction to the doings and outcomes of the educational status quo.[17] In other words, such antecedent relations between different parts of society (its social institutions) are indispensable to explaining the *delineation* of those agents who *became parties* to subsequent educational interaction (and those who did not) and whether they aligned themselves for the defence of reproduction or the pursuit of transformation.

Structural relations, transmitted to agents (as always) by shaping the situations in which they found themselves, are indispensable to accounting for their *motivation*. But structural conditioning goes further than explaining who was involved, who was not and which 'side' the participants took. It also serves to explain the *strategic action* adopted. Why did this take the form of 'substituting' independent networks of schools in England, which engaged in market competition with Anglican schooling, while in France all transformative action was focused upon the 'restriction' of religious control of educational through the central apparatus of the State? Only by introducing the different relationships between State, Church and social stratification in England and France at the end of the eighteenth century can this be understood. Who had what resources to bring to bear? Again, it is necessary to consult the prior distribution of resources (various), anterior to educational struggles in both counties, but constraining certain participants to delay entering the fray and enabling others to make swift headway. (It is common to find such distributions represented as 'mere' aggregate properties, which they are, but to neglect the structural context generating them). Given the above, it is unsurprising that outcomes too – the development of a centralised system in France and a decentralised one in England – are not fully explicable without reference to all these forms of structural conditioning. These are not (and are never) determinants, because agency too has its own properties and powers, both individually and collectively, one of the most important being to act innovatively in circumstances that were not of their making or choosing.

So far, this section has sought to recommend the 'morphogenetic approach' as an explanatory framework that helps to render structural change tractable to investigation by breaking up the flow of events into three phases, according to the formula

<Structural Conditioning → Social Interaction → Structural Elaboration>. This carves out one morphogenetic cycle, but projection of the lines forwards and backwards connects up with anterior and posterior cycles. In fact, two such cycles were analysed in the educational study used for illustration here: the one prior to the emergence of State educational systems and the one posterior to it. Their delineation was due to the conviction that *the advent of a State system represented a new emergent entity*, whose distinctive relational properties and powers conditioned subsequent educational interaction (and processes and patterns of change) in completely different ways compared with 'private ownership' in the previous cycle.

The establishment of such morphogenetic 'breaks' – signalling the end of one cycle and constituting the beginning of the next – is the business of any particular investigator and the problem in hand.

Generically, what this requires has been neatly summarised by Elder-Vass:[18] (i) a list of its [new] characteristic parts; (ii) an explanation of how these must be related to each other to form a whole rather than an unorganised heap; and (iii) an explanation of the generative mechanism constituted by the manner in which its [novel] properties and powers are produced from that particular organisation of its parts. To this, he adds (iv) a morphogenetic account of how this state of affairs comes about, which I have just been discussing and with which he seems to agree, and (v) a morphostatic account of how it is sustained and thus proves relatively enduring. Here too, I agree, but we should note that with (v), as opposed to (iv), we have now moved into the present tense. Yet, as has been seen, he also claims that the morphogenetic approach cannot account for synchronic relations sustaining parts and their relations at a specific moment in time – upon which their possession and exercise of causal powers depends. I disagree, but will have to unpack the realist commitment to continuous 'activity dependence' to show why.

To realists, nothing social, whatever its origins, is self-sustaining, which is what *inter alia* distinguishes the social from the natural world. Only a myriad of agential 'doings' (including thinking, believing and imagining) keep any given higher-level social entity in being and render it relatively enduring. In other words, whilst ever something like the centralised French educational system lasts, then move a marker, second-by-second, from the system's inception until today, and each and every moment of its 'centralisation' depends upon agential doings (including intentional inaction). However, this is not equivalent to some Giddensian notion that *every* such doing on the part of *everyone* somehow contributes to maintaining the whole (in this case, institution).[19] On the contrary, some doings are entirely irrelevant to sustaining centralisation (keeping a dog), some are more important than others, and it is only because further 'doings' exist in tension with one another that things remain the way they are (Catholic and now Muslim religious practices 'provoke' centralisation to exercise its powers in defence of the *laïcité* of education in the French Republic). Still further doings are intended to change the status quo, but have not yet succeeded in doing so.

What the morphogenetic approach allows us to do is to avoid the synchronic banality and futility of asserting that if a relational property endures this must be because of some net balance of sustaining agential doings at each moment in time (reminiscent of Merton's 'net balance of functional consequences'). Instead, in completing a morphogenetic cycle, by issuing in structural elaboration, not only is structure transformed but so is agency, as part and parcel of the same process – the *double morphogenesis*.[20] (This point entirely fails to be understood in Dépeltau's misleading discussion of what he calls 'co-determination theories').[21] As it reshapes structural relations at any given T^4, agency is ineluctably reshaping itself: in terms of domination and subordination, of organisation, combination and articulation; in terms of its vested interests and these in relation to those of other agents; in terms of the new roles and positions that some occupy and others do not; and in terms of the novel situations in which all agents now find themselves, constraining to the projects of some and enabling to the projects of others,[22] yet of significance for the motivation of all.

Very briefly, at any given T^4 something radical happens, not only to structure but also to agency. In cases of macroscopic change this affects the 'people' through transforming four 'parts' or levels of the social order: the systemic, the institutional, the role array and the positional (the life-chances of different sections of the population). Where the emergence of an educational system (at T^4) is concerned, one of its immediate effects consists in redividing the population, not necessarily exhaustively, into those with vested interests in (educational) maintenance and change respectively, according to the situations in which they now find themselves – involuntarily for the majority of people. To characterise an interest as a 'vested' one is to associate it with a particular position, the implication being that if positions (roles, institutions) change, then so do interests. As Porpora puts it,

> among the causal powers that are deposited in social positions are interests. Interests are built into a social position by the relationship of that position to other positions in the system [...] actors are motivated to act in their interests, which are a function of their social position. Again, this doesn't mean that actors always with necessity act in their interests, but if they don't they are likely to suffer.[23]

Thus, 'opportunity costs' are differentially distributed to different groups of actors for the same course of action – hence providing directional guidance *vis à vis* the course of action each group adopts.

To illustrate this point equally briefly, the emergence of a *centralised* educational system *creates* new vested interests in maintaining that organisational form (i.e. those particular relations between its parts) as constitutive and definitive of national education. For example, at the institutional apex, consider the position of the Minister of Public Instruction. One of the rare empirical generalisations one can make is that no incumbent of this (new) role, or the government of which he/she is also part, will ever voluntarily cede 'centralisation' because of the bonus that derives from an educational system that is supremely responsive to etatist direction. Lower down, consider the (new) role of Primary school teacher (successfully wrested from the hands of religious personnel and now constituting part of the *corps enseignant*). The *instituteurs*, whom Péguy accurately dubbed the 'hussars of the Republic', consistently played an important part in upholding the *laïcité* of French public instruction by actively resisting the *curé*'s influence throughout the villages of rural France during the nineteenth century. Finally, consider the (new) educational situation confronting the population at large. The various levels of instruction were carefully calibrated with entry to appropriate grades of public service and access to each level effectively mirrored the contemporary form of social stratification, thus reproducing it. Indeed, the educational work of Bourdieu is an extended analysis of how the French system engendered dispositions, reproductive of the level of instruction received and the commensurate positions subsequently assumed. In sum, the new relational properties of national education exerted causal powers, influencing individual and collective motivation sufficient for agents to act back *synchronically* in a manner that sustained centralisation.

What more does the morphogenetic approach need to do other than to conduct such an analysis in a properly detailed fashion? One more thing that concerns the *relatively* enduring nature of structures and that, in turn, serves to highlight the importance of the 'double morphogenesis' of structure and agency. A frequent difficulty with persuasive synchronic accounts – and I believe Bourdieu's concept of 'habitus' to be a case in point – is how to explain that a given relationship between parts is *ever* susceptible of transformation (indeed, he himself relied upon *external* intrusions, in common with normative functionalism). Instead, the double morphogenesis reveals how the synchronic 'forces' (re-)producing morphostasis are an agential achievement, which is constantly threatened, rather than being ones conducive to eternal life for any structure.

To begin with, the losers in a struggle for educational control, whose outcome was the emergence of a State system, do not quietly fade away; on the contrary, they retain their organisation and their objectives for instruction. They fight on and may win concessions (such as the Church reacquiring the right to own and run schools under the Loi Falloux of 1850). Paradoxical as this might seem, morphostatic analysis cannot remain the same from one time interval to another. This is because the explanation of why something endures has to accommodate such changes in its constitution – changes that 'punctuate' morphostasis diachronically. In other words, an emergent entity (such as an educational system) can retain its key relational properties and causal powers (those making it a centralised system), without it remaining *exactly* the same entity.

Similarly, to simplify greatly, the new system also *defines new groups of losers*: those with limited educational opportunities but also, for example, industrialists concerned about the absence of technical training. All groups in the above situation have vested interests in bringing about transformation, though not of the same kind. With even greater over-simplification, the crucial question for *endurance versus change* is: 'Can these groups work together?' This is an empirical question. What it means, however, is that we know where to look – and this is only contingently 'outside' – to explain why time is eventually up for that which was only *relatively* enduring. When we then address the break-up of the tense balance of forces that had consistently maintained morphostasis, we also know what to do next, and that is to examine the next (potentially) morphogenetic cycle.

Throughout this account it has been maintained that structural 'conditioning' is necessarily *mediated by* (variable) agential responses to their circumstances. Without allowing for the personal powers of agents, it is impossible to explain the variability of their actions in the same circumstances. However, some question the notion of mediation itself. Thus, Manicas asks 'why postulate the existence of structure or culture as causally relevant if, to be causally effective, these must be mediated by social actors?'[24] Since he leaves the question there, it is presumably held to be unanswerable. However, structure and culture could only be deemed causally irrelevant if what were being mediated was, in fact, invented then and there by actors whose own personal powers were entirely responsible for it. This 'ban' upon 'mediation' seems as untenable as holding that the wires bringing electricity into my house are entirely responsible for the working of my lights and electrical appliances and that the existence of a national grid and electricity generators are causally irrelevant.

This reflects a tendency among 'weak' realists to require some kind of instantiation of structure properties by agents before they are accorded any role in an explanation. In other words, far from their *impinging upon* agents, it is human subjects who literally bring them into play. Such a voluntaristic bias obviously provides rather better protection against being charged with reification. Examples would include John Searle's[25] notion of 'the Background', to which back-reference is made, for example, by listeners to disambiguate statements that require contextualisation. Similarly, Manicas's[26] relegates structural and cultural properties to being 'materials at hand', without the capacity to exert causal powers but also, from his standpoint, without any explanation of why some are within easy reach of certain actors but out of reach for others. (It is thus unsurprising that Searle's favourite sociologist appears to be Bourdieu, whilst Manicas's book is a virtual repetition of Giddens: these two authors thus favouring the theoretical stance I have termed central conflation).[27]

Culture

In developing a conceptual framework for employing analytical dualism in cultural analysis, culture as a whole is defined as referring to all intelligibilia: that is, to any item which has the dispositional ability to be understood by someone, whether or not anyone does so at a given time. Within this corpus, the Cultural System (C.S.) is that sub-set of items to which the law of contradiction can be applied – i.e. society's register of propositions at any given time. Contradictions and complementarities are *logical* properties of the world of ideas, of World Three as Popper terms it,[28] or, if preferred, of the contents of 'libraries'. We use these concepts every day when we say that the ideas of X are consistent with those of Y, or that theory or belief A contradicts theory or belief B. In so doing, we grant that a Cultural System has an objective existence and particular relations amongst its components (doctrines, theories, beliefs and individual propositions). These relationships of contradiction and complementarity are independent of anyone's claim to know, to believe, to assert or to assent to them, because this is knowledge independent of a knowing subject – such as any unread book.

However, the above is quite different from another kind of everyday statement, namely that the ideas of X were influenced by those of Y, where we refer to the influence of people on one another – such as teachers on pupils, television on its audience or earlier thinkers on later ones. This is the Socio-Cultural level (S-C) and it depends upon *causal relations* – that is, the degree of cultural uniformity produced through the ideational influence of one set of people on another through the whole gamut of familiar techniques, which often entail the use of power: argument, persuasion, manipulation, distortion and mystification.

Thus, there are two distinct notions pertaining to two distinct levels (the C.S. and S-C), which should not be elided:

- the notion of *cultural coherence* – or ideational consistency;
- the notion of *uniform practices* – or a community with a common way of life.

To run the two together, as when culture is defined as 'a community of shared meanings', conflates the 'community' (S-C) with the 'meanings' (C.S.). This confuses two elements, which are both logically and sociologically distinct. I criticised this position as the 'Myth of Cultural Integration',[29] but the notion is tenacious and Elder-Vass repeats it: 'the most fundamental feature of cultures' is that 'culture is a *shared* set of practices and understandings'. To me, such *sharing* is always an *aim* on the part of a particular group *and never a definition*, much less a state of affairs 'that tends to produce and sustain shared ways of living'.[30] However, it seems to me that there is a crucial and useful distinction to be made between:

- *Logical consistency* – that is, the degree of internal compatibility between the components of culture (C.S.), and
- *Causal consensus* – that is, the degree of social uniformity produced by the ideational influence of one set of people on another (an S-C matter).

Logical consistency is a property of the world of ideas, which requires no knowing subject, whilst *causal consensus* is a property of people and their interaction. The proposition employed here is that the two are both analytically and empirically distinct and, therefore, can vary independently of one another. Some, like Elder-Vass, object that

> the archive contains not knowledge as such but only potential knowledge: that as a material resource it contains only marks on paper (or some other medium) and that there is no informational content to such marks in the absence of a reader or other interpreter.[31]

This denial of 'informational content' to our diachronically established archive and its reductive dependency for meaning upon contemporary 'knowing subjects' can, I think, be shown to unravel.[32]

Firstly, the items lodged in the 'archive' must have the 'dispositional capacity to be understood'. This is what makes them intelligibilia rather than mere markings, such as those made by the legendary monkeys-at-the-keyboard or, in the case of stones, by natural geophysical processes. What, then, distinguishes between intelligible and random markings? Ultimately, it is their decipherability. Certainly the jury may not be convened for centuries (as with the Rosetta Stone whilst it was hidden under the sands), its members may disagree for a time (as with the Dead Sea Scrolls), and they may fail as decoders (which is why museum exhibits are often relabelled). In addition, although there is certainly a need for 'mediation', there is no *a priori* reason why the intelligible content requires a 'mind' to understand it – this task could be done by a computer and then put to use by mediating agents.

Moreover, why does Elder-Vass consider it necessary that an idea has to be in someone's head for it to have legitimate ontological status? Sometimes in everyday life an idea migrates from head to paper and back again. Suppose I make a shopping list, then it is misplaced, and I do the shop without it. I will forget some items that I do need. In that case, my full shopping needs were not in my head but on the list. Similarly, many of us keep the instructions to domestic appliances, accepting that these are more accurate guides to making them work properly than the rather vague ideas retained in our heads, which we do not trust as being correct. Then again, when we 'look something up', we are no longer a 'knowing subject' but a subject knowingly in search of knowledge. Thus, I stand by my claim that a book has 'the dispositional capacity to be understood' means the same as 'it contains ideas'.

It follows that I think it mistaken to construe books simply as World I physical artefacts. As Bhaskar maintains, 'books are social forms'[33] and have the same ontological status as 'structures', 'organizations', 'roles' and so on. In order to avoid reification he insists that 'the causal power of social forms is mediated through social agency'.[34] Thus, a book not only requires a mind to create it but also another mind(s) to understand it. This excursion merely reinforces the fact that *mediation* is always required, in culture as in structure.

Relationships between the Cultural System and the Socio-Cultural levels are summarised in Figure M.2.

At any moment, the Cultural System (C.S.) is the product of historical Socio-Cultural (S-C) interaction, maintained in the present, but having emergent properties and powers which pertain to that level. Like structure, some of its most important causal powers are those of constraints and enablements. In the cultural domain these stem from contradictions and complementarities. However, again like structure, constraints require something to constrain and enablements something to enable. Those 'somethings' are the ideational projects of people – the beliefs they seek to uphold, the theories they wish to vindicate, the propositions they want to deem true.[35]

Cultural level	Dependent upon	Type of relations
CULTURAL SYSTEM	Other ideas	Logical
SOCIO-CULTURAL	Other people	Causal

Figure M.2

14 Realism's explanatory framework

In other words, the exercise of C.S. causal powers is dependent upon their activation from the C-S level. What ideas are entertained Socio-Culturally, at any given time, result from the properties and powers belonging to that level. Obviously, we social agents do not live by propositions alone; we generate myths, are moved by mysteries, become rich in symbols and ruthless at manipulating hidden persuaders. These elements are precisely the stuff of the S-C level, for they are all matters of inter-personal influence – from hermeneutic understanding at one extreme to ideological assault and battery at the other. It is interaction at the S-C level that explains why particular groups wish to uphold a particular idea or to undermine one held by another group. Once they do, then their ideational projects will confront C.S. properties (mostly not of their own making) and unleash upon themselves these systemic powers, which they may seek to realise or to contain. However, the S-C level possesses causal powers of its own kind in relation to the C.S.: it can resolve apparent contradictions and respond adaptively to real ones, or it can explore and exploit the complementarities it confronts, thus modifying the C.S. in the process. Moreover, it can set its own cultural agenda, often in relation to its structurally based interests, by creatively adding new items to the systemic register. In these ways, the S-C level is responsible for elaborating upon the composition of the C.S. level.

In turn, the relations between them form the three phases of an analytical cycle made up of <Cultural Conditioning $\Rightarrow$ Socio-Cultural Interaction $\Rightarrow$ Cultural Elaboration> (Figure M.3). In fact, the final phase may culminate at T^4 in either morphogenesis (transformation) or morphostasis (reproduction). In both cases, T^4 constitutes the new $T^{1'}$, the conditional influences affecting subsequent interaction. This explanatory framework, which uses analytical dualism for undertaking practical cultural investigations, again depends upon two simple propositions: that any cultural structure necessarily pre-dates the actions which transform it, and that cultural elaboration necessarily post-dates those actions.

Cultural conditioning (C.S.)

This phase is concerned with the effects of people *holding* ideas which stand in particular logical relationships of contradiction or complementarity to other ideas. To hold such ideas is to activate the C.S. powers of constraint and enablement,

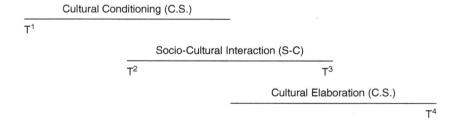

Figure M.3 Cultural morphogenesis.

Realism's explanatory framework

but why they are held is an S-C question whose answer would require investigation at that level, involving historical recourse – however short.

'Constraining contradictions' exist when there is an internal relationship between the ideas (A) advanced by a given group and other ideas (B) which are lodged in the C.S. – that cannot simply be repudiated – and yet (A) and (B) are in logical tension. Durkheim provides a superb historical example of this in his analysis of the logical inconsistencies in which Christianity was embroiled, from earliest times, because its inescapable dependence upon classicism confronted the Church with 'a contradiction against which it has fought for centuries'.[36] Since the relationship between (A) and (B) is an internal one, their contradiction could not be evaded by the simple renunciation of (B): Christians could not repudiate the classical languages in which the Gospel was enunciated nor the classical philosophical concepts through which it was theologically explicated. Although substantively very different, the 'constraining contradiction' also confronts any explanatory theory (A), which is advanced in science, but whose observational theory (B) does not provide immediate empirical corroboration – that is, if scientists think they have good reason not to jettison (A).[37]

What the 'constraining contradiction' does in practice is to confront those committed to (A), who also have no option but to live with (B) as well, with a particular *situational logic*. According to this logic, given their continuing dedication to (A) (its abandonment is always possible because conditioning is never determinism), then they are constrained to deal with (B) in a specific manner. Since (A) and (B) are logically inconsistent, then no genuine resolution is possible between them, but if (B) remains unaltered, it threatens the credibility or tenability of (A). Consequently, the situational logic directs that continued adherence to (A) entails making a *correction* of its relationship with (B) mandatory. Corrective action involves addressing the contradiction and seeking to *repair* it by reinterpretation of the ideas involved. The generic result will be some form of *syncretism* that brings about union between the antithetical but indispensable sets of ideas.[38] For protagonists of (A), their vested interest is in developing syncretic reinterpretations of (B) in order to make it compatible. However, they may be driven to more 'generous' syncretic endeavours because the unificatory thrust of the corrective repairs can be deflected by their Socio-Cultural reception. Whether or not a syncretic formula can be made to stick depends upon how it meshes with the state of S-C integration in society.

At the systemic (C.S.) level, the direct counterpart of the 'constraining contradiction' is the necessary or 'concomitant compatibility', because it bears the same formal features in reverse and its conditional influence is that of enablement. In other words, invoking idea (A) also necessarily evokes idea (B), but since the (B) upon which this (A) depends is consistent with it, then (B) buttresses adherence to (A). Consequently (A) occupies a congenial environment of ideas whose exploration, far from being fraught with danger, yields a treasure trove of confirmation and corroboration because of the logical consistency of the ideas involved. This was the generic feature that Weber analysed as linking the religious beliefs, rationale for status distribution and the economic ethos of Ancient India and China. A similar relationship obtained between classical economics and utilitarian philosophy.

16 *Realism's explanatory framework*

Modern examples are so abundant in natural science that Kuhn was tempted to portray the whole enterprise as a succession of paradigms, each of which constituted a cluster of 'concomitant complementarities'.[39]

What emerges is an enlarged and highly consistent conspectus. It represents a substantial increase in cultural density, by which this sector of the C.S. becomes especially rich in fine and subtle distinctions and develops an elaborate vocabulary to describe them. The end-product of this extensive exploration is a growth in ideational *systematisation*: that is, the 'strengthening of pre-existing relations among the parts, the development of relations among parts previously unrelated, the gradual addition of parts and relations to a system, or some combination of these changes'.[40] The intricacies of caste rights, the detailed protocols for 'normal science' and the bulging libraries of exegetical literature are produced by the same systemic conditioning.

The more complex the internal organisation of such a corpus of ideas becomes, the more difficult it is to assimilate new items without major disruption to the delicately articulated interconnections. Tight and sophisticated linkages eventually repel innovation because of its disruptive capacity. This is the result of the situational logic of *protection*. Its implications *within* the conspectus are that it progressively accommodates fewer and fewer radical innovations until, in Kuhn's words, it 'suppresses fundamental novelties because they are fundamentally subversive of its basic commitments'.[41] Weber, of course, made the same point about the effects of complex ritualisation in Hinduism being incapable of the innovative 'germination of capitalism in its midst'.[42] The implication for relations between the conspectus and its *external* environment is protective insulation against disruptive incursions – the most notable example being the Chinese Edict of Seclusion.

The situational logic of protection means brooking no rivals from outside and repressing rivalry inside. The former is at the mercy of contingent 'international relations'; the latter depends upon the success of its main Socio-Cultural thrust towards cultural reproduction in the (relevant) population. Ultimately, whether or not this sticks and endures turns upon *cui bono*; non-beneficiaries have no interest in sustaining protection.

The conditional influences of the two types of logical relations at the C.S. level (societal or sectional), just discussed, are summarised in Figure M.4.

Socio-Cultural (S-C) Interaction

The whole point of distinguishing between the Cultural System and the Socio-Cultural levels is because the orderly or conflictual relationships characteristic of the one can vary independently of the other, which is crucial to the explanation of stability or change. If conditional influences were determinants, the effects of 'correction' and 'protection' would both mean that cultural stability ensued. Yet this is not invariably the case. An economical way to explain why not is to ask what properties and powers may be possessed by agency and exercised during Socio-Cultural interaction such that the outcome is contrary to the conditioning. In other words, what accounts for discrepancies between the orderliness (or disorderliness)

	Constraining Contradictions	Concomitant Complementarities
	which condition	
Situational Logic of	Correction	Protection
C.S.	Syncretism	Systematisation
S-C	Unification	Reproduction

Figure M.4 Cultural System: types of logical relations.

of the two levels? First, why can social integration persist despite the existence of tensions within a system of ideas? Second, what explains a syncretic set of ideas *failing* to take hold in society or accounts for a systematised conspectus *failing* to be reproduced?

The answer to the first question (what explains the persistence of disproportionately high S-C integration), seems to lie in the effective exercise of cultural power. Where upholders of (A) have the position and the resources to control the diffusion of information, they can practise a variety of 'containment strategies' designed to insulate the majority of the population from dangerous familiarity with B. In this context, Lukes' three-dimensional concept of power[43] seems readily transferable to the cultural domain. Power is used to control the social visibility of contradictions and thus to prevent the eruption of S-C controversy. Its applications can vary from the straightforward first-dimensional use of censorship to the more subtle third-dimensional strategies that may induce 'misrecognition of symbolic violence' – perceptively analysed by Bourdieu,[44] although always presumed by him to be lastingly successful. However, 'containment strategies' are seen here as strictly temporising manoeuvres, most effective against the least influential.[45] Nevertheless, while a week may be a long time in science, exercises of cultural power can buy centuries of quietude in the history of a civilisation – especially when ideal interests and the structural distribution of resources are closely superimposed.

One answer to the second question (about disproportionately low S-C integration) is that independent Socio-Cultural discrepancies in orderliness occur when the social (or sectional) distribution of *material interests* does not gel with the situational logic of the Cultural System (or sub-system) at any given time.[46] Important as this is, if that were the end of the matter it would amount to saying 'cultural conditioning works *ceteris paribus* unless structural conditioning contravenes it'. It would be to retreat from advancing a theory of *cultural* dynamics because only countervailing *material* interests (and their promotive organisations) would be held capable of resisting cultural conditioning. Instead, two scenarios will be sketched, which give *ideal interests* their due – thus advancing a theory of cultural dynamics to parallel that of structural dynamics, without collapsing into it.

18 *Realism's explanatory framework*

On the 'corrective' scenario, associated with internal C.S. contradictions, the unificatory thrust of the situational logic can be deflected in three S-C ways. Cumulatively, they spell a growing disorderliness in the cultural relations between people that may ultimately precipitate a corresponding clash in the realm of ideas. Firstly, there is progressive *desertion*. At the Socio-Cultural level no one is compelled to take part in a syncretic enterprise. Exit is a permanent possibility and a steady stream of deserters attends the unfolding of any constraining contradiction. Ideational wranglings breed sceptics in the scientific as in the metaphysical domain and, as has often been remarked, the ex-member of a school of thought becomes its most virulent critic. This aggregate source of growing disorder then provides the impetus for a bolder syncretic manoeuvre – a more thoroughgoing correction, involving the interpretative adjustment of (A) itself. Ironically, these more radical syncretic moves *themselves* become bones of contention among the 'faithful'. Those who were once united in their ideational difficulties fall into *schismatism* when they try to solve them. A copybook example is the relationship between the Reformation and Counter-Reformation, which generated lasting sectarian conflict rather than restoring consensus in post-Renaissance Europe, despite both movements being equally concerned to prevent the actualisation of secular classical rationalism.

Finally, whenever the manifest Systemic unity of ideas is reduced through public wrangling, their unificatory role in society falls disproportionately. Those with an interest in so doing can then harness social disorder in order to bring about a full actualisation of (B), whose contents have unintentionally become better and increasingly widely known as syncretic formulae made more generous adaptations to it. What is crucial in order for a social group to actualise a contradiction by inducing a split along the Systemic fault-line is that it has no cross-cutting allegiances with other social groups to restrain it.[47] This is why the French revolutionary bourgeoisie rather than the leisured aristocracy (allied with the Clergy and constituting the two privileged Estates) was responsible for actualising secular rationalism, anti-clericalism and laicisation. The emergence of secularist Republicanism is a replication, in the cultural domain, of the conditions Lockwood set out for profound structural change – where social disintegration finally superimposes itself upon Systemic malintegration, forcing the latter asunder and actualising the changes that had previously been strategically contained.

On the 'protective' scenario, linked with internal 'concomitant complementarities', a substantial drop in Socio-Cultural integration is the exclusive motor of change because there is no tension to exploit within the Cultural System itself. However, the consistent conspectus does slowly generate a sufficient differentiation of interests to unleash social disorder. The root cause is the increase in C.S. *density*, as the complementary conspectus is explored and then systematised. Eventually, it becomes too great to be fully reproduced (societally or sectionally) because it has become too elaborate, expensive and time-consuming for all to share. Consequently, C.S. density turns into the enemy of S-C equality, and the resulting hierarchy of knowledgeability progressively delineates different interest groups in relation to the C.S.

As the cultural conspectus is gradually infilled and as work on systematisation reduces to mopping-up, the concentration of rewards and benefits among the S-C elite (typically the intellectual hegemony of old conservatives) means that more and more of the 'educated' become a category of 'marginals'. They have made a major investment in the C.S., but are denied much return from it as it stands, yet are firmly discouraged from making cultural innovations to increase their rewards. The application of cultural power, which can maintain orderliness among subordinates, is ineffective against the marginals: culturally they are in the know and one of the things they know is that they are not rewarded for it.

The disaffection of the marginals correspondingly reduces S-C integration, but C.S. integration still remains high. The disaffected do not kick it for they have invested too much in it, but they are opportunists, ready to migrate towards new sources of ideational variety in order to increase their pay-off. Impelled by their ideal interests, boundaries (geographical, disciplinary or paradigmatic) are crossed and the departure of these disruptive S-C elements is not resisted. In short, marginal migrants go out seeking new but complementary items (novel but consistent ideas, skills, techniques) to augment their ideal interests. From this a distinctive type of cultural change emerges, which is born of innovative amalgamation.

Cultural elaboration

Although the above two scenarios have been presented as ones that may unreel autonomously within the cultural realm, there is no denying that in fact they are usually accelerated and decelerated by their interaction with structural factors. What is of particular importance is how far structure differentiates *material* interest groups that *reinforce or cross-cut* the Socio-Cultural alignments conditioned by the Cultural System. This interplay between culture and structure is even more marked when we turn, in conclusion, to the ways in which cultural elaboration can be independently introduced from the Socio-Cultural level. However, although such social conflict may well be fuelled by structural cleavages and divisions, neither the form of cultural interaction involved nor the type of cultural changes induced can be reduced to epiphenomena of structure. This is because there is considerable cultural work to be done by agents when the ideas with which they are dealing are only contingently related. Here, agency alone is responsible[48] for bringing these ideas into conjunction and seeking to achieve social salience for them. It is also because, once they have done so, they have created new forms of situational logic in which the promotion of their own ideal interests are then enmeshed.

In contrast to the 'constraining contradiction' – where the alternative to a given set of ideas is also internally related to them, and thus constantly threatens them with its own counter-actualisation – the *accentuation* of a 'competitive contradiction' is a supremely social matter. Accentuation depends upon groups, actuated by interests, *making* a contradiction competitive by taking sides over it and by trying to make other people take their side. In brief, opposed interest groups *cause* the 'competitive contradiction' to impinge on broader sections of the (relevant) population; it does not ineluctably confront them, as is the case with 'constraining contradictions', the moment that anyone asserts (A).

Perhaps the most important illustration of the 'competitive contradiction' is ideological conflict. Were ideologies no more than passive reflections of material interests, then it would be impossible that they could advance, foster or defend such interests. To the extent that they succeed, they necessarily do so in competition with other ideologies, which perform the same task in relation to opposed interests. In the process, their ideational conflict becomes subject to its own distinctive situational logic. In contradistinction to the 'constraining contradiction', the situational logic of the 'competitive contradiction' fosters *elimination* not *correction*. In the former case, agents were driven to cope with ideas that necessarily contradicted their own (compromising, conciliating and conceding much *en route*), whereas those involved (and drawn into involvement) over a 'competitive contradiction' have every incentive to eliminate the opposition. Because partisans of ideas (A) and (B) are unconstrained by any internal relations between these ideologies, there is nothing to restrain their combativeness, for they have everything to gain from inflicting maximum damage on one another's ideas in the course of competition.

In principle, victory consists in so damaging and discrediting oppositional views that they lose all salience in society, leaving their antithesis in unchallenged supremacy. In practice, the cut and thrust between them has the entirely unintended consequence that, far from one ideology being eliminated, both contribute to one another's refinement. Charge is not merely met by counter-charge, but also by self-clarification and response (as is equally the case for competing scientific frameworks). Ironically, both sets of ideas undergo 'progressive problem-shifts',[49] thus inserting much greater *pluralism* into the Cultural System. Correspondingly, since both groups of protagonists seek to win over uncommitted agents, the Socio-Cultural effect of their refined interchanges is to increase *cleavage* within the population, as was the case during the Great Age of Ideology.

Finally, the existence of discoverable but wholly 'contingent complementarities' at the C.S. level constitutes a source of novelty, with few strings attached, that is systemically available to human agency. Both the detection of these items and their synthesis are entirely dependent upon the exercise of agential powers of creativity. Certainly, the fact that such agents are on the look-out for such items is fostered by frustration of either or both their ideal and material interests, but there is nothing automatic about discontents yielding creative innovations. Certainly, too, the C.S. existence of 'contingent complementarities' is a necessary condition for their exploitation, but the sufficient condition requires active agents to produce constructive, concrete syntheses from what is only a loose situational logic of opportunity.

When and if they do so, newly elaborated items are added to the Cultural System, which in practical terms represent novel areas of intensive *specialisation*, such as new academic disciplines or research programmes. If and when they are successful (and defective syntheses are common), institutionalisation usually follows, and, as it does so, more and more people are attracted to work upon the new source of cultural variety. In turn, variety stimulates more variety because this interplay between the C.S. and the S-C constitutes a positive feedback loop. This is the exact obverse of the negative feedback mechanism that regulates the protection and reproduction of the 'concomitant complementarity'. Not only are the logics of the two kinds of complementarities the inverse of one another, but so are their results. Cultural variety is the opposite of cultural density. Variety feeds on what looks promising but is ill-defined; density deals with what feel like certainties, but which are already over-defined. Variety pushes on to extend cultural horizons unpredictably; density stays at home to embellish the cultural environment systematically.

These differences are equally marked in their Socio-Cultural effects – *systematisation* fosters cultural reproduction, whilst *specialisation* prompts ideational diversification. The proliferation of specialist groupings is fissiparous in its social effects, for as more and more *sectional* groups are carved out, they have less and less in common with one another and with the rest of society. Sectional groups, unlike polarised ones, are not defined by their opposition to others, but by their differences from everyone. The dialectics of specialisation and sectionalism contribute to the progressive exclusion of vast tracts of the population from larger and larger portions of specialised knowledge. The division of the population into lay people and experts is repeated over and over again as each new specialism emerges. This is a horizontal form of Socio-Cultural differentiation, quite unlike the vertical stratification engendered by the 'concomitant complementarity'. The four relationships discussed are summarised in Figure M.5.

By distinguishing between the Cultural System and the Socio-Cultural levels and examining their interplay, the myth of culture as 'a community of shared meanings' – the heritage of early anthropology – has been challenged on two fronts. On the one hand, four different bodies of 'meanings' (C.S.) have been differentiated: that is, organisations of ideas whose conditional influences upon the further development of ideas are respectively *syncretic*, *pluralist*, *systematised* and *specialised*. On the other hand, the influences of the Cultural System on the Socio-Cultural level (those of *unification* and *reproduction*) and the independent effects of agents' own pursuit and promotion of ideas in society (those of *polarisation* and *sectionalism*) serve to replace the undifferentiated notion of 'community' (S-C). They point to different sequences of causal interplay between the two levels, with different outcomes, thus challenging every version of cultural conflation.

		High	Low	
	High	Concomitant Complementarity	Constraining Contradiction	Morphostasis
Social-Cultural Integration				
	Low	Contingent Complementarity	Competitive Contradiction	Morphogenesis

Figure M.5 Cultural System Integration.

Agency: the stratified model of people

The central problem of theorising agency is how to conceptualise the human agent as someone who is partly formed by their sociality but also has the capacity partly to transform their society. The difficulty is that social theorising has oscillated between these two extremes. On the one hand, Enlightenment thought promoted an 'undersocialised' view of man[50] – *Modernity's Man* – whose human constitution owed nothing to society and thus was a self-sufficient 'outsider', who simply operated in a social environment. On the other hand, there is a later but pervasive 'oversocialised' view of man, whose every feature, beyond his biology, is shaped and moulded by his social context. He, as *Society's Being*,[51] thus becomes such a dependent 'insider' that he has no capacity to transform his social environment.

From the realist point of view, the central deficiency of these two models is their basic denial that *the nature of reality* as a whole makes any difference to the people we become, or even to our becoming people. *Modernity's Man* is preformed, and his formation – that is, the emergence of his properties and powers – is not dependent upon his experiences of the world.[52] Indeed, the world can only come to him filtered through an instrumental rationality shackled to his interests whose genesis is left mysterious. Preference formation has remained obscure, from the origins of the Humean 'passions' to the goals optimised by the contemporary rational chooser. The model is *anthropocentric*, because man works on the world, but the world does not work upon man, except by attaching risks and costs to the accomplishment of his preformed designs. In short, he is closed against any experience of reality that could make him fundamentally different from what he already is.

Similarly, *Society's Being* is also a model which forecloses direct interplay with reality. Here the whole of the world comes to people sieved through one part of it, 'society's conversation'. Their very notion of being selves is merely a theory appropriated from society, and what they make of the world is a matter of permutations upon their appropriations. Once again, this model cuts man off from any experience of reality itself, which could make him fundamentally different from what social discourse makes of him. Society is the gatekeeper of reality and therefore all we become is society's gift because it is mediated through it.

What is lost, in both versions, is the crucial notion of experience of reality, namely that the way the world is can affect how we are. This is because both anthropocentrism and sociocentrism are two versions of the 'espistemic fallacy', where what reality is taken to be, courtesy of our instrumental rationality or social discourse, is substituted for what the world really is. Realism cannot endorse the 'epistemic fallacy' and, in this connection, it must necessarily insist that how the world is has a regulatory effect upon what we make of it and, in turn, what it makes of us. These effects are independent of our full discursive penetration, just as gravity influenced us, and the projects we could entertain, long before we conceptualised it.

The emergence of our 'social selves' is something that occurs at the interface between 'structure and agency'. It is therefore necessarily relational and, for it to be properly so, then independent powers have to be granted to both 'structures' and 'agents'. This is what is distinctive about the social realist approach. It grants the existence of people's emergent properties (PEPs) and also the reality of structural and cultural emergent properties (SEPs and CEPs), and sees the emergence of *agents* and *actors* as relational developments occurring between them. Conversely, *Society's Being* presents 'agency' as an epiphenomenon of 'structure', whereas *Modernity's Man* regards 'structure' as an epiphenomenon of 'agency'.[53]

Realism entails several moves to account for the emergence of social subjects, who themselves must be conceptualised as stratified. The three basic strata involved can be summarised as follows:

i   *Selfhood* or the continuous *sense of self* – that is, of being the same being over time.
ii *Primary Agents*, differentiated by virtue of their relations to socially scarce resources, which may collectively transform themselves into *Corporate Agents* seeking to transform society or to maintain the *status quo*.
iii *Social actors*, whose social identities are secured by investing themselves in social roles, which they actively personify according to their 'ultimate concerns'.

Taken together, these yield the following stratified model of agency, which develops over the life-course of any individual.

Human selfhood ⇒ ⇒ ⇒ **Social Agent** ⇒ ⇒ ⇒ **Social Actor**

(Grandparent)   *(Parent)*   *(Offspring)*

Human selfhood

Relations between humanity and the world are intrinsic to the development of human properties, which are *necessary* conditions of social life itself. Thus, I am advancing a transcendental argument specifically for the necessity of a 'sense of self' to the existence of society. The continuity of consciousness, meaning a continuous 'sense of self', was first advanced by Locke.[54] To defend it entails maintaining the crucial distinction between the evolving *concept* of self (which is indeed social) and the universal *sense* of self (which is not). This distinction has been upheld by certain anthropologists, such as Marcel Mauss,[55] to whom the universal sense of 'the "self"' (Moi) is everywhere present. This constant element consists in the fact that 'there has never existed a human being who has not been aware, not only of his body but also of his individuality, both spiritual and physical'.[56] However, there has been a persistent tendency in the social sciences to absorb the *sense* into the *concept* and thus to credit what is universal to the cultural balance sheet.

The best way of showing that the distinction should be maintained is a demonstration of its necessity: that is, a *sense of self* must be distinct from social variations in *concepts of selves*, because society could not work without people who have a continuity of consciousness. Thus, for anyone to appropriate social expectations it is necessary for them to have a sense of self upon which these impinge such that they recognise what is expected of them (otherwise obligations cannot be internalised).

To reinforce the transcendental argument, it should be noted that both the impoverished sociological models of human agency mentioned earlier are also dependent upon a continuity of self-consciousness but of which they give no account. *Society's Being* needs this sense of self in order for an agent to know that social obligations pertain to her, rather than just being diffuse expectations. She has to know that when they clash – as they did for Antigone – then it is she who is put on the spot and has to exercise a creativity which cannot be furnished by consulting the discursive canon. Unscripted performances that hold society together need an active agent who is enough of a self to acknowledge her obligation to perform and to write her own script to cover the occasion. Similarly, this continuous sense that we are one and the same being over time is equally indispensable to *Modernity's Man*. He needs this sense of self if he is consistently to pursue his preference schedule, for he has to know both that they are his preferences and how he is doing in maximising them over time.

Social agents

Agents, from the perspective of Realism, are agents *of* something. Baldly, they are agents of the socio-cultural system into which they are born (groups or collectivities in the same position or situation) and, equally, they are agents of the systemic features they transform (since groups and collectivities are modified in the process of the double morphogenesis). Fundamentally, this is a shorthand account of the morphogenesis of agency (Figure M.6): the drama of interaction may be centuries long, but the storyline is a simple one of pre-grouping and regrouping.

Everyone is inescapably an agent in some of their doings, but many of the doings of human beings have nothing to do with being an agent. Agents are real and agency involves real actions by real people, which is why we can legitimately talk about agents acting, because agency is not a construct, not another heuristic *Homo Sociologicus*. In explaining the statement that everyone is ineluctably an agent, we have to make a crucial distinction between what have been termed 'corporate' and 'primary' agents. At first glance, which probably involves selective perception

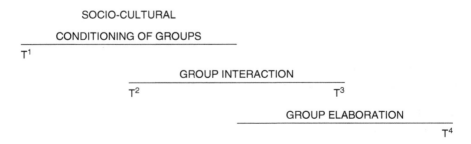

Figure M.6 Morphogenetic diagram for agency.

induced by several decades of literature on political pluralism, it may seem that the only important agents are articulate and organised interest groups. Organised interest groups are indeed special, and they pack a very special punch as far as systemic stability and change are concerned. This is because only those who are aware of what they want can articulate it to themselves and others, have organised in order to get it, and can engage in concerted action to reshape or retain the structural or cultural feature in question. These are termed 'corporate agents': they include self-conscious vested interest groups, promotive interest groups, social movements and defensive associations. Their common denominators are articulation and organisation. Who they are, where they come from and how the full array develops will be discussed shortly.

As far as Primary Agency is concerned, everyone is born into an ongoing socio-cultural system and has agential effects on stability or change, if only by merely being within it, physically and numerically. Moreover, the world – structured as they find it and are placed in it – is the one in which they live and move to have their social being; yet there is no being without doing and no doing without consequences. In short, the prior social context delineates collectivities in the same position (those with the same life chances *vis à vis* the major institutions) and within this context they have to carry on – 'carrying on' being more broadly conceived than Wittgenstein's rule-governed 'going on'.

Those falling into this category are termed Primary Agents. They differ from Corporate Agents at any given time by lacking a say in structural or cultural modelling. They neither express interests nor organise for their strategic pursuit, either in society or in a given institutional sector. (Note that a Primary Agent in one domain may be a Corporate Agent in another at any given T^1, because these categories are not fixed but develop over time.) Nevertheless, to lack a say in systemic organisation and reorganisation is not the same as to have no effect on it, but the effects are unarticulated in both senses of the word. Collectivities without a say, but similarly situated, still react and respond to their context as part and parcel of living within it. Similarities of response from those similarly placed can generate powerful, though unintended, aggregate effects.

Corporate Agency shapes the context for all actors (usually not in the way any particular agent wants but as the consequence of collective interaction). Primary Agency inhabits this context, but in responding to it also reconstitutes the environment which Corporate Agency seeks to control. The former unleashes a stream of aggregate environmental pressures and problems that affect the attainment of the latter's promotive interests. Corporate Agency thus has two tasks: the pursuit of its self-declared goals, as defined in a prior social context, and their continued pursuit in an environment modified by the responses of Primary Agency to the context which *they* confront.

At the systemic level this may result in either morphostasis or morphogenesis depending exclusively upon the outcome of interaction but, since social interaction is the sole mechanism governing stability or change, what goes on during it also determines the morphostasis or morphogenesis of Agency itself. This is the double morphogenesis during which Agency, in its attempt to sustain or transform the social system, is inexorably drawn into sustaining or transforming the categories of Corporate and Primary Agents themselves.

Two basic questions therefore arise in relation to Social Agency. What are the conditions for the morphostasis of Social Agency? This demands an account of the divide between Corporate and Primary Agents and how some given pre-grouping is *maintained* during interaction. What are the conditions for the morphogenesis of Social Agency? This calls for a discussion of how Corporate and Primary Agents are *regrouped* in the course of interaction.

In a thoroughly morphostatic scenario the two types of Agents – Corporate and Primary – are starkly delineated from one another. The distinction between them is maintained through interaction and proves long-lasting – as in those 'old and cold' systems which had at most two Corporate Agents who successfully confined the rest of the population to Primary status for centuries. Morphostatic scenarios do occur in modern societies – totalitarianism being a prime example – as well as in institutional sectors, but are more complex, vulnerable and short-lived since morphogenetic influences impinge from elsewhere.

The 'old and cold' scenario was characterised by a conjunction between structural morphostasis and cultural morphostasis. Substantively, this meant that in the cultural domain there was one set of hegemonic ideas and a culturally dominant group of proficients, who had not (yet) encountered ideational opposition and were able to reproduce ideas amongst the collectivity of Primary Agents, thus maintaining a high level of cultural unification in society. On the other hand, structural morphostasis indicates a monolithic form of social organisation with the superimposition of elites and heavy concentration of resources, which together prevent the crystallisation of opposition – this subordination of Primary Agents thus allowing the structure to be perpetuated. The reciprocal influence between the structural and cultural domains reinforces the *status quo* and in the process perpetuates the preliminary divide between Corporate and Primary Agents by precluding regrouping.

By contrast, the morphogenetic scenario displays precisely the opposite features, namely the progressive expansion of the number of Corporate Agents, of those who are numbered among them, and a divergence of the interests represented by them, thus resulting in substantial conflict between them. Accompanying this process is a complementary shrinkage of Primary Agents, due in part to their mobilisation to join burgeoning promotive interest groups and in part to the formation of new social movements and defensive associations as some of them combine to form novel types of Corporate Agency (Figure M.7).

The co-existence of a plurality of Corporate Agents seeking to push and pull systemic or institutional structure in different directions has profound effects on reshaping the context for Primary Agents and remoulding the situations in which they find themselves. Collective reactions to the new context create new environmental problems for some Corporate Agents and constitute enabling factors for others, since Corporate Agency is no longer consensual. Collective counter-reactions also take the form of new Corporate Agents, thus complicating interaction. The interplay between Primary and Corporate Agents could be applied to the wide social canvas of modernity or to more localised settings since it is meant to be

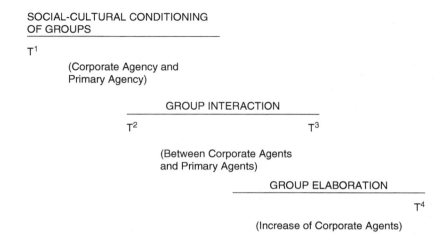

Figure M.7

generic to the elaboration of Social Agency – and agents themselves come in all shapes and sizes. The appropriate morphogenetic cycle is thus delineated according to the scope of the problem in hand. Nevertheless, each such cycle will contain the basic features of pre-grouping and regrouping. Figure M.8, therefore, draws out the typical constituents of the morphogenesis of Social Agency.

Thus, from the morphogenetic perspective, Social Agency is embedded in interaction and, hence, is ultimately a relational property of people. This involves relations to the prior socio-cultural context (which effect pre-grouping) and subsequent interactions with others (which effect regrouping). Simultaneously, the context itself changes, since we are dealing with a double morphogenesis in which the elaboration of both structure and agency are conjoint products of interaction. Structure is the conditioning medium and elaborated outcome of interaction: agency is shaped by and reshapes structure whilst reshaping itself in the process. But the complexity of this process remains hopelessly indefinite unless the interplay between them is disentangled over time to specify the where, the when and the who.

Social actors

An account of the *Social Actor* seeks to conceptualise a *social self* for an individual that, whilst dependent on society, also meets the strict criteria of identity as a particular person. It proceeds by eschewing two notions: that of an actor undertaking a pre-scripted part (too much of society – too little self), and that of one who merely dons and doffs masks behind which his private business can be conducted (too much self – too little of the social). The balance is struck by a concept of the *Social Actor* who becomes such by choosing to identify himself or herself with a particular role and to personify it in a particularistic way.

28 Realism's explanatory framework

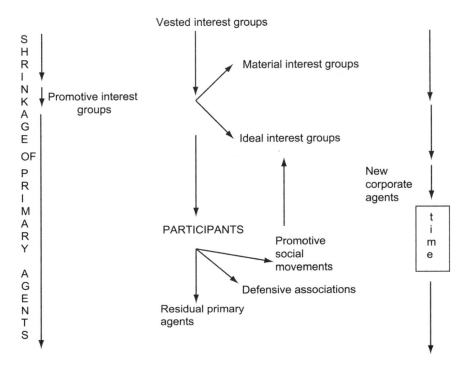

Figure M.8 Typical constituents of the morphogenesis of Social Agency.

One major result of the interactions between Corporate Agents, as discussed above, is to modify the array of roles available for incumbency. At the end of any given morphogenetic cycle, the positions which people can occupy as *Social Actors* are also transformed. Another way of putting it is that *Agency* makes more room for the *Actor*, who is not condemned to a static array of available positions in a changing society. This tendency has been marked throughout modernity. Its generative mechanism is the progressive mobilisation and subsequent interaction of more and more Corporate Agents (see Figure M.8).

We become Agents *before* we become Actors. From our families, we acquire the properties of Agents through belonging to particular collectivities and sharing their life chances – as males/females; blacks/whites; foreigners/indigenous; middle class/ working class. Infant Agents have a long way to go before they become mature Actors. But the kind of Agents that they start out being without any choice, due to parentage and social context, profoundly influences what type of Actor they can choose to become. Certain opportunities and information are open to the privileged and closed to the non-privileged. Options are not determined, but the opportunity costs of attaining them are stacked very differently for the two.

However, even within a socially restricted section of the role array, choices have to be made. Questions then arise as to 'who does the choosing – and, a little later, who does the personifying?' To answer these without slipping into social determinism we need to introduce *personal identity*. This is where we return to the crucial concept of 'selfhood'. Selfhood, the capacity of subjects to know themselves to be the same person over time, is pivotal to the development of *personal identity* and thus of individuation. Since *personal identity* derives from subjects' interactions with the world, its natural, practical and social orders, it is dependent upon the prior emergence of a *sense of self*. The latter secures the fact that the three orders of reality are all impinging on the same subject – who also knows it.

Fundamentally, *personal identity* is a matter of what we care about in the world. Constituted as we are, and the world being the way it is, humans ineluctably interact with the three different orders of natural reality: nature itself, practice and the social order. Human beings necessarily have to sustain relationships with the natural world, work relationships and social relationships if they are to survive and thrive. Therefore, no one can be indifferent about the concerns which are embedded in their relations with all three orders. A distinct type of concern derives from each of these orders. The concerns at stake are respectively those of 'physical well-being' in relation to the natural order, 'performative competence' in relation to the practical order and 'self-worth' in relation to the social order. Our emotions convey the import of these different kinds of situation to us. Thus, emotional reactions are seen as 'commentaries upon our concerns'[57] and the raw materials of our reflexive responses to the world.

However, a dilemma confronts all people. It arises because every person receives all three kinds of emotional commentaries on their concerns, originating from each order of natural reality – nature, practice and the social. Because human subjects have to live and attempt to thrive in the three orders simultaneously they must necessarily, in some way and to some degree, attend to all three clusters of commentaries. Their problem is that nothing guarantees that the three sets of emotional commentaries dovetail harmoniously together. It follows that the concerns to which they relate cannot all be promoted without conflict arising between them. For example, an evasive response to the promptings of physical fear can threaten social self-worth by producing cowardly acts; cessation of an activity in response to boredom in the practical domain can threaten physical well-being by leaving tasks unfinished; and withdrawal as a response to social shaming may entail a loss of livelihood. In other words, momentary attention to pressing commentaries may produce instant gratification of concerns in one order, but it is a recipe for disaster since we have no alternative but to inhabit the three orders simultaneously and none of their concerns can be bracketed away for long. It is on only rather rare occasions that a particular commentary has semi-automatic priority, as in escaping a fire, undertaking a test or getting married.

Most of the time, each person has to work out their own *modus vivendi* in relation to the three orders. What this entails is striking a liveable balance within our trinity of inescapable concerns. Any given *modus vivendi* can prioritise one of the three orders of natural reality, as with someone who is said to 'live for their art', but what it cannot do is entirely to neglect the other orders. Yet, which precise balance we strike between our concerns and what precisely figures amongst a subject's constellation of concerns are what give us our strict identities as *particular persons*. Eventually, our emergent *personal identities* are a matter of how we prioritise one concern as our 'ultimate concern' and how we subordinate, but yet accommodate, others to it. Constituted as we are, we cannot be unconcerned about how we fare in any order of natural reality. Therefore, these concerns can never be *exclusively* social.

That we all have concerns in the natural, practical and social orders is ineluctable, but exactly *which* concerns, and in precisely *what* configuration, is a matter of human reflexivity. We reflect on our priorities and evaluate them. The process of arriving at a configuration, which prioritises our 'ultimate concern' and accommodates others to them, is both cognitive and affective: it entails both judgements of worth and an assessment of whether we care enough to be able to live with the costs and trade-offs involved. We are fallible on both counts, but our struggling towards a *modus vivendi* between our commitments is an active process of reflexive deliberation, which takes place through 'internal conversation'. In it we 'test' our potential or ongoing commitments against our emotional commentaries, which tell us whether we are up to living this or that committed life. Since such commentaries will not be unanimous, the 'internal conversation'[58] involves evaluating them, promoting some and subordinating others, so that the concerns we affirm are also those with which we feel we can live. Since the process is corrigible (we may get it wrong or circumstances may change), the conversation is ongoing.

Developing a satisfying and sustainable *modus vivendi* is an achievement; not one which can be accomplished immediately and not one which can necessarily be maintained. For children and young people, who undoubtedly have internal conversations, the establishment of a stable configuration of commitments is a virtual impossibility because they are still learning about themselves, the world and the relations between them. Furthermore, there are destabilised commitments, often resulting from changes of circumstances, some of which are predictable (for example, in the life-cycle), whilst others stem from the contingencies of life in an open system (for instance, involuntary redundancy). These are nodal points which prompt a radical reopening of the 'internal conversation', but for all people the dialogue is a continuous reflexive monitoring of their concerns, for human commitments are promissory, provisional and subject to renewal, revision or being revoked.

The role assigned here to reflexivity focuses upon our voluntarism, because every version of the 'oversocialised' view (*Society's Being*) or the pre-programmed view (*Modernity's Man*) traduces our personal powers to live meaningful lives – they dismiss the power of *personal identity* to shape our lives around what we care about most[59] and commit ourselves to. However, when we come to the next stage, that of examining the emergence of our *social identities*, we have to deal with our *involuntary* placement as *social agents* and how this circumscribes the *social actors* that different people can *voluntarily* become. We all have some choice about the roles we adopt but few, if any, have a free choice to select from amongst the total role array when attempting to establish a *modus vivendi* for themselves.

However, there seems to be a problem with this account. If *social identity* comes from adopting a role and personifying it in a singular manner, rather than simply animating it, then it seems as though we have to call upon *personal identity* to account for who does the active personification. Yet, it also appears that we cannot make such an appeal, for it looks, on this account, as though *personal identity* cannot be attained before *social identity* is achieved – through experience of social roles, endorsement of some of them and prioritising amongst those selected. How otherwise can people evaluate their social concerns against other kinds of concerns when defining their ultimate concern? How can they determine that priority should be given to one role rather than others they occupy, when defining their *modus vivendi*? This is the dilemma. I suggest that it is only solved by conceptualising the interplay between *personal identity* and *social identity* as a dialectical process, taking place over the life-course of each individual – a dialectic whose outcome *constitutes our individuation*.

If we wish to uphold the active rather than the passive *Actor*,[60] what will not do is to allow sociological imperialism back in by letting *social identity* swamp *personal identity*. This cannot be the case for three reasons. To begin with, most of us hold several social roles simultaneously and most roles are greedy consumers. There are never enough hours in the day to be the 'good' academic, the billing lawyer or the company executive, and the 'good' parent can be on the go around the clock. Now, if all roles are 'greedy', then who or what moderates between their demands? Were we to leave this as a matter arbitrated simply by the strength of these competing role demands alone, we would again have reconciled ourselves to the passive subject. Secondly, if it is assumed that subjects themselves conduct the arbitration, then we have to ask who exactly is doing this? The answer can only be a person. However, if it is indeed the person who has these abilities, then we have to grant that if they have the capacity to 'weigh' one role against another they can also evaluate their social concerns against their other commitments – thus establishing a *modus vivendi*. This is precisely what it was argued that the 'adult' internal conversation was about. Certainly, for recent role incumbents, new and socially derived information is brought into the internal conversation, but *in relation* to the claims of other ongoing concerns. Through reflexive inner dialogue their prioritisation and accommodation is worked out.

The resultant is a personal identity *within which* the social identity has been assigned its place in the life of a subject. That place may be large ('she lives for her work') or small ('he's only in it for the money'), but there is nothing which automatically ensures that social concerns have top priority. It is the subject who prioritises, and even if conditions are constrainingly such that good reason is found for devoting many hours to, say, monotonous employment, nothing insists that subjects put their hearts into it. Thirdly, in determining *how much* of themselves anyone will put into their various concerns, they are simultaneously deciding *what* they will put in. It has to be the person who does this, and acts as he or she does in each role, precisely because they are the particular person that they have become. *In the process, their social identity also becomes defined, but necessarily as a sub-set of their personal identity.*

We can now represent this acquisition of social identity as a process of progressive individuation, which is underpinned by the self-conscious human being. This is the 'I' whose continuous sense of self is needed throughout. The 'Me' is the self-as-object who, in the individual's past, was involuntarily placed within society's

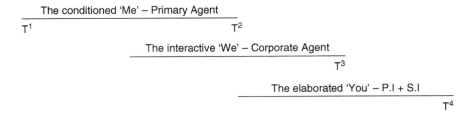

Figure M.9

resource distribution as a Primary Agent. The 'We' represents the collective action in which the self engages as part of Corporate Agency's attempt to bring about social transformation, which simultaneously transforms society's extant role array as well as transforming Corporate Agency itself. This then creates the positions which the 'You' can acquire, accept and personify, thus becoming an Actor possessing social identity. Figure M.9 summarises the argument presented in this last section.

In a nutshell, the subject, in his or her concrete singularity, has powers of ongoing reflexive monitoring of both self and society. These are far outside the register of *Modernity's Man*, who remains shackled to his own individualistic preference schedule. In parallel, this subject is also capable of authentic *creativity* that can transform 'society's conversation' in a radical way, which is foreign to *Society's Being*, ever condemned to making conventionally acceptable permutations upon it.

Conclusion: being human

The foregoing analysis aimed to secure a concept of the agent who was active and reflexive, as social realism requires: someone who has the properties and powers to monitor his or her own life, to mediate structural and cultural properties of society, and thus to contribute to societal reproduction or transformation. However, the process of being human is ongoing because throughout life we continue our reflexive work. The internal conversation is never suspended, it rarely sleeps, and what it is doing throughout the endless contingent circumstances it encounters is continuously monitoring its concerns. Inwardly, the subject is living a rich unseen life which is evaluative (rather than calculative, as is the case for *Modernity's Man*) and which is meditative (rather than appropriative, as is the lot of *Society's Being*). What this subject is doing is to conduct an endless assessment of whether what it once devoted itself to as its ultimate concern is still worthy of this devotion, and whether or not the price once paid for subordinating and accommodating other concerns is still one with which the subject can live. This is the sense in which each adult continually reinspects the 'I', the 'Me', the 'We' and the 'You' that have been part of his or her personal morphogenesis, and then applies his or her autonomous personal powers to pursue their replication or transformation. In the process, subjects actively contribute to their own ongoing personal development and to the continuous shaping of natural reality and its three orders – nature, practice and the social.

Notes

1 I leave it to others in this volume to introduce the broader context: specifically, the 'stratified realist ontology', 'open systems', 'contingency' and the critique of 'empiricism'.
2 See Roy Bhaskar, *The Possibility of Naturalism*, Harvester Wheatsheaf, Hemel Hempstead, 1979, pp. 25–6. This preliminary version was refined in his *Reclaiming Reality*, Verso, London, 1989, p. 77f.
3 John Parker, *Structuration*, Open University Press, Buckingham, 2000, Ch. 6.
4 Frédéric Vandenberghe, 'The Archers: A Tale of Folk (Final Episode?)', *European Journal of Social Theory*, 8:2, 2005, pp. 227–37.
5 Significantly, Margaret S. Archer, *Social Origins of Educational Systems*, Sage, London, was published in 1979, the same date at which Bhaskar's *The Possibility of Naturalism* first appeared. These are therefore two independent but convergent developments.
6 David Lockwood, 'Social integration and system integration', in G.K. Zollschan and H. W. Hirsch, *Explorations in Social Change*, Houghton Mifflin, Boston, 1964. This can be seen as a preliminary move towards a stratified social ontology.
7 Walter Buckley, *Sociology and Modern Systems Theory*, Prentice Hall, Englewood Cliffs NJ, 1967, p. 58.
8 Ibid., p. 18.
9 William Outhwaite, 'Agency and Structure', in J. Clark, C. Modgil and S. Modgil (eds), *Anthony Giddens: Consensus and Controversy*, Falmer Press, London, 1990, p. 71.
10 'A state educational system is considered to be a nationwide and differentiated collection of institutions devoted to formal education, whose overall control and supervision is at least partly governmental, and whose component parts and processes are related to one another.' Archer, *Social Origins*, p. 54.
11 Dave Elder-Vass, 'For Emergence: refining Archer's account of social structure', *Journal for the Theory of Social Behaviour*, 37:1, 2007, pp. 25–44.
12 Ibid, p. 30.
13 However, this will necessarily be an incomplete and non-predictive account, given that all structures and the conditions of their existence are at the mercy of contingency in an open system.
14 Roy Bhaskar, *Reclaiming Reality*, Verso, London, 1989, 'People and society [. . .] do not constitute two moments of the same process. Rather they refer to radically different things' (p. 76).
15 For example, by obliterating the decentralised organization of the English educational system in the last two decades of the twentieth century.
16 R. Keith Sawyer, *Social Emergence: Societies as Complex Systems*, Cambridge University Press, Cambridge, 2005, p. 83 (my italics).
17 A very brief summary of this study can be found in Margaret S. Archer, *Realist Social Theory: The Morphogenetic Approach*, Cambridge, Cambridge University Press, 1995, pp. 324–44 (*La Morfogenesi della Società*, Milan, FrancoAngeli, 1997, pp. 369–86.)
18 Elder-Vass, 'For Emergence'. Note, that for purposes of presentation, I have shifted his original point (v) to become point (iii), which appears to make no difference to his argument.
19 For example, as in his paradigmatic case of language: 'when I utter a grammatical English sentence in casual conversation, I contribute to the reproduction of the English language as a whole.' Anthony Giddens, *Central Problems in Social Theory*, Macmillan, London, 1979, pp. 77–8.
20 See Archer, *Realist Social Theory*, p. 74 and Ch. 8.
21 François Dépeltau, 'Relational Thinking: A Critique of Co-Deterministic Theories of Structure and Agency', *Sociological Theory*, 26:1, 2008, pp. 51–73.
22 See Margaret S. Archer, *Structure, Agency and the Internal Conversation*, Cambridge University Press, Cambridge, 2003, pp. 1–16 (*La conversazione interiore*, Erickson, Gardolo, 2006).

23 Douglas V. Porpora, 'Four concepts of social structure', *Journal for the Theory of Social Behaviour*, 19:2, 1989, p. 208.
24 Peter T. Manicas, *A Realist Theory of Social Science*, Cambridge University Press, Cambridge, 2006, p. 72
25 John R. Searle, *The Construction of Social Reality*, Penguin Books, London, 1996, Ch. 6.
26 Peter T. Manicas, *A Realist Philosophy of Social Science*, Cambridge University Press, Cambridge, 2006. '[P]ersons are the dominant causal agents in society – even while, of course, they work with materials at hand' (p. 75).
27 For a discussion of what I have termed 'central conflation', see Margaret S. Archer, *Culture and Agency*, Cambridge University Press, Cambridge, 1988, Chs 2, 3 and 4. Also Archer, *Realist Social Theory*, Chs 3 and 4.
28 Karl Popper, *Objective Knowledge*, Clarendon Press, Oxford, 1972, p. 298 f.
29 M.S. Archer, 'The Myth of Cultural Integration', *British Journal of Sociology*, 36:3, 1985, pp. 333–53.
30 D. Elder Vass, 'The Emergence of culture', in G. Albert and S. Sigmund (eds), *Soziologische Theorie kontrovers* (Kölner Zeitschrift für Soziologie und Sozialpsychologie Special Issue 50), pp. 351–63, VS Verlag, Wiesbaden, 2010, states 'culture by definition is shared by a group' (p. 6) and 'culture is inherently shared' (p. 14).
31 Ibid.
32 Margaret S. Archer and Dave Elder-Vass, 'Realists debate Culture' (forthcoming).
33 Bhaskar, *The Possibility of Naturalism*, p.40.
34 Ibid., p. 26.
35 For a theory of the formation of agents' 'projects' in the light of their personal concerns and consideration of their social contexts, see Archer, *Structure, Agency and the Internal Conversation. La conversazione interiore*.
36 Emile Durkheim, *The Evolution of Educational Thought*, Routledge & Kegan Paul, London, 1977, p. 22.
37 Imre Lakatos, 'Falsification and the methodology of scientific research programmes', in I. Lakatos and A. Musgrave (eds), *Criticism and the Growth of Knowledge*, Cambridge University Press, London, 1970, p. 99 f.
38 Indispensability need not be symmetrical – that is, bilateral.
39 Thomas S. Kuhn, *The Structure of Scientific Revolutions*, Chicago University Press, Chicago, 1962.
40 A.D. Hall and R.E. Hagen, 'Definition of system', in Joseph A. Litterer (ed.), *Organisation, Systems, Control and Adaptation*, Vol. II, Wiley, New York, 1969, p. 36.
41 Kuhn, *Scientific Revolutions*, p. 5.
42 Max Weber, in H.H. Gerth and C.W. Mills, *From Max Weber*, Routledge & Kegan Paul, London, 1967, p. 413.
43 Steven Lukes, *Power: A Radical View*, Macmillan, London, 1974.
44 Pierre Bourdieu and Jean-Claude Passeron, *La Reproduction*, Ed.de Muinuit, Paris, 1964.
45 See *Culture and Agency*, pp. 189–95.
46 See *Realist Social Theory*, Ch. 7
47 A.W. Gouldner, 'Reciprocity and Autonomy in Functional Theory', in N.J. Demerath and R.A. Peterson, *System, Change and Conflict*, Free Press, Collier Macmillan, New York, 1967.
48 Clearly this implies the existence of irreducible properties and powers pertaining to agents. For a specification of these, see Margaret S. Archer, *Being Human: The Problem of Agency*, Cambridge, Cambridge University Press, 2000.
49 Lakatos, 'Falsification', p. 158f.
50 'Man' and especially 'rational man' was the term current in Enlightenment thinking. Hence, I reluctantly abide with the term 'man', as standing for humanity, when referring to this tradition, its heirs, successors and adversaries.

51 The generic view that there are *no* emergent properties and powers pertaining to human agents – that is, ones which exist between human beings as organic parcels of molecules and humankind as generated from a network of social meanings. The best example of this model is provided by the work of Rom Harré. The leitmotif of his social constructionism is the following statement: 'A person is not a natural object, but a cultural artefact'. *Personal Being*, Basil Blackwell, Oxford, 1983, p. 20.
52 This was the model of man which was eagerly seized upon by social contract theorists in politics, Utilitarians in ethics and social policy and liberals in political economy. *Homo Economicus* is a survivor. He not only lives on as the anchorman of microeconomics and the hero of neoliberalism but is also a colonial adventurer and, in the hands of Rational Choice theorists, he bids to conquer social science in general. As Gary Becker outlines this mission, 'The economic approach is a comprehensive one that is applicable to all human behaviour'. *The Economic Approach to Human Behaviour*, Chicago University Press, Chicago, 1976, p. 8.
53 This is dealt with much more thoroughly in my *Being Human*.
54 Locke put forward a definition which has considerable intuitive appeal, such that a person was 'a thinking intelligent being, that has reason and reflection, and can consider itself as itself, the same thinking thing in different times and places' (*Essay* II, xxvii, 2). From Bishop Butler onwards, critics have construed such continuity of consciousness exclusively in terms of memory and then shown that memory alone fails to secure strict personal identity. See, for example, Bernard Williams, *Problems of the Self*, Cambridge University Press, Cambridge, 1973. A defence of a modified neo-Lockean definition is provided by David Wiggins, 'Locke, Butler and the Stream of Consciousness: and Men as a Natural Kind', *Philosophy*, 51, 1976, pp. 131–158, which preserves the original insight.
55 Marcel Mauss, 'A category of the human mind: the notion of person; the notion of self', in M. Carrithers, S. Collins and S. Lukes (eds), *The Category of the Person*, Cambridge University Press, Cambridge, 1989, pp. 1–25.
56 Ibid., p. 3.
57 Margaret S. Archer, 'Emotions as Commentaries on Human Concerns', in Jonathan H. Turner, *Theory and Research on Human Emotions*, Elsevier, Amsterdam, 2004.
58 Archer, *Structure, Agency and the Internal Conversation*.
59 Harry G. Frankfurt, *The Importance of What we Care About*, Cambridge University Press, Cambridge, 1988.
60 For this distinction, see Martin Hollis, *Models of Man: Philosophical Thoughts on Social Action*, Cambridge University Press, Cambridge, 1977.

1 Thinking and theorizing about educational systems

In the beginning

This book is where the Morphogenetic Approach was first developed and presented in 1979. Revisiting it gives me the opportunity to repay some debts and also to re-endorse this explanatory framework by replying to some of its critics. Let me briefly revert to the theoretical landscape in which this approach to explaining the emergence of State educational systems was conceived. In the social sciences, those were the days of 'the two sociologies',[1] when explanations based upon action and chains of interaction increasingly diverged from those that focused upon systems and culminated in the endorsement of systemic autopoiesis without actors. In the philosophy of social science these two sociologies were underwritten by Methodological Individualism and Methodological Holism, in which the ultimate constituents of the social world were respectively held to be 'other people' or 'social facts'.[2] *Social Origins of Educational Systems* should be seen as a howl of protest against this theoretical and philosophical background.

The original Introduction shows the importance I attached to resisting both of these types of approaches, ones I later critiqued as 'upward conflationism' and 'downward conflationism'.[3] The following quotation set the terms of the theoretical challenge to which the whole book was the response:

> It is important never to lose sight of the fact that the complex theories we develop to account for education and educational change *are theories about the educational activities of people* . . . [However] our theories will be *about* the educational activities of people even though they will not explain educational development strictly *in terms* of people alone.[4]

This is a statement about the need to acknowledge, to tackle and to combine agency and structure rather than conflating them. It was made difficult in two ways. On the one hand, there was no existing *stratified social ontology* that justified different emergent properties and powers pertaining to different strata of social reality, being irreducible to lower strata and having the capacity to exercise causal powers. Instead, notions of 'emergence' and of their causal powers[5] met with resistance and the charge of reification.

However, the properties and powers of State educational systems are considered here to be both real and different from those pertaining to educational actors – even though deriving from them. The problem was twofold: how to justify the existence of both sets of properties and how to theorize their interplay. The articulation of a stratified social ontology for the social order was the achievement of Roy Bhaskar's *Possibility of Naturalism*, also published in 1979.[6] Retrospectively, the concurrence of our two books was advantageous because although Bhaskar's social ontology would have provided a more robust basis than the 'sheepish' Methodological Collectivism[7] upon which I perforce relied in this study, its absence at the time induced me to develop a thoroughgoing explanatory framework for analysing the interplay of structure and agency. This was the first appearance of the Morphogenetic Approach, which I view as the 'methodological complement'[8] of the Critical Realist ontology that developed simultaneously.

On the other hand, in 1979 the landscape tilted again with the publication of Anthony Giddens' *Central Problems in Social Theory*.[9] Its key claim that 'structure is both medium and outcome of the reproduction of practices'[10] was the most blatant statement in the English-speaking world that the 'problem of structure and agency' should be 'transcended' by treating the two components as interdependent and inseparable. In other words, 'central conflation' had arrived and purported both to nullify Bhaskar's stratified social ontology and to render my morphogenetic approach redundant. I will not recapitulate my criticisms of structuration theory, made from 1982 onwards,[11] which basically held it guilty of *sinking* the differences between structure and agency rather than *linking* them. In turn, Bhaskar adopted this critique of Giddens[12] and critical realists generally came to accept that different emergent properties and powers are proper to different levels of social organization, and that those pertaining to structure are distinct and irreducible to those belonging to agents. Thus, it follows that critical realism is necessarily ontologically and methodologically opposed to 'transcending' the difference between structure and agency. Instead, the name of the game remains how to conceptualize the interplay between them, which is what the morphogenetic approach set out to do from the beginning.

Philosophical underlabouring and forging an explanatory toolkit

When taken together, two theorists enabled the 'morphogenetic approach' to be advanced in 1979. What it aimed to do was to develop a framework for giving an account of the *existence* of particular structures at particular times and in particular places. The phenomenon to be explained was how State educational systems (SES) came into existence at all and, more specifically, why some were *decentralized* (as in England) whilst others were *centralized* (as in France) and what consequences resulted from these differences in relational organization. Thus, the 'morphogenetic approach' first set out to explain where such forms of social organization came from – that is, how emergents in fact emerged.

Thanks to David Lockwood's seminal distinction between 'system' and 'social' integration,[13] it was possible to conceive of the two (taken to refer to 'structure' and 'agency') as exerting different kinds of causal powers – ones that varied independently from one another and were factually distinguishable over time – despite the lack of a well-articulated social ontology. Thanks to Walter Buckley, my attention was drawn to 'morphogenesis': that is, 'to those processes which tend to elaborate or change a system's given form, structure or state',[14] in contrast to 'morphostasis', which refers to those processes in a complex system that tend to preserve the above unchanged. However, Buckley himself regarded 'structure' as 'an abstract construct, not something distinct from the on-going interactive process but rather a temporary, accommodative representation of it at any one time',[15] thus tending to 'dodge questions of social ontology'.[16]

Although the study is ontologically bold in advancing the relational organization of different structures of educational systems as being temporally prior to, relatively autonomous from and exerting irreducible causal powers over relevant agents, there was something less courageous in acceding with the Methodological Collectivists (Gellner and Mandelbaum) that such claims must be open to 'potential reduction' because their justification rested only on 'explanatory emergence'.[17] A more robust social ontology of causal powers and generative mechanisms was needed to underpin this explanatory programme and allow it to shed its apologetic attitude. This is what Bhaskar provided in *The Possibility of Naturalism*, describing his own role as 'underlabouring' for the social sciences.

Nevertheless, his realist social ontology does not explain why, in Weber's words, given social matters are 'so, rather than otherwise'. A social ontology explains nothing and does not attempt to do so; its task is to define and justify the terms and the form in which explanations can properly be cast. Similarly, the Morphogenetic Approach also explains nothing; it is an explanatory framework that has to be filled in by those using it as a toolkit with which to work on a specific issue, who then do purport to explain something. Substantive theories alone give accounts of *how* particular components of the social order originated and came to stand in given relationships to one another. The explanatory framework is intended to be a very practical toolkit, not a 'sensitization device' (as 'structuration theory' was eventually admitted to be); one that enables researchers to advance accounts of social change by specifying the 'when', 'how' and 'where' and avoiding the vagaries of assuming 'anytime', 'anyhow' and 'anywhere'.[18]

In this book I am doing two jobs at once: developing the toolkit and also putting it to work to offer an explanation of the social origins of State educational systems and of the difference that their relational organization makes to subsequent processes and patterns of educational change. Part I of the book uses this framework to account for the *diachronic* development of State educational systems and their differences in structural organization, which can be summarized as centralized or decentralized. Part II moves on to explain the *synchronic* effects of emergent centralization and decentralization, whilst ever these two forms of relational organization were maintained. The briefest outline of this explanatory framework is needed before turning to some of the debates it has provoked.

The origins of the morphogenetic approach

Although all structural properties found in any society are continuously activity-dependent, analytical dualism allows 'structure' and 'agency'[19] to be separated and their interplay examined in order to account for the structuring and restructuring of the social order or its component institutions. This is possible for two reasons. Firstly, 'structure' and 'agency' are *different kinds of emergent entities*,[20] as is shown by the differences in their properties and powers, *despite* the fact that they are crucial for each other's formation, continuation and development. Thus, an educational system can be 'centralized' whilst a person cannot, and humans are 'emotional', which cannot be the case for structures. Secondly, and fundamental to how this explanatory framework works, 'structure' and 'agency' operate diachronically over different time periods because: (i) structure necessarily pre-dates the action(s) that transform it and (ii) structural elaboration necessarily post-dates those actions, as represented in Figure 1.1.

It aims to make structural change tractable to investigation by breaking up the temporal flow – which is anything but 'liquidity' – into three sequential phases: <Structural Conditioning → Social Interaction → Structural Elaboration>. This carves out one morphogenetic cycle, but projection of the lines forwards and backwards connects up with anterior and posterior cycles. Two such cycles are analysed in the current study: the one prior to the emergence of State educational systems and the one posterior to them (the book ends with the state of educational affairs in 1975). The delineation of Cycle I and II followed the preliminary judgement that *the advent of a State system represented a new emergent entity*, whose distinctive relational properties and powers conditioned subsequent educational interaction (processes and patterns of change) in completely different ways compared with the previous cycle, in which educational control derived from private ownership of educational resources. The establishment of such morphogenetic 'breaks' – signalling the end of one cycle and constituting the beginning of the next – is always the business of any particular investigator and the problem in hand.

Figure 1.2 illustrates how the explanatory framework is used throughout the book and should disabuse the prevalent mistaken view that the morphogenetic approach dated from 1995.[21]

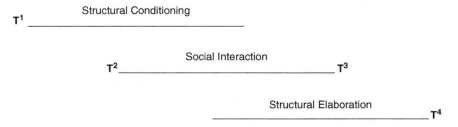

Figure 1.1 The basic morphogenetic sequence.

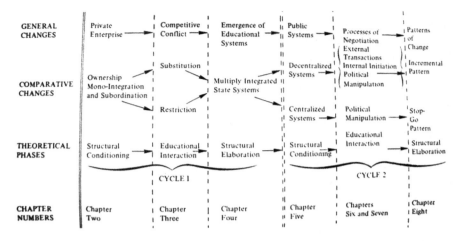

Figure 1.2 Summary use of the Morphogenetic Approach in the book.

Why study State educational systems and how?

This is merely a particular version of the question 'Why study social institutions at all?' Some social theorists do not,[22] and substitute the investigation of 'practices', 'transactions', 'networks', 'activities' and so forth. Those doing so find themselves driven to introduce a 'qualifier' whose job is to register that these doings are not free-floating but are anchored temporally and spatially, the most common being the term 'situated'. However, to talk, for example, about 'situated practices' may seem to give due acknowledgement to the historical and geographical contextualization of doings such as 'transactions' but only serves to locate them by furnishing the co-ordinates of their when or where. Simply to provide these spatial and temporal co-ordinates is not to recognize the fact that all actions are contextualized in the strong sense that the context shapes the action and therefore is a necessary component in the explanation of any actions whatsoever, since there is no such thing as non-contextualized action (contra Dépelteau).[23]

Thus, the point is how this context should be conceptualized. Some attempt a minimalist response and basically construe the situated nature of all doings as the accumulated deposit of past actions. This merely re-poses the problem: what was the historical context of such past doings themselves? If ultimate regress is not to result, such theorists have to cease backtracking at some point and take the contemporary historical, contextual properties as given. They do so as a heuristic necessity and expressly refuse to grant that these historical contextual properties should be accorded causal powers. Such properties are indeed treated as an 'accumulation', at most supplying a situational inheritance to be drawn upon by those actors present, but not as something they inevitably confront and that necessarily enters into the shaping of their actions and the trajectories they take. (See Anthony King, for example).[24]

There is a voluntarism in such approaches that even at the experiential level struck me as unrealistic. As a post-doctoral student moving from London to Paris in the late 1960s, the organization of courses at the Sorbonne, with booklets of lecture notes for sale around the corner, which invited their regurgitation and was reinforced by a lack of seminar discussion, represented a context that fostered standardized performance and stylistic standardization. Writ large, it was this experience of two very different educational systems that prompted the present book, but it would not have done so without the conviction that the contexts of teaching and learning in England and France derived from systemic differences that fundamentally shaped their pedagogical practices.

In other words, the structure of social institutions (of education, in this case) mattered to what took place within them and who had a say in this. These two educational systems had been structured in the past but exerted causal powers in the present because of the lasting differences in their relational organizing structures. If that was the case, then an exploration of the social origins of these very different educational systems was necessary, though not sufficient, to explain the differences in their enduring properties and powers. Those social origins in both countries (as in Russia and Denmark, which were added later) were ones of intense struggle in terms of cultural aims and educational ideals, and in terms of material resources and objective interests on the part of different groups vying for educational domination but with none ever achieving outright, unopposed control. To me, this meant then, as it still does, that society's institutional complex was the product of group conflict, which meant construing the social order as a *relationally contested organization*. This signified that the development of society's institutions could not be represented as processes of functional adaptation or as complex adaptive systems. Today, I would extend this and deny that contemporary educational systems can be characterized as either *self-governing* or *self-organizing*. They became what they were and are what they are because of the *relational contestation* between interested parties and the compromises and concessions temporally reached that give a temporary structure to the organization of education.

Then, as now, such a generic starting point had little in common with the work of sociologists of education, who set themselves the entirely different project of advancing *general theories* – including *universal propositions* – about the educational process in society. As such, they theorized about 'process without system'. Despite the kindness received from both Pierre Bourdieu and Basil Bernstein, I could not accept their three main theoretical assumptions whose combined effect was to deprive the structure of educational systems of any importance: (i) that schools, colleges and universities were permeable membranes, penetrated through osmosis by social stratification, thus reproducing class differences in the pedagogical process; (ii) that the definition of instruction at all levels was conducive to the morphostatic maintenance of class relations and that teachers were condemned reflexively to 'mis-recognize' their homeostatic practices; (iii) that differences in the organizational structure of education could be deprived of significance by selectively accentuating similarities and neglecting differences, thus homogenizing the structure of educational systems. Their combined effects are summarized in Figure 1.3 below.

42 Theorizing about educational systems

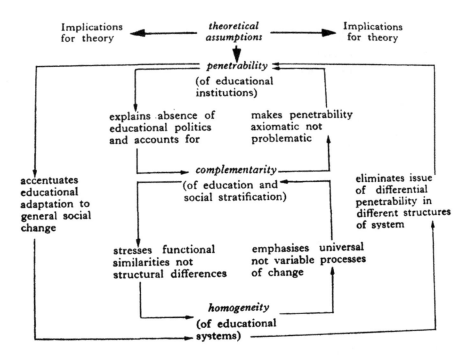

Figure 1.3 Assumptions making the structure of the Educational System unimportant.
Source: Margaret S. Archer, 1983, "Process without System", *Archives Européennes de Sociologie*, 24:1083, p. 219.

The argument advanced in the chapters that follow rejects all three of those assumptions and the explanatory procedures to which they led. Instead, I counterposed the following two propositions.

First, that the advent of a State educational system (SES) in any country marked a radical change from the prior historical situation in which the existence of educational provisions was a matter of *private ownership*, giving those who furnished its physical and human resources untrammelled control in the educational domain. The advent of an SES, defined as 'a nationwide and differentiated collection of institutions devoted to formal education, whose overall control and supervision is at least partly governmental, and whose component parts and processes are related to one another',[25] was a structural transformation with far-reaching consequences. The development of SESs universally signalled crucial changes in *who* could gain access, *what* definition of instruction was imposed for what ends, and for *which* positions and roles in society entrants were being prepared. Clearly, with the advent of SESs, the attachment of education to the State introduced some element of political influence that had previously been far from universal.

The problem was how to theorize the emergence of SESs, given the overview that every form of institutionalization is the outcome of *relational contestation*.

The theoretical approach had to be more specific because it needed to embrace the fact that different forms of strategic interaction (*legal restriction* or *market substitution* of the previous privately owned provisions) were responsible for generating an SES in different countries. It had also to explain how these different strategic forms of interaction resulted in SESs whose common characteristics ('unification' by the State, 'systematization', referring to the principled connection between educational components, 'differentiation' from other social institutions and 'specialization' of pedagogical activities) differed in strength and importance according to the strategy that had generated the SES. Specifically, the relative strength of the two pairs of characteristics, 'unification' plus 'systematization' and 'differentiation' plus 'specialization', represented the difference between *centralized* versus *decentralized* educational systems. This is held to be the most significant and far-reaching difference between State educational systems. Providing analytical histories of the emergence of centralized compared with decentralized SESs is the task undertaken in Part I of the book.

Second, the advent of an SES represented a great break with the previous socio-educational context. It constituted a new institutional structure, differentially serving more parts and portions of given societies and valorizing different sections of the total cultural system in its definition of instruction. *Cui bono* at the time an SES emerged was never a matter of osmosis but the consequence of which groups (materially or ideationally motivated) had won out most and which least. However, with the advent of an SES, both the (temporal and temporary) beneficiaries and the less successful (frustrated, obstructed and partially excluded) groups could no longer resort to unbridled conflict to defend their gains or to redress their grievances. Educational change now became a matter of *negotiation*, replacing the exchange of injurious acts previously intended to eliminate other educationally active parties through strategies of *market substitution* or *political restriction*. These were no longer possible because no group could now complete with the powers and resources of the State. Instead, three new processes for negotiating educational change universally came into play: *Political Manipulation, External Transactions* and *Internal Initiation*. However, their *differential importance* varied with the social origins of the particular SES. *Which* of the two strategies had resulted in the emergence of an educational system profoundly influenced *who* proved most and least influential in negotiating further educational changes, in the service of *what* ends, and *how* they brought these modifications and reforms about. Once again, this is utterly unlike osmosis; it guarantees no universal beneficiary – even the State – and there is no sense in which it automatically underwrites the form of social stratification prevailing in any country. On the contrary, for the first time education comes to play a central role in confirming and transforming the class structure of modernity. All of this is the subject matter of Part II of the book.

The book meets some of its critics

How any social form comes to exist – in this case State educational systems – is crucial for explaining the emergent properties and powers that derive from the new relational organization of its parts. What the first morphogenetic cycle accounts for is how education was transformed from a 'heap' (of disparate private educational provisions) into a 'whole' (an SES, subject to governmental regulation and with coordinated component establishments). It supplies an analytical history of emergence, indispensable for explaining the new emergent powers pertaining to the nationwide SESs – ones that did not exist even for the broadest networks of educational institutions previously owned and operated by the Churches in Europe.

The second cycle, dealing with the SESs in action, is vital to account for (i) the novel workings of this new structure in general, (ii) for how the particular relational organization of centralized and decentralized SESs structurally conditioned different processes and patterns of change and (iii) why once SESs had developed they remained in existence despite ongoing struggles and resultant changes.

Broadly, there have been two sets of critics whose targets are respectively the first and the second cycles. In the former group are those such as Peter Manicas, who would argue that the social origins of SESs – as novel structures with novel workings – are dispensable in sociological explanation. Manicas is basically endorsing an elisionist account[26] that requires the instantiation of structural properties by agents before they can be accorded any explanatory role. In line with structuration theory, he claims that, far from structural properties impinging upon agents, it is agency that brings them into play by instantiating them. Yet, for example, parents do not instantiate compulsory school attendance and nor do teachers instantiate school inspection; both depend upon *prior* legislation and its sanctions. Since such laws differ from country to country, how they came into existence needs to be explained. Equally, the major preoccupation of sociologists of education, namely the differential educational achievement of pupils from different socio-economic backgrounds, cannot be adequately conceptualized. Manicas would consider the structural and cultural properties attaching to pupils' social backgrounds as being 'materials at hand',[27] without the capacity to exert causal powers. From this standpoint we would be deprived of any ability to account for why some of these 'materials' (structural and cultural) are within easy reach of certain social groups but out of reach for other ones.

Conversely, others have claimed (although they rarely evidence having read this book) that any morphogenetic cycle, such as the first one discussed here, is *only history* and has dubious connections with emergence. I will not delay over the bizarre assertion that the explanatory framework regards anything as being emergent *because it is historical*. On this view, all antiques would qualify as emergents! In similar vein, Keith Sawyer maintains that Cycle I is *only history* and cannot account for the making of emergent powers and their constraint, enablement and motivation of (subsequent) agents. Hence, Sawyer's misleading comment that I am arguing that 'it is emergence over time – morphogenesis – that *makes* emergent properties real and *allows* them to *constrain* individuals' (my italics).[28]

It seems obvious that Sawyer cannot dismiss explanations of how something (such as an SES) came into existence and that this 'may require' what I term an 'analytical history of its emergence'.[29] It puzzles me sociologically why this only 'may' rather than 'must' be required in every case. It is because Sawyer's choice of words endorses Fodor's[30] notion of 'wild disjunction', such that a higher-level property (such as an SES) can be 'multiply realized' by a wildly disjunctive set of lower-level properties. Even were this to be granted, it is hard to see how it dispenses with analytical histories of emergence in the plural. Indeed, I give two instances of the 'multiple realizability' of SESs (those deriving from *restriction* and *substitution* respectively), and 'wild disjuncture' seems a wildly inappropriate description of the two action sequences analysed in Part I. There is not space to enter this discussion here, save to point out that the whole point of Part I is to show that the interaction involved is systematically related to the development of SESs and to their relational organizing structures. Wild disjunctures never enter the picture.

However, Sawyer's fire is predominantly directed not at the social origins of educational systems but at maintaining that the explanatory approach cannot supply an account of how the relational organizational structures of SESs can constrain (and, I would add, enable and motivate) individuals and groups; that is, he holds it incapable of furnishing a synchronic account of reflexive downward causation in Part II. Here he joins hands with Dave Elder-Vass.

The latter differs from Sawyer in readily conceding that the morphogenetic approach usefully supplies the diachronic account that he holds to be universally necessary in order to explain *how* any emergent property comes to exist. Nevertheless, he proceeds to argue that

> morphogenesis does *not* explain how an entity can possess emergent properties and powers. Such an explanation always depends on the existence of a specific set of *synchronic* relations between the parts: morphogenesis explains the development of a such a set of relations over time, but the operation of a causal power at any given moment depends upon the presence of those relations *at that specific moment in time*.[31]

In other words, we have now moved over to a critique of Cycle II, namely how can an SES exert causal powers *once* it exists?

When he first advanced this argument in 2007, it was hard to understand how it squared with the commitment in realism to the 'activity dependence' of all social forms. To realists, nothing social, whatever its origins, is self-sustaining, which is what *inter alia* distinguishes the social from the natural world. Only a myriad of agential 'doings' keep any given higher-level social entity in being, underwrite its causal powers and render it relatively enduring. I agree; whilst ever something like the centralized French educational system lasts, then move a marker, second-by-second, from the system's inception until today, and each and every moment of its 'centralization' depends upon agential doings.

This is not equivalent to some Giddensian notion that *every* doing on the part of *everyone* somehow contributes to maintaining the whole (in this case, an SES with a centralized relational organization).[32] On the contrary, how different groups of agents are positioned in relation to the emergent educational system at the end of Cycle I profoundly affects what they can do, seek to do and do in fact do at the start of Cycle II. The relational organization of education is ineluctably handed onto them and what they do with it does lie in their hands – even though their hands are not free because of the emergent structure with which they have to live *pro tem* and the fact that groups supporting it and challenging it are significantly defined by it. To me, 'one of the main antecedent effects of structures . . . consists of dividing the population, not necessarily and not usually exhaustively into those with vested interests in maintenance and change according to the positions in which they find themselves involuntarily'.[33] This is how the diachronic segues into the synchronic and the latter is incomprehensible without allowing for this continuity.

Although in *The Causal Power of Social Structures*[34] Elder-Vass has come to adopt morphogenetic and morphostatic analysis, his 'solution' to the problem he voiced about with my approach is 'solved' by confining morphogenesis to what initially brings about a 'set of relations', such as an SES, whilst morphostasis is held to account for what synchronically 'stabilizes' something like an SES and the working of its causal powers over any further tract of time. This dichotomization creates more problems than it solves precisely because it erects a wall between the diachronic and the synchronic, effectively placing morphogenesis on one side and morphostasis on the other. It entails a misunderstanding of 'morphogenesis', working through positive feedback, and 'morphostasis', which works through negative feedback, and the crucial fact that both are *always in play*. This is properly understood by Italian commentators who rightly refer to the explanatory framework as the M/M approach.[35]

In Cycle I, for example, the Churches defending their networks of schools were acting morphostatically in the face of assertive groups seeking educational transformation. The interaction between those groups seeking educational change versus those defending stability *together* shaped the SES to emerge. The point is simply that in Cycle II their interaction does not cease (all lines in Figure 1.1 are continuous) because those who have won most have not gained everything they want and those who have lost out most do not throw in the sponge but battle on.

In other words, the 'break' represented by the emergence of a SES does *not* issue in an untrammelled morphostasis, with all hands on deck and working through negative feedback to maintain the new educational status quo. Synchronically, what the emergence of an educational system at T_4 does at the end of Cycle I is to redivide the relevant population (through the *double morphogenesis* of agency) into those with vested interests in maintenance (morphostasis of the new SES) and those interested in further change (that may be morphogenetic but can be regressive), according to the new educational situations in which people and groups now find themselves.[36] But these conflicting interests (material and ideal) will now, in Cycle II, have to work through different processes for defensive purposes or for further change *because* the relational organization has become different *through* their earlier contestation and that of their predecessors. This is the downwards causation initially exerted by what their own interaction had brought about at the end of Cycle I.

On the one hand, this means, for example, that no government has ever since voluntarily ceded the centralization inherited from Cycle I because of the objective advantages it perceives as deriving from an SES responsive to political direction. Such actions can indeed be seen as morphostatic and stabilizing. However, that same diachronically emergent SES is also and simultaneously modified significantly by old and new social groupings seeking morphogenetically to align education more closely to their interests. For any SES – as for all institutions – the change it represents is a compromise rather than the morphogenetic ideal of any group. It is the satisfaction/dissatisfaction of group interests, together with the further interaction of the relevant parties, that explains future structural stability and change. In short, the SES *remains a relationally contested organization* in Cycle II, which is not a period of unchallenged morphostasis (they never are) in which the pressures for 'stabilization' mean that nothing other than negative feedback becomes the rule.

Elder-Vass does not endorse the social order as a *relationally contested organization*. This is what leads him to slide away from the realist canon that the *combined* outcomes of morphostasis and morphogenesis are always activity-dependent (upon agential interests, aims and doings). Instead, he introduces a 'third party', as it were, the evolutionary adaptation over which systems theorists such as Buckley hesitated,[37] but that recent converts to complexity theory are busy rehabilitating in social theory. As he puts it, 'The concepts of morphostasis and morphogenesis, then are capable of elaboration and combination in ways that enable us to start describing *complex adaptive systems* that are reminiscent of social structures.'[38] Because I have never encountered a satisfactory sociological answer to the question 'adaptive to what', I stand by the statement in the original introduction that 'education is fundamentally about what people have wanted of it and have been able to do to it',[39] which includes the generation of emergent properties, their causal powers and their subsequent elaboration.

Afterword

The book's last chapter does highlight how, prior to 1975, centralized systems were already using 'sub-division' to provide more specialization, especially for the market economy, but without yielding central control and coordination. In parallel, decentralized systems were limiting local and professional powers in order to enhance education's responsiveness to political direction. However, what could not be foreseen was the lurch of all SESs towards a centralized structure during the 1990s, in the context of globalization and of centrist politics, despite a disingenuous rhetoric about 'devolution'. In the past, the main problem with centralized systems was that they were always out of synchrony with the surrounding environment because of their over-control, whilst the historical problem of decentralized systems was internal anarchy due to their under-coordination.

Today's shift towards almost universal educational centralization universalizes the mismatch between educational systems and the global environment. This cannot be adequately explained by empirical generalizations about 'marketization', 'financialization' and 'commodification'. Nor can the sociology of education persist in structure-blindness and continue to discuss class, gender and ethnic educational inequalities as 'processes without system'. Isn't it time for the analysis of Cycle III?

Notes

1 Alan Dawe, 1970, 'The Two Sociologies', *British Journal of Sociology*, 21:2, pp. 207–18.
2 See Margaret S. Archer, 1995, *Realist Social Theory: The Morphogenetic Approach*, Cambridge, Cambridge University Press, Chapter 2.
3 Margaret S. Archer, 1988, *Culture and Agency*, Cambridge, Cambridge University Press, Chapters 2, 3 and 4.
4 Margaret S. Archer, 1979, *Social Origins of Educational Systems*, London and Beverly Hills, Sage, p. 2.
5 Rom Harré and Edward H. Madden, 1975, *Causal Powers: A Theory of Natural Necessity*, Oxford, Blackwell.
6 Roy Bhaskar, 1979, *The Possibility of Naturalism*, Hemel Hempstead, Harvester.
7 Ernest Gellner says social institutions and so on are not simply mental abstractions but are, 'I am somewhat sheepishly tempted to say, "really there"': 'Holism versus Individualism' in May Brodbeck (ed.), 1968, *Readings in the Philosophy of the Social Sciences*, New York, Macmillan, p. 264.
8 See Margaret S. Archer, 2011, 'Morphogenesis: Realism's explanatory framework', in A.M. Maccarini, E. Morandi and R. Prandini (eds), *Sociological Realism*, London and New York, Routledge, pp. 55–94.
9 Anthony Giddens, 1979, *Central Problems in Social Theory*, London, Macmillan.
10 Giddens, *Central Problems*, p. 69.
11 Margaret S. Archer, 1982, 'Morphogenesis versus structuration', *British Journal of Sociology*, 33, pp. 455–83.
12 Roy Bhaskar, 1993, *Dialectic: The Pulse of Freedom*, London, Verso, p. 54.
13 David Lockwood, 'Social integration and system integration', in G.K. Zollschan and H.W. Hirsch, *Explorations in Social Change*, Boston, Houghton Mifflin, 1964. This can be seen as a preliminary move towards a stratified social ontology.
14 Walter Buckley, 1967, *Sociology and Modern Systems Theory*, Prentice Hall, Englewood Cliffs NJ, p. 58.
15 Ibid., p. 18.
16 William Outhwaite, 1990, 'Agency and Structure', in J. Clark, C. Modgil and S. Modgil (eds), *Anthony Giddens: Consensus and Controversy*, London, Falmer Press, p. 71.
17 Maurice Mandelbaum, 1955, 'Societal Facts', *British Journal of Sociology*, 6, p. 229.
18 Archer, 1979, *Social Origins of Educational Systems*, original Introduction, p. 23.
19 The same is true of culture – see my 1988 and 1995 publications.
20 Roy Bhaskar, 1989, *Reclaiming Reality*, London, Verso, 'People and society [. . .] do not constitute two moments of the same process. Rather they refer to radically different things' (p. 76).
21 This error is often repeated despite a brief summary of this book being used for illustration in Archer, *Realist Social Theory*, pp. 328–44. The notable exceptions are John Parker, 2000, *Structuration*, Buckingham, Open University Press, Ch. 6, Frédéric Vandenberghe, 2005, 'The Archers: A Tale of Folk (Final Episode?)', *European Journal of Social Theory*, 8:2, pp. 227–37, and Pierpaolo Donati in numerous works.
22 This is particularly common in US work on educational development, which deals instead with 'mass education'.
23 François Dépelteau, 2008, 'Relational Thinking: A Critique of Co-Determinist Theories of Structure and Agency', *Sociological Theory*, 26:1, pp. 51–73. Action and interaction are always context-dependent and concept-dependent.
24 Anthony King, 2004, *The Structure of Social Theory*, London, Routledge.
25 Archer, *Social Origins of Educational Systems*, p. 54.
26 Basically that of Giddens: see Peter Manicas, 2006, *A Realist Theory of Social Science*, Cambridge, Cambridge University Press.

27 Manicas writes: '[P]ersons are the dominant causal agents in society – even while, of course, they work with materials at hand.' *A Realist Philosophy of Social Science*, p. 75.
28 R. Keith Sawyer, 2005, *Social Emergence: Societies as Complex Systems*, Cambridge, Cambridge University Press, p. 83.
29 Ibid., p. 84.
30 See Ibid., p. 67.
31 Dave Elder-Vass, 2007, 'For Emergence: refining Archer's account of social structure', *Journal for the Theory of Social Behaviour*, 37:1, p. 30.
32 For example, as in his paradigmatic case of language: 'when I utter a grammatical English sentence in casual conversation, I contribute to the reproduction of the English language as a whole'. Giddens, *Central Problems*, pp. 77–8.
33 Archer, *Realist Social Theory*, p. 203.
34 Dave Elder-Vass, 2010, *The Causal Powers of Social Structures*, Cambridge, Cambridge University Press.
35 Andrea M. Maccarini, 2011, 'Towards a new European sociology', in A.M. Maccarini, E. Morandi and R. Prandini (eds), *Sociological Realism*, London and New York, Routledge, pp. 95–121. He writes that the M/M approach 'stands for "morphogenetic/morphostatic", and is used to emphasize that in principle neither of the two possible outcomes has priority over the other' (p. 115).
36 To characterise an interest as a 'vested' one is to associate it with a particular position, the implication being that if positions (roles, institutions) change, then so do interests. As Porpora puts it, 'among the causal powers that are deposited in social positions are interests. Interests are built into a social position by the relationship of that position to other positions in the system [. . .] actors are motivated to act in their interests, which are a function of their social position. Again, this doesn't mean that actors always with necessity act in their interests, but if they don't they are likely to suffer.' Douglas V. Porpora, 1989, 'Four concepts of social structure', *Journal for the Theory of Social Behaviour*, 19:2, p. 208.
37 Walter Buckley, 1998, *Society – A Complex Adaptive System: Essays in Social Theory*, Amsterdam, Gordon and Breach. Note the very proper hesitations on p. 74.
38 Elder-Vass, *The Causal Powers of Social Structures*, p. 38 (my italics).
39 Archer, *Social Origins of Educational Systems*, original Introduction, p. 2.

2 On predicting the behaviour of the educational system

Predicting the Behavior of the Educational System
THOMAS F. GREEN, DAVID P. ERICSON & ROBERT SEIDMAN, 1980
Syracuse University Press
pp. 200

This is a book to be read three times – once with unreserved admiration for its bold conception and economic execution; secondly with serious sociological reservations; and thirdly with great care to sift out the achievements from the ambitions. The work *is* a major contribution, although it will take me the whole of this review to establish precisely what Green, Seidman and Ericson have achieved.

Essentially the authors have two major aims. The first is to elucidate a 'logic' of the educational system, its structure and dynamics. The second is to validate the claim that the educational system has a 'life of its own'. This means providing an account such that 'the behavior of the system, its inherent processes, may become intelligible in a way that is *independent* of differences in political and economic ideology' (p. xiii).

Basically I will argue that the claim concerning the 'logic' of educational systems cannot be sustained, whereas the claim that they have a 'life of their own' can be established. Green and his colleagues see the two claims as intimately, though not inextricably, related. In denying the existence of this (and probably any) inherent 'logic' of the system I am obviously separating the two claims, and consequently many of the propositions about the 'life' of the system then have to be reformulated to eradicate their logical status and to restore sociological contingency.

Reformulation can be accomplished by replacing many of the law-like statements with 'if . . . then' propositions. What remains is not the pass-key to the workings of any modern educational system (on the analogy of micro economics to the market economy) but a corpus of theory about how they do work under certain conditions – which is all the more useful because the conditions involved are indeed very common. Perhaps the authors are right that they will become yet more pervasive: if so, they will become more important, but this will not transform their conditional status.

The 'logic' of the system is grounded in Green's belief that 'though the system is instantiated in many places, it is "*the* system" everywhere in precisely the same way that though the nation state is exemplified in many places, it is the *same* reality in each that we point to with the phrase "*the* nation state"' (p. xiv). He is referring to twentieth-century manifestations of educational systems and to their unnoticed uniformities. The first problem begins to arise because Green refuses to define what the educational system is, whilst simultaneously insisting that it is the same everywhere. Instead he is 'content to rely upon the fact that the reader will bring to the text an adequate conception of what is meant by "the educational system"' (p. xv). Because we talk about it, we know what it is – perhaps our ordinary language use even reveals a popular understanding that 'the system' is one. The trouble is that this commonsense conception of the reader rapidly turns out to mean common American experience. Green begins by stating that 'All we require, by way of definition, is to consult that conception and we shall discover that it refers (1) to a set of schools and colleges (2) related by a medium of exchange, and (3) arranged by some principles of sequence' (p. xvi). However, 'commonsense' has now incorporated into the groundwork of the theory two features (the second and third) which are not found everywhere outside the USA. Particularly when they are spelt out, they appear to be systemic variables: features which varied greatly during the history of different systems and which still display comparative variations.

This is clearest where 'sequence' is concerned. Although Green stresses that there can be different *rules* of sequence, he thinks of the system in terms of 'levels' (meaning primary, secondary and higher) through which people pass sequentially. Indeed, later he refers more explicitly to a 'single ladder of success' (p. 88). Thus the *principle* of sequence

> states that the system of schools is organised into levels, so that if a person has completed the nth level of the system, that will constitute sufficient reason for concluding that he has completed the level of $n - 1$, but not a sufficient reason for concluding that he has completed or will complete the level of $n + 1$.
>
> (p. 8)

But what are $n - 1$ and $n + 1$? In a system like the French where the 'single ladder of success' has been fought for throughout the twentieth century (and barely won), there were two separate sequences, amounting almost to two parallel systems, as the *premier degré* sprouted 'secondary' and even 'tertiary' tops and the *second degré* grew downwards into *lycée* preparatory classes. Here $n - 1$ meant two different things for pupils of the same age or stage in their school career – a year lower in the 'primary system' or a year lower in the '*lycée* system': similarly, taking n as the start of schooling, $n + 3$ for the bourgeois pupil meant entry to the *lycée* sector, but $n + 12$ (or more years) would not mean that the lower-class pupil had ever left the primary sector.

In short, some systems were not designed for their 'levels' to operate sequentially: the very concept of levels is extremely problematic in such countries. What Green assumes to be universal is what I have termed elsewhere the *positive* principle of Hierarchical Organisation,[1] the point being that historically and comparatively the *negative* principle has been just as important – indeed, many modern systems are still marked by it since their levels do not represent strong ladders.

The same can be said about educational institutions being related by a 'medium of exchange' (mutually recognised certificates, diplomas or transcripts) whose 'existence permits us to speak of a single educational system' (p. 5). This is held to be more fundamental for defining the system than whether educational institutions share a common legal authority – the former is viewed as sufficient for the existence of a system, the latter is seen as neither necessary nor sufficient. The significance attached to this characteristic may accurately reflect the state of affairs in the USA, given the great freedom of her institutions to negotiate mutual recognition and to establish their own equivalences. However, there are many countries in which the very award and acknowledgement of qualifications, let alone the entitlements deriving from them, are subject to such tight political control that the concept of a 'medium of exchange' has little meaning without reference to the State.

Green admits that the notion of a 'medium of exchange' does not yield a clear-cut definition of the boundaries of the system, but defends it as it reflects and preserves 'our ordinary judgement that the boundaries of the system are vague' (p. 7). It is true that they are in the USA and most other decentralised systems, but in centralised ones the boundary is more clearly marked and patrolled by the polity.

These two points about Green's basic conceptualisation of 'the educational system' criticise him for failing to undertake a full analysis of the *structure of systems*, in the plural. Instead, the edifice of the 'logic' is built on ethnocentric foundations. An equally serious defect attends the elucidation of the 'logic'. This is the product of inference, not causality. Explanation consists in using the method of 'practical rationality' which makes 'explicit the rules, beliefs, or principles that are required as premises in the system so that its observed behavior becomes rationally intelligible. The premises of such practical arguments are the reasons for the behavior of the system' (p. xvii). In turn, practical reasons always presuppose the existence of human interests. Now Green is scrupulously careful never to deal in terms of disembodied interests of the system: only groups or individuals can have interests or give reasons. However, the interests he identifies are *generalised* and *abstract* ones *imputed* to the State, parents, society and the teachers – they are interests *in* certain things and not the empirical interests *of* particular groups. Methodologically imputing motives is always problematic, but here I object less to *what* is imputed than to the fact that imputation *dispenses with analysis of social interaction* and the interests actually salient in it at the time. For these are the real processes which drive the system – which are responsible for structuring it and for its restructuration.

Instead, the practical rationality of the system is driven by *abstract* interests: for example, the State has an interest in an aggregate level of economic independence and in a minimum level of civil obedience within the total population, in opposition to parents, whose interests are maximal and non-aggregate – they seek the best for their child. My criticism of Green for failing to analyse the structure of systems and for dispensing with interaction come together here in opposing his use of such abstractions. To deal only with abstract interests (and their derivatives) prevents interests from ever being seen (a) as *vested interests* in a *particular structure* – that is, firmly anchored in time and space and conditioned by that specific educational reality – or (b) as elements whose *results* depend exclusively upon *interaction* taking place in that *context*.

Let me briefly illustrate the significance of these two points of criticism (failure to analyse the structure of systems or to examine educational interaction within them) with reference to Green's delineation of the 'hierarchical principles' (i.e. part of the 'logic') of educational organisation. Now all three of these principles, the Downward Drift of Learning,[2] the Self-Regulating Hierarchies of the System as Employer and the Hierarchies of Status,[3] make implicit assumptions about structure, in addition to the fundamental principle of 'sequence' already mentioned. Furthermore, all three rest entirely upon generalised descriptions of interactional outcomes, which at best project trends into laws and at worst simply fail to work in systems very different from the American decentralised model (e.g. Eastern Europe). I will concentrate on the middle principle now.

The argument about the Self-Regulating Hierarchies of the System as Employer goes as follows. First, there is an undeniable trend for the educational system to become a bigger market for its own products, and with it comes a growing internal capacity to define the instruction which fits individuals to assume positions in schools and colleges. Secondly, professionalisation develops and teachers press the belief that the system must be staffed by products of the system at the highest level, which itself moves upwards. Thirdly, the principle of 'uniform growth' is then set in train, namely that the 'system will tend to require any level, L, to be staffed by persons who have completed $L + n$ in the system and that n will decline as L increases' (p. 66). Finally, from this is deduced the long-run tendency of the system to expand continually to the point where it is staffed entirely by those who have completed the highest level.

Now structural differences can intervene decisively to distort this conclusion, and here we meet one implication of the erroneous incorporation of 'sequence' as a fundamental and universal feature of systems. The first statement about self-employment is true, but *uniform* growth does not follow from it: that is, if the system expands at the earliest level it does not necessarily expand at the graduate level. It does not do so in the absence of a 'single ladder' of levels: in the bifurcated French system the primary sector (*degré*) was staffed by the primary sector for a century and a half. Certainly this implied growth, even upwards growth (of the *écoles normales* producing the *instituteurs*), but not *uniform* growth – there was no proportional expansion at the top of the system because the training of primary school teachers was politically pegged lower down in the system.

Next what Green is describing under the term of professionalisation is the generalised outcome of a long, hard and, in some countries, only partially successful *struggle* for upgrading and self-determination. Empirically he is right that there has been substantial secular progress towards these goals, but in eschewing the interaction involved he fails to have any purchase not only on historical variations between systems but also on the contemporary interactional dynamics which could annul, suspend or modify his principle of uniform growth. In his 'logic', for there to be a logic, this generalised outcome has to be extrapolated into a law. Yet if we give proper attention to interaction, to the fact that this growth is simply what the profession wants (its vested interest), then its attainment becomes properly contingent upon the acquiescence of other groups (conditioned by their vested interests).

When there is an over-supply of the educated – that is, *prima facie* grounds for no growth – Green argues that the tendency of the system will, on the contrary, be to expand or to raise its qualifications or both. This undoubtedly is what the profession would like to see, but continued expansion depends upon their convincing the polity to increase the number of positions (e.g. on the grounds that smaller classes are better) or convincing external interest groups in health, industry or the prisons of their need for the 'qualified'. Neither group *necessarily* is convinced – sometimes they are and sometimes they are not – which is why we need to address interaction rather than assuming that the 'practical argument of the system' is always victorious.

Similarly, when there is an under-supply of the educated, the most likely course of action might seem to be a lowering of qualifications until all positions are filled. Not so, argues Green: 'as a general rule ... the practical argument of the system will not permit us to lower qualifications for positions. ... They will tend to remain unchanged' (p. 73). Certainly they will if the profession has its way, but this depends, as Green admits, on structural and interactional constraints – on demographic growth, on 'the rate of economic growth, and the strength of will and political influence possessed by the leadership of the system' (p. 74, note 15).

Considered in an historical and comparative perspective, these constraints are as important as the tendency. Rather than enshrine the latter in a principle, with the expectation that it will be mirrored in practice, outcomes can only be understood by the interplay between structure and interaction. This does not condemn us to the study of uniqueness and specificity (in growth rates or any other respect), for we can theorise about this interplay, but our propositions will be less than universal and of contingent not logical status.

This leads me to a final comment on the supposed rationality of educational structures and dynamics, which underpins this quest for the 'logic'. To see, as Green does, that educational control is forged by the structure of *abstract* interests and change of the system is fired by them is synthetically to endow educational development with rationality and is artificially to absolve it of the accumulation of unintended consequences – ones which bear no relation to the aims of any group, yet which have to be either accommodated or confronted by all groups. Thus, to Green, the structure and behaviour of the system are understood when we discover the 'practical arguments that explain its behavior' (p. xvi). Structure and change are presumably held to be incomprehensible unless linked to such arguments. Hence if the system is rational these arguments always can be found – exit unintended consequences not attributable to them or their interplay. Thence to account for the system growing very large he has to invoke a strong, pervasive, normative principle connecting educational attainment to social reward.

Thus to Green it would be hard to understand how the system could grow very large unless it is believed to be in the interests of people to acquire the benefits of the system, and believed to be in their interests because it is a legitimate way to secure a greater share of non-educational social goods than they would otherwise be likely to secure (p. 45).

Now I do not want to deny that strenuous *attempts* are made by certain social groups so to legitimate most systems, but I do contest that we have to assume their success – that is, the *existence* of consensual values – in order to explain growth. It does *not* seem hard to me to understand it in other ways.

In the dynamics of relative advantage and deprivation we have parental interests operating without any necessary value-commitment (many parents and pupils would like to settle for less education were there no objective penalty involved); in political authorisation and funding we have motives such as the undercutting the control of others, defensive incorporation or maintenance of the support-base which are negative and pragmatic (the State would often settle for less education if other groups would not abhor the vacuum); in the acceptance of the educated person by the employers we have even less reason to impute legitimacy, given their absence of any alternative (plenty of employers might settle for less education were there a pool of the non-scholarised to draw upon – after all, they fought long enough to retain this reservoir).

In short, if we are dealing with principles, I would advance the opposite one – namely, *the growth of the educational system is what nobody wanted*. It is the irrational and unintended consequence of a parallelogram of forces (the polity, the profession, external interest groups and parents, with different interests and divergent values). This growth displays regularities but it does not embody logic.

Having rejected the 'logic' there remains Green's exceptional contribution to our understanding of the 'life' of the system, which starts in Chapter VI, 'The System in Motion'. Its value lies in a rare appreciation of the importance of time and scope in sociological theory. Now, to Green, the 'life' is dependent on the 'logic' of systemic change over time, 'according to certain regularities established by the practical arguments of the system' (p. 90). I believe, on the contrary, that it is essential to restore contingency, but that this is not particularly hard to do in this case. Indeed, Green goes quite a long way towards this himself when he prefaces his important discussion of the 'law' of zero-correlation by a series of operative conditions. It assumes: (1) endorsement of the norm of educational efficacy for social placement; (2) sequential organisation, 'the single ladder of success'; (3) that everyone completes the nth level of the system; and (4) beyond the nth level, the system is selective. From this it follows, 'without restriction, that if there is a level within the system that everyone completes, then completing that level can have no bearing whatever upon any social differences that may subsequently arise within the population' (p. 90). This tautological proposition turns out to be extraordinarily fruitful, but I believe that the conditions upon which its corollaries depend are more numerous than the four acceded above.

Green is aware of these additional conditions but does not give them full force. His argument, basically, is that as the zero-correlation is approached there will be pressures, under the four conditions, to expand schooling to $n + 1$, and, when it is reapproached at $n + 1$, the target moves to $n + 2$ and keeps moving up under these dynamics. The entire argument hinges on *completion* of the nth level being an *un*differentiated attribute – literally a leaving certificate. If, on the other hand, such a certificate is differentiated by specialism (or even by being graded) then the tautology breaks down, for employers could now use it selectively for placement. For instance, if everyone gained four 'O' levels, different combinations could then have different relationships to the occupational structure and its rewards. Green accepts this and goes on to state that the differentiation of, say, vocational programmes at the nth level is an *alternative* response to zero-correlation – even further, he admits that expansion at $n + 1$ may itself be differentiated (thus, of course, undercutting the necessity for any iteration beyond $n + 1a$, $n + 1b$, $n + 1c'$). So, ultimately, given the approach of the zero-correlation, three different things can happen. Thus contingency *has* to be restored: and I would argue that a proper examination of structure and interaction has to be undertaken to explain *which* of these *will* happen.

Furthermore, this is not something about which we need to remain theoretically mute. Different structures of system vary in both degree and tolerance of differentiation, just as different forms of interaction intensify it or reduce it (the two not being unconnected). However, although aware of these alternatives, Green's argument *proceeds* on the basis of the first response: that is, simple undifferentiated expansion to $n + 1'$. This is wrong sociologically, as I hope I have just demonstrated; and it means that the corollaries of the zero-correlation are wrongly given too much fixity of status. But it is rescuable by recasting one's reservations in terms of conditionals. We can use the formulation that 'if there is undifferentiated expansion to $n + 1$ (or beyond) . . . then' many of Green's corollaries do follow.

The most important inference involves both time and scope: namely that the value of completing the nth level, as a basis for allocating social benefits, is a curvilinear function of the proportion of each age cohort that does complete it. Different parts of this growth curve represent the changing utilities of attainment and a shifting balance of benefits and liabilities. When the system starts to expand at the nth level the benefits of those reaching it rise also (as is reflected in the higher incomes they command); as the curve peaks off then the benefits flatten out (there is a narrowing of income differentials between those leaving school and those completing the nth year), but, as the curve approaches universal enrollment at n, income differentials rise sharply again, for non-completion has now become a liability. Thus increases in scale over time mark a shift from the distribution of social benefits to the distribution of social liabilities – they are emergent properties of systemic growth which warrant the claim that the system has a 'life of its own'. The liabilities produced, for instance, are generated by 'the mere expansion of the system, and not by the behavior of the labor market. This is a partial declaration of the independence of the educational system from the economy' (p. 106).

Various further corollaries, exemplifying other aspects of the systems 'life', also follow. The social meaning of attainment is transformed whenever the zero-correlation is approached, for the chief instrumental worth of education is that it then merely gives access to more education. Correspondingly, the motivation of pupils shifts under these new objective conditions. Completing the nth level is no longer done to secure any benefit, but is endured in order to avoid penalisation. (Slowly collective learning tells them that gaining the diploma is no big deal but that its lack is a disaster.) Finally, who are the social groups who regularly find themselves occupying the three sections of the growth curve? As zero-correlation is reached there must always be a group of last entry (which picks up the liabilities) and this, empirically, comes from the lower socio-economic categories. Meanwhile, the target moves to $n + 1$, where, especially if it is selective, the higher socio-economic groups are first in and collect the benefits.

I would make identical points about Green's equally fruitful discussion of the 'Dialectics of Best and Equal', which also has the supreme merit of incorporating time and scope as major theoretical variables. Again, the attempt is to uncover a 'logic'. According to this, when system scale is small, the relative variabilities of pupils that can be recognised are few and their magnitudes have to be large, thus producing the smallest number of distinct educational groups and programmes (realisation of the 'equal' principle in effect). Where the system is large, the relative variabilities are many, their magnitudes can be small and the largest number of distinct educational groups and programmes are produced (effective realisation of the 'best' principle). Again, this is not a matter of 'logic'.

The first proposition about the small-scale system has immediate appeal (straight away we think of the all-age school), but it is again contingent upon action, or more precisely in this case upon inaction: for the personal tutor had his heyday[4] when the system was small, and, on Green's 'medium of exchange' criterion, he must be considered as part of it. Again, the propositions can be reformulated conditionally: given the collective pursuit of equality, then

> up to a certain point in its expansion, the system can treat the population as homogeneous, but at another point it shall have to either approach the population as hetereogeneous or probably cease its expansion. And ceasing its expansion would mean ceasing in the attempt to maximise the equal principle.
>
> (p. 126)

Again, he is right that scope makes a difference. *First*, it conditions demands – in the attempt to scholarise the entire cohort (or to equalise opportunity or outcome) the racial, linguistic or handicapped groups are treated differently (they are institutionalised separately) in order to produce the same level of attainment; after a time the complaint arises that the system is not providing them with the same as others, so a new demand surfaces for deinstitutionalisation in order to get the same treatment as others. *Second*, it changes the objective capacity of the system[5] to respond to small differences and thus to maximise the 'best for each' principle. *Third*, it constrains the type of policy to be adopted at a particular stage of expansion if a particular goal, such as equality, is to be achieved.

In these three senses the system does have a 'life of its own'. But it is a life which was endowed by social interaction – it is the heritage of unintended consequences of past actions. It is also a life which continues to be contingent upon social interaction. Ultimately we as social actors sustain it, though temporally and temporarily we are conditioned by it. This complex interplay of macroscopic policy formation and microscopic pursuit of individual interests in fact constitutes the life-support of the system – not any inexorable 'logic'.

Notes

1 See Margaret S. Archer (1979) *Social Origins of Educational Systems* (London, Sage), pp. 176–8 ff.
2 The Downward Drift of Learning assumes that since learning takes time and since there are technological imperatives for the rapid dispersal of the skills needed to support the use or marketing of the relevant technology, then the 'practical reasoning' of the system reinforces a downward drift in the specification of what is to be learned. The examples Green gives are those of typing skills and computer programming. In fact, the occurrence of the downward drift, in the case of the typing example, depend partly on a decentralised structure which allowed a progression from: (1) skill development by the retailer to (2) informal instruction to (3) business schools to (4) the public schools. Equally it depended upon the actual transactions between external interest groups (retailers and private marketer-teachers), public authorities (who first resisted and then accepted incorporating the course) and finally the profession (who undertook to offer this elective). Not only would the sequence leading from private initiative to public practice hardly exist in very centralised systems, but also the downward drift is no foregone conclusion in decentralised ones. It is contingent upon interaction and, as Teune & Mlinar have recently demonstrated, the 'distribution of diversity' is a systems problem not a universal systemic characteristic. See Henry Teune and Zdravko Mlinar (1978) *The Developmental Logic of Social Systems* (London, Sage), especially chapters 1, 2 and 3.
3 The Hierarchies of Status proposition is that

> the natural tendency the natural sequence of change in the academic procession is a move away from diversity towards uniformity. . . . This principle suggests, for example, that unless there are explicit constraints or interventions to prevent it, junior colleges and community colleges will aspire more and more to become like four-year liberal arts colleges and finally universities.
>
> (p. 78)

But the American reference point is one of extreme structural licence rather than typicality. Although Green is probably right about our universal proclivity to play these kinds of academic games in our professional interaction, the stringency of the constraints that are met can systematically impair them or terminate them at some point (e.g. the introduction of the present bifurcated system of higher education in England, which prevents further upgrading to university status on the part of aspiring colleges or polytechnics).
4 To anticipate the obvious rejoinder, I agree that this was largely the privilege of the rich, even the very rich, although the educative role of the upper-middle-class mother in the home is usually neglected here. However, 'who benefited' is not the point at issue now. Nor is the *limited* distribution of this practice, for we are discussing a time when the whole of education was limited in extent.
5 Here I do mean the State educational system. It will have been clear throughout that, unlike Green, I believe in the conceptual utility of defining the system and doing so in a way which attaches greater importance than he does to the connection of the system to the State. It may illuminate some of the points made to present the working definition which I have had in mind when writing this paper. A State educational system is considered to be a nationwide and differentiated collection of institutions devoted to formal education whose overall control and supervision is at least partly governmental and whose component parts and processes are related to one another: *Social Origins of Educational Systems*, p. 54.

3 The myth of cultural integration*

The conceptualization of culture is extraordinary in two respects. It has displayed the weakest analytical development of any key concept in sociology and it has played the most wildly vacillating role within sociological theory.

i At the *descriptive* level, the notion of 'culture' remains inordinately vague despite little dispute that it is indeed a core concept. In every way 'culture' is the poor relation of 'structure'. Definition of the former has not undergone an elaboration equivalent to that of the latter. Consequently there is no ready fund of analytical terms for designating the components of the cultural realm corresponding to those which delineate parts of the structural domain (roles, organizations, institutions, systems, etc.). Methodologically such is the poverty of conceptualization that there are as yet no 'units' for describing culture: essentially cultures are still 'grasped' in contrast to structures, which are now 'analysed'. Basically the notion of cultures *being* structured is uncommonly rare outside of structuralism: instead of different 'cultural structures' there are endless 'cultural differences'.

ii At the *explanatory* level the status of culture oscillates between that of a supremely independent variable, the superordinate power in society, and, with a large sweep of the pendulum, a position of supine dependence on other social institutions. Hence, in various sociological theories, culture swings from being the prime mover (credited with engulfing and orchestrating the entire social structure) to the opposite extreme, where it is reduced to a mere epiphenomenon (charged only with providing an ideational representation of structure).

Together this descriptive vagueness and these theoretical vagaries mean that culture occupies no clear place in sociological analysis. What culture is and what culture does are issues bogged down in a conceptual morass. From this no adequate sociology of culture has been able to emerge. Obviously such a state of affairs begs for explanation and I believe that the reason for it is embedded in the generic assumptions of an all-pervasive 'myth of cultural integration'. This myth embodies 'one of the most deep-seated fallacies in social science . . . the . . . assumption of a high degree of consistency in the interpretations produced by societal units'.[1]

Yet it projected an image of culture which proved so powerful that it scored the retina, leaving a perpetual after-image, which distorted subsequent perception.

Originating at the descriptive level, the myth created an archetype of culture(s) as the perfectly woven and all-enmeshing web, whose intricate construction only added to its strength. Today, instead of analogy, one would simply say that the myth portrayed culture as the perfectly integrated system, where every element was interdependent with every other – the ultimate exemplar of compact and coherent organization.

Held in thraldom by this archetype, theorists of various persuasions concerned themselves only with *how* to accommodate it in their theories: there was no question of whether it should be given house-room. Their problem was to find a place *for* the Myth since the Myth itself was not problematic. In turn the Myth derived power and durability precisely because it was endorsed by schools of sociological thought which were otherwise hostile to one another, if not antipathetic.

That the same theorists who were in bitter dispute over the extent of structural integration (institutional complementarity or contradiction) could simultaneously agree on the subject of *cultural* integration only buttressed this mythology. Moreover, the fact that they produced differing versions of the myth helped to insulate its core premise from scrutiny: the *existence* of cultural integration could never be at issue in a debate on the rival mechanisms held to be responsible for it. Thus profound differences over *how* cultural unity was achieved only served to reinforce a fundamentalist accord upon the generic nature of cultural coherence.

The most proximate and powerful origins of the myth are undoubtedly the heritage of anthropology. Despite definitional wrangling over the term 'culture' there was substantial concord amongst anthropologists about its main property – strong and coherent patterning. This central notion of culture as an integrated whole,[2] grounded in German historicism (historismus), echoes down the decades. Malinowski's conceptualization of 'an individual culture as a coherent whole'[3] reverberates through Ruth Benedict's 'cultural patterns',[4] Meyer Shapiro's 'cultural style'[5] and Kroeber's 'ethos of total culture patterns',[6] to resurface in Mary Douglas's notion of 'one single, symbolically consistent universe'.[7] Two features of this heritage should be underlined. On the one hand, its strong aesthetic – rather than analytical – orientation led to an endorsement of '"artistic" hermeneutics as the method for grasping the inner sense of cultural wholes';[8] on the other, this approach, based on the intuitive understanding of cultural configurations, entailed a crucial prejudgment: namely an insistence that coherence was there to be found – that is, a mental closure against the discovery of cultural inconsistencies.[9]

This *a priori* assumption that there always was a discoverable coherence in culture and this total reliance on inspirational grasp as the method for discovering it spilt over to soak the most diverse varieties of sociological theory. The myth surfaced intact in functionalist thought, transmitted by Sorokin. His insistence on the internal logic of culture, which would be apprehended by sweeping up a mountain of cultural fragments whose inner coherence could then be intuitively deciphered, was finally enshrined in the Parsonian central value system – that *a prioristic* guarantor of further societal integration. If Parsons had taken on board and given

The myth of cultural integration 61

pride of place to a notion of an overt and readily detectable cultural system (being somewhat more analytical in his attempt to grasp it through his 'pattern variables'), linguistic structuralism did the reverse. It accepted incoherence as being the surface characteristic of overt and seemingly unconnected cultural symbols, but then revealed their underlying structuration by a hidden code – again grasped intuitively, by some form of deciphering or interpolation, though always lacking any external context of justification. Finally, the myth received monumental reinforcement by its adoption into western humanistic Marxism. The notion of 'hegemonic culture' and its offspring, the 'dominant ideology' thesis, embodied the same assumption about cultural coherence: certainly it was inspired by sectional interests, generally it distorted the nature of reality and, undoubtedly, the consensus it generated was the product of manipulation; but, nevertheless, mystification and misguidedness did not deny it the basic property of coherence shared equally by the Parsonian normative system. Significantly, the now-familiar reliance on aesthetic grasp dominated Marxist methodology here, as evidenced by the growing pre-occupation of Euro-Marxists with literary criticism[10] – with laying bare the ideological impregnation of works of art by a kind of 'class decoding' which had distinct affinities to the enterprise of linguistic structuralism.

Now the conventional anthropological approach to culture in fact contained two distinct strands within the concept:

i the notion of a *cultural pattern* with an underlying unity and a fundamental coherence;
ii the notion of *uniform action*, identified with the above and stemming from it to produce social homogeneity.

In other words, to view culture as 'a community of shared meanings' meant eliding the community with the meanings. In so doing a vital analytical distinction was obfuscated and this was to have far-reaching consequences when the myth was transmitted to sociology, for the myth contains a basic analytical confusion between two elements which are both logically and sociologically distinct. Teasing them out involves separating the two strands (a) and (b) which were tautly intertwined in the anthropological image.

What remain inextricably confounded in the myth of cultural consistency are

i LOGICAL COHERENCE – that is, the degree of internal compatibility between the components of culture (however these two terms are defined).
ii CAUSAL CONSENSUS – that is, the degree of social uniformity produced by the imposition of culture (again, however these two terms are defined) by one set of people on another.

The former concerns *the consistency* of our attempts to impose ideational order on experiential chaos; the latter concerns *the success* of attempts to order other people. Logical Coherence is a property of the world of ideas: Causal Consensus is a property of people.

The main proposition advanced here is that the two are logically and empirically distinct; hence, they can vary independently of one another. Thus it is perfectly conceivable that any social unit from a community to a civilization could be found whose principal ideational elements (knowledge, beliefs, norms, language, mythology, etc.) do indeed display considerable logical coherence – i.e. the components are consistent not contradictory – yet the same social unit may be low on causal consensus. For example, this may be especially true where the 'culture' in all its logical coherence is the prerogative of an elite (priesthood, caste, intelligentsia, estate or ruling class). Because of this the non-elites will behave differently (absence of social uniformity) because they are shaped by non-identical, since more restricted, ideas.

Restricted access may give rise to defective or divergent syntheses of the cultural stock resulting in schism through the differential accentuation of the cultural elements received. Furthermore, such action is the joint product of the notions inculcated and the response to enforced inculcation. Unlike the elite, these actors are not responding to the power of precept alone but also to preceptual power. Power relations are the causal element in cultural consensus building and, far from unproblematically guaranteeing behavioural conformity, they can provoke anything from ritualistic acceptance to outright rejection of the culture imposed.

It should be noted that these cases where high logical coherence is accompanied by low causally induced consensus do not depend upon the existence of cultural alternatives within the social unit in question. Although these are generally extremely important in amplifying the lack of social uniformity, their presence is not a necessary precondition for the independent variation of logical coherence and causal consensus in the cultural realm. In brief, this distinction can be sustained *even if* we uncritically accept the existence of a single unified central value system or cultural scheme.

Equally, the opposite situation can be found in society: causal consensus may be high whilst logical coherence is low. Again, there is nothing inconceivable about a social unit whose members display considerable cultural accord in their basic values, interpretations and language yet where the cultural system itself is riven with inconsistencies. Successful imposition does not require high coherence of the cultural package imposed. Partly this is because humankind does not necessarily notice inconsistency or unexceptionally find it intolerable (individually we all give houseroom to incompatible mental furnishings through intellectual idleness, patches of ignorance, nostalgia or closing the emotional shutters). More important empirically are, again, the power relations implicated in imposition. Whether we are talking about parental socialization or political indoctrination, the success achieved may reflect coercion rather than conviction. As in the glaring case of German fascism, considerable behavioural uniformity can co-exist with *both* substantial doctrinal inconsistencies and significant mental reservations in the population.

Thus my basic proposition is that it is essential to distinguish logical coherence from causal cohesion in order to gain an analytical grip on the cultural components and upon socio-cultural dynamics. This distinction would closely parallel that between system integration and social integration,[11] made by Lockwood, in the structural domain. Indeed, much of the following argument seeks not merely to bring the analysis of culture on a par with that of structure but also to suggest that the two can be analysed in very similar generic terms. In line with this conviction, what has so far been discussed as the logical coherence of culture will henceforth be referred to as 'cultural system integration'. Similarly, causal cohesion will now be termed 'socio-cultural integration'. As in the structural field, so here, the point of this distinction is to improve our explanatory purchase upon cultural statics and dynamics.

Lockwood rightly argued that neither element alone provided the sufficient conditions of structural change. On the one hand, system integration could be low, but unless its contradictions were actualized and amplified by sectional social groups they could be contained and stasis would persist because of this high social integration. Alternatively, group antagonism could be profound (low social integration) without leading to significant change in society unless it was linked to systemic contradictions. Obviously the cultural parallels require a detailed specification, which will follow later, but for the moment the key point is that in both structural and cultural fields the analysis of stability and change depends upon making such analytical distinctions.

The error underlying the Myth of Cultural Integration was that it elided this crucial distinction: the basic deficiency of the anthropological heritage *as appropriated in sociology* was that it resisted making any analytical distinctions at all. The net effect of this insistence upon cultural compactness was that it precluded any theory of cultural development springing from internal dynamics. Logically the component parts of any complex have to be accorded some autonomy if they are to interact and to change (or actively to maintain) one another or the state of the whole. Yet this is precisely what the image of a coherent pattern, a uniform style or an all-pervading ethos effectively denied. Consequently, *internal* dynamics were surrendered to external ones – the forces for development were located anywhere other than within the cultural system itself. At their most sociological they were pictured as diffusing inwards from the exterior; at their least, as giant mirrors of individual psychology[12] whose traits were independent of their cultural context.

However, the interest of this myth for sociology does not concern its genesis, maintenance and vitality in the history of thought, but instead relates to its analytical premises and consequences. Its evergreen quality is mainly of significance in protecting and protracting these. Thus I now want to link three things together over time, but the linkage to be accentuated between them concerns conceptual continuity. Obviously this is mirrored in the history of ideas, but it is not their chronology that will be traced here:

i   the genesis of the myth of cultural integration in anthropology;
ii sociological support for the myth;
iii the weak analytical development of a sociology of culture.

My main argument is that the current theoretical deficiencies in the sociological analysis of culture are directly attributable to the conflation of *cultural system integration* with *socio-cultural integration* – a confusion of the two which could be found within the anthropological heritage but which was intensified by the myth of cultural integration in all its subsequent sociological manifestations. Consequently, the premises and implications enshrined in the myth must be disentangled and demolished before culture can assume a proper place in sociological analysis.

The origins of the myth

The image of cultural coherence is grounded in traditional society. It is most persuasive where traditionalism prevails largely because the enduring enruttedness of primitive society can immediately be taken as exemplifying the force of cultural consistency. (This logical leap is far too precipitous and requires close reinspection.) Almost automatically, however, the durability of routine was attributed to its enmeshment in an all-pervasive perfectly integrated cultural system which had imposed itself as the printed circuit of the primitive mind. Thus in the classic statement about compact coherence among the Azande we should note that Evans-Pritchard in fact elides the cultural, structural and personality systems:

> In this web of belief every strand depends upon every other strand, and a Zande cannot get out of its meshes because it is the only world he knows. The web is not an external structure in which he is enclosed. It is the texture of his thought and he cannot think that his thought is wrong.[13]

Not only was this taken as the epitome of the primitive cultural system by many social theorists, but certain anthropologists also sponsored the extension of such imagery beyond traditional society. Thus it percolated up the centuries or the 'stages' of social development – a seepage undoubtedly encouraged by a neglect of the 'interregnum', that vast tract representing the majority of human history which fell between the increasingly popular dichotomies of primitive and modern, undeveloped and developed, traditional and scientific societies. Thus in 1924 we find Edward Sapir generalizing the myth from one side of the gap to the other: both sides displayed cultural coherence and so, by extension, did the phases and forms in between:

> A genuine culture is perfectly conceivable in any type or stage of civilization. . . . It is merely inherently harmonious, balanced, self-satisfactory . . . It is a culture in which nothing is spiritually meaningless, in which no important part of the general functioning brings with it a sense of frustration, of misdirected or unsympathetic effort.[14]

Hence the 'anthropological image', with its co-insistence upon a complete interdependence (every strand depending upon every other) and an inherent harmony of the whole cultural system (balanced, self-satisfactory), passed into sociology. And this despite the existence of at least one school of thought that had consistently repudiated the association of interdependence with harmony – the Marxist tradition, accentuating contradictions between interdependent parts and their disruptive social potential.[15]

But, before moving on to the sociological inheritance, it is important to enter certain severe objections to the conception of cultural integration where it originated – in relation to primitive society. First, it is a strange tribute to the influence of German historicism and romanticism that something like Zande culture, which Evans-Pritchard himself called 'a thing of shreds and patches',[16] should have become the supreme exemplar of coherent integration. As Gellner comments, it

> is ironical that this culture of shreds and patches, incorporating at least 20 culturally alien groups and speaking at least 8 diverse languages in what is but part of its total territory, should have come to have been systematically invoked, by philosophers making facile and superficial use of anthropology, as an illustration of the quite erroneous view that cultures are islands unto themselves, *whose supposedly coherent internal norms of what is real and what is not real may not be challenged*.[17]

The irony is compounded if it is recalled that the famous passage about the tightly interwoven cultural strands which completely enmesh the Zande population is immediately qualified in the text. This reads on,

> Nevertheless [a caveat perhaps so large as to swamp the initial proposition] Zande 'beliefs are not absolutely set but are variable and fluctuating to allow for different situations and to permit empirical observations and even doubts'.[18]

Evans-Pritchard himself attempts to save his argument from this obvious objection by introducing the notion of a kind of moving cultural equilibrium whereby the Azande 'adapt themselves without undue difficulty to new conditions of life':[19] adaptation preserving coherence. This theme, of course, echoes down the corridors of later functionalist thought. But, given that he has acceded to the presence of doubts and to the importing or implanting of external influences, why should we assume that these are unproblematically reintegrated into a new form of cultural coherence?

The assumption has not in fact been acceded to universally. The work of certain later anthropologists has questioned this view of *cultural system integration* as generic to primitive societies. There is, for example, Edmund Leach's record of Burmese tribesmen alternating between two quite incompatible visions of their society.[20] There are the frequent instances of frontier dwellers who literally and linguistically bestride two different (thus potentially inconsistent) cultures, and there is the well-documented effect of exogamy in marriage rules which enforces exposure to and incorporation of cultural differences to varying degrees. These are simply a few examples of the occurrence of cultural pluralism and the accompanying incursion of inconsistencies. Usually, however, these have been deprived of cultural significance through an easy acceptance of adaptive reintegration; but, as Gellner argues, the implications of this view are unacceptably unrealistic. It presumes that there can be no syncretism, no doctrinal pluralism, no deep treason, no dramatic conversion or doctrinal oscillation, no holding of alternative belief systems up one's sleeve, ready for the opportune moment of betrayal.[21]

It denies the readiness of opportunistic gurus, ambitious younger sons or disgruntled minorities to capitalize upon cultural ambiguities and discontinuities that would advance their ambitions. If the standard view does not give us the noble savage it leaves us with the primitive cultural dope, unable to exploit the intricacies of his own *Lebenswelt*. Yet, if it is indeed the case that pluralism is common, inconsistency is pervasive and syncretism in general practice, why has the image *of high cultural system integration* possessed such staying power? Why, too, has there been the complementary and stubborn resistance to assigning cultural inconsistencies any importance in mainstream social theory? Two reasons are usually given to account for this situation by those who, like me, see perversity and prejudice in its perpetuation. Both reasons are rooted in the debate about the nature of the so-called primitive mind. Although they themselves are mutually opposed, they jointly repulse the notion of cultural inconsistencies and their social importance.

On the one hand, the long-lasting school of thought that has endorsed some concept of a 'savage mind' has enshrined a mentality that is constituted entirely differently from our own. No amount of information or instruction would alter its basic difference in constitution, its (romanticized or regrettable) fusion with nature, which, in turn, repudiates clear distinctions between the mundane and the spiritual, the animate and the inanimate, the self and others or other things. What is crucial in this generic concept of a 'savage mind' is that it is one where the rules of identity and contradiction do not operate. For, from this perspective, these are not 'the' rules, they are 'our' rules, part of a wholly different mentality. Consequently the reactions which *we* might expect towards inconsistency and incoherence are predicated upon *our* own mental constitution. Hence cultural discontinuities are theoretically discounted from this point of view, which holds them unimportant because the 'savage mind' discountenances them. It cannot act upon what it does not sense. For us to accord theoretical significance to unsensed contradictions would be an unwarranted act of cultural importation, to proponents of this kind of theory.

I have no interest here in debating the demerits of this 'booming buzzing confusion' portrayal of primitive mentality except on one point. Since a substantial amount of evidence indicates that the perceptual discrimination of primitive people in everyday and experimental settings is just as acute as that of their investigators, and that their linguistic capacities for differentiation in various areas (snow, cattle, kin) may well exceed that of the anthropologist, there are no grounds on which to *presume* that the cultural inconsistencies we perceive and could/would act upon *must necessarily* remain inert to the 'savage mind' and therefore *will be of no significance* in primitive society. What I am more concerned to stress is the odd affinity in this connection shared by those holding a diametrically opposed view of primitive mentality.

Ironically, the harshest opponents of the 'pre-logical mind' notion seek to make their case by a demonstration of the total coherence of primitive thought. Intense

The myth of cultural integration 67

hermeneutic ingenuity is deployed to defend seemingly contradictory statements/ beliefs from the charge of incoherence: extensive interpretative schemes are erected to decode superficially inconsistent elements by revealing their underlying compatibility. Once again the effect is systematically to deprive cultural inconsistency of any social or theoretical significance – not by arguing that such contradictions are unsensed but by contending that they are 'merely' sensed: that is, they are apparent rather than real. But, as Gellner argues, the

> trouble with such all-embracing logical charity is . . . that it is unwittingly quite *a priori*: it may delude anthropologists into thinking that they have *found* that no society upholds absurd or self-contradictory beliefs, whilst in fact the principle employed has ensured in advance of any inquiry that nothing may count as prelogical, inconsistent or categorically absurd though it may be. And this, apart from anything else, would blind one to at least one socially significant phenomenon: the social role of absurdity.[22]

However, without diminishing the significance of these two views for founding and buttressing the myth of high cultural system integration – through their *a prioristic* denial of the existence or the significance of inconsistency – I believe that there is an even more pervasive reason for accounting for its longevity. This reason is more general, as it also characterizes the work of many who remain completely agnostic about the constitution of primitive mentality. Basically it consists in attributing the massive uniformity of behaviour, displayed over time, in 'cold' societies, to the *binding logic of the cultural system*. In other words, the predominance of routine, repetition and reproduction in the traditional society are interpreted as properties of high cultural system integration. Primitive peoples are seen as inexorably trapped in a coherent cultural code which generates the behavioural uniformities observed. Thus, to give a recent example, Giddens writes of 'societies confined implacably within the grip of tradition'[23] because of the 'ontological security' conferred by unquestioned codes of signification and forms of normative regulation. Now in all such cases there seems to be a fundamental confusion between the 'grip of tradition' (which I do not denigrate) and its source in the bindingness of the cultural logic. In brief, *high cultural system integration is consistently being confused with high socio-cultural integration*.

The uniform and lasting patterns of behaviour accredited to properties of the cultural system are never considered to be engendered and encouraged by contingencies of the traditional terrain.[24] In other words, the force of tradition is seen as the force of the traditional belief system rather than of the traditional way of life. On the contrary, I would argue that it is the latter which fosters uniformity and continuity in collective patterns of behaviour, whereas it is an illusion foisted on traditional life that its regularities are *orchestrated* by an overarching cultural system. Instead, they are merely manifestations of high socio-cultural integration. That is to say that, given a relatively stable environment, individuals could largely live inductively from past contexts to future ones *because* they were engaged in unchanging activities. But this was due to the stability of the structured context, which promoted high socio-cultural integration since customary practices did continue to 'work', rather than to their constrained enmeshment by an integrated belief system. On the contrary, it should be ventured that it was precisely this high level of day-to-day and generation-to-generation workability of practices which created an optical illusion about the coherence of cultural systems and simultaneously discouraged the thorough exploitation or exploration of their contradictions.

Instead, the two are elided, the effects of socio-cultural integration having generally been seen as the consequences of cultural system integration. Even a thinker such as Bauman, who conceptualizes 'culture as praxis', gives more power to the systemic elbow. The *univers du discours*, from which meanings are derived, is seen as 'foisting itself, with the force of an external inevitability, on each particular member of the community and on each particular communication-event'.[25] What is much rarer to find in the literature is any full-blooded assertion that the crucial element in traditionalism is the *social* integration aspect. Gellner provides this, but also recognizes the controversial nature of his following proposition: where

> relationships are fairly well-known (because the community is small, and because the types of relationship are small in number), shared culture is not a precondition of effective communication.

In support of this he cites Lévi-Strauss's example of a Red Indian band in the Brazilian jungle, made up of two smaller groups, neither of which understood the other's language. Here, given

> the smallness of the total group, and the simplicity of the problems and situations facing it, this absence of linguistic communication did not apparently prevent it forming an effective co-operating group.[26]

In fact I suspect that Gellner is deliberately over-accentuating his case in stating that, given a highly structured society, then culture is not indispensable in order to put gunpowder under the myth of cultural system integration and integration through cultural systems. What I think he is really accentuating is the independent contribution of socio-cultural integration to traditionalism, dissociated from any orchestration by a binding cultural system. For the reasons why he holds that 'an affective co-operating group', or other kinds of repetitive relationship, can work are *not* without a cultural dimension: those involved

> have long ago sized each other up: each knows what the other wants, the tricks he may get up to, the defences and counter-measures which, in the given situation, are available, and so on.[27]

But this, of course, is at the socio-cultural level.

Even if I am guilty of misconstruing Gellner's intentions, such an interpretation of his position is at least of value in pointing up the fact that much of the uniformity that has been confused with and attributed to the bindingness of cultural belief

The myth of cultural integration 69

systems merely reflects a high degree of socio-cultural integration. Another, more contentious, way of putting this is *that traditionalistic practices are not necessarily shared because the cultural system is binding, but can be binding because they are shared at the socio-cultural level*. In fact I think that this is not an *a prioristic* matter; it is a view which strengthens but is not essential to the main argument – namely the necessity of distinguishing analytically between the two types of cultural integration, the systemic and the social. So far this necessity has been established negatively by reference to the errors arising from elision of the two elements; next I will seek to establish the positive advantages of this analytic distinction.

Four flaws in the original myth

So far I have tried to show *how* the myth of cultural integration originated in terms of its constitutive assumptions – the most basic one being the conflation of cultural system integration with socio-cultural integration. Now I want to disentangle certain sins of commission and omission perpetrated within the myth in relation to these two elements. For the crucial point here is that their combined effect serves to extinguish exactly those features whose combination could give explanatory purchase on cultural change. In teasing them out the object is, of course, complementary: it is to delineate those components whose interplay would form the kernel of a theory of cultural development.

1

Where *cultural system integration* is concerned, the main sin of omission has been touched upon already – the refusal to recognize or attach any importance to the existence of inconsistencies at this level. Commitment in advance to cultural coherence blinds us to the possibility that social change may occur through the replacement of an inconsistent doctrine or ethic by a better one, or through a more consistent application of either. It equally blinds us to the possibility of, for instance, social control through the employment of absurd, ambiguous, inconsistent or unintelligible doctrines; even if they never occurred it would be wrong to employ a method which excludes their possibility *a priori*.[28]

What Gellner is pointing to here are certain far-reaching social consequences which *may* result from systemic cultural contradictions. Whether these do occur depends, I will argue, on conditions in the socio-cultural realm. So far Gellner has touched on a necessary but insufficient condition for consequential cultural change, which is suppressed by the upholders of systemic consistency.

Simultaneously he has done something else of equivalent importance. This is to explode the assumption that the *interdependence* of cultural elements automatically equals the *integration* of the cultural system (as exemplified in the image of each strand depending on every other and forming an escape-free web). Quite simply, what he demonstrates is that when inconsistencies obtain between interdependent elements, as in the case of the role expectations attaching to *igurramen* of the High Atlas (who must behave generously, appear unmaterialistic and yet remain prosperous), then *cultural manipulation* is inescapable (in the above case in order to balance the books). In other words, far from a coherent cultural system being passively received, its active mediation is required if it is to be translated into a semblance of social coherence. Thus interpretative manipulation is involved, whether to sustain the cultural system or to change it.

In brief, the theoretical incorporation of inconsistency at the systemic level does two things. It specifies certain necessary conditions for stability or change in the cultural system. Every contradiction represents a potential for change. Whether it does lead to this, rather than to active containment, depends on the activities of groups and individuals at the socio-cultural level. Thus the second implication of giving due attention to the flaws in cultural system integration is the necessity of distinguishing this level analytically from socio-cultural integration – for the latter determines the fate of these discontinuities – that is, whether they are amplified into recognizable changes or damped down to preserve the picture of social continuity.

2

Still at the level *of cultural system integration* an equally important sin of commission is covertly committed in the process of conceptualization. The presence of a high degree of interdependence among cultural components is taken as a straightforward manifestation of high systemic integration. Already we have seen the fallacy of assuming that because the strands are tied together they necessarily form a neat web. This erroneously presumes that interdependent elements must be compatible; and, empirically, we have seen that this is not always the case. However, the coherence of the cultural system may not derive from the harmonious integration of its parts, as tends to be assumed (for we have seen that harmony and interdependence need not be synonymous). Instead, the coherence presented, and any integrative force it exerts, may be due not to something the cultural system possesses (harmonious integration of parts) but to something it lacks, namely autonomous elements (relatively independent of the connected components). To use the traditional imagery, these would be 'loose ends' unknit with the main web. Empirically they might be things such as pockets of deviant cultic practice, novel practices penetrating from frontier regions or ancient mythological survivals. If at all extensive, such autonomous elements would constitute a fund of alternatives at the systemic level. The myth, however, is committed to the absence of such 'loose ends'.

The crucial point here is that cultural coherence may not stem from the integration of the cultural system but from a lack of alternatives to it. And this, itself, is a property of the system. Too frequently it has been presumed to be a property of the socio-cultural level. Primitive people, because of their low individuation, are held to lack a *sense* of alternatives (rather than alternatives being systemically unavailable). Thus Horton exemplifies this view when he writes that 'in traditional cultures there is no developed awareness of alternatives to the established body of theoretical tenets; whereas in scientifically oriented cultures, such an awareness is highly developed.'[29] But the (systemic) existence of options cannot be elided with people's sense of them. In modern societies a variety of options are known to be available, but some people can also close their minds to this plurality; in traditional societies we cannot assume that everyone has a closed mind until we know whether they have any option. Once again, this point serves to bring home the need to distinguish between the two levels.

Equally this question of alternatives (like our discussion of inconsistencies) is linked to the conditions of cultural stability or change. The existence of alternatives at the systemic level, or the presence of *variety*, as it is termed in information theory,[30] is essential for *adaptive systems*. This mathematical theory postulates some source which continuously generates variety (new signals, symbols, messages) and some receiver who can put this variety to use. Now, I am concerned here not with the 'adaptive' aspect or with the notion of 'successful mapping' (through which the fund of variety is sorted into those modifications which most closely match the environment and those which do not) but simply with the question of change (which may turn out to be non-adaptive – always assuming that this term can be operationalized). However, in the context of cultural change, information theory does contain two invaluable insights: (1) that alternatives (variety) must be available to be drawn upon at the systemic level; and (2) that there must be receivers at the socio-cultural level who are willing and able to make use of them. (Yet again the distinction between the levels is indispensible.)

To put some meat on the bones of this abstract discussion let us briefly refer to Roger C. Owen's example of the interpenetration of certain independent Indian patrilocal bands of Northern Baja, California.[31] Here the source of variety at the systemic level was the operation of the exogamy rule for marriage partners. This meant the continuous importation of females from other bands that were linguistically and culturally different. The local band was thus a hybrid residence unit in terms of language and culture, where the children differed from either parent in their bi-lingual and bi-cultural characteristics. Here, in other words, the children constituted the group which could draw upon the pool of variety. To Owen, who pursued the notion of adaptation, this meant that

> contained in any given population would be a diversified set of adaptive symbols derived from the females: to any situation of rigorous selective stress, there would be available a number of possible responses, thus giving to the culturally hybrid band a high survival potential.[32]

I would prefer to say more simply that this unit had a high systemic potential for change, requiring actualization by its bi-cultural agents.

3

Turning now to *socio-cultural integration*, the main sin of omission here was a conventional unwillingness to concede that there was *ever* enough differentiation in the population to make interpretative innovations, to manipulate cultural loopholes or to exploit inconsistencies. Now I would not for a moment deny that the relatively low levels of social differentiation in most traditional societies do act as a severe drag upon large-scale collective action for cultural and any other sort of change. But, at the same time, it seems to me that our modern notions of the kind of collectivity which introduces significant modifications, and also the kinds of modification which count as significant, have blocked an appreciation of smaller-scale differences *and* the qualitative changes which they can introduce.

Now certainly in the Durkheimian tradition low social differentiation is closely associated with low personal individuation; and, in general terms, I do not contest this. However, 'individuation' is a comparative social term, never meant by Durkheim, at least, to rob tribal man of any element of individual*ism*: indeed, it was precisely his egotism, self-seeking and opportunism which required normative control. Yet all such character traits tended to be banished by the makers of the original myth. This was particularly true of the holistic anthropologists

> the individuals they so respect and exalt, jealously guarding them against subsumption under the typical or the general, are always *collective wholes* . . . Historicists may like individuality; yet as good holists, they feel no affection towards *individualism*.[33]

Homogeneous individuals as standard bearers (in both senses) of shared cultural uniqueness were the humanoids of this type of theorizing. These were the oversocialized populaces that made for high socio-cultural integration. What is lacking here is the acceptance of a few individual personality differences – a bit of gumption, a sense of grudge or grievance, an eye to the main chance, a touch of adventurism. For these are all that need to be postulated as the initial mechanisms through which the contradictions of the cultural system begin to be exploited.

Unfortunately, and partly because of this dominant orientation in anthropology, what we lack is a 'high politics' of traditional society. There seems to be a glaring paucity of case studies dealing with individual machinations to gain power, to establish independence or to generate legitimacy, which would have been very revealing about the cultural elaboration associated with these manoeuvres. There is another reason for this neglect that is just as powerful. Quite simply, the manifestations of early cultural elaboration that I have in mind were often not recognized as such. Shifts in cosmologies, in doctrinal emphasis, in symbolic combinations or in ritualistic practices have not been accorded much significance because they did not represent an obvious shift towards cultural modernity. Very probably they do not, but this does not mean that they are merely a kind of symbolic Brownian motion inside a sealed cultural vessel. Instead, by elaboration, accretion, syncretism or reinterpretation, a winding path may lead away from the original cultural system. Though there is no reason to assume that this will either constitute or join the highway to modernity, this is *not* to deprive it of subsequent social significance.

4

Finally, to view socio-cultural integration as the product of the bindingness of the cultural system involves an equally serious error of commission: namely the

The myth of cultural integration 73

assumption that the shared beliefs, values and symbols will continue to integrate society whilst ever the cultural system remains intact. As far as change is concerned, it is presumed to be a one-way relationship that works from the top down. I believe it is more realistically conceptualized as a two-way relationship, but, once again, this would depend upon utilizing analytical dualism for dealing with the interplay between the two levels. In support of the latter approach let us pursue the implications of the view that culture is *not* always shared because it is binding but may sometimes be *binding because shared*. The latter allows the socio-cultural level the possibility of pushing open the door to cultural change through actions which diminish integration-through-sharing and to do so independently of any co-terminus alteration in the cultural system.

Undoubtedly integration-through-sharing is a powerful binding force in traditional societies. By its very nature it discourages innovation. Where there is a high level of co-action this does serve to promote co-thought,[34] especially when we are dealing with subsistence living. As a generalization, it does seem to be the case that there is rough parity between the available variety and active variety of cultural elements in such societies and that they are pretty equally distributed. There is no significant vocabulary of concepts, meanings, beliefs or knowledge for some to draw upon, thus distinguishing themselves from others and fragmenting socio-cultural integration. Second, although this does not preclude individualistic innovation (primitive creativity should not be ruled out *a priori*), it is the individual who accumulates variety in the co-action system and who then confronts severe difficulties over its retention and transmission. In other words, cultural poverty is like physical poverty: grinding. Primitive cultural accumulation is almost as difficult as primitive capital accumulation and is, of course, related to it. So far these may look like further good reasons for not anticipating an independent contribution to cultural change from the socio-cultural level. They are *not*; they are simply reasons why this contribution will be slow and hard-won.

On the one hand, the generalization about available variety and active variety being on a par is nothing more than that – it represents an 'average type' of traditional society, not a universal characterization of traditional societies. For in many such social groupings small pools of variety do exist in the form of surviving practices that can be activated and legitimated through a claim to represent the authentic 'tradition'. At any time this diversity may also be augmented by external contact or, more probably, the latter sets up a tripartite, though rudimentary, pluralism between cultural recusants, conventionalists and converts. Then we have only to return to the postulate of elementary differences in personality and interests for the erosion of sharing to be set in train. The second argument about the difficulties of accumulation is basically that the train can never gather enough speed to leave the station. Undeniably there is strength in the assertion that, without the written word, cultural variations and innovations will be condemned to protracted recapitulation and oral embroidery. But this, it seems to me, is a general characteristic of any form of cultural transmission in traditional societies: it is not particular to, or more difficult for, ideas outside the mainstream. This would be the case only if the individual alone accumulated them. But whilst he/she may be the first to originate or adopt them,

74 *The myth of cultural integration*

we cannot universally assume that such people will be unsuccessful in transmitting them to their families, to a particular locality or to some subgroup with the same opportunism or general outlook as themselves. Only by assuming complete homogeneity at the level of structure, geography and personality *as well as* culture can lack of success be a foregone conclusion. Without this assumption there is no reason why slow cultural fissiparousness cannot undermine previous socio-cultural integration by eating into the 'sharedness' which was its mainstay.

In sum, four major criticisms have been made of the original myth, and are summarized below:

- refusal to recognize or attach importance to inconsistencies within the cultural system;
- inattention to the presence or absence of alternatives at the systemic level;
- unwillingness to concede any modicum of differentiation in the population;
- rejection of any condition capable of damaging socio-cultural integration.

When considered in conjunction these points totally preclude a theory of cultural change because they eliminate precisely those elements essential to one. At each of the four points it has been seen that there is a common defect – the lack of any distinction between properties of the cultural system and the features of socio-cultural integration. In brief, it is this central aspect of the myth which militates against examination of the interplay between the two levels and thus obstructs the investigation of cultural dynamics.

Yet the origin of the myth was grounded in primitive society, which at least accounts for the playing down of inconsistency, alternatives, diversity and discontinuity, though it does not exculpate those who advanced theories that were predicated upon their total absence. Even if the

> discovery of incoherence were never more than a contributory rather than a sufficient cause, it still would not be legitimate for us to employ a method which inherently prevents any possible appreciation of this fact. When anthropologists were concerned primarily with stable societies (or societies held to be such), the mistake was perhaps excusable: but nowadays it is not.[35]

Instead the myth has gone from strength to strength, as at its origins it continues to draw its power from the elision of cultural system integration with socio-cultural integration.

In the first place its appeal was redoubled as it was buttressed from two different, and usually opposed, schools of thought. However, it is vital to be clear that the one reinforced it in an entirely different way from the other. In the first case (typical of normative functionalism) the myth was restated in terms of 'downwards' conflation. Here cultural system integration engulfs socio-cultural integration through processes of orchestration, regulation and internalization. In the opposite case (represented by neo-Marxism) the myth was reinstated in the form of 'upwards' conflation. Basically the socio-cultural level swallows up the cultural system as the effect of social domination and ideological manipulation. Finally, just as both of these versions were becoming rather frayed under the wear and tear of criticism, the myth was suddenly revitalized by a brand new exposition of it – this time taking the form of 'central' conflation (typified by the 'structuration' approach).[36] This was not merely a new shot in the arm: rather, it extended an eternal life-support system to the myth by seeking to banish the analytical dualism, upon which the present critique depends, for good. To these theorists the myth did indeed elide the systemic and socio-cultural levels, *but* rightly so: since the two were mutually constitutive and consequently inseparable, it was therefore improper to analyse them dualistically. That this full-frontal defence of the inexorable duality of culture was even less capable of providing a theory of cultural change[37] than the two preceding forms of conflation is taken here to constitute the final condemnation of the whole conflationary procedure.

The common denominator of the various conflationists who buttress the myth of cultural integration is that they elide logical relations with causal connections and then judge this ensemble to make a coherent whole. On the contrary, an approach based on analytical dualism challenges this judgment and the premises upon which it is founded. Instead, by distinguishing logical relations (pertaining to the cultural system) from causal ones (pertaining to the socio-cultural level) and allowing of their independent variation, the interface between them becomes a problematic area for intensive exploration. The results of this would identify the *conditions* for integration in the cultural realm, without that state of affairs being taken as a foregone conclusion – any more than it can be in the structural domain. Cultural integration is demythologized by rendering it contingent upon the particular patterning of interconnections *at* the two different levels and *between* the two different levels.

Notes

* I would like to thank Percy Cohen, Ernest Gellner, John Heritage and José G. Merquior for helpful discussions or comments when this paper was in preparation.
1 Amitai Etzioni, *The Active Society*, Free Press, London, 1968, p. 146.
2 'Culture' in the German romanticist tradition stemming from Herder referred to a unique collective pattern of life, an integrated whole, pertaining to particular peoples. It was viewed as a 'meaningful' historical product, transmitted within the collectivity but not transferable beyond it. Herder's concept of culture as an integrated whole is closely akin to the notion of Gestalt.
3 B. Malinowski, *A Scientific Theory of Culture*, University of North Carolina Press, Chapel Hill NC, 1944, p. 38.
4 Ruth Benedict, *Patterns of Culture*, London, Routledge & Kegan Paul, 1961. She in fact used the terms 'pattern' and 'style' interchangeably in this work: coherence of a given culture is indicated by her usage of the 'broken cup' metaphor for cases where any mixing of cultures occurs.
5 Cf. 'Style', in Sol Tax (ed.), *Anthropology Today*, University of Chicago Press, Chicago, 1962, p. 278.
6 A.L. Kroeber, *Anthropology; Culture, Patterns and Processes*, Harcourt Brace, New York, 1963. See sections 122 (integration) and 125 (ethos/eidos and values).
7 Mary Douglas, *Purity and Danger*, Routledge & Kegan Paul, London, 1966, p. 69.
8 J.G. Merquior, *The Veil and the Mask*, Routledge & Kegan Paul, London, 1979, p. 48.

9 Ernest Gellner, 'Concepts and Society', in Bryan R. Wilson (ed.), *Rationality*, Blackwell, Oxford, 1979, p. 36 f.
10 Perry Anderson, *Considerations on Western Marxism*, Verso, London, 1979, pp. 75–8.
11 David Lockwood, 'Social Integration and System Integration', in G.K. Zollschan and W. Hirsch (eds), *Explorations in Social Change*, Houghton Mifflin, Boston, 1964, pp. 244–257.
12 'Cultures are individual psychology thrown large upon the screen, given gigantic proportions and a long time span': Ruth Benedict, 'Configurations of culture in North America', *American Anthropologist*, 34, 1932, p. 24.
13 E.E. Evans-Pritchard, *Witchcraft, Oracles and Magic Among the Azande*, Oxford University Press, Oxford, 1937, p. 195.
14 Edward Sapir, *Culture, Language and Personality*, University of California Press, Berkeley CA, 1949, p. 90. What Sapir's views lacked in typicality was more than compensated by their congruence with functionalism and its universalistic pretensions. Later on they retained salience as they were to gel equally well with cultural projects based on linguistic relativism.
15 As Lockwood rightly argued, Max Weber was equally aware of the potential for strains and conflicts developing between interdependent parts, as is illustrated by the example of patrimonialism. See Lockwood, 'Social Integration and System Integration', pp. 253–5.
16 E.E. Evans-Pritchard, *The Position of Women in Primitive Society and Other Essays in Social Anthropology*, Faber and Faber, London, 1965, p. 110.
17 Ernest Gellner, *Legitimation of Belief*, Cambridge University Press, Cambridge, 1974, pp. 143–4 (my italics).
18 Evans-Pritchard, *Witchcraft, Oracles and Magic*, p. 195.
19 Ibid., p. 13.
20 Edmund Leach, *Political Systems of Highland Burma*, Bell & Sons, London, 1954.
21 Gellner, *Legitimation of Belief*, p. 156.
22 Gellner, 'Concepts and Society', p. 36.
23 Anthony Giddens, *Central Problems in Social Theory*, Macmillan, London, 1979, p. 219.
24 Merquior, *The Veil and the Mask*, p. 51.
25 Zygmunt Bauman, *Culture as Praxis*, Routledge & Kegan Paul, London, 1973, p. 5.
26 Ernest Gellner, *Thought and Change*, Weidenfeld & Nicolson, London, 1964, p. 154.
27 Idem.
28 Gellner, 'Concepts and Society', pp. 42–3.
29 Robin Horton, 'African Traditional Thought and Western Science', *Africa*, 37:2, 1967, p. 154.
30 Claude E. Shannon and Warren Weaver, *The Mathematical Theory of Communication*, University of Illinois Press, Urbana IL, 1963.
31 Roger C. Owen, 'The Patrilocal Band: A Linguistically and Culturally Hybrid Social Unit', *American Anthropologist*, 67, 1965, pp. 675–690.
32 From an earlier unpublished version of this paper cited by Walter Buckley, *Sociology and Modern Systems Theory*, Prentice Hall, Englewood Cliffs NJ, 1967, p. 91.
33 Merquior, *The Veil and the Mask*, p. 53.
34 Henry Teune and Zdravko Mlinar, *The Developmental Logic of Social Systems*, Sage, London and Beverly Hills CA, 1978, pp. 94–5, 107, 127.
35 Gellner, 'Concepts and Society', p. 47.
36 See Giddens, *Central Problems in Social Theory*.
37 Margaret S. Archer, 'Morphogenesis versus Structuration', *British Journal of Sociology*, 33:4, 1982, pp. 455–483.

4 The vexatious fact of society

Social reality is unlike any other because of its human constitution. It is different from natural reality whose defining feature is self-subsistence: for its existence does not depend upon us, a fact which is not compromised by our human ability to intervene in the world of nature and change it. Society is more different still from transcendental reality, where divinity is both self-subsistent and unalterable at our behest; qualities which are not contravened by responsiveness to human intercession. The nascent 'social sciences' had to confront this entity, society, and deal conceptually with its three unique characteristics: first, that it is inseparable from its human components because the very existence of society depends in some way upon our activities; second, that society is characteristically transformable; it has no immutable form or even preferred state – it is like nothing but itself, and what precisely it is like at any time depends upon human doings and their consequences; third, however, neither are we immutable as social agents, for what we are and what we do as social beings are also affected by the society in which we live and by our very efforts to transform it.

Necessarily then, the problem of the relationship between individual and society was *the* central sociological problem from the beginning. The vexatious task of understanding the linkage between 'structure and agency' will always retain this centrality because it derives from what society intrinsically is. Nor is this problem confined to those explicitly studying society, for each human being is confronted by it every day of their social life. An inescapable part of our inescapably social condition is to be aware of its constraints, sanctions and restrictions on our ambitions – be they for good or for evil. Equally, we acknowledge certain social blessings such as medication, transportation and education: without their enablements our lives and hopes would both be vastly more circumscribed. At the same time, an inalienable part of our human condition is the feeling of freedom: we are 'sovereign artificers' responsible for our own destinies and capable of remaking our social environment to befit human habitation. This book begins by accepting that such ambivalence in the daily experience of ordinary people is fully authentic. Its authenticity does not derive from viewing subjective experiences as self-veridical. By themselves, the strength of our feelings is never a guarantee of their veracity: our certitudes are poor guides to certainty. Instead, this ambivalence is a real and defining feature of a human being who is also a social being. We *are* simultaneously free and constrained and we *also* have some awareness of it. The former derives from the nature of social reality; the latter from human nature's reflexivity. Together they generate an authentic (if imperfect) reflection upon the human condition in society. It is therefore the credo of this book that the adequacy of social theorizing fundamentally turns on its ability to recognize and reconcile these *two aspects* of lived social reality.

Thus we would betray ourselves, as well as our readers, by offering any form of social scient*ism* with 'laws' which are held to be unaffected by the uses and abuses we make of our freedoms, for this renders moral responsibility meaningless, political action worthless and self-reflection pointless. Equally, we delude one another by the pretence that society is simply what we choose to make it and make of it, now or in any generation, for generically 'society' is that which nobody wants in exactly the form they find it and yet it resists both individual and collective efforts at transformation – not necessarily by remaining unchanged but by altering to become something else which still conforms to no one's ideal.

From the beginning, however, betrayal and delusion have been common practice when approaching the vexatious fact of society and its human constitution. The earliest attempts to conceptualize this unique entity produced two divergent social ontologies which, in changing guises, have been with us ever since. Both evade the encounter with the vexatious ambivalence of social reality. They can be epitomized as the 'science of society' versus the 'study of wo/man': if the former denies the significance of society's human constitution, the latter nullifies the importance of what is, has been and will be constituted as society in the process of human interaction. The former is a denial that the real powers of human beings are indispensable to making society what it is. The latter withholds real powers from society by reducing its properties to the projects of its makers. Both thus endorse epiphenomenalism by holding respectively that agency or structure are inert and dependent variables. In this way they turn the vexatious into something tractable, but only by evading the uniqueness of social reality and treating it as something other than itself – by making it exclusively super-ordinate to people or utterly subordinate to them.

Furthermore, what society is held to be also affects how it is studied. Thus one of the central theses of this book is that any given social ontology has implications for the explanatory methodology which is (and in consistency can be) endorsed. This connection could not have been clearer in the works of the founding fathers. We need to remain equally clear that this is a necessary linkage – and to uphold it. The tripartite link between ontology, methodology and practical social theory is the *leitmotif* of this whole text.

Thus early protagonists of the 'Science of Society' began from an uncompromising ontological position which stated that there was indeed a Social Whole whose *sui generis* properties constituted the object of study. Thus, for Comte, 'Society is no more decomposable into individuals than a geometrical surface is into lines, or a line into points.'[1] Similarly, for Durkheim: 'Whenever certain elements combine, and thereby produce, by the fact of their combination, new phenomena, it is plain that these new phenomena reside not in the original elements but in the totality formed by their union.'[2] Here 'Society' denoted a totality which is not reducible and this therefore meant that the explanatory programme must be anti-reductionist in nature. Hence, the methodological injunction to explain one 'social fact' only by reference to another 'social fact'. Correct explanations could not be reductionist – that is, cast in terms of individual psychology – *because* the nature of social reality is held to be such that the necessary concepts could never be statements about individual people, whether for purposes of description or explanation. Consequently, practical social theories were advanced in exclusively holistic terms (explaining suicide rates by degrees of social integration) and without reference to individual human motivation. This, then, was a direct and early statement of what I term 'Downwards Conflation'[3] in social theorizing, where the 'solution' to the problem of structure and agency consists in rendering the latter epiphenomenal. Individuals are held to be 'indeterminate material', which is unilaterally moulded by society, whose holistic properties have complete monopoly over causation, and which therefore operate in a unilateral and downward manner. The contrary standpoint is represented by Individualism.

Those who conceived of their task as the 'study of wo/man' insisted that social reality consisted of nothing but individuals and their activities. Thus, for J.S. Mill,

> Men in a state of society are still men. Their actions and passions are obedient to the laws of individual human nature. Men are not, when brought together, converted into another kind of substance with different properties, as hydrogen and oxygen are different from water.[4]

Similarly, for Weber, references to collectivities such as the family, state or army are 'only a certain kind of development of actual or possible actions of individual persons'.[5] Having defined social reality individualistically, it followed for both thinkers that explanations of it must be in terms of individuals. Hence, for Mill, 'The effects produced in social phenomena by any complex set of circumstances amount precisely to the sum of the effects of the circumstances taken singly.'[6] If society is an aggregate, then, however complex, it can be understood only by a process of disaggregation, and explanation therefore consists in reduction. For Weber, too, though collectivities such as business corporations may look like non-people, since they are made up of nothing else then they 'must be treated solely as the resultants and modes of organization of the particular acts of individual persons'.[7] Since an aggregate is the resultant of its components, this means that in practical social theorizing we are presented with 'Upwards Conflation'. The solution to the problem of structure and agency is again epiphenomenal, but this time it is the social structure which is passive, a mere aggregate consequence of individual activities, which is incapable of acting back to influence individual people. Thus, people are held to monopolize causal power, which therefore operates in a one-way, upwards direction.

Already in *stating* the manner in which early social analysts confronted society, it has not been possible to do so without touching upon three different aspects which are intrinsic to *any* solution offered. Since the purpose of this book is to proffer a particular kind of solution and one which is intended to be of use to those engaged in substantive social analysis, it is crucial to be clear about the three necessary components – ontology, methodology and practical social theory – and their interconnections. I have already stated one basic thesis, namely that the social ontology adopted has implications for the explanatory methodology endorsed, and indicated how this was the case at the start of the discipline. However, it is equally the case that the methodology employed has ramifications for the nature of practical social theorizing – and in the two early paradigms this led paradigmatically to opposite versions of conflationary theory.

I believe we should never be satisfied with these forms of conflationary theorizing, which either deny people all freedom because of their involvement in society or leave their freedom completely untrammelled by their social involvements. The fact that neither Durkheim nor Weber managed to hold consistently to his own explanatory injunctions when conducting practical social analyses might have induced some reflection upon the adequacies of their methodological charters and ontological commitments. However, the nineteenth-century parting of the ways between the 'science of society' and the 'study of wo/man' passed, virtually unaltered, into the twentieth-century debate between Holism and Individualism in the philosophy of 'social science'. And there it continued to reproduce the deficiencies of both downwards and upwards conflation in practical social theorizing by re-endorsing much the same explanatory methodologies and social ontologies as had traditionally been advanced.

Both are deficient and have been regularly criticized, but the current state of the art still harbours them, together with numerous variants and claimants to the status of 'alternatives'. Because of this, commentators regularly used to signal 'crisis', whereas postmodernists now celebrate 'fragmentation' in social theory. My principal contention is that we cannot extricate ourselves from this theoretical morass without recognizing the tripartite connections between ontology, methodology and practical social theory and ensuring consistency between them. There have, however, been two different responses to the present situation, whose consequences are instructive. On the one hand, some have been tempted to uncouple practical social theory from its underpinnings, to survey the array of perspectives and suggest an eclectic pragmatism in order to have the best of all worlds. Such 'perspectivism' simultaneously denies that there are serious underlying reasons for theoretical variety and slides via instrumentalism into a marriage of inconsistent premises. On the other hand, some social theorists have returned to work exclusively on the reconceptualization of social reality. As such, they may be playing a useful role in the division of sociological labour, but if they suggest that their ontological exertions suffice, the theoretical enterprise simply cannot be resumed on this unfinished basis. The practical analyst of society needs to know not only *what social reality is*, but also *how to begin to explain it*, before addressing the particular problem under investigation. In short, methodology, broadly conceived of as an explanatory programme, is the necessary link between social ontology and practical theory.

This is what this book is intended to supply: an explanatory methodology which is indeed pivotal, called the morphogenetic approach. (The 'morpho' element is an acknowledgement that society has no pre-set form or preferred state: the 'genetic' part is a recognition that it takes its shape from, and is formed by, agents, originating from the intended and unintended consequences of their activities). In order to play its part in the chain 'ontology – methodology – practical social theory', such an explanatory framework has to be firmly anchored at both ends.

First, this means that it has to be consistently embedded in an adequate social ontology. Yet I have already begun to intimate that the study of society got off on the wrong footing in both the Individualist and Holist conceptions of reality, and in so far as these do still remain as very serious contenders, it will be necessary to break with both. Second, the morphogenetic approach is meant to be of practical utility for analysts of society. In itself, of course, an explanatory framework neither explains, nor purports to explain, anything. Nevertheless, it performs a regulatory role, for, though many substantive theories may be compatible with it, this is not the case for all, and an explanatory methodology therefore encourages theorizing in one direction whilst discouraging it in others. The primary regulative function that the morphogenetic framework seeks to assume is one that refuses to countenance *any form of conflationary theorizing* at the practical level.

Although frequent references will be made to its substantive applications (usually drawn from my own work on education and culture), what other practitioners would make of it is left to their discretion in relation to their own substantive problems. Instead, the major concern of this book is with the link between this explanatory methodology and social ontology, precisely because existing combinations are found wanting in themselves and are also guilty of fostering conflation between structure and agency, which is then registered at the level of practical theorizing.

Traditions of conflation

Generically, conflation in social theory represents one-dimensional theorizing. As in the old 'individual versus society' debate or its later expression as the 'structure and agency' problem, traditional conflationists were those who saw this as a matter of taking sides and who could come down with great conviction on one or the other. Their common denominator was this readiness to choose and consequently to repudiate sociological dualism where the different 'sides' refer to different elements of social reality, which possess different properties and powers. In contradistinction, the *interplay and interconnection* of these properties and powers form the central concern of non-conflationary theorizing, whose hallmark is the recognition that the two have to be related rather than conflated. Instead, classical conflationists always advance some device which reduces one to the other, thus depriving the two of independent properties capable of exerting autonomous influences, which would automatically defy one-dimensional theorizing. The most generic traditional device was epiphenomenalism through upwards or downwards reduction, although the precise mechanism employed showed some variation – aggregation/disaggregation, composition/decomposition or the homologies of miniaturization/magnification.

Traditionally, too, the major divide which theorists have sought to overcome in these ways has been labelled differently in various schools of thought and countries. Although there are differences in nuances, I regard the fundamental issues raised by those debates variously named 'individual and society', 'voluntarism and determinism', 'structure and agency' or 'the micro- versus macro-' as being fundamentally identical. Instead of attempting to see these as standing in some ascending order of complexity (*contra* Layder[8]), I regard their differential accentuation as little more than historical and comparative variations on the same theme. In particular, discussion in the UK has consistently concentrated upon the 'problem of structure and agency', whilst in the USA the preoccupation has been with 'the problem of scope',[9] which has now resurfaced, renamed as the 'micro-macro link'.[10] However, nomenclature should not mislead us for, as Jeffrey Alexander emphasizes, these are versions of exactly the same debate: 'The perennial conflict between individualistic and collectivist theories has been re-worked as a conflict between micro-sociology and macro-sociology.'[11]

Here the parallel form of conflationary theorizing takes the form of the displacement of scope which 'is committed whenever a theorist assumes, without further ado, that theoretical schemes or models worked out on the basis of macro-sociological considerations fit micro-sociological interpretations, or vice versa'.[12] In the downwards conflationary version, a homology was asserted between the societal system and the small group which was held to constitute a miniaturized version of the former because orchestrated by the same central value system. Hence the one-dimensionality of Parsons' processes for analysing 'any system of action', whatever its scope. Since to him 'there are continuities all the way from two-person interaction to the USA as a social system', it follows that 'we can translate back and forth between large scale social systems and small groups'.[13] This licence to start wherever one wants and to move 'back and forth' with ease depends upon the validity of the homological premise, namely that the same properties (no more, no less and no different) are indeed found throughout society.

The upward conflationary version simply made the opposite homological assumption: that is, that society is simply the small group writ large. This led interpretative sociologists in particular to place a 'big etc' against their microscopic expositions and to hold out the expectation that explanation of the social system could be arrived at by a process of accretion. This aggregative ethnographic programme depended upon the validity of exactly the same homological premise about there being no more, no less and no different properties characterizing different levels of society.[14] This central premise will be challenged in every chapter of the present work.

The final and most important similarity between these parallel debates in the UK and the USA was their firm rooting in empiricism. The conviction that social theory must confine itself to observables, since the perceptual criterion was held to be the only guarantor of reality, provided British individualists with their trump card (for who could doubt the existence of flesh-and-blood people?) and the collectivists with their stumbling block (since how could they validate the existence of any property unless they could translate it into a series of observational statements about people?). The American debate was even more unabashed in its positivism, since its defining terms, the 'micro-' and the 'macro-', necessarily dealt only with an observable property: that is, *size*.

Since I have maintained that it was one and the same debate going on on either side of the Atlantic, then I seriously want to question whether 'the main story'[15] in

American social theory or anywhere else should be about size *per se*. In fact, to disassociate the United States' version of the debate from this empirical observable feature is paralleled by the more comprehensive task of disassociating the British debate from empiricism altogether. In other words, it is my view that only by rejecting the terms of these traditional debates and completely revising them on a different ontological basis can we get away from one-dimensional conflationary theorizing and replace it by theories of the interdependence and interplay between different kinds of social property.

Thus in the American debate there is a substantial consensus, which I seek to challenge, that unequivocally considers the problem of how to relate the micro and the macro as being about how to forge a linkage between social units of different *sizes*. Thus Munch and Smelser,[16] reviewing the field in 1987, produced seven different definitions of the terms 'micro' and 'macro', which (with the exception of Peter Blau) all firmly associated the former with the small scale and the latter with the large scale. In other words, despite their differences, Layder's recent fomulation would generally be accepted as uncontroversial by them.

> Micro analysis or "microsociology" concentrates on the more personal and immediate aspects of social interaction in daily life. Another way of saying this is that it focuses on actual face-to-face encounters between people. Macro analysis or "macrosociology" focuses on the larger-scale more general features of society such as organizations, institutions and culture.[17]

Instead, this seems to me highly controversial, and to represent a tradition with which social theory should break. It needs to be replaced by an emphasis upon the incidence of emergent properties that delineate different strata – an emphasis which does not assume that observable differences in the size of groups automatically means that they constitute distinct levels of social reality.

Although no one would deny that empirically there are big and small units in society, this does not necessarily mean that they possess properties whose linkage presents any particular problems. That is, the real 'aspects' or 'features' of social reality are not by definition tied to the *size* of interacting elements (the *site* of the encounter, or for that matter, the *sentiment* accompanying interaction). Thus, I am in complete agreement with Alexander's statement

> that this equation of micro with individual is extremely misleading, as indeed, is the attempt to find any specific size correlation with the micro/macro difference. There can be no empirical referents for micro or macro as such. They are analytical contrasts, suggesting emergent levels within empirical units, not antagonistic empirical units themselves.[18]

In the same way, I want to maintain that 'micro' and 'macro' are *relational* terms meaning that a given stratum can be 'micro' to another and 'macro' to a third, and so on. What justifies the differentiation of strata and thus the use of the terms 'micro' and 'macro' to characterize their relationship is the existence of *emergent properties* pertaining to the latter but not to the former, even if they were elaborated from it. But this has nothing to do with size, site or sentiment.

Emergent properties are *relational*, arising out of combination (e.g. the division of labour from which high productivity emerges), where the latter is capable of reacting back on the former (e.g. producing monotonous work) and has its own causal powers (e.g. the differential wealth of nations), which are causally irreducible to the powers of its components (individual workers). This signals the *stratified nature of social reality* where different strata possess different emergent properties and powers. However, the key points in this connection are (a) that emergent strata constitute the crucial entities in need of linking by explaining how their causal powers originate and operate, but (b) that such strata do not neatly map onto empirical units of any particular magnitude. Indeed, whether they coincide with the 'big' or the 'small' is contingent and thus there cannot be a 'micro'–'macro' problem which is defined exclusively by the relative size of social units.

Thus, in the course of this book, frequent references will be made to 'the societal'. Each time, this has a concrete referent – particular emergent properties belonging to a specific society at a given time. Both the referent and the properties are real, they have full ontological status, but what do they have to do with 'the big'? The society in question may be small, tribal and work on a face-to-face basis. Nor do they have anything to do with what is, relatively, 'the biggest' at some point in time. We may well wish to refer to certain societal properties of Britain (the 'macro' unit for a particular investigation), which is an acknowledged part of bigger entities, such as Europe, developed societies or the English-speaking world. We would do so if we wanted to explain, for example, the role of the 'Falklands factor' in recent elections and in so doing we would also incidentally be acknowledging that people who go in for it take their nationalism far from 'impersonally', and that the 'site' of neo-colonialism may be far distant.

Similarly, the existence of small-scale interpersonal encounters does not make these into a sociological category, much less if this is on the presumption that they are somehow immune to 'factors' belonging to other strata of social reality, possessed of some much greater freedom for internal self-determination and presumed to be inconsequential for the system of which they are part. To the social realist there is no 'isolated' micro world – no *lebsenswelt* 'insulated' from the socio-cultural system in the sense of being unconditioned by it, nor a hermetically sealed domain whose day-to-day doings are guaranteed to be of no systemic 'import'.

On the contrary, the entrance and exit doors of the life world are permanently open and the understanding of its conditions, course and consequences are predicated upon acknowledging this. For example, small-scale interactions between teachers and pupils do not just happen in classrooms but within educational systems, and those between landlords and tenants are not in-house affairs but take place on the housing market. Both pupils and teachers, for instance, bring in with them different degrees of bargaining power (cultural capital as expertise) – that is, resources with which they were endowed in wider society by virtue of family, class, gender and ethnicity. Equally, the definition of instruction which they literally encounter in schools is not one that can freely be negotiated *in situ* but is determined outside the classroom, and, at least partially, outside the educational system altogether.

Thus one of the biggest deviations in the 1970s sociology of education (which had its parallels in other specialisms) was not the determination to study those neglected educational processes and practices taking place within but the methodological decision that this could be done by shutting the classroom door and bolting the school gates because everything needed to explain what went on within was found inside the small enclosure. Yet closure is always a misleading metaphor which conceals the *impact* of external systemic and social properties and also the *import* of internal 'micropolitics' for reproduction and change of the social and the systemic. For, on the one hand, both teachers and pupils are enmeshed in broader *socio-cultural relations* that they carry with them into the classroom, and whose first effect is which type of school class they enter! Once there, teachers and pupils cannot freely negotiate the relationships they jointly will, given the impact of curricular controls, public examinations and the job market. On the other hand, classroom interaction is *never* without systemic *import*, whether this works for reproduction or for transformation.

Construed in this manner, then, the crucial linkage to make and to maintain is not between the 'micro' and the 'macro', conceived of as the small and interpersonal in contrast to the large and impersonal, but rather between the 'social' and the 'systemic'. In other words, systemic properties are always the ('macro') *context* confronted by ('micro') social interaction, whilst social activities between people ('micro') represent the *environment* in which the ('macro') features of systems are either reproduced or transformed. But in neither the structural nor the cultural domains is this necessarily to talk about the big in relation to the small, for emergent properties can figure at all 'levels'. Yet since they arise from and work through only social interaction, then this crucial interplay requires examination at any level.

Two implications follow from this. Firstly, that the central theoretical task is one of linking two *qualitatively* different aspects of society (the 'social' and the 'systemic', or, if preferred, 'action' and its 'environment') rather than two *quantitatively* different features, the big and the small or macro and micro. The main point here is that qualitative differences defy linkage by aggregation, homology or, in short, by conflation. Instead, it is a matter of theorizing their mutual impact and import – which need not be reciprocal. (This accounts for why it is necessary to deal with the positive feedback producing morphogenesis and to distinguish it from the negative feedback reinforcing morphostasis). As Alexander puts the task of linking action and its environments, 'The collective environments of action simultaneously inspire and confine it. If I have conceptualized action correctly, these environments will be seen as its products; if I can conceptualize the environments correctly, action will be seen as their result.'[19] Although in general agreement, I would prefer to talk about conditional influences in order to avoid the deterministic overtones of the above.

The second implication is that if the misleading preoccupation with *size* is abandoned, then the linkages which need forging to account for the vexatious fact of society are those between the 'people' and the 'parts' of social reality, or, as Lockwood[20] put it, between 'social' and 'system' integration: that is, how orderly or conflictual social relations (properties of people) mesh with congruent or incongruent systemic relations (properties of parts of society). In short, we come back full circle to the one problem of 'structure and agency'. Consequently it is necessary to return to the debate which traditionally underpinned it – between individualism and collectivism – for that is where the root divide is grounded. No apologies are made for revisiting this 1950s terrain, although I will try to review it in the sparest terms. Instead, my apologia is that unless individualism and collectivism are uprooted, reinspected and rejected once and for all, because of their radical ontological and methodological deficiencies, then social theory will remain bogged down in the fallacy of conflation and practical social analysis will remain shackled to the unworkable explanatory programmes represented by upward and downward conflationism.

The purpose and the plan of the book

The overriding aim is to come to terms with the vexatious fact of society and its human constitution, which, it is held, cannot be achieved through any form of conflation of these two components. However, 'coming to terms' means two related things – ontological and methodological – for the aim of the social theorist is twofold. On the one hand, the task is to explicate in what general terms 'society' should be conceptualized. Since theories are propositions containing concepts and since all concepts have their referents (pick out features held to belong to social reality), then there can be no social theory without an accompanying social ontology (implicit or explicit). On the other hand, the point of theory is practical. It is never an end in itself but a tool for the working social analyst which gives explanatory purchase on substantive social problems through supplying the terms or framework for their investigation. Thus my aim cannot be to advance some abstract account of the vexatious fact of society which solves a theoretical problem (how to avoid conflationary formulations) but one which remains at such a high level of abstraction that it is of no assistance to those who are vexed by some particular aspect of it. Although books may be written in this way, I want to sustain the point that what social reality is held to be cannot but influence how society is studied. In other words, there is always a connection between social ontology and explanatory methodology (however covert and however unhelpful). The final section of the introduction is devoted to justifying the proposition that this is a necessary and a two-way linkage.

In the next chapter I seek to demonstrate the consistency of these two within both Individualism and Collectivism. It follows from this that we are still trapped in the *conjoint* ontological/methodological terms set by this traditional debate – with the unacceptable consequence that upward and downward conflation are perpetuated in social theory. Chapter 3 argues that it is therefore only by rejecting the terms of the traditional debate and replacing both their ontologies and methodologies that a basis can be developed for non-conflationary theorizing. However, this chapter also begins to show that rejection does not mean replacement by a new consensus but rather the reopening of another debate about how to link structure and agency. It outlines the (now) four different positions systematically. It follows that the burden of choice has not been removed from contemporary practitioners; nor, in replacing the terms of the traditional debate, has conflationism disappeared from social theorizing.

On the contrary, there is now a parting of the ways between those who seek to *transcend* the duality of structure and agency in one conceptual move by considering the two as being mutually constitutive and necessarily linked to form a duality such that agents cannot act without drawing upon structural properties whose own existence depends upon their instantiation by agents. This core notion of structure as the simultaneous medium and outcome of action is central to Giddens's structuration theory. Chapter 4 analyzes how this leads directly to central conflation in social theory – as a relatively new variant, though an idealist version of it can be found in the social constructionism of Berger and Luckmann.[21] Although superior in many ways to its predecessors, it nonetheless shares the problematic nature of all forms of conflationary theory. In this case, the difficulty is not that of ephiphenomenalism (that is, of either structure or agency being dependent, inert and therefore causally uninfluential) but that endorsement of their mutual constitution precludes examination of their interplay, of the effects of one upon the other and of any statement about their relative contribution to stability and change at any given time.

Conversely, social realism which accentuates the importance of emergent properties at the levels of both agency and structure, but considers these as proper to the strata in question and therefore *distinct* from each other and *irreducible* to one another, replaces the terms of the traditional debate with entirely new ones. Irreducibility means that the different strata are *separable* by definition precisely because of the properties and powers which only belong to each of them and whose emergence from one another justifies their differentiation as strata at all. Three *differentia specifica* are denoted by the concept of emergence:

- Properties and powers of some strata are anterior to those of others precisely because the latter emerge from the former over time, for emergence takes time since it derives from interaction and its consequences, which necessarily occur in time.
- Once emergence has taken place the powers and properties defining and distinguishing strata have relative autonomy from one another.
- Such autonomous properties exert independent causal influences in their own right and it is the identification of these causal powers at work which validates their existence, for they may indeed be non-observables.

Chapter 5 is devoted to spelling out the ontological distinctiveness of social realism and clearly distinguishing it from the ontology of praxis endorsed by proponents of the mutual constitution of structure and agency. Unfortunately, because both realists and structurationists have rejected the terms of the old debate between Individualism and Collectivism, there has been an over-hasty tendency to assume their mutual convergence and to lump them together as *an* alternative to the positions taken in the traditional debate. Instead, the crucial point is that we are now confronted by two new and competing social ontologies.

Moreover, these ontological differences bear out the conviction that what social reality is held to be serves to regulate *how* we are enjoined to study it. Because it is based four-square upon the notion of emergent properties the methodological implications of social realism are quite different from the explanatory framework advanced by structurationists because the latter explicitly reject emergence itself. Quite simply, if the different strata possess different properties and powers, and structure and agency *inter alia* are deemed to be distinctive strata for this very reason, then examining their interplay becomes crucial. When applied to structure and agency, the realist social ontology *entails* the exploration of those features of both that are prior or posterior to one another and of which causal influences are exerted by one stratum on the other, and vice versa, by virtue of these independent properties and powers. The 'people' in society and the 'parts' of society are not different aspects of the same thing but are radically different in kind. This being so, then social realism implies a methodology based upon analytical dualism, where explanation of why things social are so and not otherwise depends upon an account of how the properties and powers of the 'people' causally intertwine with those of the 'parts'. Analytical dualism means emphasizing linkages by unpacking what was referred to earlier as the 'impact' and 'import' of and between different strata. This focal concern with *interplay* is what distinguishes the emergentist from the non-emergentist, whose preoccupation is with *interpenetration*. The cognate terms of the latter, such as instantiation and mutual constitution, all involve compacting strata rather than disentangling them, hence resulting in central conflation at the level of practical social theorizing.

It is the social realists' insistence upon ontological emergence which introduces analytical dualism as its methodological complement and which eventually culminates in the only form of non-conflationary theorizing to develop to date. The centrality of analytical dualism to social realism is laid out in Chapter 6. However, generalized explanatory programmes, necessary as they are and necessarily related as they be to their underlying ontology, are not the end of the story. There is a final element needed if theory is to be of utility to the working analyst of society, and this is practical social theory itself. Analytical dualism is the guiding methodological principle underpinning non-conflationary theorizing but the injunction to examine the interplay between the 'parts and the people', the 'social and the systemic', 'structure and agency', or 'action and its environments', although indispensable, is also incomplete. The social analyst needs practical guidelines as well as good principles; she requires explicit sociological guidance about how to approach the problem in hand in addition to philosophical assurance that they are taking the right basic approach.

Here the morphogenetic/morphostatic framework is put forward as the practical complement of social realism because it supplies a genuine method of conceptualizing how the interplay between structure and agency can actually be analyzed over time and space. It is based on two basic propositions:

i   That structure necessarily pre-dates the action(s) leading to its reproduction or transformation.
ii That structural elaboration necessarily post-dates the action sequences which gave rise to it.

As embodiments of analytical dualism, both are opposed to conflation since what is pivotal are the conditional and generative mechanisms operating *between* structure and agency. This would be a logical impossibility were the two to be conflated (in any manner or direction). Thus the last three chapters are devoted to the morphogenetic cycle, the three phases which are involved – structural conditioning → social interaction → structural elaboration – and their direct parallels for culture and for agency itself. The morphogenetic approach is thus presented as the practical methodological embodiment of the realist social ontology, the two together representing a distinctive alternative to both the upward and downward conflationary theorizing of the old debate and to the central conflation with which many now seek to replace it. It constitutes a distinctive linkage between social ontology, explanatory methodology and practical social theorizing. The remainder of this chapter will argue the unavoidability of such a tripartite linkage and how it was indeed consistently advanced and defended within the traditional terms of the debate, but also how these terms were inadequate and thus how the linkages between them were correspondingly both unacceptable and unworkable. Their rejection was merited and overdue: the central question today is whether they should be replaced by a novel version of conflationary theorizing or whether the future of fruitful social theory lies in developing the neglected option of non-conflation. The purpose of this book is to give justification for endorsing the non-conflationary option – both in principle and in practice.

Social ontology and explanatory methodology: the need for consistency

In any field of study, the nature of what exists cannot be unrelated to how it is studied. This is a strong realist statement, which I endorse but cannot explore here. Instead, I want to examine the more modest proposition that what *is held* to exist must influence considerations about how it should be explained. In other words, what social reality is deemed to consist of (and what is deemed non-existent) does affect how its explanation is approached.

It is certainly not being maintained that the relationship between the two is one of logical implication. This cannot be the case. For it must remain possible to uphold the existence of something which need never enter our explanations (a deity indifferent to Creation), or that some things exist socially which carry no particular implications about how we should study them or what importance should be assigned to them in explanations. For example, because both pleasure and pain are undeniably part of our social lot, this does not entail that all social action must be explained as the pursuit of pleasure and the avoidance of pain. This requires a justification of the connection, which Utilitarians would adduce and others would find unconvincing on the grounds that there is significantly more to social life than that.

Nevertheless, the social ontology endorsed does play a powerful *regulatory* role *vis-à-vis* the explanatory methodology for the basic reason that it conceptualizes social reality in certain terms, thus identifying what there is to be explained and also ruling out explanations in terms of entities or properties which are deemed non-existent. Conversely, regulation is mutual, for what is held to exist cannot remain immune from what is really, actually or factually found to be the case. Such consistency is a general requirement and it usually requires continuous two-way adjustments between ontology and methodology to achieve and to sustain it as such.

Of course, the achievement of consistency is no guarantee against error, as will be argued of both the Individualist and Collectivist programmes. Nevertheless, consistency is a necessary pre-condition, and to establish this now is to define one of the conditions which those seeking to replace both Individualism and Collectivism must meet when advancing alternative social ontologies and associated methodological programmes. For whatever their defects, both Individualism/Methodological Individualism and Collectivism/Methodological Collectivism provide clear illustrations of two programmes whose respective advocates both strove for internal consistency and were well aware of the reasons why this was necessary. These reasons can be broken down into three, which are binding on all who study 'the social', but examining them also serves to introduce the distinctive ways in which Individualists and Collectivists responded, thus setting the terms of the debate between them.

Description and explanation: the ties that bind them

The most fundamental consideration is that description and explanation are not discrete from one another and therefore we cannot be dealing with separate debates about the two. What social reality is held to *be* also *is* that which we seek to explain. It is denoted as being such and such by virtue of the concepts used to describe it and their use is inescapable since all knowledge is conceptually formed. There is no direct access to the 'hard facts' of social life, at least for the vast majority of us who cannot subscribe to the discredited doctrine of immaculate perception. By describing it in particular terms we are in fact conceptually denoting that which is to be explained. In other words, our ontological concepts serve to define the explanandum, and different social ontologies describe social reality in different ways, as is the case with Individualists and Collectivists. Necessarily this circumscribes the explanans to such statements as could potentially explain social reality *as it has been defined* by each of them.

Now it might be objected that nobody disagrees that in social reality there are both individuals (X) and groups (Y), nor that there are attributes of groups (Y^1), such as efficiency and power, that are not just the sum of individual properties, nor even that there are some attributes of groups (Y^2) (such as organization, stability or cohesiveness) that cannot be properties of people. This of course is the case: the crux of the matter, however, is not whether groups exist but what constitutes them. In other words, how should they properly be described? Here the Individualist insists that anything about groups and their properties (Y, Y^1, $Y^{2\prime}$) can be eliminated by redefining them in terms of people (X, $X^{1\prime}$) and that such redescription is a matter of necessity because if our concepts do not denote something about people, then to what else can they meaningfully refer? The answer given was – only a reified entity (as if there were no alternative response).

Consequently, to the individualist, however much longhand it takes to produce the acceptable redescription (of, say, group stability, in terms of members' preferences for remaining together), it must be possible in principle and accomplished in practice. Here the Collectivist counters that an activity such as withdrawing money from a bank account cannot be described (and there description and explanation are the self-same process of making an activity intelligible) without reference to 'group concepts' such as 'banking' or 'legal tender', since the rules of deposit accounts are internal to the concept of cashing a cheque. Try to eliminate the former and misdescription results in the misunderstanding that anyone will hand over money when presented with a written slip of paper. The Individualist responds that this presents no great problem because the referents of these 'group concepts' can be redefined or 'translated' into statements about what the individuals involved are doing; a banking institution can be descriptively reduced to the activities of people engaged in it. In turn, the Collectivist dissents because descriptions of these activities will necessitate the introduction of other non-individual concepts, such as the role of the cashier, which again invokes the notion of 'banking' because patterns of action themselves are unintelligible without it (e.g. to understand why cashiers don't hand out money at parties).[22]

In other words, the significance of the concepts employed to *describe* reality also circumscribe those that can legitimately be entertained as *explaining* it. This is most obvious in cases like the above, where explanation *consists* in identification – that is, something becomes intelligible to us through correct description. In that case, far from being separate, the descriptive and explanatory processes are identical. Indeed, in the methodological tradition stemming from Dithey to Winch, this is held to be the appropriate mode of explanation in social analysis. Yet whether we believe that we have finished the job of explaining by (descriptive) identification or are only just beginning it, there is no way in which the process of description can be omitted and the concepts deemed appropriate for this task always circumscribe those that can then consistently be allowed to explain it.

Since the Individualist describes society as constituted by individuals (their dispositions, relations, beliefs, etc.) and nothing else, then some types of explanations – that is, those employing concepts inconsistent with the above – are automatically ruled out. Since 'group properties', which are synonymous with holistic entities to the Individualist, have been descriptively defined out of existence, they cannot re-enter through the methodological door in order to explain social life. Consequently, explanations as well as descriptions must be in terms of X and not Y (individual properties and not group properties), otherwise what is at best a shorthand construct (Y) or at worst a reified entity is being assigned real causal power which properly can belong only to that which really is real – that is, to individuals (Xs and Xs in combination).

Here the Collectivist reasserts that, since adequate descriptions of social life cannot be given without references to irreducibly social 'remainders' (i.e. we cannot eradicate 'banking' and 'role of cashier' from an intelligible description of cashing cheques), then these indispensable descriptive terms can, and usually must, *also* figure in our explanations. Collectivists then use the fact that it is impossible to give descriptions in purely individual terms to challenge the Individualists' assertion that the only admissible form *of explanation* is one framed in terms of 'individual dispositions'. For, the Collectivist argues, these too cannot be identified without invoking the social context and to do so entails using concepts which are again irreducibly social. Thus Gellner maintains that as 'a matter of causal fact, our dispositions are not independent of the social context in which they occur; but they are not even independent logically, for they cannot be described without references to their social context'[23] (i.e. we cannot identify the dispositions of 'voters' without referring to 'elections', of 'soldiers' without 'armies', or of 'bank tellers' without 'banks').

Although it is possible, of course, to advance individual predicates of a non-social kind, such as those pertaining to human beings as material objects (genetic make-up), or ones that, whilst presupposing consciousness, still presuppose nothing about any feature of society (aggression or gratification), no theorist could seriously entertain the prospect of explaining social complexity in its entirety on the basis of predicates that we share with the animals.[24]

For on this basis we cannot explain that which distinguishes human society from animal society (the explanandum), while the explanans itself, the individual, would simultaneously have been misdescribed by confining personal qualities to the properties of animals, thus omitting that which is uniquely characteristic of people. Hence Bhaskar concludes critically that

> the real problem appears to be not so much that of how one could give an individualistic explanation of social behaviour, but that of how one could ever give a non-social (i.e. strictly individualistic) explanation of individual, at least characteristically human, behaviour! For the predicates designating properties special to persons all pre-suppose a social context for their employment. A tribesman implies a tribe, the cashing of a cheque a banking system. Explanation, whether by subsumption under general law, adversion to motives or rules, or redescription (identification), always invoke irreducibly social predicates.[25]

In short, explanation cannot proceed without prior description, yet what something is defined as being through the concepts which describe it determines what exactly is to be explained, which necessarily circumscribes the explanatory project.

Ontology as conceptual regulation

Social ontologies perform a yet stronger regulatory role, for they govern *those concepts which are deemed admissible* in explanation as in description. Precepts for proper concept formation come from the social ontology that is endorsed, as this logically *determines* the types of descriptive concept that can be employed.[26] Of course, for the Individualist which particular concepts are chosen is not determined: all that is logically required is that they must be individualistic and what is prohibited is the attribution of non-observable properties to equally non-observable group entities in any acceptable description of social life. This, in turn, *regulates* what kinds of concepts can consistently appear in the explanatory methodology. Because the ontology contains judgements about the 'ultimate constituents' (and non-constituents) of social reality, it thus governs what sorts of concepts may properly be countenanced for any purpose whatsoever.

Thus Watkins, as an Individualist, is explicit about how ontology carries over to influence explanation because the 'metaphysically impregnated part of methodology' seeks to establish the appropriate material (as opposed to formal) requirements 'which the *contents* of the premises of an explanatory theory in a particular field ought to satisfy. These requirements may be called regulative principles.'[27] Significantly, he expands on this to the effect that 'Fundamental differences in the subject-matters of different sciences – differences to which formal methodological rules are impervious – ought, presumably, to be reflected in the regulative principles appropriate to each science.' In other words, our subject matter, social reality, ought to regulate how we explain it. The fact that there is disagreement over what really exists socially does nothing to undermine Watkins's point that the ontology *held* by different students of society, their different conceptions of social reality, will indeed regulate how they try to explain it – in different ways. To regulate is not to dictate: there can be lively debate about the most useful concepts to employ within a given view of what social reality is, but equally that view of what exists (and thus constitutes our subject matter) does serve to rule out certain concepts from explanations, just as atheists cannot attribute their well-being to divine providence.

The actual debate between Individualists and Collectivists provides the clearest illustration of the regulative role that ontology performs for methodology. In the following instances a major protagonist from each side begins with an uncompromising statement about the 'ultimate constituents' of social reality and then proceeds immediately to state the terms in which it should be studied. Thus, for Individualism, Watkins states that

> the ultimate constituents of the social world are individual people who act more or less appropriately in the light of their dispositions and understanding of their situation. Every complex social situation, institution or event is the result of a particular configuration of individuals, their dispositions, situations, beliefs, and physical resources and environment. There may be unfinished or half-way explanations of large scale social phenomena (say, inflation) in terms of other large-scale phenomena (say, full employment); but we shall not have arrived at rock-bottom explanations of such large-scale phenomena until we have deduced an account of them from statements about the dispositions, beliefs, resources and inter-relations of individuals.[28]

On the other hand, Mandelbaum draws just as tight a link between the Collectivist ontology and the concepts that can be used to refer to social reality and that also explain it:

> If it be the case, as I wish to claim, that societal facts are as ultimate as are psychological facts, then those concepts which are used to refer to the forms of organization of a society cannot be reduced without remainder to concepts which only refer to the thoughts and actions of specific individuals.

His explanatory aim is then 'to show that one cannot understand the actions of human beings as members of a society unless one assumes that there is a group of facts which I shall term "societal facts"'.[29]

Here, ontological considerations are used not merely to justify a congruent methodological stand-point but to actively regulate the associated explanatory programmes. For both Individualists and Collectivists, what society is held to be made to be made up of serves to monitor the concepts that can properly be used to describe it and which in turn may legitimately figure in explanatory statements. No explanation is acceptable to either camp if it contains terms whose referents misconstrue the nature of social reality as they see it – whether such misconstruction is due to sins of conceptual omission or commission. Ontology, I am arguing, acts as both gatekeeper and bouncer for methodology.

Certainly, the ontological question 'what constitutes social reality?' is different from the question asked about methodology: 'does it work?' However, in the Individualist/Collectivist and Methodological Individualist/Methodological Collectivist debates the nexus between the two is so tight that the stern voice of Individualistic ontology asserts that its own explanatory programme, containing only concepts referring to individuals, 'must work in principle'. Equally it insists that its opponents' explanations deal in unacceptable terms (reified entities, social substances or unreduced group properties) and therefore must be rejected out of hand *because* of this. Even when the latter appear to work, they are only 'half-way explanations' which cannot become complete or 'rock bottom' until the group concepts they contain have been reduced to individual terms. In parallel, the Collectivists' ontological commitment to irreducible social properties leads them to assert that individualist explanations must fail in principle because of what they leave out (reference to the social context), and that where they do appear to work in practice this is because such necessary references have been smuggled in by incorporating them into the individual (belief systems become the individuals' beliefs, resource distributions are disaggregated into people's wealth, the situation confronted becomes a person's problem etc.). On the whole, Collectivists tend to be less ontologically strident, given the holistic skeleton in the family cupboard, and generally respond by using their explanatory successes to boost confidence and strengthen their ontological foothold. This constitutes the third reason why the two debates (the ontological and the methodological), far from being separate, are in a relationship of mutual regulation.

Explanation and ontological revision

Since the nature of social reality, like any other for once, is a matter of fact which is independent of the prior commitments of any theorists about what exists, then if and when an incongruous method of explanation gives evidence of working, or the congruent methodological programme breaks down in practice, this should result in a reinspection of those commitments themselves. What we think social reality is cannot be a separate matter from what we find it to be. The reciprocal regulation that I am arguing obtains between ontology and methodology is one which obviously has to work in both directions. Thus when a Collectivist explanation containing 'group variables' seems to be powerful, or even unavoidable (containing irreducible references to social entities such as 'banking'), then methodology has raised a question for ontology. What is at issue is the ontological status of the entities denoted by the collective terms.

Collectivists were shyly tentative about drawing robust ontological conclusions from the frequent success of their explanatory programme. Gellner went as far as to contend that 'if something (a) is a causal factor (b) cannot be reduced, then in some sense it "really and independently exists"'.[30] What is being suggested here is that a causal criterion of existence is acceptable, rather than always and only employing the perceptual criterion (observability) as entrenched in empiricist Individualism. To have pressed home this argument and extracted its full ontological value (given that it was first advanced in 1956) needed not only a complete break with empiricist assumptions, positivistic prescriptions and the underlying Humean notion of causality but also an articulated alternative. In its absence, the furthest Gellner went was the cautious assertion that factors which were causally efficacious and also irreducible had a real and independent existence 'in some sense'.[31] He was completely correct, but unable to substantiate it without a philosophy of social science which warranted unobservable concepts, employed a causal criterion to establish their reality and departed from the constant conjuncture model of causality. This, of course, raised the whole question of 'in what sense?' By using the phrase at all, did he imply that 'social properties' existed in a different sense from 'individual properties'? And, if so, was this precisely the sense which anti-Holists had been so concerned to eradicate, namely the imputation of a reified existence to insubstantial concepts? (Retrospectively it seems certain that the phase indicated only an inability to be any clearer until much more work had been done on the causal criterion of existence and the whole empiricist framework challenged.) As matters stood, the Collectivist method of explanation had indeed reinforced the Collectivist ontology, but this was stated in such a tentative manner that it only served to keep the already converted going. Collectivists could expect no converts, precisely because they had failed to give a clear answer as to the ontological status of the entities denoted by collective terms.

Even if Individualists did not acknowledge the implications of successful Collectivist explanations (or the significance of being unable to eliminate all 'societal' concepts from explanation) for what 'really and independently exists', nevertheless the frequent failure of their own methodological programme should have been

96 *The vexatious fact of society*

a cause for ontological concern. In practice, their own reductionist programme hinged on the development of 'composition laws'. Here reduction consists in advancing explanatory statements made up of nothing apart from propositions about individual dispositions together with a specification of how people's behaviour differs according to the membership and size of the group in which they are participating. This specification means establishing a series of relevant empirical generalizations, the composition laws, which would then enable the computation of complex situations involving more people from simpler ones involving the behaviour of smaller numbers. Provided all concepts (like a hierarchical group) are *defined* in individualistic terms (some people having authority over others) and the composition laws are known, then reduction can take place and complex group behaviour can be explained in terms of the behaviour of individuals in groups. At least, this is what the methodological programme promises, but since composition laws are no more than empirical generalizations, the possibility of their breakdown cannot be excluded and in fact is more common than cases in which reduction has been accomplished.

However, the Methodological Individualist is not arguing that satisfactory means for achieving reduction *have* been found, or even that promising solutions are in sight, but only that *in principle* such reduction is possible. Yet such a 'principle' cannot serve as the basis for practical methodological injunctions of this kind. Whether or not there are composition laws cannot be decided 'in principle' on logical grounds: it is a matter of fact[32] – and one which poses problems for the Individualists' prior ontological commitment. For those instances where the reductionist explanatory programme breaks down, especially given their frequency, actually call for a re-evaluation of the social ontology which led to the expectation that it would (let alone must) work. There is an ontological problem not just because the definition of what exists, and can therefore legitimately be conceptualized, has produced a methodology whose concepts and laws cannot cope with the whole of social reality but also because of what happens when such an explanation fails. In these cases, where all concepts have been defined individualistically but the composition laws break down at some level of complexity, then it has to be admitted that a new factor has come into play at that point. Its inclusion is necessary for successful explanation and this thus constitutes a case of 'explanatory emergence'. Whether or not the emergent factor, which now has to be incorporated if the explanation is to work, happens to look innocuously individualistic (like 'fear of large groups', which makes the difference between small talkative seminars and the silence which ensues when the same people are asked to comment during a lecture), the fact remains that it has come into play and is identifiable *only* in the new context of the lecture itself.

In 'some sense', but undeniably one which is indispensable for explanation, the lecture group is having an effect independent of its membership – and this despite the fact that it can indeed be described in individualistic terms (i.e. the people present and what they do). Such frequent methodological findings (cases again of causal efficacy) should have raised some ontological disquietude, for clearly there are 'things at work' beyond individuals and their interpersonal relations or combinations which leads to the question of *their ontological status* and whether it is compatible with an individualist conception of social reality.

In short, the practical results of the explanatory programmes associated with Methodological Collectivism and Individualism (relative success and failure respectively) called for ontological re-examination on each side. Instead, the Collectivists remained unduly tentative, settling for their explanatory variables existing 'in a sense', without pursuing the causal criterion of reality to confirm their ontological status as real and independent. On the other hand, the Individualists remained so committed to their ontological principle (that the ultimate constituents of social life were nothing but people) that they were deaf to their own methodological findings that something beside 'other people' was at work in society. Since both proved reluctant to go back to the ontological drawing board and revise their views of social reality in the light of knowledge about it, stalemate ensued.

Conclusion

It was in this context of deadlock that the suggestion was advanced that two separate debates were being compacted together, unnecessarily and unhelpfully, in the confrontation between Individualists and Collectivists. The first, it was claimed, concerned the terms used to describe society and was therefore a matter of their meaning and whether their referents were logically meaningful. The other, it was held, was a matter of fact since it dealt with explanation and concerned the possibility or impossibility of reducing all explanatory predicates to individual terms – something upon which logic cannot arbitrate. One point of insisting upon this separation was to offer the terms of a truce between the two standpoints which got them (and us) out of stalemate. However, if the two debates are genuinely separate then it is possible to decide the descriptive debate in favour of the Individualists or the Collectivists and the explanatory debate the other way round. Effectively, this is what the peace treaty first put forward by Brodbeck did, since it can be summed up in the formula 'descriptive individualism plus explanatory emergence'. Individualism was handed the honours in the descriptive debate: '*In principle*, of course', even when dealing with vague and open terms such as the Reformation, 'all such concepts must be definable in terms of individual behaviour' (though in practice it was conceded that we often cannot do it).[33] Collectivism, however, had rather the better of the explanatory confrontation. Hence, to the peace-makers,

> Emergence at the level of explanation should be carefully distinguished from what we earlier called descriptive emergence. The latter phrase refers to the occurrence of a property of groups, like the so-called group mind, which is not definable in terms of the individuals making up the groups. Explanatory emergence, however, refers to laws of group behaviour, which, *even though their terms are defined as they should be*, are still not derivable from the laws, including whatever composition laws there are about individual behaviour. This is *in fact* the case at present.[34]

98 The vexatious fact of society

Thus Brodbeck considers it profitable to continue exploring these laws applying to social complexes – that is, to pursue the Collectivist explanatory programme – always hoping that the connections established will then suggest suitable modes of reduction.

There are, it seems to me, profound objections to this procedure for ending the stalemate. To begin with, although Brodbeck herself is advocating a particular compromise position, it is premised on the separateness of 'the two debates' and, if this is really the case, then one could end up adopting either kind of ontology and then endorsing either type of methodology or vice versa. Even though Sztompka has shown that some combinations are unlikely, neither are they impossible.[35] Yet the whole point of this introduction has been to argue that, although the relationship between ontology and methodology is not so close as logical implication, it is still a tight one of *mutual* regulation.

In summary, the reasons for this are, first, that we are not dealing with discrete activities where description and explanation are concerned, and cannot be because explanation requires identification of what is to be explained, which the descriptive terms supply. Thus the same corpus of concepts is used in both and links them together. Second, in general and avowedly in this debate, different ontologies furnish different 'regulative principles' about the methodology appropriate to do the explaining. Negative regulation is unavoidable, for you cannot develop a method to explain that which is held not to exist. Positive regulation conditions how it is permissible to go about explanation and enunciates principles about the form of methodology to be adopted. However, adequate explanations can end up a long way from their ontological starting point and this may introduce another form of regulation, which operates in reverse, by calling for revision of the original conception of reality. Third, then, methods of explanation – their workings and findings, successes and failures – also have reciprocal ontological implications because preconceptions about the nature of social reality cannot be immune from discoveries about it. In both Individualism and Collectivism the latter should have prompted revisions of very different kinds in the ontological commitments of their advocates, but did not do so.

One of the implications of the stalemate reached between Individualism and Collectivism was that one had to swallow them whole (ontology and methodology together) or not at all, yet there was nothing else on offer. The corresponding attraction of the proposed truce was that of mixed medicine – or a half dose. Here lies my practical objection to it. Once social analysts have been assured that ontology and methodology are separate issues, why should they not conclude that they can merely select the methodology which pragmatically seems most useful to them (thus sliding rapidly into instrumentalism), because, if ontology is a separate concern, then it need to be no concern of theirs. Equally, once social theorists have been persuaded of the separation, what prevents an exclusive preoccupation with ontological matters, disregarding their practical utility and effectively disavowing that acquiring knowledge about the world does and should affect conceptions of social reality? This is a recipe for theoretical sterility. An ontology without a methodology is deaf and dumb; a methodology without an ontology is blind. Only if the two do go hand in hand can we avoid a discipline in which the deaf and the blind lead in different directions, both of which end in cul-de-sacs. Brodbeck herself is most careful not to fall into this trap, but what does 'separatism' do other than to set it for others?

Ironically, the peace treaty was intended to have exactly the reverse effect, for the impetus behind it was that the practising social theorist needed not only an acceptable social ontology but also the most powerful explanatory methods available. This is the very last thing I would contest. Equally, I am fully convinced that neither Individualism/Methodological Individualism nor Collectivism/Methodological Collectivism can meet these two requirements. Yet, because I am maintaining that ontology and methodology are not separate matters, I am still committed to saying they must be swallowed whole or not at all: since I am also arguing that neither of them meets the basic requirements, my conclusion has to be 'don't drink'. This caution against drinking and driving has to be justified by showing that neither position does or can meet the two requirements (ontological rectitude and explanatory power) and thus cannot take us where we need to go. The justification itself will consist in showing that it is empiricism which bedevils both standpoints. This is the force behind my injunction to abstinence rather than temperance where Individualism and Collectivism are concerned, and my final objection to Brodbeck's temperate compromise is that it too is unashamedly empiricist.[36]

Only with the demise of the view that all knowledge is obtained from human sense experience did 'individuals' (because alone capable of experiencing) lose their automatic primacy and could non-observable features of society avoid the question mark hanging over their existence (because incapable of being experienced as sense data). Eventually this enabled the terms in which society was conceptualized and explained to be reformulated, and those in which Individualism and Collectivism had cast them to be rejected.

Yet, as always, there are ties that bind ontology and methodology together and these need to be ones which are internally consistent and *also* provide a working basis for practical social theorizing. Thus the main question to ask about the standpoints which later made a bid to replace both Individualism and Collectivism is how far they succeeded in both tasks. However, to understand the impetus behind replacing the two traditional approaches we need to appreciate *how* Individualism and Collectivism failed and *why* neither could supply the practical social theorist with an adequate conception of either 'structure' and 'agency', or provide a satisfactory programme for explaining the linkages between them.

I began by endorsing the authenticity of the human experience – that we are both free and constrained – considering the touchstone of adequate social theorizing to be how well it captures these insights. However, there is no contradiction in upholding this lay outlook as authentic whilst denying the empiricist view that all knowledge is obtained from human experience. For, fundamentally, the lay reflection on the human condition in society is not itself empiricist. Those ambivalent feelings of freedom and constraint of ours derive from what we are as people and how we tacitly understand our social context. Yet lay reflections on ourselves and our society are never restricted to sense-data or the supposed 'hard facts' it yields – for much of the

100 *The vexatious fact of society*

time we think and act in terms of 'group properties' such as elections, interest rates, theories and beliefs. On the contrary – and therefore the main reason why empiricism must be deficient – we ourselves as reflective beings are not empiricists: we would not be recognizable as people if we were, nor capable of recognizing enough of our social context to live competently within it if we tried to be.

Notes

1. A. Comte, *Système de politique positive*, L. Mathias, Paris, 1951, vol. II, p. 181.
2. E. Durkheim, *The Rules of Sociological Method*, Free Press, New York, 1962, p. xlvii.
3. See Margaret S. Archer, *Culture and Agency*, Cambridge University Press, Cambridge, 1989, ch. 2.
4. J.S. Mill, *A System of Logic Ratiocintive and Inductive*, People's Editions, London, 1884, p. 573.
5. Max Weber, *The Theory of Social and Economic Organization*, Free Press, New York, 1964 (orig. 1922), p. 102.
6. Mill, *System*, p. 583.
7. Weber, *Theory*, p. 101.
8. Derek Layder, *Understanding Social Theory*, Sage, London, 1994, p. 3.
9. Helmut Wagner, 'Displacement of scope: a problem of the relationship between small-scale and large-scale sociological theories', *American Journal of Sociology*, 69:6, 1964, pp. 571–84.
10. Jeffrey Alexander, Bernhard Giesen, Richard Munch and Neil Smelser (eds), *The Micro-Macro Link*, University of California Press, Berkeley CA, 1987. 'In the last debate the discipline of sociology resuscitated an old dilemma in a new form – a form, unfortunately, that has done little to resolve the dilemma itself.' Jeffrey Alexander, 'Action and its environments', in Alexander et al. (eds), *The Micro-Macro Link*, University of California Press, Berkeley CA, 1987, p. 289.
11. Alexander, 'Action and its environments'.
12. Wagner, 'Displacement of scope', p. 583.
13. T. Parsons, 'The social system: a general theory of action', in R.R. Grinker (ed.), *Toward a Unified Theory of Human Behavior*, Basic Books, New York, 1956, p. 190.
14. For a more extended discussion of these points see Margaret S. Archer, 'The problems of scope in the sociology of education', *International Review of Sociology*, ns 1, 1987, pp. 83–99.
15. Layder, *Social Theory*, p. 2f.
16. Richard Munch and Neil Smelser, 'Relating the micro and macro', in Alexander et al. (eds), *The Micro-Macro Link*, pp. 356–7.
17. Layder, *Social Theory*, p. 1.
18. Alexander, 'Action and its environments', p. 290.
19. Ibid., p. 303.
20. David Lockwood, 'Social integration and system integration', in G.K. Zollschan and H.W. Hirsch, *Explorations in Social Change*, Houghton Mifflin, Boston, 1964.
21. P. Berger and T. Luckmann, *The Social Construction of Reality*, Doubleday-Anchor, New York, 1967. See also the comments upon this model by Roy Bhaskar, *The Possibility of Naturalism*, Harvester, Hemel Hempstead, 1989, p. 32f.
22. Maurice Mandelbaum, 'Societal facts', in John O'Neill (ed.), *Modes of Individualism and Collectivism*, Heinemann, London, 1973, p. 225.
23. Ernest Gellner, 'Holism versus individualism', in May Brodbeck (ed.), *Readings in the Philosophy of the Social Sciences*, Macmillan, New York, 1971, p. 267.
24. See Steven Lukes, 'Methodological individualism reconsidered', *British Journal of Sociology*, 19:2, 1968, pp. 119–29. Lukes also mentions a third type of predicate,

where explanation is in terms of social behaviour which, whilst involving some minimal social reference, is unspecific as to any particular form of group or institution. He sees no reason why explanations should be confined to such (pp. 124–6).
25 Bhaskar, *Naturalism*, p. 28.
26 May Brodbeck, 'Methodological individualisms: definition and reduction', in Brodbeck (ed.), *Readings*. Here it is argued that descriptive individualism 'is required by the logic of concept formation within the individualistic, empiricist framework' (p. 301).
27 J.W.N. Watkins, 'Methodological individualism and social tendencies', in Brodbeck (ed.), *Readings*, p. 269.
28 Watkins, 'Methodological individualism', pp. 270–1.
29 Mandelbaum, 'Societal facts', p. 223f.
30 Gellner, 'Holism versus individualism', p. 256.
31 Gellner could only conclude that a 'full clarification of these issues would probably be possible only if we were clear about what is meant by causation in social contexts' (Ibid., p. 261).
32 A. MacIntyre, 'On the relevance of the philosophy of the social sciences', *British Journal of Sociology*, 20:2, 1969, pp. 219–26. 'Nothing but the progress of scientific enquiry in the formulation of scientific theories can decide whether individual properties are always to be explained by reference to social properties, or social by reference to individual, or sometimes one and sometimes the other. As mutually exclusive theses both methodological individualism and holism are attempts to legislate *a priori* about the future progress of the human sciences' (p. 225).
33 Brodbeck, 'Methodological individualisms', p. 286.
34 Ibid., p. 301.
35 Piotr Sztompka, *Sociological Dilemmas*, Academic Press, New York, 1979, ch. 3.
36 Obviously, since I reject the premises upon which this compromise is based (separatism) and the epistemological terms in which it is advanced (empiricism), there is little point in providing a more detailed critique. However, in fairness to Brodbeck it should be noted that her 1973 article 'On the philosophy of the social sciences', in O'Neill (ed.), *Modes of Individualism and Collectivism*, marks a shift towards realism compared with the naked empiricism of the 1968 paper, which is also reprinted in this collection. On the other hand, the author herself failed to signal this move towards embracing a much more relational ontology.

5 Morphogenesis versus structuration
On combining structure and action[1]

The fundamental problem of linking human agency and social structure stalks through the history of sociological theory. Basically it concerns how to develop an adequate theoretical account which deals simultaneously with men constituting society and the social formation of human agents. For any theorist, except the holist, social structure is ultimately a human product, but for any theorist, except advocates of psychologism, this product in turn shapes individuals and influences their interaction. However, successive theoretical developments have tilted *either* towards structure *or* towards action, a slippage which has gathered in momentum over time.

Initially this meant that one element became dominant and the other subordinate: human agency had become pale and ghostly in mid-century functionalism, whilst structure betook an evanescent fragility in the reflowering of phenomenology. Eventually certain schools of thought repressed the second element almost completely. On the one hand, structuralist Marxism and normative functionalism virtually snuffed out agency – the acting subject became increasingly lifeless whilst the structural or cultural components enjoyed a life of their own, self-propelling or self-maintaining. On the other hand, interpretative sociology busily banished the structural to the realm of objectification and facticity – human agency became sovereign whilst social structure was reduced to supine plasticity because of its constructed nature.

Although proponents of these divergent views were extremely vociferous, they were also extensively criticized and precisely on the grounds that both structure and action were indispensable in sociological explanation.[2] Moreover, serious efforts to readdress the problem and to reunite structure and action had already begun from *inside* 'the two Sociologies' (Dawe 1970), when they were characterized in this manichean way. These attempts emerged after the early sixties from 'general' functionalists (e.g. Blau 1964; Gouldner 1976; Buckley 1967; Etzioni 1968; Eisenstadt and Curelaru 1977), 'humanistic' marxists (e.g. Lockwood 1964; Pizzorno 1968; Touraine 1968; Wellmer 1971; Habermas 1971 and 1972; Anderson 1976) and from interactionists confronting the existence of strongly patterned conduct (e.g. Goffman 1964; Sacks et al. 1974). Furthermore, they were joined in the same decade by a bold attempt to undercut the problem by disclosing 'hidden structures' which simultaneously governed overt structural organization and observable action patterns (Lévi-Strauss 1963; Sebag 1964; Piaget 1968; see also Boudon 1968; Glucksman 1974; Bottomore and Nisbet 1979).

Building on these bases in a very eclectic manner, two new perspectives have *since* begun to mature which *directly tackle* the relationship between structure and action and seek to unite them. One is the 'morphogenetic approach',[3] advanced within general systems theory, whose best-known exponent is Walter Buckley (Buckley 1967; 1968; see also Maruyama 1963). Its sociological roots go back to the three kinds of theoretical revisionism mentioned in the last paragraph, but the other part of its pedigree is cybernetics. The second perspective is 'structuration', recently spelt out by Anthony Giddens. Whilst integrating some of the same revisionist material, this approach leans much more heavily on the newer linguistic structuralism, semiotic studies and hermeneutics.

Both the 'morphogenetic' and 'structuration' approaches concur that 'action' and 'structure' presuppose one another: structural patterning is inextricably grounded in practical interaction. Simultaneously both acknowledge that social practice is ineluctably shaped by the unacknowledged conditions of action and generates unintended consequences which form the context of subsequent interaction. The two perspectives thus endorse the credo that the 'escape of human history from human intentions, and the return of the consequences of that escape as causal influences upon human action, is a chronic feature of social life' (Giddens 1979, 7). Where they differ profoundly is in *how* they conceptualize it, and *how*, on that basis, they theorize about the structuring (and restructuring) of social systems.

Structuration and morphogenesis

Structuration

In dealing with 'structuration' this paper concentrates exclusively upon Anthony Giddens's book *Central Problems in Social Theory: Action, Structure and Contradiction in Social Analysis* (1979), since its density and range require close textual attention. Giddens's whole approach hinges on overcoming *three dichotomies* and it is these dualisms which he strips away from a variety of sources, then recombining their residues:

(a) First, he insists on an account of human agency which is intrinsically related to the subject acting in society, thus seeking to transcend the dualism between voluntarism and determinism. Hence, both deterministic attempts to get behind the 'backs of actors' (as in organic functionalism and orthodox Marxism) and the excessive voluntarism which neglects the structural context (as in contemporary action theories) are equally condemned.

(b) Second, he seeks to mediate the dichotomy between subject and object by assigning a prime role to the knowledgeability of actors in producing and reproducing their society, whilst acknowledging that they necessarily employ societal properties in the process. Thus structuralism and functionalism are criticized for subordinating the individual to society and Giddens aims to

transcend the subject/object dualism by elaborating on common elements in the work of Marx and the later Wittgenstein which construe the generation of society as the outcome of praxis.
(c) Finally, he rejects any theory which represses time by separating statics from dynamics and analysing the two separately. For, to Giddens, any theory embodying the interdependence of structure and action is predicated upon grasping the temporal and spatial locations which are inherent in the constitution of all social interaction. Thus the division between synchrony and diachrony must also be transcended in order to capture the temporal release of unintended consequences and their subsequent influence on later action.

Because of this rejection of the three dichotomies, 'structuration' is quintessentially concerned with *duality not dualism*, with amalgamating the two sides of each divide. This is to be achieved through the central notion of the 'duality of structure', which refers to

> the essential recursiveness of social life, as constituted in social practices: structure is both medium and outcome of the reproduction of practices. Structure enters simultaneously into the constitution of the agent and social practices, and 'exists' in the generating moments of this constitution.
> (Giddens 1979, 5)

This involves an image of society as a continuous flow of conduct (not a series of acts) which changes or maintains a potentially malleable social world. In turn, it obviously proscribes any discontinuous conceptualization of structure and action – the intimacy of their mutual constitution defies it. 'Structuration' is predicated upon the 'duality of structure': analytically it disengages continuities or transformations in the reproduction of social systems. Because of the dynamic interplay of the two constituent elements 'structuration' does not denote fixity, durability or even a point reached in development. 'Structuration' itself is ever a process and never a product.

In elaborating his theory of 'structuration', however, Giddens completely ignores existing efforts to perform the same task of reuniting structure and action from within general systems theory.

Morphogenesis

This perspective has an even better claim than the former to call itself a 'non-functionalist manifesto',[4] since a major part of its background was the growing disenchantment on the part of neo-functionalists with every remnant of the Organic Analogy – with the over-integrated view of social structure and the over-socialized view of man; with the assumption of immanent equilibration unrelated to human decision-making; with its failure to incorporate time – a double failure involving the absence of an analytical *history* of systemic emergence (grounded in human interaction, taking place in prior social contexts) *and* a failure to appreciate that the structural elaboration thus produced carries over to *future time*, providing new contexts for subsequent interaction.

'Morphogenesis' is also a process, referring to the complex interchanges that produce change in a system's given form, structure or state (morphostasis being the reverse), *but it has an end-product*, structural elaboration, which is quite different from Giddens's social system as merely a 'visible pattern'. This to him can best be analysed as recurrent social practices, whereas to general systems theorists the elaborated structure has properties which cannot be reduced to practices alone, although these are what generated both it and them.

The emergent properties[5] that characterize socio-cultural systems imply discontinuity between initial interactions and their product, the complex system. In turn this invites *analytical dualism* when dealing with structure and action. Action, of course, is ceaseless and essential both to the continuation and further elaboration of the system, but subsequent interaction will be different from earlier action because conditioned by the structural consequences of that prior action. Hence the morphogenetic perspective is not only dualistic but sequential, dealing in endless cycles of structural conditioning/social interaction/structural elaboration, thus unravelling the dialectical interplay between structure and action. 'Structuration', by contrast, treats the ligatures binding structure, practice and system as indissoluble, hence the necessity of *duality* and the need to gain a more indirect analytical purchase on the elements involved.

Hence Giddens's whole approach turns on overcoming the dichotomies which the morphogenetic perspective retains and utilizes – between voluntarism and determinism, between synchrony and diachrony and between individual and society. In 'place of each of these dualisms, as a single conceptual move, the theory of structuration substitutes the central notion of the *duality of structure*' (Giddens 1979, 5). The body of this paper will:

(a) question the capacity of this concept to transcend such dichotomies in a way which is sociologically useful;
(b) defend the greater theoretical utility of *analytical dualism*, which underpins general systems theory; and
(c) seek to establish the greater theoretical utility of the morphogenetic perspective over the structuration approach.

The 'duality of structure' and voluntarism/determinism

Basically what Giddens is seeking to enfold here are two views of social institutions – institutions as causes of action (which has certain deterministic overtones) and institutions as embodiments of action (which has more voluntaristic connotations). Condensed in the brief statement that 'structure is both medium and outcome of the reproduction of practices' (1979, 69) is his method of bridging this dichotomy. The central notion of the 'duality of structure' makes up the bridge by dropping two planks from opposite banks so that they lie juxtaposed. First he advances the essential contribution made by knowledgeable actors in generating/transforming

106 *Morphogenesis versus structuration*

recurrent social practices – which in turn creates the 'visible pattern' that constitutes the social system for Giddens. Simultaneously, he lays down the fundamental proposition that when actors produce social practices they necessarily draw upon basic 'structural properties' – these essential factors being viewed as a matrix of rules and resources.

Ideally what he wants to integrate is the way in which the active creation of social conditions is itself unavoidably conditioned by needing to draw upon structural factors in the process. Perhaps this is clarified by consulting the kind of practical images Giddens has in mind. The references to agents producing recurrent social practices summon up a picture of the 'ruttedness' of routine action – in bureaucracy, for instance, where life is constantly breathed into inert rules which then deaden their animators through routinization.[6] But this is not the only picture he invokes. There is also metamorphosis, the generation of radically new practices when agency rides on the coat-tails of structural facilitation to produce social change of real magnitude. Although the 'duality of structure' spans both images, it provides no analytical grip on *which* is likely to prevail under what conditions or circumstances. The theory of 'structuration' remains fundamentally non-propositional.

In other words, the 'central notion' of the 'structuration' approach fails to specify when there will be 'more voluntarism' or 'more determinism'. In fact, on the contrary, the 'duality of structure' *itself* oscillates between the two divergent images it bestrides – between (a) the hyperactivity of agency, whose corollary is the innate volatility of society, and (b) the rigid coherence of structural properties associated, on the contrary, with the essential recursiveness of social life.

(a) Hyperactivity is an ineluctable consequence of all rules and resources being defined as *transformative*, in contradistinction to the rigid transformational grammar of linguistics. Resources are readily convertible, rules endlessly interpretable; the former providing material levers for transforming the empirical domain, the latter transfiguring codes and norms. Consequently the spatio-temporal constitution of society is ordered in terms of the mediations and transformations made possible by these two structural properties, as manipulated by agents. However, it follows that, if structural properties are inherently transformative, then actors generically enjoy very high degrees of freedom – at any time they could have acted otherwise, intervening for change or for maintenance. Hence the counterfactual image of hyperactivity in which actors explore and exploit these generous degrees of freedom. Hence, too, the outcomes must be correspondingly variegated: society is not just 'potentially malleable' (Giddens 1979, 56), but becomes highly volatile if 'the possibility of change is recognized as inherent in every circumstance of social reproduction' (Giddens 1979, 210).

(b) The other side of the 'duality of structure' is intended to rectify the image and introduce a more recognizable picture of social life. Instead I believe over-correction takes place, generating a counter-image of 'chronic recursiveness' in society. Basically this arises because actors have to draw upon rules and resources in social interchange and these structural properties are thus *reconstituted* through such interaction. However, Giddens goes further than this, now endorsing the kind of linguistic analogy disavowed in (a). Thus when actors do draw upon rules and resources they necessarily invoke the whole matrix of differences which constitute structures, 'in the sense in which the utterance of a grammatical sentence presupposes the absent corpus of syntactical rules that constitute the language as a totality' (Giddens 1979, 71).

In this way Giddens commits himself to an enormous coherence of the structural properties such that actors' inescapable use of them embroils everyone in the stable reproduction of social systems. The pendulum swings so far the other way that we are now presented with another over-integrated view of man, for the 'duality of structure' relates the smallest item of day-to-day behaviour to attributes of far more inclusive social systems:

> when I utter a grammatical English sentence in a casual conversation, I contribute to the reproduction of the English language as a whole. This is an unintended consequence of my speaking the sentence, but one that is bound in directly to the recursiveness of the duality of structure.
> (Giddens 1979, 77–8)

This rigidity of the recursive image is open to criticism on two counts. On the one hand, rules and resources are not so coherently organized as grammar, often lacking the mutually invocating character of syntax (to have a council house does not *necessarily* mean no telephone, low income, job insecurity etc.). On the other hand, action is not really so tightly integrated by these structural properties: not only may some of the smallest items of behaviour be irrelevant to the social system, certain larger ones may also be trivial, mutually cancelling or self-contained in their effects, whilst still other actions can produce far-reaching aggregate and emergent consequences – yet these different possibilities remain undifferentiated by Giddens. What is wrong with this image, as with the previous one, is that it does not allow for *some* behaviour engendering replication whilst *other* action initiates transformation. Rather than transcending the voluntarism/determinism dichotomy, the two sides of the 'duality of structure' embody them respectively: they are simply clamped together in a conceptual vice.

This *oscillation between contradictory images derives from Giddens not answering 'when' questions* – when can actors be transformative (which involves specification of degrees of freedom) and when are they trapped into replication (which involves specification of the stringency of constraints)? These answers in turn require analysis of the potential for change, which is rooted in systemic stability/instability, and the conditions under which actors do/do not capitalize on it. Although Giddens admits that structures are both facilitating and constraining – indeed, it is one of the major theoretical tasks to discover what aspects of social organization govern the interconnection between the two (1979, 69–70) – this is precisely, with one exception, what he does not do. His theory consistently avoids concrete propositions of this type.

Stringency of constraints

The reason for this omission is his principled but misguided distaste for the constraint concept (contaminated by functionism) (1979, 50–2): the exception, his analysis of contradiction, is of course, on the contrary, an example of systemic facilitation. Specification of the stringency of constraints is sedulously avoided at all three levels of analysis – structural properties, social institutions and social systems. *Structural Properties* are integral to social constitution and reconstitution, but when do they throw their weight behind the one or the other? Generally in sociology this has been tackled through an appreciation that some properties are more resilient or engender more resistance to change than others at any given time. This specification of the strength of constraints is both impossible in Giddens's conceptualization and unacceptable to him. First his properties (defined reductively as rules and resources) are outside time and space, having a *'virtual existence' only when instantiated by actors*. Second, since what is instantiated depends on the *power of agency and not the nature of the property*, then properties themselves are not differentially mutable. Excessive voluntarism enters through these two doors, which are conceptually propped open.

However, why should one accept this peculiar ontological status for structural properties in the first place? Where resources are concerned he argues that what exists in a spatio-temporal sense is only a 'material existent' which, to become operative as a resource, has to be instantiated through power relations in conjunction with codes and norms (1979, 104). This is an argument of *necessary* accompaniment and it is not a very convincing one, for the so-called 'material existents' often constrain in their own right. Examples include various kinds of scarcity which can arise without power or normative regulation and involve nothing other than physiological signification, such as famine, over-population or shortage of skills or land. In what possible sense do these require instantiation? *They are there* and the problem is how to get rid of them or deal with them.

Less obviously, why should World Three knowledge, even if it lives on only in libraries, be regarded as outside time and space? It is there continuously and thus awaits not instantiation but activation.[7] Yet when it is activated it contains its own potentials and limitations independent of the constructions and regulations imposed upon it. The fact that resources and their uses *are* usually entangled with rules of signification and legitimation and that these do make a difference should not be confounded with them making all the difference. Indeed, the rules themselves are usually contested and are so precisely because the distribution or use of real resources is at stake. The latter in turn can also affect signification and regulation, instead of the relationship being exclusively the other way round.

Furthermore, the quality of the structural properties makes its own contribution to differential malleability, independent of the amount of power actors bring to bear. Some properties can be changed relatively quickly (tax rules), some take longer to change (demographic or knowledge distributions), some prove highly resistant to change (bureaucracy, gender distinctions, ethnicity), and some are unchangeable (exhausted natural resources or environmental ruin). Even more importantly, central configurations of rules and resources (the Law, the Constitution, or capitalism) display this differential mutability *among* their internal components.

The key point here is that during the time it takes to change something then that thing continues to exert a constraint which cannot be assumed to be insignificant in its social consequences whilst it lasts. Nations can fall, polities be deposed and economies bankrupted *while* efforts are being made to change the factors responsible. As a general theoretical proposition this holds good however short the time interval involved. Yet this is what Giddens spirits away by making structural properties atemporal and according them only a pale 'virtual existence'.

Social Institutions are conceptualized as standardized practices, enduring and widespread in society (Giddens 1979, 80). In dealing with social *practices* rather than with institutional *operations*, the earlier conceptual exercise (in which structural *properties* were transmuted into agents' *power*) *is* directly paralleled. It has identical effects; it amplifies voluntarism and minimizes constraint. The combined accentuation of actors' institutional knowledgeability and under-emphasis of how institutions work 'behind our backs' (or before our faces, for that matter) produces a complementary neglect of institutional characteristics in their own right. What this omits are characteristics of which people may well be aware (such as centralization, electoral systems or inflation), but which constrain them nonetheless (as well as others which constrain without much 'discursive penetration' of them, such as international monetary policy or high science).

Here explanatory reductionism attends treating the *effects* of, say, centralization as reducible to the exercise of power by determinate actors.[8] The voluntaristic bias means that institutions are what people produce, not what they confront – and have to grapple with in ways that are themselves conditioned by the structural features involved.[9] For Giddens institutional recursiveness never reflects the durability of constraint: it always represents the continuity of reproduction.

Social system

Only at this level does Giddens concede that 'unintended consequences of action stretch beyond the recursive effects of the duality of structure' (1979, 78), producing what others would term 'emergent properties', but which he calls 'self-regulating properties'. Immediately and categorically he asserts that it is their *facilitating effects* upon which theory should centre – 'the self-regulating properties of social systems must be grasped via a theory of *system contradiction*' (1979, 76). The reason for this one-sidedness is that to Giddens contradictions represent cracks through which radical change can be forced by social conflict – '*ceteris paribus*, conflict and contradiction have a tendency to coincide' (1979, 144). But is he warranted in concentrating on systemic contradiction alone and in ignoring systemic compatibilities altogether?

From the morphogenetic perspective contradictions, though very important, are only one of many deviation-amplifying mechanisms. To Maruyama the latter

> are ubiquitous: accumulation of capital in industry, evolution of living organisms, the rise of cultures of various types, interpersonal processes which produce

mental illness, international conflicts, and the processes that are loosely termed as 'vicious circles' and 'compound interests': in short, all processes of mutual causal relationships that amplify an insignificant or accidental initial kick, build up deviation and diverge from the initial condition.

(Maruyama 1963, 164)

Obviously some of the above examples involve conflict, but 'felicitous circles' and 'compound interests' do not, yet they contribute to structure-building. The close relationship between conflict and change belongs more to the history of sociology than to theories of self-regulation in complex systems.

Giddens's studious neglect of compatibilities – those relations and exchanges among components which tend to preserve or maintain a system's given form, organization or state – derives partly from his valid rejection of functional equilibration but perhaps owes more to the fact that such morphostatic processes are experienced as *constraints* by others in social life. Nevertheless, in complex sociocultural systems the positive and negative feedback loops producing, respectively, morphogenesis and morphostasis also circulate simultaneously.

This means that Giddens provides an inherently partial account of the systemic conditions of change and stability. His attempt to bow out of this by contesting that there is 'little point in looking for an overall theory of stability and change in social systems, since the conditions of social reproduction vary so widely between different types of society' (1979, 215) fails on three counts. First it implies a descent into specificity (not necessarily historical uniqueness) which Giddens himself tends to eschew throughout the book. Second, in pinpointing 'contradiction' as the focus of theoretical analysis he *is* specifying a general condition of change and to do so must have eliminated other contenders. Third, he does indeed provide an overall theory of stability, if rudimentary in form, to which we will now turn.

Degrees of freedom

As we have seen, the systematic underplaying of constraints artificially inflates the degrees of freedom for action. To correct this Giddens counterposes two factors which limit them, thus tempering hyperactivity and volatility: that is, his 'attempt to show the essential importance of tradition and routinization in social life' (1979, 7). However, while a full specification of constraints details who is limited, when and how, distinguishing these people from others with vested interests in stability, Giddens stresses only that society forms actors in general terms by inducing habitual action. Yet 'habit' lumps together a variety of conditions promoting stability in a way that is not only methodologically unhelpful but also positively misleading in its implication that *all* that is required for destabilization is a change of habit.

Thus, instead of a specification of degrees of freedom related to systemic features and the action contexts they create, Giddens provides a general account of 'deroutinization' detached from variations in structural configurations. Primarily it is treated as a passive process in which external events (war, cultural contact, industrialization) disrupt ingrained habits. In practice this repudiates Weber's tenet, embodied in the studies of world religions, that it is only through acknowledging both the restrictions that social organization imposes on people and the opportunities for action that are rooted in the internal instability of social structures that we arrive at detailed theories of deroutinization, rationalization and change.

At most Giddens allows that there are 'critical situations' or 'critical phases' where the drastic disruption of routine corrodes the customary behaviour of actors and heightens susceptibility to alternatives. Then 'there is established a kind of "spot welding" of institutions that forms modes of integration which may subsequently become resistant to further change' (1979, 229). Not only is the concept of a 'critical situation' dubious because of its *post hoc* designation, but also this formulation begs more questions than it answers. What makes a phase 'critical' – are structural factors not always germane? What produces a particular crisis – do specific systemic features not generate distinctive crises?[10] What produces subsequent resistance? Logically *this* cannot be attributed to the long-term sedimentation of habits.

Does Giddens's formulation fare any better if we look at it the other way round – that is, focusing not on what curtails freedom (tradition and routinization) but on the conditions under which higher degrees of freedom prevail? Unfortunately this is not the case, the reason being that the 'transformative capacity' of actors is immediately conflated with the concept of power. On the contrary, I would maintain that degrees of freedom are logically independent of the power of agents, the relationship between them being one of contingency. Systemic patterning determines a given potential for transformation, but:

(a) this may not be capitalized upon by those with the power to do so;
(b) its exploitation does not necessarily involve power;
(c) considerable power can be deployed in this context without producing any transformation.

The example of our decentralized educational system should clarify points (a) and (b), for this provides considerable structural degrees of freedom for innovation and change. Sometimes these remain unexploited, not because teachers lack the power to innovate but because they do not want transformation; sometimes they are used for the internal initiation of change without any application of power. Always to Giddens 'transformative capacity is harnessed to actors' attempts to get others *to comply with their wants*' (1979, 93). This was not the case with the foundation of experimental schools nor with the move to progressive schooling, which involved a cumulative change in educational philosophy (see Selleck 1972) that could be termed compliance only by rendering that term vacuous (i.e. to accept anything is to comply with it). To clinch point (c), degrees of freedom may be large, but powerful contestants can lock in immobilism, as in cases of political 'centrism', such as Fourth Republic France. In other words, there are even some circumstances under which the use of power and the achievement of transformation are antithetic.[11]

Once again the contrast between the structuration approach and the morphogenetic perspective becomes pointed. In the latter structural elaboration can arise from three sources of interaction (besides their unintended consequences): the confluence of desires, power induced compliance or reciprocal exchange. Therefore in any given case the relationship between power and morphogenesis remains to be determined. Structuration, on the other hand, makes transformation logically dependent on power relations alone.[12]

Whilst structuration attempts to *transcend* the voluntarism/determinism divide by a single conceptual leap (the 'duality of structure'), morphogenesis *tackles* the respective weightings of the two aspects by analysing the stringency of constraints and degrees of freedom in different structural contexts and for different social groups. The hare and the tortoise analogy is equally pertinent to the way these perspectives approach the next 'dualism'.

'Structuration' and synchrony/diachrony

Giddens maintains that 'the conception of structuration introduces temporality as integral to social theory; and that such a conception involves breaking with the synchrony/diachrony or static/dynamic divisions' (1979, 198). While agreeing wholeheartedly that the incorporation of time is a condition of theoretical adequacy, one may doubt whether 'structuration' does integrate the temporal dimension adequately. Just as the attempt to transcend the voluntarism/determinism dichotomy produced two images of hyperactivity and routinization that were not successfully united, so in this attempt to overcome the static/dynamic division two equivalent images emerge – those of chronic recursiveness and total transformation – but are not successfully reconciled. The reason for this is identical in both cases: his unwillingness to examine *the interplay between* structure and action because the two presuppose one another so closely (1979, 53).

Immediately following his discussion of the system and its self-regulating properties he proposes 'two principal ways in which the study of system properties may be approached' (1979, 80). This involves an exercise of 'methodological bracketing'. Institutional analysis brackets strategic action and treats structural properties as 'chronically reproduced features of social systems' (1979, 80). This image of recursiveness figures prominently, but many would deny that these features necessarily are 'chronic': though they *may* be long lasting they are nevertheless temporary (e.g. feudalism) or may change frequently (e.g. resource distributions). Instead, through this kind of institutional analysis, they acquire a spurious methodological permanence.

On the other hand, to examine the constitution of social systems as strategic conduct, Giddens brackets institutional analysis and studies actors' mobilization of resources and rules in social relations. This leads immediately to the reverse image – '*Change, or its potentiality, is thus inherent in all moments of social reproduction*' (1979, 114). Here an equally spurious changeability appears as a product of this methodological device – systemic malleability is *not only high but is constant over time*. On the contrary, many would argue that it is variable and that its temporal variations are partially independent of strategic action, however intensely it is mobilized or knowledgeably it is conducted. This methodological bracketing has again produced the pendular swing between contradictory images – of chronic recursiveness and total transformation.

Giddens might reply in defence that, since both occur simultaneously in reality, then no contradiction is involved as the social system is inherently Janus-faced. But hardly anyone would deny this – that is, that there are long tracts of steady institutional replication (sometimes eroded by cumulative action) or that collective action can reshape social structure (without necessarily erasing every familiar regularity or routine). What most of us seek, instead of these truisms, are theoretical propositions about when (more) recursiveness or (more) transformation will prevail – a specification which would necessitate unravelling the relations between structure and action. This Giddens refuses to give on principle because to specify their inter-relationship would involve dualistic theorizing. Yet, ironically, what does his bracketing device do other than traduce this very principle, since it merely transposes dualism from the theoretical to the methodological level – thus conceding its *analytical* indispensability.

More importantly, this bracketing approach has serious implications concerning time that seem to contradict the aim of making temporality integral to explaining the system and its properties. To Giddens what is bracketed are the two aspects of the 'duality of structure', institutional analysis and strategic conduct being separated out by placing a methodological *époche* upon each in turn. But because they are the two sides of the same thing, the pocketed elements must thus be co-terminous in time (the symmetry of the *époches* confines analysis to the same *époque*); and it follows from this that *temporal relations between* institutional structure and strategic action *logically cannot be examined*.

The attempt to reunite the two elements under the rubric of 'structuration' consists in the introduction of three 'modalities', drawn upon by actors strategically but at the same time constituting the institutional features of the system – 'interpretative scheme', 'facility' and 'norm'.[13] To Giddens the 'level of modality thus provides the coupling elements whereby the bracketing of strategic or institutional analysis is dissolved in favour of an acknowledgement of their interrelation' (1979, 81). But the interrelationship is not really at issue (or more precisely it is only an issue for hard-line ethnomethodologists and extreme structural determinists). The real theoretical issue is not whether to acknowledge it but how to analyse it, and how to explain the systemic properties it generates and elaborates. Yet little of this can be tackled from an approach which precludes theorizing about the *temporal relations* between structure and action.

The basic notion of the 'duality of structure' militates against the latter because it resists untying structure and action, except by the bracketing exercise. In turn this means that Giddens cannot acknowledge that structure and action work on different time intervals (however small the gap between them). This, ironically, leads him to underplay the full importance of time in sociology. What he stresses is that theorizing must have a temporal dimension: what he misses is time as an actual variable in theory. In consequence, he asserts that 'social systems only exist through their continuous structuration in the course of time' (1979, 217), but is unable to provide any theoretical purchase on the *structuring over time*.

114 Morphogenesis versus structuration

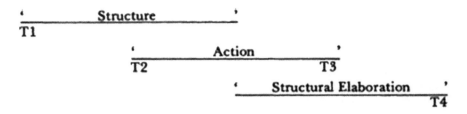

Figure 5.1 The basic morphogenetic sequence.

The morphogenetic argument that structure and action operate over different time periods is based on two simple propositions:

- that structure logically predates the action(s) which transform it;
- that structural elaboration logically postdates those actions, which can be represented as shown in Figure 5.1.

Although all three lines are in fact continuous, the analytical element consists only in breaking up the flows into intervals determined by the problem in hand: given any problem and accompanying periodization, the projection of the three lines backwards and forwards would connect up with the anterior and posterior morphogenetic cycles. This represents the bedrock of an understanding of systemic properties, of *structuring* over time, which enables explanations of specific forms of structural elaboration to be advanced. (Since time is equally integral to morphostasis there is no question of the temporal being equated with change in general systems theory.) 'Castro's example' will be used to demonstrate how time is incorporated as a theoretical variable since it lends itself to simple quantitative illustration.

After the revolution Castro confronted an extremely high rate of illiteracy which he sought to eliminate by the expedient of 'each one teach one'. Now let us make a number of arbitrary and hypothetical assumptions about a situation such as the Cuban one, namely that the proportion of the total population literate at the start was 5 per cent (15 per cent or 25 per cent), that to become literate took precisely a year, and that the policy was 95 per cent successful (no society ever achieving 100 per cent literacy). From these the diagram shown in Figure 5.2 can be produced. For all its oversimplification, the curves demonstrate some vital points about the relationships between time and the morphogenetic sequence.

Structure

The initial structural distribution of a property (i.e. the aggregate consequence of prior interaction) influences the time taken to eradicate it (five years versus two years for the outer and inner curves) through its effect on the population capable of transforming it. Certainly only some kinds of property would approximate to this exponential pattern of change (skills, knowledge, capital accumulation,

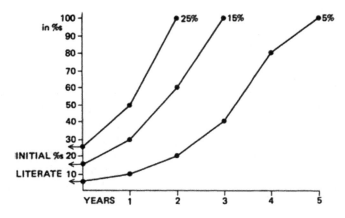

Figure 5.2 Total population.

demographic distribution), but this does not affect the basic point that all structures manifest temporal resistance and do so generically through conditioning the context of action. Most often, perhaps, their conditional influence consists in dividing the population (not necessarily exhaustively) into social groups working for the maintenance versus the change of a given property, because the property itself distributes different objective vested interests to them at T2 (rather than abilities, as in the example used). This would be the case where properties such as citizenship, political centralization or wage differentials were concerned.

Furthermore, what the diagram serves to highlight is that the initial structural influence does not peter out immediately, even given a collective determination to transform it (indeed, here the major burden of illiteracy is only dispersed towards the end, in the last or penultimate time interval). In other words, it takes time to change *any* structural property and that period represents one of constraint, for some groups at least. No matter how short, it prevents the achievement of certain goals (those which motivate attempts to change it). Structural influences extend beyond T2 and it is essential to know whether this is because they (temporally and temporarily) resist collective pressures to change, remain because they represent the vested interests of the powerful, or are in fact 'psychologically supported' by the population. To regard every institutional regularity as the result of 'deep sedimentation' is to assimilate them all to the latter category. Yet without these distinctions it remains inexplicable *when* (or whether) the property will be transformed.

Action

On the one hand, action initiated at T2 takes place in a context not of its own making. In our example, those who were literate initially were not responsible for their *distribution* in the population; this group property resulted from the restrictive educational policies of others, probably long dead.[14] Here it appears impossible to follow the methodological individualist and assert that any structural property influential after T2 is attributable to contemporary actors (not wanting or not knowing how to change it), because knowledge about it, attitudes towards it, vested interests in retaining it and objective capacities for changing it have already been distributed and determined by T2. Yet, without analysing these, we cannot account for *when* the '*longue durée*' is broken, *who* is primarily responsible for it or *how* it is accomplished (by collective policy, social conflict, incremental change etc.).[15]

On the other hand, between T2 and T3 agency exerts two independent influences: one temporal, the other directional. It can speed up, delay or prevent the elimination of prior structural influences. In our example, (i) popular commitment to self-instruction could reduce the time taken to eliminate illiteracy, thus improving on all three curves (though not obliterating them entirely because of the need for personnel to prepare, disseminate and guide in the use of materials), while (ii) lack of enthusiasm or ability to teach amongst literates and lack of willingness to participate and learn amongst illiterates can delay the process[16] and damage the project. (Determinism is not built into the morphogenetic perspective.) Simultaneously agents, although partly conditioned by their acquirements (whose contents they did not themselves define), can exercise a directional influence upon the future cultural definition of 'literacy', thus affecting the substance of elaboration at T4. (Voluntarism has an important place in morphogenesis but is ever trammelled by past structural and cultural constraints and by the current politics of the possible.)

Structural elaboration

If action is effective then the transformation produced at T4 is not merely the eradication of a prior structural property (illiteracy) and its replacement by a new one (literacy), it is the structural elaboration of a host of new social possibilities, some of which will have gradually come into play between T2 and T4. Morphogenetic analysis thus explains the timing of the new facilitating factors and can account for the inception, in this instance, of, say, a national postal service, mail-order businesses, bureaucratization and less obvious but more significant developments such as international communication, with its ramifications for religion, technology, political ideology and so on. From the 'structuration' perspective, these remain the capricious exploits of indeterminate 'moments'.

Simultaneously, however, structural elaboration restarts a new morphogenetic cycle, for it introduces a new set of conditional influences upon interaction that are constraining as well as facilitating. T4 is thus the new T1, and the next cycle must be approached afresh analytically, conceptually and theoretically. Giddens is completely correct that laws in the social sciences are historical in character (i.e. mutable over time), but whereas his endorsement of this view rests principally on the reflexive knowledge and behaviour of actors (1979, 243–4), mine resides on changes in the social structure itself that require us to theorize about it in different ways since our subject matter has altered. A new explanandum calls for a new explanans, though this does not rule out the possibility that the latter can be subsumed under a more general law.

Morphogenesis versus structuration 117

Paradoxically, for all Giddens's stress upon the importance of time, it is the past *in* the present and the future *in* the present which matter for him, the present being a succession of 'passing moments' in which, quoting William James approvingly, 'the dying rearward of time and its dawning future forever mix their lights' (1979, 3). This continuous flow defies periodization. Consequently he has to stress the quintessential polyvalence of each 'moment', both replicatory and transformatory (reproduction always carries its two connotations). Yet he is nevertheless driven to recognize the existence of 'critical phases' in the long term and to accord (excessive) theoretical significance to them (as times of institutional spot-welding). What is lacking in Giddens's work is the length of time between the 'moment' and the 'critical phase' – in which the slow work of structural elaboration is accomplished and needs theorizing about.

Social systems and the individual/society dichotomy

Giddens's basic aim here is to bring together the development of the individual as a social product and the generation of society by human agency within a single theoretical framework. Essentially this means giving a 'parts–whole' account which explains the *articulation* of the two components. Giddens's account accepts the 'problem of scope' (see Wagner 1964): he rightly rejects homology as a solution, denying that the system is small-scale interaction writ large, or that the small is a miniaturized version of the large. His distinction between social and systems integration widens this rejection to include any view that presumes that what integrates the individual into society automatically explains what integrates society itself – thus illegitimately conflating social integration with systemic integration. Such views foreclose the possibility of society consisting of groups in tension, yet he argues that those who have accepted such tension as their premise (such as Merton) have then wrongly relinquished an understanding of *the totality as in some way implicated in the parts* (Giddens 1979, 111). It is this implicative 'parts–whole' relationship that he seeks to develop. Already two controversial points should be noted.

On the one hand, he implies that all current theories endorsing intergroup tension at the level of social integration also share the defects of Mertonian functionalism at the systemic level: that is, they cannot handle the mutual implication of parts and whole. This might be challenged from a number of different perspectives, but what is of particular relevance here is that it would be rejected by those who expressly broke with functionalism to achieve an implicative but non-homological 'parts–whole' account – such as Gouldner, Blau, Etzioni or Buckley – namely, just those theorists who began to explore morphogenesis in the context of general systems theory. (Interestingly, given the sweep and erudition of Giddens's work, these are the sociologists who never receive sustained attention.)

On the other hand, although Giddens accepts *a* 'problem of scope' he does not see this as intimately allied to transcending micro–macro dualism in sociological theory. On the contrary, instead of conceptualizing scope as the problem of charting a methodological path leading from the smallest-scale interaction to large-scale complex systems, Giddens transmutes the notion of successive concrete *levels* of increasing size into one of abstract 'dimensions', which affect all sizes of group and operate simultaneously. Thus the 'crunching-up', which has already been discussed, of transformation and recursiveness (equally salient and eternally operative) and of moment and totality (no sequence, only simultaneity), is now joined in his 'dimensional approach' by a compacting of the micro- and the macro-, which are not teased out in scale or time. Can this yield an adequate, let alone a superior, account of the 'parts–whole' relationship?

Giddens's articulation between the two is achieved through his concepts of 'modalities' and 'structural principles', which are intimately related to one another. We have seen that the three modalities – 'interpretative scheme', 'norm' and 'facility' – serve to articulate interaction and structure. Through being drawn upon by actors in the production of interaction whilst also constituting the structural media of systems, 'the "modalities" of structuration represent the central dimensions of the duality of structure' (1979, 81). All three dimensions are combined in different ways to produce the range of social practices generated within the intersecting sets of rules and resources that ultimately express features of the totality. How, then, are we to grasp the observable regularities (the 'visible pattern') produced through this dimensional interplay? (Giddens, of course, rejects the procedure of separating out 'upward' and 'downward' influences or disentangling interconnections between 'context' and 'environment'.)

His answer is given at length because of the need to dwell on his precise formulation:

> Each of the three sets mentioned above thus has to be interpolated as elements of cycles of social reproduction producing systemness in social relations. In the context of such interpolation, we can identify structural elements that are most deeply embedded in the time–space dimensions of social systems . . . I shall refer to such structural elements as *structural principles*. Structural principles govern the basic institutional alignments in a society.
>
> (1979, 106)

They may operate at all of the three levels of system integration: homeostasis, feedback or reflexive self-regulation (1979, 141). Difficulties in this 'parts–whole' account surround both the *identification* of the two key concepts and their *interrelationship*.

The 'structural principles' are *abstractions*, manifesting themselves as institutionalized connections governing the reproduction of a particular social system or type of society. How, then, can they be grasped unequivocally? In practice Giddens advances two different procedures, though they are not clearly distinguished as such.

The first method turns on his distinction between 'primary principles' and 'secondary' or derivative ones. 'Primary principles', he argues, can be identified as being fundamentally and inextricably involved in systemic reproduction because they enter into the very structuring of what that system is. In other words, they can be detected *directly* by virtue of their *centrality*. However, when practical examples are adduced the procedure appears to lead to considerable equivocation. For instance, he claims that in Marx's characterization of early capitalism the 'forces/relations of production scheme may be read as asserting the universal primacy of allocation over authorization', but in what Giddens calls 'class-divided societies' (where accumulation is not dominated by private capital) the principle is reversed, authorization having primacy over allocation, as in the early civilizations (1979, 162–3). Not only are such 'principles' far from self-evident, they are incapable of commanding public assent. Indeed, the whole 'industrial society' debate is precisely about what its central principles are, the various terms used providing a good indication of divergence over what is considered to be central – 'technological society', 'affluent society', 'consumer society', 'welfare society', 'managerial society' or 'new industrial state'.

The distinction between 'primary' and 'secondary' principles is open to the same objection (and has fuelled the above debate, a major aspect of which is whether we should talk about industrial *economies* or are justified in speaking more extensively about industrial *societies*). In other words, all such 'structural principles' are in fact contested. Their ultimate status is that of hypotheses advanced by investigators and *not* that of structural elements integral to societies.

Giddens's alternative method for the identification of 'structural principles' is interpolation of the 'modalities' that will reveal the most deeply embedded structural elements, as the earlier quotation stated. Here the 'structural principles' are not identified (at the macro-level) by inspecting the system itself, as in the method above, but rather *indirect* identification takes place instead, by examining the mechanisms (at the micro-level) producing systemness, which the principles govern. In other words, governance is detected through its effects. Yet this method of identification does not seem any more satisfactory for it has exactly the same weakness as the first, namely that indirect interpolation has the same contested nature and hypothetical status as does the direct induction of principles. Since there are no grounds of validation that would command public agreement, each and every interpolation must remain equivocal.

Moreover, the latter method not only fails to solve the problem of identifying 'structural principles' but also reveals a major difficulty surrounding the *relationship* between the 'principles' and the 'modalities'. This is crucial because it is their articulation which constitutes the mainstay of Giddens's 'parts–whole' account. In the latter method the combination(s) of the 'modalities' is held to be governed by principles operative at higher levels (homeostasis, feed-back or reflexive self-regulation), otherwise the 'principles' are not identifiable through the 'modalities'. Here social interchange at lower levels is being presented as the product of the system (incidentally a much stronger influence than the structural conditioning of the micro- by the macro endorsed in general systems theory). But this is not consistent with Giddens's own conceptualization of the 'modalities' and specifically the *generative* powers with which he endows them – put another way, it conflicts with the micro-level acting back on the macro-level.

To him, for all that the three 'modalities' are media (structural components) of the system, they nevertheless have significant autonomy as drawn upon creatively by actors. If each 'mode' presupposes unprogrammed transformations, then their combinatory possibilities are open not closed, problematic not given. This Giddens considers as quintessential to the duality of structure. Yet, if this autonomy is granted, then the combinations of these three dimensions actually manifested in interaction are not necessarily governed by the 'structural principles'. In other words, any regularities detected via interpolation of the 'modalities' need not be the effects of the 'principles' but may reflect the regular exploitation of autonomy by agency. Giddens wishes to say that they are both, but if he wants to have it both ways then he is left with no method for detecting his 'principles'.

Once again the duality notion has produced two unreconciled images: the one presents the 'principles' as governing the 'modalities' (the macro- dominating the micro-), the other portrays the 'modalities' as cyclically transforming the 'principles' (the micro- directing the macro-). The attempt to interrelate them fails on logical grounds and the attempt to identify the principal components also fails on practical grounds. The unsuccessful articulation of the two key concepts which these failures imply undercuts the claim to have advanced a superior 'parts–whole' account.

The 'parts–whole' account proffered from the morphogenetic perspective links structure and interaction in an entirely different way – the structured whole being understood in terms of the social processes which articulate relations between individuals and groups. In contrast to the structuration approach, there is investigation of *processes* instead of imputation of '*principles*' and identification of *mechanisms* in place of the interpolation of '*modalities*'. This account of the whole as a negotiated order is based foursquare on the following assumptions, which Giddens barely acknowledges and grossly underplays:

- interaction generates emergent properties which must figure in explanatory statements;
- scope is a crucial variable which precludes an undifferentiated theory covering the micro- and macroscopic;
- the dynamics producing and elaborating the complex whole can be modelled.

By working through these sequentially I will seek to show that not only a better 'parts–whole' account results but also one which fulfils Giddens's desiderata of treating society as consisting of parts in tension and of understanding the totality as implicated in its parts (Giddens 1979, 111).

Emergence is embedded in interaction: in the latter 'we are dealing with a system of interlinked components that can only be defined in terms of the interrelations of each of them in an ongoing developmental process that generates emergent phenomena – including those we refer to as institutional structure' (Buckley 1967, 125). Emergent properties are therefore relational: they are not contained in the elements themselves, but could not exist apart from them. As Blau puts it, 'although complex social systems have their foundation in simpler ones, they have their own dynamics with emergent properties' (Blau 1964, 20). The latter can arise at all levels from small-scale interaction upwards, although as scope grows they are

Morphogenesis versus structuration 121

increasingly distanced from everyday psychological dispositions but never ultimately detached from interaction. The highest orders of emergence are nothing more than the relations between the results of interaction. Nevertheless, these 'feed back' to condition subsequent interaction at lower levels.

It follows that the problem of scope cannot be side-stepped if an adequate 'parts–whole' account is to be given. In this perspective the task

> is to specify and conceptualize the processes and mechanisms by which the more complex and indirect sociative structures or communication matrices are generated out of less complex, less indirect and patterned sociative processes – on how the former feed back to help structure the latter; and on how each may continually interact to help maintain or to change the other.
> (Buckley 1967, 128)

Thus *the first implication* of a full acceptance of emergence is the need to *disentangle the micro–macro connections* which lead to the genesis of social structures. Although the problem of scope has not yet been fully transcended, Blau's analytical history of emergence is what later morphogenetic accounts must improve on.

Blau provides a starter motor at the micro-level in exchange relations, derives integration (reciprocal exchange) and differentiation (power stemming from lack of reciprocity) directly from these elementary transactions and shows how macro-level political organization, with its inherent tension between legitimation and opposition, are indirect consequences of them. This painstaking derivation of large-scale structures from small-scale interaction gives much more analytical purchase on the social system and its parts than does Giddens's procedure of positing 'modalities' and conceptualizing their interplay as dimensional permutations. In the latter the middle ground of transactions, accommodations, aggregations and emergence is dealt with by conceptual manipulation rather than processual exploration. In the former institutional structure is understood as generated by determinate social processes taking place under specified conditions.

The second implication of emergence is the need to grapple with the ongoing interplay between micro- and macro-levels, where the broader context conditions the environment of actors whose responses then transform the environment with which the context subsequently has to deal, the two jointly generating further elaboration[17] as well as changes in one another. Analytical complexity is enormous precisely because morphogenesis is a multi-level affair and no level can be dropped or conflated without making the unwarranted assumption that some level has ultimate primacy. The multiple feedback models of general systems theory are basic tools for teasing out the dynamics of structural elaboration: though complex to operationalize, they are not defied by complexity. This kind of modelling can yield up the practical mechanisms of morphogenesis which provide a better explanatory grip on complex social systems than do hypothetical 'structural principles'.

It should be clear from the foregoing that Giddens's two criteria for a satisfactory 'parts–whole' account are met. From the morphogenetic perspective the whole is implicated in the parts in two senses – it emerges from them and it acts back upon them – though the full implicative force can be grasped only *over time*, since feedback takes time. Part of this force is therefore lost by truncating mutual implication into the moment/totality relationship. Equally, the parts themselves are in tension and the nature of the tension produces the state of the whole. Inevitably social processes generated to meet certain requirements represent impediments to other groups. Integrative and differentiating processes come into conflict, as do legitimate organizations and the opposition provoked by the constraints they exert.[18] As Blau argues from this, the 'perennial adjustments and counter-adjustments find expression in a dialectical pattern of social change' (Blau 1964, 314), much of which would be lost by unduly restricting analytical focus to certain tensions, hypothesized but not substantiated as 'primary'.[19]

Conclusion

The differences explored between the morphogenetic perspective and the structuration approach stem from an initial parting of the ways over the endorsement of 'analytical dualism' or the adoption of the 'duality of structure'. The following points summarize how 'analytical dualism' *tackles* the dichotomies which the 'duality of structure' fails to transcend.

- The specification of degrees of freedom and stringency of constraints makes it possible to *theorize about variations* in voluntarism and determinism (and their consequences), whereas conceptual insistence on the simultaneity of transformative capacity and chronic recursiveness inhibits any theoretical formulation of the conditions under which either will predominate.
- The analytical separation of structure and interaction over time permits of theorizing about temporal structuring and restructuring, which is precluded when the conceptual bonding of the synchronic and the diachronic produces a seamless web of 'instantiations'.
- The analytical distinction between subject and object over time allows for theorizing about the influences of men on society and vice versa, avoiding the 'desperate incorporation' (Gellner 1971, 267) of society into man or the dubious imputation of 'principles' articulating the two.

It should be clear from the foregoing discussion that the 'analytical dualism' advocated is artificial and methodological: it implies no commitment to the philosophical dualisms which Giddens rightly attacks.

Postscript

However, it would be unfair to conclude without noting Giddens's view that the two approaches are engaged upon different sociological enterprises. To him the 'identification of structures can in no sense be regarded as the only aim of sociological investigation. The instantiation of structure in the reproduction of social systems, as its medium and outcome, is the proper focus of sociological analysis'

Morphogenesis versus structuration 123

(Giddens 1979, 106). However, this distinction is not one of substance, as is implied, but harks back to a difference of origins, to potent images of society carried over from analogical starting points: that is, from cybernetics and linguistics respectively.

In view of this the contrast appears particularly inapposite as far as the morphogenetic perspective is concerned, for general systems theory has already shed that part of its cybernetic heritage which led it to focus on the identification of structures. It has abandoned the sterile exercise of terminological redescription in which to translate conceptions of social structure into the language of systems theory was either the end product or was confused with an understanding of the logic or social systems.[20] Indeed, it is now explicitly recognized that basic cybernetic models are of no help in identifying, much less in theorizing about, complex social systems. Essentially a 'simple, cybernetic feedback model of explicit group goal-seeking does not fit most societies of the past and present because of a lack in those societies of informed, centralized direction and widespread, promotively interdependent goal behaviours of individuals and sub groups' (Buckley 1967, 206). Hence the morphogenetic perspective now concentrates *on the socio-cultural system in its own right, identifying and explaining the real and variegated structures which have emerged historically and theorizing about their concrete elaboration in the future.*

It is these italicized features which properly distinguish between the two perspectives. For the structuration approach has shaken off much less of the linguistic analogy and this means that Giddens still addresses the social system indirectly, hoping that its variations can be subsumed under the principles governing the analogue that will also provide the key to its transformations.

Although Giddens states clearly 'I reject the conception that society is like a language' (1979, 4), the late Wittgenstein stalks the text – to know a form of life is to know a language (1979, 251). Thus the key concepts themselves come direct from linguistics: the 'recursive character of language – and, by generalization, of social systems also' (1979, 18) – is the source of the 'duality of structure': the notion that society, like language, should be regarded as a 'virtual system' with 'recursive properties' (1979, 47) comes direct from Saussure. Certainly he breaks away from some of these starting points, Saussure in particular, but his ultimate aim is the closer integration of semiotic studies with social theory in order to develop 'a theory of codes, and of code production, grounded in a broader theory of social practice, and reconnected to hermeneutics' (1979, 48). As Gellner aptly commented in a wider context, a culture, a form of life and, we can add, a code, 'is a *problem* – never a *solution*' (Gellner 1964, 184 ff.). What Giddens has done in shackling sociology to semiotics is in fact to transfer several problems to our domain – insubstantiality, indeterminacy and intractability.

His approving quotation from Eco gives the full flavour of insubstantiality, light years away from the examination of real structures.

> Semiotics suggests a sort of molecular landscape in which what we are accustomed to recognize as everyday forms turn out to be the result of transitory chemical aggregations ... revealing that where we thought we saw images

there were only strategically arranged aggregations of black and white points, alternations of presence and absence.

(cited in Giddens 1979, 106)

To ground this view of codes in a 'broader theory of social practice' merely adds the indeterminacy problem, for practices themselves are seen as transformations of virtual orders of differences (of codes in time and space). Societal changes thus become indeterminate, they are like the shaking of a kaleidoscope – shifting patterns produced by the manipulation of oppositions by the population at large.

Finally, given the mutuality of codes and practices (in which we cannot simply identify pre-existing codes which generate messages because messages also enter into the reconstitution of codes in the duality of structure), their interplay becomes analytically intractable, for how can we 'break in' to the circuit? (Analytical dualism is, of course, the device employed in morphogenesis to deal with *its* ongoing circular systemic processes, but this is proscribed here.) In practice the answer is, by imputation, interpretation or interpolation – as was seen with the 'structural principles' – but this merely reinvokes Lévi-Strauss's problem of the absent context of justification.

The difference in sociological enterprise, as Giddens initially stated it, is illusory. The morphogenetic perspective is not only concerned with the identification and elaboration of social structures but is preoccupied above all with the specification of the mechanisms involved – with the feedback 'process that contains both negative (stabilizing or rigidifying) elements and positive (structure-elaborating, or increasingly disorganizing) features' (Buckley 1967, 137). This is the way in which institutional structures help to create and recreate themselves in an ongoing developmental process. The ultimate difference is not one of enterprise, for an adequate theory of stabilization, disorganization and elaboration obviously incorporates the instantiation of structure, just as an adequate theory of instantiation must specify the conditions of morphostasis and morphogenesis. The theory of structuration remains incomplete because it provides an insufficient account of the *mechanisms* of stable replication versus the genesis of new social forms, and will do so while ever it resists unpacking these two connotations of 'reproduction'.

Notes

1 I am extremely grateful to Duncan Gallie, John Heritage and Ian Proctor for making many helpful criticisms and constructive points when this paper was in draft form.
2 The most detailed argument for the indispensability of both structure and action appeared in the late 1960s (Cohen 1968). See also Blau (1976); Blau and Merton (1981).
3 Morphostasis 'Refers to those processes in complex system-environment exchanges that tend to preserve or maintain a system's given form, organization or state. Morphogenesis will refer to those processes which tend to elaborate or change a system's given form, structure or state' (Buckley 1967, 58–9).
4 A label Giddens appropriates (1979: 7).
5 See Brodbeck (1971). For my own defence of this concept and its place in theorizing about social structure see Archer (1979: 5–42).

Morphogenesis versus structuration   125

6 I am indebted to Dr John Heritage for this insight.
7 Activation need not involve power relations unless Giddens's premise that all action is logically tied to power is accepted. See Giddens (1979, 88).
8 As Gellner succinctly puts it, group variables 'can indeed only exist if their parts exist – that is indeed the predicament of all wholes – but their fates *qua* fates of complexes can nevertheless be the initial condition or indeed the final condition of a causal sequence' (Gellner 1971, 263).
9 For example I have tried to show at length how a centralized system of education conditions subsequent patterns of educational interaction and profoundly influences the processes by which change can be introduced in ways quite different from those characteristic of decentralized systems. See Archer (1979: esp. ch. 5, 265–8).
10 Amitai Etzioni provides the boldest illustrations of this point in his discussions of 'under'- and 'over'-managed societies and their typical and very different kinds of crises (Etzioni 1968).
11 It should be clear from the foregoing that I endorse Lukes's approach to the concept of power rather than that of Giddens. Once again this is a question of dualism versus duality. Lukes maintains analytical dualism by seeking to draw a line between structural determination and the exercise of power. Hence he talks of 'where structural determination ends and power begins' (Lukes 1977, 18) and is predictably chastized by Giddens for tending to 'repeat the dualism of agency and structure' (Giddens 1979, 91). Giddens wants to overcome this divide by defining power as 'transformative capacity', hence maintaining duality by viewing structure as implicated in power relations and power relations as implicated in structure. Now Lukes does not deny these interconnections but he avoids Giddens's compacting of the two elements which blurs the distinction between responsible action and determined action, severing the tie between power and responsibility which is essential to Lukes. On the contrary, he tries to discover, explain and assess the weight of structural limitations on action which delimit the zone in which it is proper (and profitable) to speak of power relations. Thus to Lukes, in general, 'although the agents operate within structurally defined limits, they none the less have a certain relative autonomy and could have acted differently' (Lukes 1977, 6–7). What is then required in this dualistic approach 'is a sustained discussion of the nature of, and conditions for, autonomy (and its relation to social determination)' (Lukes 1974) – in other words, a specification of the degrees of freedom *within which* power can be exercised.
12 The following statement that 'power within social systems can thus be treated *as involving reproduced relations of autonomy and dependence in social interaction*' (Giddens 1979, 93) is significant in view of the connection he makes between power and transformative capacity. What is neglected throughout the book is *interdependence*, where two parties can achieve joint control over something (thus directing subsequent transformations of it) on the basis of *reciprocal* exchange between them. Yet transformative capacity can depend just as much upon balanced transactions as upon power relations.
13 I shall say more in the next section about the location of these modes and will only concentrate now on their significance for time.
14 One of Auguste Comte's rare and valid aphorisms was that human society has more dead than living members.
15 'Institutions are constituted and reconstituted in the tie between the *durée* of the passing moment, and the *longue durée* of deeply sedimented time – space relations' (Giddens 1979, 110).
16 The curves *are* purely hypothetical, without being wholly unrealistic (i.e. they embody no known counterfactuals). Certainly exponential growth will probably be distorted as universal literacy is approached, because pockets of high resistance are encountered (made up, for example, of the geographically inaccessible, those culturally antagonistic, the very old and those who are diffident or discouraged). Simultaneously, however, social learning will have improved teaching techniques between T2 and T3, thus offsetting resistance to

some (unknown) extent. In any case the diagram specifically excludes 100 per cent success, and it makes no difference to the argument if literacy is only achieved at the 85 per cent level, say, rather than the 95 per cent used for illustration.
17 I have provided an extended illustration of these context/environment/elaboration interplays in relation to growth in school enrolment, 'Theorizing about the expansion of Educational Systems' in Archer (1982).
18 'Such conflicting social forces give rise to alternating patterns of structural change' (Blau 1964, 321).
19 Percy Cohen has convincingly demonstrated the supreme difficulty of designating or distinguishing 'primary', core or fundamental features of a social system from minor, superficial or peripheric ones. The same arguments hold for processes of social change.

'Even if there were no problems of *identifying* core elements of a system, there would still be a problem of distinguishing basic from superficial changes. This is important for the following reason: even if one identifies factor A as strategic in relation to B, C, D and E, this does not mean that these other, non-core features do not change at all without an initial change in A, nor does it mean that changes in them have no effect at all on changes in A . . . The crucial question is: do changes in A produce *radical* changes in B, C, D or E, while changes in B, C, D and E produce only superficial changes in A? And if the answer to this question is affirmative, does one have some measure for distinguishing radical changes from superficial ones? And, if one does have such a measure, when does one apply it? For the short-run effect of B on A might be superficial, while the long-run effect might be radical! The gist of all this discussion is that one can only know *ex post facto* whether a particular change was or was not a change in a "core" feature of the social structure' (Cohen 1968, 177; see 176–8).
20 An ambitious attempt, which nevertheless manifests this defect, to unify the concepts used in all the social sciences by translating them into the terminology of systems theory is Kuhn (1976).

Bibliography

Anderson, P. 1976 *Considerations on Western Marxism*, London: New Left Books.
Archer, M.S. 1979 'In Defence of Macro-Sociology', in M.S. Archer (ed.), *Social Origins of Educational Systems*, London and Beverly Hills CA: Sage, pp. 5–11.
Archer, M.S. 1982 'Theorizing about the expansion of Educational Systems', in M.S. Archer (ed.), *The Sociology of Educational Expansion*, London and Beverly Hills CA: Sage, pp. 3–64.
Blau, P.M. 1964 *Exchange and Power in Social Life*, New York: Wiley.
Blau, P.M. (ed.) 1976 *Approaches to the Study of Social Structure*, London: Open Books.
Blau, P.M. and Merton, R.K. 1981 *Continuities in Structural Inquiry*, London and Beverly Hills CA: Sage.
Bottomore, T. and Nisbet, R. 1979 'Structuralism', in T. Bottomore and R. Nisbet (eds), *A History of Sociological Analysis*, London: Heinemann, pp. 557–98.
Boudon, R. 1968 *A quoi sert la notion de 'structure'*, Paris: Gallimard.
Brodbeck, M. 1971 'Methodological Individualisms: Definition and Reduction', in M. Brodbeck (ed.), *Readings in the Philosophy of the Social Sciences*, New York: Macmillan, pp. 280–303.
Buckley, W. 1967 *Sociology and Modern Systems Theory*, Englewood Cliffs NJ: Prentice Hall.
Buckley, W. (ed.) 1968 *Modern Systems Research for the Behavioural Scientist*, Chicago: Aldine.
Cohen, P.S. 1968 *Modern Social Theory*, London: Heinemann.

Dawe, A. 1970 'The Two Sociologies', *BJS*, 21(2), pp. 207–18.
Eisenstadt, S.N. and Curelaru, M. 1977 'Macro-Sociology', *Current Sociology*, 25(2), pp. 1–73.
Etzioni, A. 1968 *The Active Society*, New York: Free Press.
Gellner, E. 1964 *Thought and Change*, London: Weidenfeld & Nicolson.
Gellner, E. 1971 'Holism Versus Individualism', in M. Brodbeck (ed.), *Readings in the Philosophy of the Social Sciences*, New York: Macmillan, pp. 254–68.
Giddens, A. 1979 *Central Problems in Social Theory: Action, Structure and Contradiction in Social Analysis*, London: Macmillan.
Glucksman, M. 1974 *Structuralist Analysis in Contemporary Thought*, London: Routledge & Kegan Paul.
Goffman, E. 1964 'The Neglected Situation', *American Anthropologist*, 66(6), pp. 133–6.
Gouldner, A.W. 1976 'Reciprocity and Autonomy in Functional Theory', in N.J. Demerath and R.A. Peterson (eds), *System, Change and Conflict*, New York: Free Press.
Habermas, J. 1971 *Toward a Rational Society*, London: Heinemann.
Habermas, J. 1972 *Knowledge and Human Interests*, London: Heinemann.
Kuhn, A. 1976 *The Logic of Social Systems*, San Francisco CA: Jossey-Bass.
Lévi-Strauss, C. 1963 *Structural Anthropology*, New York: Basic Books.
Lockwood, D. 1964 'Social Integration and Systems Integration', in G.K. Zollschan and H.W. Hirsch, *Explorations in Social Change*, Boston MA: Houghton Mifflin, pp. 244–57.
Lukes, S. 1974 *Power: A Radical View*, London: Macmillan.
Lukes, S. 1977 *Essays in Social Theory*, London: Macmillan.
Maruyama, M. 1963 'The Second Cybernetics: Deviation Amplifying Mutual Causal Processes', *American Scientist*, 51, pp. 164–79.
Piaget, J. 1968 *Structuralisme*, Paris: P.U.F.
Pizzorno, A. 1968 'A propos de la méthode de Gramsci', *L'Homme et la Société*, 8, pp. 161–71.
Sacks, H., Schegloff, E.A. and Jefferson, G. 1974 'A Simplest Systematics for the Organization of Turn-Taking in Interaction', *Language*, 50(4), pp. 696–735.
Sebag, L. 1964 *Structuralisme et Marxisme*, Paris: Payot.
Selleck, R.J.W. 1972 *English Primary Education and the Progressives, 1914–39*, London: Routledge & Kegan Paul.
Touraine, A. 1968 *Le Mouvement de Mai ou le Communisme Utopique*, Paris: Seuil.
Wagner, H.R. 1964 'Displacement of Scope: A Problem of the Relationship between Small Scale and Large Scale Sociological Theories', *American Journal of Sociology*, 69(6), pp. 571–84.
Wellmer, A. 1971 *Critical Theory of Society*, New York: Herder & Herder.

6 For structure: its reality, properties and powers
A reply to Anthony King[1]

Every social theorist or investigator has a social ontology. This may be quite implicit but it is also unavoidable because we can say nothing without making some assumptions about the nature of social reality examined. Philosophers of social science, until about fifteen years ago, used to represent the basic parting of the ways as the division between Methodological Individualists (who held that social reality could be reduced to the doings and beliefs of 'other people') and Methodological Collectivists (who held that 'social facts' were irreducible, but nonetheless real and influential). Some certainly still hold to these traditional generic positions.[2] Thus Anthony King has recently come to the defence of 'interpretive sociology' and of its methodologically individualist ontology, though it is not entirely clear whether he is defending 'interpretivism' alone or the ontological position in general, which is shared by such disparate exponents as Rational Choice theorists.

However, for many of us working on the allied problem of 'structure and agency' or the links between micro- and macro- phenomena, it seemed that the old debate should not be continued, but rather that its very terms ought to be superseded. We were more concerned with how structure shaped interaction, and interaction, in turn, reshaped structure, than with promises of reductionism or, for that matter, 'constructionism', which merely seemed to place a 'big etcetera' alongside micro-sociological propositions.[3] Undoubtedly we found the reductionist charter incoherent in its very individualism. As Bhaskar wrote,

> the real problem appears to be not so much that of how one could give an individualistic explanation of social behaviour, but that of how one could ever give a non-social (ie, strictly individualistic) explanation of individual, at least characteristically human behaviour! For the predicates designating properties special to persons all pre-suppose a social context for their employment. A tribesman implies a tribe, the cashing of a cheque a banking system. Explanation, whether by subsumption under general laws, advertion to motives and rules, or redescription (identification), always involves irreducibly social predicates.[4]

From a very different point of view, Giddens also set reductionism aside because 'the same structural characteristics participate in the subject (the actor) as in the object (society). Structure forms "personality" and "society" simultaneously'.[5] Equally, we felt no better aided by Methodological Collectivists, who went no further than a vindication of 'irreducibly social remainders', which the Individualists could not expunge from their analyses, but who did not begin to articulate the ontology of social structure. Hence there were two different attempts to query the terms of the old debate and to replace it with distinctively new social ontologies. Here King erroneously runs these together, for Giddens's 'ontology of praxis' is as opposed to the realists' 'ontology of emergence' as ever the two old positions were embattled – something which is recognised by the new protagonists.[6] Thus, in defending methodological individualism he has two battles on his hands, which it is important to stress, for *both* would need undermining in order to leave the world safe for interpretivism. However, I will confine myself to defending my own realist position here and leave structuration theorists to defend their own.

To begin with, realist social theory tackles the structure/agency problem from a position of *analytical* dualism, and not philosophical dualism as King states. It is analytical because it sees great utility in differentiating the two in order to examine their interplay, something which is of particular importance to practical analysts of society. However, as can be seen from the basic morphogenetic diagram, which he reproduced, there is never a moment at which *both* structure and agency are not jointly in play. As far as the basic scheme is concerned, its phases of 'Structural Conditioning' → 'Social Interaction' → 'Structural Elaboration' are ones in which

> all three lines are in fact continuous, the analytical element consists only in breaking up the flows into intervals determined by the problem in hand: given any problem and accompanying periodization, the projection of the three lines forwards and backwards would connect up with the anterior and posterior morphogenetic cycles.
>
> (RST: 76)

What makes analytical differentiation possible are the two simple propositions: that structure necessarily pre-dates the actions which transform it and that structural elaboration necessarily post-dates these actions (RST: 90), which of course is precisely what practising sociologists want to examine in various fields. There is no philosophical dualism because (a) structures are only held to emerge from the activities of people, and (b) structures only exert any effect when mediated through the activities of people. Structures are ever relational emergents and never reified entities existing without social interaction: the converse would be tenets of dualism.

However, it is these emergent properties to which King objects and against which he offers the standard methodologically individualistic defence, namely that they should properly be construed as nothing but the effects of 'other people'. Here it is not clear whether he fully understands that to realists *all* emergent properties are *relational*, for he refers to 'numerical', 'relational' and 'bureaucratic' as different 'types of structural emergence' (p. 208). Instead, 'to talk about "emergent powers" is simply to refer to a property which comes into being through social combination.

These are literally "existential emergents". They exist by virtue of inter-relations, although not all relationships give rise to them' (RST: 51). Those that do are ones whose internal and necessary relations generate their internal and external causal powers, such as the landlord–tenant relation, which allows the extraction of rent, or the power of mass production, which emerges from the division of labour.[7] Those which do not are social relationships which lack natural necessity: relations between their participants are external and contingent (such as in a sewing bee, where everyone confines themselves to their own work). The crucial distinguishing feature of an 'emergent property' is that,

> itself being a relational property, (it) has the generative capacity to modify the powers of its constituents in fundamental ways and to exercise causal influences *sui generis*. This is the litmus test which differentiates between emergence on the one hand and aggregation and combination on the other.
> (RST: 174)

This needed clarification because often King's criticism of particular examples stops short at a *descriptive* individualism, which, as Brodbeck showed[8] is inoffensive, if unhelpful, in explanation, rather than going on to deal with the 'properties and powers' of emergents, which is their real contribution to explanation.

The force of my defence, therefore, is that *contra* King's claim that 'appeals to autonomous structures are simply errors of description' (p. 213), we are indeed talking about structural properties and powers which defy reduction and are about causal influence that no redescription can eliminate from explanatory accounts. Let me re-present the force of this in the three examples which he claims successfully to have reduced.

i My discussion of literacy *rates* has to be taken as precisely that: the influence that an initial distribution of literacy exerts upon those *proportions* of the population who have the skills to change it, and the different amount of time which this distributional feature entails before illiteracy is eliminated. Now Watkins, the post-war doyen of methodological individualism, maintained that 'no social tendency exists which could not be altered *if* the individuals concerned both wanted to alter it and possessed the appropriate information'.[9] My example takes a tendency, illiteracy, and presumes the consensual desire to alter it. Of course, descriptively, as King says, during transformation 'all that occurs there is that individuals interact with other individuals, teaching them to read', and this eventually changes the society into a literate one. Similarly, in history those who were literate were 'just other people in the past, who have learnt to read' (p. 211). No-one could possibly disagree, which should indicate that this can hardly be the point. Rather, it is that however much of Watkins' desire for change they have (and let us grant them all the appropriate teaching information), *their impact* is necessarily constrained by their proportional representation in the population. Quite simply, the lower it is the longer it takes, as I illustrated graphically.

For structure 131

This is exactly the same as arguing that only the reproductive behaviour of child-bearing people can transform a demographic structure, but that the speed of transformation depends upon their proportional relationship to the rest of the population. In short, more than desire plus knowledge is needed to explain change, its magnitude and speed. Why does this matter, since *eventually* we all agree that people's concerted, knowledgeable action can transform the *status quo* into national literacy? Well, as I commented, the individualists' assumption has to be that whilst all are working to alter a 'social tendency', nothing of importance will happen during the period when they are constrained to *go on* working for its transformation. This cannot be decided by theoretical *fiat*. On the contrary, elections can be lost, businesses can fail and economical dependency increase whilst all hands are on deck trying to reverse a structural property and its undesirable but influential powers – that is, those which explain the unwanted consequences just illustrated.

ii In much the same vein, King considers my discussion of the *relational power* unleashed by the division of labour to be a matter of 'misdescription' because (descriptively) it 'is reducible to all the workers on the shop floor, who together create a mutual social situation' (p. 213). Well, of course they do, just as before the industrial revolution craft workers and farm workers created mutual 'social situations', but the *productive relationships* of those like Adam Smith's early pin-workers created something more – the power of mass production. This, King argues,

> is not emergent from or irreducible to all of them. It is very precisely all of the individuals working in the division of labour and to say otherwise is to misdescribe social reality, creeping unwittingly toward social metaphysics, where social life is described by reference to an entity beyond everyone.
> (p. 213)

Yet, in the most serious sense, the power of the (first-order) emergent property, mass production, did exceed those of everyone involved, because it was no aggregate of their individual productivity but the relational resultant of their *combined productive activity*.

Moreover, first-order emergent properties lead to second-order ones, or to the results of the results of emergent properties. After all, why was Adam Smith discussing pin-making anyway, other than to point to the fact that differential development in the powers of mass production had led to the differential *Wealth of Nations*? As the first in, we British did best, and, as the wealthiest of nations, this second-order emergent property then gave us the power to colour the globe pink. We cannot explain British colonialism by unobjectionable descriptions of needle-sharpeners and eye-makers: yet we would give a very defective explanation of it if we omitted the wealth-generating powers of Britain *in relation* to those of other countries. Moreover, third-order effects, such as the academic privileges which today's native English-speaking academics enjoy, cannot be *explained* as other than the unintended resultant of these powers, exercised seriatim, but irreducible to the individual people involved. What will not do as an explanation is the truistic descriptive statement that more books are written in English than in other languages, for this begs the whole question.

iii The realist analysis of how structural emergent properties impinge upon agents, by generically shaping the situations which they confront, is conducted at three levels – the positional, that of roles and that of institutions. As a hierarchy, these are nested such that what goes on structurally at higher levels impacts downwards: institutional contradictions influence role clashes, just as the role array available affects positional life chances – whilst agential activities work upwards for change. Thus there is a serious misunderstanding when King isolates 'roles' as 'a third set of emergent properties' (p. 214), for I am not presenting disparate clutches of emergent properties to make an ontological point but presenting a systematic analysis of social structuring itself and its dynamics in terms of the relations between the 'parts' of society and the 'people'.

The divergence here is that King believes he can provide an analysis of roles which is confined to the level of the 'people' and their intersubjectivity alone (p. 215). On the contrary, I argue that at

> the level of roles each of which is necessarily and internally related to others (doctor/patient; landlord/tenant; teacher/pupil) and to material requirements such as hospitals, pharmaceutical supplies, equipment and trained personnel, the distinction between the 'systemic' and the 'social' is the difference between roles and their occupants.
>
> (RST: 186)

Therefore we fundamentally disagree about what roles are, for King's view is that what 'structures an individual's practices in that role is *not the role itself* but rather the intersubjectivily created notion of what that role is' (p. 215). Yet to enter a role is not just to confront other people's subjective expectations, it is to become involuntarily involved in structures and their situational conditioning. To marry entails legal responsibilities, financial liabilities, canonical obligations and juridical restrictions upon exit, all of which may prompt agential avoidance, but the alternative of 'partnership' is merely to exchange one form of structural conditioning for another, since the law still arbitrates on child custody, entitlements to common goods and eligibility for certain benefits. These constraints are not reducible to intersubjectivities, which can be flouted (at a price): instead, the divorcing parent who abducts the children is flouting a law and one which retains its constraining power – until such time as collective action may transform it. Moreover, agents are aware of this (not that their awareness makes it the case) and act with an eye to constraints. Catholics know that the difficulties of obtaining an annulment will *force* them to choose between remarriage or communicant membership. It is this over which they agonise, for which they join support groups and sometimes pressure groups working for change – ones whose success would involve overturning canonical doctrine and its hierarchical support, and thus cannot be thought of as simply 'getting the Pope to change his mind'.

At this point King makes the predictable riposte about things like laws and hierarchies, namely that they could be different if only everyone interpreted things differently: 'it could be transformed if everyone or vast numbers of individuals began to interpret their social relations differently and, therefore, began to engage in new social practices' (p. 222). Yet, when Watkins used the same argument about the reversibility of all social tendencies in the present tense, he admitted that this 'central assumption of the individualistic position' was 'an assumption which is admittedly counter-factual and metaphysical'.[10] It is both, for it entails a 'stop-the-world-while-we-get-off-and-change-it' condition. On the contrary, realists not only know that the social world goes on but also that *how* it goes on is profoundly conditioned by the vested interests which a given structure has distributed prior to current action sequences. In other words, the realist analysis of structural elaboration is based on the ways in which once 'relevant populations' have *been* defined, then their structural interests in sustaining or reformulating such definitions condition social interaction and change. Because changes never conform exactly to any one group's requirements (due to compromise and concession between interested parties), social structure is the resultant that nobody ever wants in exactly its current form, which is precisely what fosters continuing morphogenesis. But without reference to the prior distribution of vested interests in generating reproduction or transformation, and without any purchase upon the differential opportunity costs of different courses of action for those differently placed, then changes in intersubjectivities alone must remain indeterminate, volatile and kaleidoscopic as sources of change. Because of the temporal priority, relative autonomy and causal efficacy of structural properties and their influential powers, there never is and never can be a social *tabula rasa* from which to conduct interpersonal negotiations – supposing otherwise is what is counter-factual and metaphysical.

The epistemic fallacy

So far the argument has been an action replay of the traditional cut and thrust between methodological individualists and their opponents. King then introduces a curious argument about my 'solipsistic error', namely that '[t]he key error which Archer makes in her derivation of social structure is to draw the sociological conclusion of the existence of a social structure from the perspective of a single individual's knowledge of their freedom and constraint' (p. 217). Now this arose from a comment to my readers that most of them did wake up every morning aware of *both* their freedom to make their lives and *simultaneously* of the constraints which attended most of their projects. This I do regard as authentic discursive awareness, and thus stressed that it is a problem for each and every human being rather than an abstruse concern of social theorists. This I firmly hold to, but it is *not* how I 'derive' social structure. Note the stress in my formulation which follows upon how our knowledge is an imperfect guide to reality.

> We *are* simultaneously free and constrained and we *also* have some awareness of it. The former derives from the nature of social reality; the latter from human nature's reflexivity. Together they generate an authentic (if imperfect) reflection upon the human condition in society.
>
> (RST: 2)

Our epistemology is *about* something ontological – that is, real – and it is imperfect because all human knowledge is fallible. The existence of structural properties and powers is established by the *causal criterion* – that is, in terms of their generative effects. Matters of ontology are not settled by interviewing people about them! Because agents have some discursive penetration, this is neither accurate nor complete and I later go on to show how its very incompleteness can mean that individuals often pay prices (e.g. for counteracting their enablements) quite uncomprehendingly – but pay they surely do. 'The constraints and enablements of the situations we confront are not the same as our powers of description or conceptualisation' (RST: 197).

Thus, to realists, knowledge about a state of affairs can never be taken *for* that state of affairs. To confuse our knowledge about reality with how reality is means committing the 'epistemic fallacy'.[11] Thus nothing could be more in contradiction with realism than that I should take an epistemological observation and use this as a biographical basis for ontological statements, yet this is what I am supposed to do: 'this one commonsensical perspective is then drawn upon as the grounds for ontological conclusions' (p. 217). In fact the boot is on the other foot: interpretive sociologists cannot avoid committing the epistemic fallacy because their ontology is irredeemably epistemic! What it addresses are networks of meanings, but not what they are about; definitions of the situation, but not whether the situation conforms to them; the 'taken-for-granted', but not whether it validly can be. This is true solipsism where people are epistemologically licensed to make what they will of the world: the only interpretivist caveat is 'providing they can negotiate this understanding with other people', but the world itself is disallowed any role as an ontological regulator in what warranted assertions can be made about it. *Par contre*, I believe my readers have *some* notion of their freedoms and constraints because of the way the world is, but the world is not this way *because* they happen to have such notions. And this, of course, has nothing to do with the stance of one particular individual, as King curiously wants me to say; it is true of each and every person and of all of them taken together.

The epistemic fallacy has always created problems for interpretive sociologists and particularly when they cannot but acknowledge real but non-interpretivist properties of society. King gets into these difficulties when conceding that the 'distribution of wealth is real', but 'is dependent upon a myriad of past interactions between individuals according to their understanding of the capitalist market' (p. 221). Here the 'capitalist market' is allowed to exist and to be understood variously. Thus matters of ontology and epistemology are now allowed to be distinct. Indeed they are, but if so the realist wants to know about their interplay and is particularly concerned to explain how this 'capitalist market' can be misrecognised in popular understanding through ideological manipulation. To raise the latter is to introduce further ontological considerations about things like power and it is here that interpretivism effectively capitulates.

The clearest example of this is provided by Peter Berger's eventual generalisation that 'he who has the bigger stick has the better choice of imposing his definitions',[12] which immediately raises questions about the prior social distribution of influential power. Similarly, Silverman's interpretivist attempt[13] to specify the conditions under which particular definitions of situations will become institutionalised detailed the following elements: (i) the existing world-taken-for-granted by participants; (ii) the ends pursued by actors and the attachment to particular patterns of interaction that this implies; (iii) the strategies actors perceive as available to them and the resources they can call upon to attain their ends; (iv) the actions in which they engage and their ability to convince others of their legitimacy. Here, point (ii) assumes the existing social structure – that is, the standardised forms of action and interaction – point (iii) the existing distribution of scarce resources and point (iv) the existing distribution of social values. While these are indeed necessary assumptions, they all have to be granted to be prior to, autonomous from yet causally influential upon current intersubjective negotiations.

What this goes to show is the accuracy of Cohen's judgement when interpretivism first raised its head.

> In all sociological inquiry it *is* assumed that some features of the social structure and culture are strategically important and enduring and that they provide limits within which particular social situations can occur. On this assumption, the action approach can help explain the nature of the situations and how they affect conduct. It does not explain the social structure and culture as such, except by lending itself to a developmental inquiry which must start from some previous point at which structural and cultural elements are taken as given.[14]

These are not 'heuristics' as King suggests, nor pragmatic stopping points in infinite reductive regress, which he also suggests, but rather, as he concedes, there does come a point 'in employing the interpretive approach and focusing on the specific interactions of individuals, when the sociologist is going to have to assume certain background conditions which are not reduced to their micro dimensions' (p. 223).

This is actually where the honest interpretivist has to end up. Thus Blumer, whom King took as canonical of symbolic interactionism, does concede that 'social organisation enters into action only to the extent to which it shapes situations in which people act and to the extent to which it supplies fixed sets of symbols which people use in interpreting their situations'.[15] Yet this 'only' is all that the social realist needs. *Realist Social Theory* is a book about how structures shape the situations in which people act; this is how structure is mediated to them. *Culture and Agency*[16] is a book about how cultural beliefs shape ideational situations for those who hold them; this is how culture influences them. What this enabled me to show was how patterns of action and interpretation were shaped by the socio-cultural constraints and enablements of these situations and how, in turn, this marked the ways in which agents reshaped their socio-cultural context through morphogenesis or morphostasis. Although he has come so far, Blumer is of course unwilling to engage in an analysis of structural or cultural conditioning sufficient to reveal its systematic rather than episodic character. That task is where realist social theory makes its signal contribution. Nevertheless, even his atemporal and ahistorical recognition of such factors protects against the difficulties encountered by those interpretive sociologists who consider the definition of the situation to be independent of its objective properties.

Notes

1 Anthony King, 'Against structure: a critique of morphogenetic social theory', *Sociological Review*, 47:2, 1999, 199–227, focusing on my *Realist Social Theory: the Morphogenetic Approach*, Cambridge University Press, Cambridge, 1995. Henceforth, RST in the text. I gratefully acknowledge the support provided by a three-year ESRC Research Fellowship, during which time this article was prepared.
2 For a good array of the main contributions to the original debate, see John O'Neill (ed.), *Modes of Individualism and Collectivism*, Heinemann, London, 1973.
3 H.R. Wagner, 'Displacement of scope: a problem of the relationship between small scale and large scale sociological theories', *AJS*, 69:6, 1964: 583.
4 Roy Bhaskar, *The Possibility of Naturalism*, Harvester Wheatsheaf, Hemel Hempstead, 1989: 28.
5 Anthony Giddens, *Central Problems in Social Theory*, Macmillan, London, 1979: 70.
6 King erroneously states that Bhaskar approves of Giddens's formulations in structuration theory. However, note the following: 'The social cube should be thought of as a cubic flow, differentiated into analytically discrete moments . . . as rhythmically processual and phasic to the core. This is the feature which, as Margaret Archer has convincingly demonstrated, distinguishes it from structuration, or more generally from any "central conflation", theory' (Roy Bhaskar, *Dialetic: the Pulse of Freedom*, Verso, London, 1993: 160).
7 'Fundamentally, what distinguishes an "emergent property" is its real homogeneity, namely that the relations between its components are internal and necessary ones rather than seemingly regular concatenations of heterogeneous factors – of unknown provenance, undetermined internal influence and uncertain duration. In contradistinction, the primary distinguishing feature of any emergent property is the natural necessity of its internal relations, for what the entity is and its very existence depends upon them. To *focus* on the *internal and necessary* relations between components as constitutive of an emergent property is to set them apart from relations which are external and contingent. In the latter case, two entities or items can exist without one another and it is thus neither necessary nor impossible that they stand in any particular relation to one another, for the nature of either does not depend upon this' (RST: 173).
8 May Brodbeck, 'Methodological Individualisms: definition and reduction', in May Brodbeck (ed.), *Readings in the Philosophy of the Social Sciences*, Macmillan, New York, 1971.
9 J.W.N. Watkins, 'Methodological Individualism and Social Tendencies', in May Brodbeck (ed.), *Readings in the Philosophy of the Social Sciences*, Macmillan, New York, 1971.
10 Watkins, 'Methodological Individualism and Social Tendencies': 271.
11 Cf. Roy Bhaskar, *Reclaiming Reality*, Verso, London, 1989: 38.
12 P.L. Berger and T. Luckmann, *The Social Construction of Reality*, Doubleday, New York, 1966: 101.

13 D. Silverman, *The Theory of Organizations*, Heinemann, London, 1970: 213.
14 P.S. Cohen, *Modern Social Theory*, Heinemann, London, 1968: 93.
15 H. Blumer, 'Society as Symbolic Interaction', in A.M. Rose (ed.), *Human Behaviour and Social Processes: An Interactionist Approach*, Routledge and Kegan Paul, London, 1962: 160.
16 Margaret S. Archer, *Culture and Agency: the place of culture in social theory*, Cambridge University Press, Cambridge, 1989. This book and its successor, *Realist Social Theory*, clarify the difference between cultural and structural constraints and enablements. They deal respectively with Cultural emergent properties and Structural emergent properties.

7 The private life of the social agent
What difference does it make?[1]

As realism gains ground in social theory, it seems fair to admit that it has made a greater contribution to the reconceptualisation of structure than it has to that of agency. However, if the 'problem of structure and agency' is to be resolved then equivalent attention has to be given to both terms. Moreover, realism's stratified ontology, which has proved so useful in delineating the properties and powers that emerge at different levels of social structure, is just as pertinent to agency. This is what will be examined here. Specifically, it is those strata that pertain to every mature social agent, namely 'selfhood', 'personal identity' and 'social identity', that will be the focus of attention.[2] The implications of distinguishing these different personal emergent properties (PEPs) will be discussed throughout in relation to other theories that fail to make these distinctions. What difference a realist approach to agency makes to social investigation will be indicated in the conclusion.

There are two aspects to the 'problem of agency', and both are fundamental. *Technically*, the central problem of agency is to conceptualise the human agent as someone who is both partly formed by their sociality, but who also has the capacity partly to transform their society. *Morally*, the problem is to put forward a model that is *recognisably human*; one that retains Arendt's notion of the 'Human Condition' as entailing a reflexive 'Life of the Mind'. As agents, we are what Charles Taylor (1985, 65) calls 'strong evaluators', and this must be recognised: for we do not take a detached, third-person, scientific stance to our own lives or to our societies.

Basically, I argue that two 'models of man' have dominated social theorising for the past 200 years, and that neither can cope with the technical or moral problems raised by the 'problem of agency'.[3] These models can be called 'Modernity's Man' and 'Society's Being'.

In cameo, the Enlightenment allowed the 'Death of God' to issue in titanic man. With the secularisation of modernity went a progressive endorsement of human self-determination, of people's powers to come to know the world, to master their environment and thus to control their own destiny as the 'measure of all things'. As the heritage of the Enlightenment tradition, Modernity's Man was a model that had stripped down the human being until he had one property alone, that of instrumental rationality, namely the capacity to maximise his preferences through means–ends relationships and so to optimise his utility. In this model, *Homo economicus* stood forth as the lone, atomistic and opportunistic bargain-hunter – a completely impoverished model of man.

Technically, what this model of man could not deal with were phenomena such as voluntary collective behaviour, leading to the creation of public goods; normative behaviour, when *Homo economicus* recognises his dependence upon others for his own welfare; and, finally, expressive solidarity, a willingness to share, or altruism. Crucially, this model could not cope with the human moral capacity to transcend instrumental rationality and to have 'ultimate concerns'. These are concerns that are not a means to anything beyond them, but are commitments, which are constitutive of who we are and an expression of our identities. Who we are is a matter of what we care about most. This is what makes us moral beings. None of this caring can be impoverished by reducing it to an instrumental means–ends relationship, which is presumed to leave us 'better off' relative to some indeterminate notion of future 'utility'.

Nevertheless, this was the model of man that was eagerly seized upon by social contract theorists in politics, utilitarians in ethics and social policy and liberals in political economy. *Homo economicus* is a survivor. He lives on not only as the anchorman of microeconomics and the hero of neoliberalism but also as a colonial adventurer and, in the hands of rational choice theorists, he bids to conquer social science in general. As Gary Becker outlines this mission, '[t]he economic approach is a comprehensive one that is applicable to all human behaviour' (1976, 8).

The rise of postmodernism during the last two decades represented a virulent rejection of Modernity's Man, but it spilt over into the dissolution of the human subject and a corresponding inflation of the importance of society. The 'Death of Man' joined the 'Death of God'. Now, in Lyotard's words, 'a *self* does not amount to much' (1984, 15), and, in Rorty's follow-up, '[s]ocialisation [. . .] goes all the way down' (1989, 185). To give humankind this epiphenomenal status necessarily deflects all real interest onto the forces of socialisation, as in every version of social constructionism. People are indeed perfectly uninteresting if they possess no personal powers that can make a difference to shaping their own lives or their own society. Consequently, to Foucault, '[m]an would be erased, like a face drawn in sand at the edge of the sea' (1970, 387).

Society's Being is social constructionism's contribution to the debate, which presents our entire human properties and powers, beyond our biological constitution, as the gift of society. Our selfhood is a grammatical fiction, a product of learning to master the first-person pronoun system, and thus quite simply a theory of the self that is appropriated from society. As Harré puts it, '[a] person is not a natural object, but a cultural artefact' (1983, 20). We are nothing beyond what society makes us, and it makes us what we are through our joining 'society's conversation'. Society's Being thus impoverishes humanity, by subtracting from our human powers and accrediting all of them – selfhood, reflexivity, thought, memory, emotionality and belief – to society's discourse.

What makes actors act has now become an urgent question within constructionism, because the answer cannot ever be given in terms of people themselves, who have neither the human resources to pursue their own aims nor the capacity to find reasons good if they are not in social currency. Effectively, this means that the constructionists' agent can only be moved by reasons *appropriated* from society, and thus is basically a *conventionalist*. The human dilemma has been eliminated from the human condition.

Reclaiming the human agent

It is maintained that the most basic of our human powers, beyond our biology, is our 'selfhood' – a *continuous sense of self* or reflexive self-consciousness. Even the two defective models need it. Society's Being requires this sense of self in order for a social agent to know that social obligations pertain to her, rather than just being diffuse expectations that would have no takers, and that, when they clash, it is she who is put on a spot. Equally, Modernity's Man needs this sense of self if he is consistently to pursue his preference schedule, for he has to know both that they are his preferences and also how he is doing in maximising them over time.

To the social realist, relations between humanity and the world are intrinsic to the development of human properties, all of which exist only *in potentia*, yet are *necessary* conditions for social life itself. Thus, I am advancing a transcendental argument, for the necessity of a *sense of self* to the existence of society. The continuity of consciousness, meaning a continuous *sense of self*, was first advanced by Locke.[4] To defend it entails maintaining the crucial distinction between the evolving *concept* of self (which is indeed social) and the universal *sense* of self (which is not). This distinction has been upheld by certain anthropologists, such as Marcel Mauss (1989, 3), to whom the universal sense of 'the "self" (Moi) is everywhere present'. This constant element consists in the fact that 'there has never existed a human being who has not been aware, not only of his body but also of his individuality, both spiritual and physical' (1989, 3). However, there has been a persistent tendency in the social sciences to absorb the *sense* into the *concept*, and thus to credit what is universal to the cultural balance sheet.

The best way of showing that the distinction should be maintained is through a demonstration of its necessity – namely, that a *sense of self* must be distinct from social variations in *concepts of selves* because society would be unable to work without people who have a continuity of consciousness. Thus, for anyone to appropriate social expectations, it is necessary for them to have a *sense of self* upon which these impinge, to the extent that they recognise what is expected of them (otherwise obligations cannot be internalised).

Hence, for example, the individual Zuni has to sense that his two given names, one for Summer and one for Winter, apply to the *same* self, which is also the rightful successor of the ancestor who is held to live again in the body of each who bears his names. Correct appropriation (by the proper man for all seasons) is dependent upon a continuity of consciousness, which is an integral part of what we mean by selfhood. No generalised social belief in ancestral reincarnation will suffice; for, unless there is a self which (pro)claims *I* am *that* ancestor, then the belief which is held to be general turns out to be one which has no actual takers! Nor is this situation improved by vague talk about 'social pressures' to enact roles or assume genealogical responsibilities. On the contrary; this is incoherent, for it boils down to meaning that everyone knows what roles should be filled, but no one has enough of a *sense of self* to feel that these expectations apply to them. The implication for society is that nothing gets done, for without selves which sense that responsibilities are their own and which also own expectations, then the latter have all the force of the complaint that 'someone ought to do something about it'. Thus, no version of socialisation theory can work with Durkheim's 'indeterminate material'; human beings have to be determinate in this one way at least, that of acknowledging themselves to be the same beings over time. In other words, Zuni society relies upon a *sense of self*, even though *concepts of the self*, within Zuni culture, are unlike ours.[5]

This sense of selfhood is necessarily reflexive. If Antigone did not know that she herself were both King Kreon's niece and also Polynices' sister, then she would have no dilemma about whether to obey the royal prohibition on burial of traitors or to comply with the family duty to bury her brother. However, in this context, Antigone makes a moral decision. It cannot be a socially scripted one because she lacks normative guidelines; her dilemma arises precisely from the fact that those two sets of social norms clash. Nevertheless, she acts, and to understand how and why, we have to know who she is. The rest of the paper concentrates on this very issue; on how we become particular people (possessors of strict personal identity), but people whose personality is not divorced from their sociality, without which we would not be recognisably human. However, this sociality must not be allowed to reswamp us, or we collapse back into Society's Being. Therefore, I will proceed in two stages, differentiating between:

1 our personal identities, which arise from our citizenship of the whole world; and
2 our social identities, which are made under social conditions that are not of our choosing.

The emergence of personal identity

Fundamentally, *personal identity* is a matter of what we care about in the world. Constituted as we are, and the world being the way it is, humans ineluctably interact with three different orders of reality: the natural, the practical and the social. Humans necessarily have to sustain organic relationships, work relationships and social relationships if they are to survive and thrive. Therefore, we cannot afford to be indifferent about the concerns that are embedded in each of these three orders. Our emotions convey the imports of these different orders to us. A distinct type of concern derives from each of these three orders: 'physical well-being' in the natural order; 'performative skill' in the practical order; and 'self-worth' in the social order. Emotions are seen as our reflexive responses to all three, because they are 'commentaries on our concerns'.

However, a dilemma now confronts all people. It arises because every person receives all three kinds of emotional commentaries on their concerns, originating from each of these orders of reality – natural, practical and social. Because they have to live and attempt to thrive in these three orders simultaneously, they must necessarily, in some way and to some degree, attend to all three clusters of commentaries. This is their problem. Nothing guarantees that the three sets of first-order emotions dovetail harmoniously, and therefore it follows that the concerns to which they relate cannot all be promoted without conflict arising between them. For example, evasion in response to the prompting of physical fear can threaten social self-worth by producing cowardly acts; cessation of an activity in response to boredom in the practical domain can threaten physical well-being; and withdrawal as a response to social shaming may entail a loss of livelihood. In other words, momentary attention to pressing commentaries might literally produce instant gratification of concerns in one order, but it is a recipe for disaster since we have no alternative but to inhabit these three orders simultaneously, and none of their concerns can be bracketed away for long. It is only on rather rare occasions that a particular commentary has semi-automatic priority, as in the act of escaping a fire, undertaking a test or getting married.

Instead, each person has to work out their own *modus vivendi* in relation to these three orders. What this entails is striking a liveable balance within our trinity of inescapable concerns. This *modus vivendi* can prioritise one of these three orders of reality, as in the case of someone who is said to 'live for their art', but what it cannot do is to neglect entirely the other orders. Yet which precise balance we strike between our concerns, and what precisely figures among an individual's concerns, are what gives us our strict identity as *particular persons*. Eventually, our emergent *personal identities* are a matter of how we prioritise one concern as our 'ultimate concern', and how we subordinate but yet accommodate others to it; for, constituted as we are, we cannot be unconcerned about how we fare in all three orders of reality. Because our concerns can never be exclusively social, and since the *modus vivendi* is worked out by an active and reflective agent, *personal identity* cannot be the gift of society.

The challenge of constructing a *modus vivendi* out of our many commitments is an active process of reflection, which takes place through an 'inner conversation'. In it we 'test' our potential or ongoing commitments against our emotional commentaries, which tell us whether we are up to living this or that committed life. Since the commentaries will not be unanimous, the inner conversation involves evaluating them, promoting some and subordinating others, so that the ultimate concerns we eventually affirm are also those with which we feel we can live. Since the process is fallible (we may get it wrong or circumstances may change), so the conversation is ongoing. I believe that our 'interior conversations' are the most utterly neglected phenomenon in social theory, which has never examined the *process* of reflection that makes us the particular active subjects that we are. This I have begun to unpack as an interior dialogue between the acting 'I', a process of forging *personal identity* by coming to identify the self as the being-with-this-constellation-of-concerns.[6]

As a result of this act of identity formation, a new source of imports comes into being. We now interpret and articulate imports in the light of our commitments that define us, and this brings with it a transformation of emotional commentary. In short, our new commitments represent a new sounding board for the emotions. For example, if marriage is one of our prime concerns, then an attractive opportunity for infidelity is now also felt as a threat of betrayal; its import is that of a *liaison dangereuse*, because we are no longer capable of the simplicity of a purely first-order response. Our reactions to relevant events are emotionally transmuted by our ultimate concerns. This is reinforced because our commitments also *transvalue our pasts*: the vegetarian is disgusted at once having enjoyed a rare steak, and the 'green' inwardly shudders at once having worn a fur coat. This provides positive reinforcement for present commitments. But the same process also works prospectively, because our lives become organised around our ultimate concerns. We consort and concelebrate with those sharing our commitments. 'Discomfort' is the transvalued feeling that keeps us apart from those with counter-commitments. For instance, feminists report unease in predominantly male gatherings, which struggle for political correctitude.

The resulting *modus vivendi*, which depends upon durable and effective transvaluation, is an achievement. For children and young people, who undoubtedly have inner dialogues, the establishment of a stable configuration of commitments is a virtual impossibility, because they are still learning about themselves, the world and the relations between them. Nor is its achievement a maturational certainty. Some remain at the mercy of their first-order pushes and pulls, drifting from job to job, place to place and relationship to relationship. Drift means an absence of *personal identity* and the accumulation of circumstances that make it harder to form one. The downward spiral of homelessness or addiction is downwards precisely because it condemns people to a preoccupation with the satisfaction of first-order commentaries – the next night or the next fix. Furthermore, destabilised commitments are the result of changes in one's circumstances, some of which are predictable (for example, changes in the life cycle), while others occur because of the contingencies of life in an open system (for instance, involuntary redundancy). These are nodal points that prompt a radical reopening of the 'internal conversation', but for all people the dialogue is a continuous reflexive monitoring of our concerns, for our commitments are promissory and provisional: subject to renewal or revision.

This exploration of our reflexivity has focused upon our voluntarism, because every version of the 'oversocialised' view (Society's Being), or the preprogrammed view (Modernity's Man), traduces our personal powers to live meaningful lives; they dismiss the power of *personal identity* in shaping our lives around what we care about most and commit ourselves to. Nevertheless, we do not make our personal identities under the circumstances of our choosing. Specifically, when we come to the next stage, that of examining the emergence of our *social identities*, we have to deal with our involuntary placement as *social agents* and how this affects the *social actors* that some of us can voluntarily become.

The emergence of social identity

Social identity is the capacity to express what we care about in the context of appropriate social roles. The emergence of our 'social selves' is something that occurs at the interface of structure and agency. It is therefore necessarily relational, and, for it to be properly so, independent powers have to be granted to both structures and agents. This is what is distinctive about the social realist approach. It grants the existence of people's emergent properties (PEPs) and also the reality of structural and cultural emergent properties (SEPs and CEPs), and sees the emergence of agents and actors as relational developments occurring between them. Conversely, Society's Being presents agency as an epiphenomenon of structure, while Modernity's Man regards structure as an epiphenomenon of agency.

Now, seemingly we have a dilemma. If *social identity* comes from adopting a role and personifying it in a singular manner, rather than simply energising it, then it seems as though we have to call upon *personal identity* to account for precisely who does the active personification. Yet it also appears that we cannot make such an appeal, for it looks, on this account, as though *personal identity* cannot be attained before *social identity* is achieved. How, otherwise, can people evaluate their social concerns against other kinds of concerns when ordering their ultimate concerns? This is the dilemma.

The only way out of it is to accept the existence of a dialectical relationship between *personal* and *social identity* (PI and SI, respectively). Yet if this is to be more than fudging then it is necessary to venture three 'moments' of the interplay (PI → SI) that culminate in a synthesis whereby both personal and social identities are emergent and distinct, although they contributed to one another's emergence and distinctiveness.

The first moment is held to be one in which nascent *personal identity* holds sway over nascent *social identity* (PI ← SI). Confronted with a choice – let us say the first decision to be made about one's occupational future – what resources does he or she have to draw upon? The answer has to be experience of the three orders of reality, natural, practical and social, even though as minors they are able to attempt only 'dry runs' at the internal conversation about them. Firstly, their experience of the natural realm is not negligible. Through play, sport, travel and outdoor activities it is at least extensive enough to perform a regulatory function in the process of deciding on an occupation. My older son, a frustrated explorer, calls it 'life in a fleece'; the younger one, who hated riding, will never be found applying for stable management. Secondly, and similarly, constant interaction in the practical order has supplied positive and negative feedback about the kinds of performative skills from which satisfaction is derived, through exposure to a host of common activities such as painting, drawing, music, construction, sewing, mechanics, gardening, computing, religious practice, childcare, cooking and household maintenance. Thirdly, in their involuntary social roles, children are reflexive beings, and it is they who determine which of the arenas that they have experienced might become the locus of their own self-worth. The child, and especially the teenager, basically asks: 'Do I want to be like that?' In other words, they inspect not only their own involuntary roles but also the lifestyles of those who have put them there. These are sifted into elements worthy of replication versus others meriting rejection. 'I like studying x, but I don't want to teach' is a frequent verdict of many undergraduates.

The key point here is that there would be no process at all unless the nascent *personal identity* brought something to the task of role selection. Otherwise we would be dealing with an entirely passive procedure of role assignment through socialisation, and be back to Society's Being.

Of course, their preliminary choices are fallible because the crucial missing piece of information is the experience of having made the (occupational) choice itself. Yet, without taking the plunge, there is no other way in which it can be acquired. But in its acquisition the individual herself undergoes change. This is why it is legitimate to disengage a *second 'moment', where the nascent social identity impacts upon the nascent personal identity* (SI ← PI). All 'first choices' are experiments, guided by the nascent personal identity, but at this point the 'terms and conditions' of investing oneself in the role, and of choosing to identify with it, also become manifest. What appointees have to ask (internally) is whether they wish to invest themselves in this occupation for the future. Reflexively, their answer can be 'no' to endorsing this particular social identity, in which case their choice is corrigible; they can search for an alternative source for their social identity. However, in the process of experimentation they will have undergone certain subjective and objective changes. Subjectively, they have acquired some new self-knowledge, which will impact upon their personal identity: they are now people who *know* that they are bored by x, disillusioned by y and uneasy with z. Yet they have also changed objectively, because the opportunity costs have altered for their revised 'second choice' and corrected positions may be harder to come by (for example, the greater struggle experienced by mature students when compared with 'ordinary' undergraduates).

Once subjects have found a satisfying social role, whether on the first or subsequent corrected attempts, they have a decision to make, namely: 'How much of myself am I prepared to invest in it?' *This is the moment of synthesis between personal and social identity, which takes the (PI → SI) form.* Those who have experienced enough of a role to wish to make some of its associated interests their own have also changed, to the degree that they now *know* that they do indeed find such activities to be worthwhile. Quite literally they have lost their disinterested stance, because they now see their self-worth as being constituted by occupying this role. However, most roles are greedy consumers: there are never enough hours in the day to be the 'good' academic, billing lawyer or company executive, and a 'good' parent can be on the go around the clock. Does this mean that this crystallising social identity swamps personal identity?

This cannot be the case for three reasons. Firstly, most of us hold several social roles simultaneously. Now, if all of them are 'greedy', then who or what moderates between their demands? Were we to leave this as a matter that is simply arbitrated by the strength of these competing role demands then we would have reconciled ourselves again to the passive subject. Secondly, if it is assumed that subjects themselves conduct the arbitration then we have to ask who exactly is doing it? The answer can only be a person. However, if it is indeed the person who has these powers then we have to grant that they have the capacity to 'weigh' one role against another, and also to evaluate their social concerns against their other commitments. As was argued above, this is precisely what the 'adult' internal conversation is about. Thirdly, in determining *how much* of themselves anyone will put into their social concerns, they are deciding simultaneously *what* they will put in. So, we need a person to do the active personifying. Thus, *our social identity becomes defined, but necessarily as a subset of personal identity.* The result is a personal identity *within which* the social identity has been assigned its place in the life of an individual. That place may be large ('she lives for her work') or small ('he's only in it for the money').

Unless we acknowledge this, we will go far astray by making assumptions that the same constraints and enablements have a standardised impact upon all agents who are similarly placed. Instead, in every social situation, objective factors, such as vested interests and opportunity costs for different courses of action, are filtered through agents' subjective and reflexive determinations. Actions are not mechanically determined, nor are they the subject of a uniform cost–benefit analysis that works in terms of a single currency of 'utiles'. Rather, it is the agent who brings her own 'weights and measures' to bear, which are defined by the nature of her 'ultimate concerns'.

What difference does realism's concept of the agent make?

The aim of this analysis has been to secure a concept of the agent who is active and reflexive; to conceptualise people who have the properties and powers to monitor their own lives, to mediate structural and cultural properties of society and thus to contribute to societal reproduction or transformation. However, the process of being human is ongoing, because throughout life we continue our reflexive work. The internal conversation is never suspended, it rarely sleeps, and what it is doing throughout the endless contingent circumstances it encounters is continuously monitoring its concerns. Inwardly, the subject is living a rich, unseen moral life that is evaluative (rather than calculative, as is the case for Modernity's Man) and which is meditative (rather than appropriative, as is the lot of Society's Being). What these subjects are doing is conducting a continuous assessment of whether what they once devoted themselves to, as their ultimate concern(s), are still worthy of this devotion. Equally, they are assessing whether the price that was once paid for subordinating and accommodating other concerns is still one with which they can live.

What difference does this conception of the active agent make to social theory? In a nutshell, this moral individual has powers of ongoing reflexive monitoring of both self and society. These are far outside the register of Modernity's Man, who remains shackled to his own individualistic preference schedule. In parallel, this subject is also capable of authentic *creativity*, which can transform 'society's conversation' in a radical way that is foreign to Society's Being, who is condemned to expressing mere conventional permutations on society's conversation.

In turn, regarding the 'internal conversation' as central to the problem of agency has technical implications for explanation. These arise from the fact that attaching such importance to the inner dialogue means upholding a modified view of first-person epistemic privilege. This does not entail endorsement of any of those excessive historical claims made about self-knowledge: that it is omniscient (Hume), infallible (Descartes), indubitable (Hamilton) or incorrigible (Ayer). Instead, what is presumed is only that difference in privileged access which leads to the basic asymmetry between first-person and third-person accounts of mental states. When speaking myself, in private as in public, the presumption that I know what I mean necessarily gives me, but not you, knowledge of what I believe I expressed in my thought or utterance. In speaking to herself, the agent's deliberations are made up of sayings that she holds to be true of herself; and speakers themselves cannot wonder whether they generally mean what they say, whilst hearers or hypothetical eavesdroppers are liable to considerable interpretative errors.[7] It is freely admitted that an agent may be wrong *in* her beliefs concerning herself, but not *about* them. What she does with self-warrant is to question and answer herself about her mental states and their mutual relationships, knowing what she means as she tells herself about them.[8] In so doing, she does what no one else can. This is sufficient to leave her with privileged authority in her own life. In basing her private and public conduct upon her reflexive deliberations, she draws on meanings known *directly* to her, which can only be known *indirectly* by others, through fallible interpretations.

What this serves to reinforce is the fundamental nature of the 'problem of agency'. It would cease to be either fundamental or problematic if third parties were able to read the agents' minds as well as the agents do themselves. Facts about agents' mental doings would then become just further psychological data to be integrated with other societal data into an explanatory framework. This, of course, was the fallacy of 'downwards conflation' and its presumption that the forces of socialisation simply imprint themselves upon agency (norms, values, attitudes and so on). As beliefs, conceived of as 'indeterminate material', it fallaciously advanced a third-person sociology precisely because it denied properties and powers to agents – properties and powers which underpin their first-person authority. Consequently, there was a denial of personal emergent properties (PEPs) and a precipitous slide into determinism.

Conversely, whenever there is acceptance of first-person authority and of its basic asymmetry with third-person accounts then the problem of agency can never be bypassed. Those who accept this will not be found advancing 'hydraulic' accounts about the effects of social factors on people, classes, groups or collectivities. However, the danger is often that this results in an intransigent individualism concerning our dispositional states (desires, beliefs, attitudes and evaluations). For consistency, advocacy of such personal uniqueness should defy any form of generalisation, and therefore would constitute an impasse as far as sociological explanation is concerned. The usual way in which methodological individualists and those from the hermeneutic tradition have sought to evade this dead end for sociology is by postulating 'typical individuals' (their beliefs, desires, and so on) acting in 'typical contexts'. To posit such typicality presumes aggregation, which is the only way that the methodological individualist considers it legitimate to move from the micro- to the macro- level: that is, the typical strategy of the 'upward conflationist'. But such a move is basically incoherent, because the process of generalisation completely substitutes third-person interpretations for first-person authoritative accounts, and usually ends up by endorsing some form of agential essentialism. For example, this methodological aggregation would reduce capitalism to typical capitalists confronting typical situations with the typical optimising strategy of *Homo economicus*. Capitalism is therefore presented as the simple outworking of the inherent greed of individual entrepreneurs. This interpretation misrepresents both structure, by denying the relations of natural necessity that are constitutive of capitalism (by presenting it as an aggregate of discrete situations confronted by discrete agents), and agency, by essentialising personal greed as the dispositional drive that accounts for this social form.

What is distinctive about social realism, but needs to be developed further, is that the reflexive deliberations of agents do indeed have their 'intrinsic' effects (that is, they modify the lives of subjects), but also their 'extrinsic' effects (that is, they mediate societal properties (SEPs and CEPs)). We make our lives, at least in part, by deliberating *upon* the structural and cultural contexts in which we find ourselves involuntarily. Unlike 'central conflationists', who amalgamate structural properties and agential properties into an undifferentiated amalgam of 'practices' (see, for example, Giddens 1993; 1995; 1997), realism upholds the subject/object distinction. It does so in order to explore the interplay between them, and thus to determine who is responsible for morphogenesis/morphostasis – where, when and how. Analysis of the stringency of constraints and of the degrees of freedom differentially pertaining to different groups of agents will go a long way towards explaining the 'who', the 'when' and the 'where' of social transformation versus reproduction. But to capture the 'what' and the 'how' we have to introduce agential deliberations which, however public they become, have necessarily made their detour through the reflexivity of every agent's 'internal conversation'.

It is the 'projects' that we subjectively design which determine whether we activate the *powers* of structural or cultural properties or leave them unexercised. It is our deliberations that determine what we will make of the constraints and enablements which we confront, what opportunity costs we are prepared to pay and whether we consider it worthwhile to join others in the organised pursuit of change or the defence of the status quo. Agential subjectivity thus mediates socio-cultural objectivity. But this must never be regarded as a standardised procedure, such as information processing or the development of a generalised 'habitus', for two reasons. First, it is evaluative through and through, and the key to variability in valuations is supplied by personal identity and its subset, social identity. Second, the significance of insisting that agents' knowledge of their own mental states is not omniscient, infallible, indubitable or incorrigible is that there can indeed be social factors that affect our outlooks (by narrowing or broadening our horizons, inducing resignation or fuelling ambition) without the agent correctly diagnosing them or even having any degree of discursive penetration of them. However, precisely in order to establish this convincingly one urgently needs to know what is (and, equally importantly, is not) going on in the internal dialogue.[9] One way or another, we will be unable either to account for or comprehend the processes by which agents reproduce or transform structures unless we examine their internal conversations.

The private life of the social subject holds the key to the 'problem of agency'. This key fits into the structural lock, represented by socio-cultural constraints and enablements. Together they open the door through which we can proceed to resolve the bigger 'problem of structure and agency'.[10]

Notes

1 This paper was written while holding an ESRC research fellowship.
2 I have dealt with the 'higher-level' properties and powers that differentiate Primary Agents from Corporate Agents, or 'agents' from 'actors', in Archer (1995), Chapter 8; consequently, they will not be re-examined here.
3 'Man' was the term current in Enlightenment thinking. I reluctantly abide by it, as standing for humanity, when referring to this tradition, its heirs, successors and adversaries.
4 Locke put forward a definition which has considerable intuitive appeal, such that a person was 'a thinking intelligent being, that has reason and reflection, and can consider itself as itself, the same thinking thing in different times and places' (Locke 1690, II, xxvii, 2). From Bishop Butler onwards, critics have construed such continuity of consciousness exclusively in terms of memory and then shown that memory alone fails to secure strict personal identity. See, for example, Williams (1973). A defence of a modified neo-Lockean definition is provided by David Wiggins (1976), which preserves the original insight.
5 For an empirical account of how our *sense of self* emerges from our practical relations with reality, see Archer (2000), Chapter 4.
6 See Archer (2000), Chapter 7.
7 On this issue see Davidson (1984).
8 On this issue see Alston (1971).
9 The problem of 'generalisation' confronted by methodological individualists, as mentioned above, does not confront social realism because the stratified model of agency which deals with selves, primary agents, corporate agents and actors does not reduce all forms of agency to the personal or individual level.
10 See Archer (2003).

Bibliography

Alston, W. (1971) 'Varieties of privileged access', *American Philosophical Quarterly*, 8(3): 223–41.
Archer, M. (1995) *Realist Social Theory: The Morphogenetic Approach*, Cambridge: Cambridge University Press.
—— (2000) *Being Human: The Problem of Agency*, Cambridge: Cambridge University Press.
—— (2003) *Human Reflexivity: Mediating between structure and agency*, Cambridge, Cambridge University Press.
Becker, G. (1976) *The Economic Approach to Human Behaviour*, Chicago: Chicago University Press.
Davidson, D. (1984) 'First-person authority', *Dialectica*, 38(2–3): 101–11.
Foucault, M. (1970) *The Order of Things*, New York: Random House.
Giddens, A. (1993) *Central Problems in Social Theory: Action, Structure and Contradiction in Social Analysis*, London: Macmillan.
—— (1995) *The Constitution of Society*, Cambridge: Polity Press.
—— (1997) *New Rules of Sociological Method: A Positive Critique of Interpretative Sociologies*, Cambridge: Polity Press.
Harré, R. (1983) *Personal Being*, Oxford: Blackwell.
Locke, J. (1690) *An Essay Concerning Human Understanding*, ed. J.W. Yolton, London: Everyman.
Lyotard, J.-F. (1984) *The Postmodern Condition: A Report on Knowledge*, Minneapolis MN: University of Minnesota Press.

Mauss, M. (1989) 'A category of the human mind: the notion of person; the notion of self', in M. Carrithers, S. Collins and S. Lukes (eds), *The Category of the Person*, Cambridge: Cambridge University Press, 131–58.
Rorty, R. (1989) *Contingency, Irony and Solidarity*, Cambridge: Cambridge University Press.
Taylor, C. (1985) *Human Agency and Language*, Cambridge: Cambridge University Press.
Wiggins, D. (1976) 'Locke, Butler and the stream of consciousness, and men as a natural kind', *Philosophy*, 51(196): 131–58.
Williams, B. (1973) *Problems of the Self*, Cambridge: Cambridge University Press.

8 The ontological status of subjectivity
The missing link between structure and agency

Introduction

One of the few propositions upon which social theorists agree is the truism 'no people; no society'. Accord stretches a bit further because no-one seriously maintains that 'society is like people'. Society remains different in kind from its component members, even if it is conceptualised as being no more than the aggregate effect of people's doings (and conceptions) or the pattern produced by them.

The crucial difference is that no aggregate or pattern truly possesses self-awareness,[1] whereas every single (normal) member of society is a self-conscious being. Thus, however differently the social may be conceptualised in various schools of thought (from an objective and emergent stratum of reality to an objectified social construct with the ontological status of 'facticity'), the social remains different from its component members in this crucial respect. It lacks self-consciousness. Therefore, it follows that a central problem for social theorists must be to provide an answer to the question 'What difference does the self-awareness of its members make to the nature of the social?'

Historically, the answers given have varied from 'all the difference', as the response common to idealists, to 'no difference at all', as the reply of hard-line materialists. Today, the variety of answers has increased but the question remains because it cannot be evaded. For example, social constructionists cannot dodge the issue by regarding any societal feature as a product of 'objectification' by its members because each and every individual can mentally deliberate about what is currently objectified in relation to himself or herself (they can ask 'Should I take this for granted?'). Conversely, no objectified 'entity' can be reflexive about itself in relation to individuals (it can never, as it were, ask 'Could this construct be presented more convincingly?'). The ineluctability of this issue led Hollis and Smith (1994) to maintain that 'argument about [the] "objective and subjective", . . . is as fundamental as argument about [the] "collective and individual"'. Not only are these two issues of equal importance but also they are closely intertwined.

The 'problem of structure and agency' has a great deal in common with the 'problem of objectivity and subjectivity'. Both raise the same question about the relationship between their component terms, which entails questioning their respective causal powers. Once we have started talking about causal powers it is

152 *The ontological status of subjectivity*

impossible to avoid talking about the ontological status of those things to which causal powers are attributed or from which they are withheld.

However, a popular response to these two (recalcitrant) problems is the suggestion that we should *transcend* both of them by the simple manoeuvre of considering them to be the two faces of a single coin.[2] Transcending the divide rests upon conceptualising 'structures' and 'agents' as ontologically inseparable because each enters into the other's constitution and therefore they should be examined as one mutually constitutive amalgam.[3] In a single leap-frog move, all the previous difficulties can be left behind. This manoeuvre has direct implications for the question of 'objectivity and subjectivity'. If 'structure' and 'agency' are conceptualised as being inseparable, because they are maintained to be mutually constitutive, then this blurring of subject and object necessarily and seriously challenges the possibility of reflexivity itself. If the two are an amalgam, it is difficult to see how a person or a group is able to reflect critically or creatively upon their social conditions or context.

Part 1: The impossibility of eliminating subjectivity

Critical Realists are necessarily 'against transcendence' precisely because, on ontological grounds, they are 'for emergence'. Ontologically both structure and agency are conceptualised as distinct strata of reality because they have different, irreducible and causally efficacious properties and powers. For example, structures can be centralised, whilst people cannot, and people can exercise reflexivity, which structures cannot do. In this case, there is no alternative to theorising about the interplay between 'structure' and 'agency' as strata of reality that are irreducible to one another. Moreover, as the above example shows, the same goes for 'objectivity' and 'subjectivity'.

My intention is to examine these interconnected issues of 'subjectivity and objectivity' and 'structure and agency' through briefly reviewing the answer given by Realists to the question 'how does structure influence agency?' Central to the Critical Realist answer is Roy Bhaskar's (1989a, 25–6) statement that 'the causal power of social forms is mediated through social agency'. This is surely correct, because unless the emergent properties of structure and culture are held to derive from people and their doings and to exert their effects through people, then Realism would obviously be guilty of reification. Nevertheless, it is not complete because what is meant by that crucial word 'through' has not been unpacked.

Generically, the word 'through' has been replaced by the process of 'social conditioning'. However, to condition entails the existence of something that is conditioned, and because conditioning is not determinism, then this process necessarily involves the interplay between two different kinds of causal powers – those pertaining to structures and those belonging to agents. Therefore, an adequate conceptualisation of conditioning must deal explicitly with the interplay between these two powers. This involves a specification, first, of *how* structural and cultural powers impinge upon agents and, second, of *how* agents use their own personal powers to act 'so rather than otherwise' in such situations.

Thus, there are two elements involved, the 'impingement upon' (which is objective) and the 'response to it' (which is subjective). Realists, myself included, have concentrated upon the former to the neglect of the latter. This one-sidedness is illustrated in Figures 8.1 and 8.2.

The place of social conditioning in realist social theory

On the whole, I think we have satisfactorily conceptualised the objective side by specifying that cultural and structural emergent properties impinge on people by shaping the social situations that they confront. Often this confrontation is involuntary, as with people's natal social context and its associated life-chances. Often it is voluntary, like getting married. In either case, these objective conditioning influences are transmitted to agents by shaping the situations that those agents live with, have to confront or would confront if they chose to do x, y or z. Sometimes they impinge as constraints and enablements and sometimes by distributing different types of vested interests or objective interests to different groups of people in either reproducing or transforming their social conditions.

However, since Realists are not determinists, what we have omitted to examine is why people do not respond in uniform fashion under the same circumstances. Subjects who are similarly situated can debate, both internally and externally, about the appropriate course of action and come to different conclusions, which is one reason why Humean constant conjunctions are not found. At best, what are detected are empirical tendencies in action patterns, consonant with objective influences having shaped them. These must remain nothing more than trends, partly because contingencies intervene, but partly because a second causal power is necessarily at play – namely, the personal power to reflect upon one's circumstances and to decide what to do in them or about them.

In short, the conceptualisation of this process of mediation between structure and agency has not been fully adequate because it has not fully incorporated the role played by human subjectivity in general. In particular, it omits the part of reflexivity in enabling agents to design and determine their responses to the structured circumstances in which they find themselves.

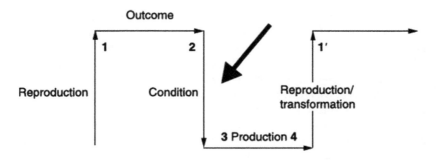

Figure 8.1
Source: Bhaskar (1989b, 94).

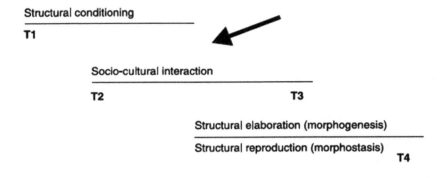

Figure 8.2
Source: Archer (1995, 157).

The process of 'conditioning' thus entails the exercise of two sets of causal powers: those of the property that 'conditions' and those of the property that is 'conditioned'. Let us look at this concretely in relation to constraints and enablements. The obvious point is that a constraint requires something to constrain and an enablement needs something to enable. These are not intransitive terms because if *per impossible* no agent ever conceived of any course of action then neither could be constrained nor enabled. This is impossible because by virtue of our biological constitution and life in society we have to conceive of courses of action (deciding what to eat tonight cannot be consigned to reflex or routine action, otherwise why are we aware of giving some thought to it?).

Similarly, the mere existence of a top-heavy demographic structure does not constrain a generous pensions policy at all, unless and until somebody advances the policy of giving generous pensions. Only when that project has been mooted does the top-heavy demographic structure in relation to a small active population become a constraint, *ceteris paribus*. Equally, in the cultural realm, if there is a contradiction between two beliefs or two theories it remains a purely logical matter, existing out there in the 'Universal Library',[4] until and unless someone wants to uphold one of those ideas or assert one of those ideas or do something with one of those ideas.

Consequently, the incorporation of agential powers into the conceptualisation of conditioning entails the following three points. First, that social emergent properties, or rather the exercise of their powers, are dependent upon the existence of what have been termed 'projects', where a project stands for any course of action intentionally engaged upon by a human being. These projects, *as subjectively conceived by agents*, are necessary for the activation of social emergent properties, i.e. their transformation into powers. Second, only if there is a relationship of congruence or incongruence between the emergent social property and the project of the person(s) will the latter activate the former. If there is congruence this represents enablement, and if there is incongruence that constitutes constraint. Third, and most importantly for this paper, agents have to respond to these influences by using their own personal powers to deliberate reflexively over how to respond. This is the difference between human agents and other kinds of animate or inanimate matter. What is also unique about the reflexivity of human beings is that it can involve anticipation. A constraint need not have impinged or impacted, it could just be foreseeable.

Because the response of the agent to a constraint (or enablement) is a matter of reflexive deliberation, it can take very different forms: from compliance through evasion and strategic action to subversion. The one thing that is rarely, if ever, found is a complete uniformity of response on behalf of every agent who encounters the same constraint or the same enablement.

Therefore, it is essential to distinguish between the objective existence of structural (and cultural) emergent properties and the exercise of their causal powers, since the realisation of their causal powers requires them to be activated by agents. Hence, the efficacy of any social emergent property is at the mercy of the agents' reflexive activity. Outcomes vary enormously with agents' creativity in dreaming up brand new responses, even to situations that may have occurred many times before. Ultimately, the precise outcome varies with agents' personal concerns and degrees of commitment, together with the costs different agents will pay to see their projects through in the face of structural obstacles and hindrances. Equally, they vary with agents' readiness to avail themselves of enablements.

Were someone determined to deny the independent influence of human subjectivity, the second mode of conditioning that Realists have conceptualised could be brought into play. It might be stressed that emergent properties also motivate us towards various courses of action. They do not just constrain and enable us. This is true, but it would not serve to sustain the above argument because these social properties are held to work precisely through agential subjectivity itself, by moulding it in a particular manner. Usually they are considered to work without full personal awareness and often as what sociologists call the 'unacknowledged conditions of action'. Yet, if they are genuinely unacknowledged then such causal influences should be exerted in blanket form on all people. There would be no difference in response, according to their subjective reception by different individual agents (or groups of agents), if all were totally unaware of them. Only a uniform response from the population in question would justify ignoring their personal subjectivity on the grounds that this has been externally shaped. Yet, such differences are common. Therefore the examination of agential subjectivity and reflexive variability becomes even more important in order to understand differences of response under the same ('unacknowledged') conditions.

There are indeed structural properties, such as vested interests, that can motivate by encouraging and discouraging people from particular courses of action. However, these have first to be found good by a person before they can influence the projects she entertains. For a person to find a vested interest good does not entail that she has full discursive penetration of the property, as if she were endowed with all the qualities of a good sociologist. In fact, agents do not have to know everything that is going on, or there would be no such things as 'unacknowledged conditions'. There are indeed, but all those conditions need to do in order to shape her motivation is to shape her circumstances. Take a young academic, born in this country with English as her mother tongue. What she recognises or takes for granted about her situation are aspects of its ease: books are translated quickly, English is one of the official languages at conferences and used in the best-known journals, etc. What she does not need to have is discursive penetration about why her situation is so comparatively easy and rewarding. She does not need to acknowledge that she is a beneficiary of neo-colonialism, which gives English the status it has today in academe. In order for her motivation towards her academic career to be enhanced all she has to acknowledge is, for example, the ease and fluency with which she makes interventions at international conferences.

However, this same young academic may have a baby and then determine that babies and academic careers are incompatible. Our hypothetical social determinist might then argue that without the 'hegemonic discourse of maternity' she would not have so determined. Yet, given this (past) hegemony, how would one account for the minority of women who continued with their careers whilst others resigned? Of course, further social factors could be adduced, but the dogged social determinist then confronts infinite regress. The only way out of this impasse is to allow that personal emergent properties give us the ability to make variable responses under the same objective social circumstances.

Equally, structural factors do constitute deterrents capable of depressing agential motivation. They do so by attaching different opportunity costs to the same course of action (such as house purchase) for different parts of the population. This is how 'life chances' exert causal powers, but their outcomes are only empirical tendencies. What they cannot explain is why x becomes a home owner and y does not, if both are similarly socially situated. That is a question of the agents' own concerns and deliberations, which govern whether or not they find the cost worth paying. The simple fact that somebody is faced with a deterrent in the form of an opportunity cost does not mean they are necessarily deterred any more than does the fact that people inherit vested interests mean that they are bound to defend them – Tony Benn renounced a knighthood in order to sit in the House of Commons.

Thus, there is no one-to-one relationship between social position and individual disposition in terms of actions and their outcomes. Instead, there is always some variability in the courses of action taken that is attributable to personal subjectivity. Without acceptance of this we are thrown back upon empirical generalisations of the kind 'the greater the cost of a project, the less likely are people to entertain it'. Not only is that no explanation whatsoever (merely a quest for Humean constant conjunctions) but also, far from having eliminated human subjectivity, it relies upon a banal and highly dubious form of it.

Because human subjectivity cannot be kept out of any such account, the overwhelming tendency has been for sociological investigators to insert their own subjectivity in place of the agents' reflexivity. Often we Realists have been guilty of putting things such as vested interests or objective interests into our accounts of action as a kind of dummy for real and efficacious human subjectivity. There are many worse exemplars, and probably the worst is Rational Choice Theory, which imputes instrumental rationality alone[5] to all agents as they supposedly seek to maximise their preference schedules in order to become 'better off' in terms of some indeterminate future 'utiles'. Subjectively, every agent is reduced to a bargain hunter and the human pursuit of the *Wertrationalität* is disallowed.[6] Bourdieu (1977; 1990), too, was often guilty of endorsing an empty formalism about subjectivity, such that people's positions ('semi-consciously' and 'quasi-automatically') engendered dispositions to reproduce their positions. Such theoretical formulations seem to lose a lot of the rich and variable subjectivity that features prominently in *La Misère du Monde*.

Part 2: The ontological implications of incorporating subjectivity

Instead, let us explore the theoretical and practical implications of giving agential powers their proper due. This is what the rest of this chapter is about: namely, conceptualising the interplay between personal subjective properties and powers and objective societal properties and powers. Specifically, what are the implications of maintaining that personal reflexivity mediates the effects of objective social forms upon us? In other words, 'reflexivity' is being advanced as the answer to how 'the causal power of social forms is mediated *through* human agency'. It performs this mediatory role by virtue of the fact that we deliberate about ourselves in relation to the social situations that we confront, certainly fallibly, certainly incompletely and necessarily under our own descriptions because that is the only way we can know anything. To accord human reflexivity that role, even provisionally, means at least entertaining that we are dealing with two ontologies, the objective pertaining to social emergent properties and the subjective pertaining to agential emergent properties.

What is entailed by the above is that subjectivity is (a) real, (b) irreducible and (c) possesses causal efficacy. Before examining these three implications, it is probably helpful to specify what kinds of subjective properties and powers are under consideration as constitutive of this mediatory process. I have termed this process the Internal Conversation[7] to designate the manner in which we reflexively make our way through the world. This is what makes (most of us) 'active agents', people who can exercise some governance in their lives, as opposed to 'passive agents' to whom things just happen.[8]

Being an 'active agent' hinges on the fact that individuals develop and define their ultimate concerns: those internal goods that they care about most[9] and whose precise constellation makes for their concrete singularity as persons.[10] No-one can have an ultimate concern and fail to do something about it. Instead, each seeks to develop a concrete course(s) of action to realise that concern by elaborating a project(s), in the (fallible) belief that to accomplish the project(s) is to realise one's concern(s). If such courses of action are successful, which can never be taken for granted, everybody's constellation of concerns, when dovetailed together, becomes translated into a set of established practices. This constitutes their personal *modus vivendi*. Through this *modus vivendi*, subjects live out their personal concerns within society as best they can. In shorthand, these components can be summarised in the formula: Concerns → Projects → Practices. There is nothing idealistic about this, because 'concerns' can be ignoble, 'projects' illegal and 'practices' illegitimate.

These are the kinds of mental activity that make up the strange reality of reflexivity, as part of broader human subjectivity. Because the implication under consideration is ontological and not epistemological, its acceptance entails the endorsement of plural ontologies. This should not in itself be a problem for Critical Realism. The reality of what has been termed 'Internal Conversation' (also known as 'self talk', 'rumination', 'musement', 'inner dialogue', 'internal speech', etc.) does not mean that when we deliberate, when we formulate our intentions, when we design our courses of action or when we dedicate ourselves to concerns, that such mental activities are like chairs or trees: they are not. Yet, this has nothing whatsoever to do with whether or not they are real, because reality itself is not homogeneous. The whole of reality cannot be confined to and defined in terms of the Enlightenment notion of 'matter in motion'. Indeed, in post-positivistic science, physical reality is made up as much by quarks and genomes as it is by old stagers such as magnetism and gravity or even older stagers such as rocks and plants.

Abandonment of that Enlightenment assumption paves the way to the acceptance of plural ontologies. It is now more than 30 years since Popper distinguished his Three Worlds as ontologically distinct sub-worlds: the world of physical states, the world of mental states and the world of objective ideas. What is important about this for the present argument is that Popper put his finger on the genuine oddity about World Two, the world of mental states: namely, that it is both objectively real and yet has a subjective ontology.

Reality

Conscious states such as holding an Internal Conversation can only exist from the point of view of the subject who is experiencing those thoughts. In other words, Internal Conversations have what John Searle (1999, 42) terms a first-person ontology. This means they have a subjective mode of existence, which is also the case for desires, feelings, fantasies, beliefs and intentions. That is, only as experienced by a particular subject does a particular thought exist. Just as there are no such things as disembodied pains, there are no such things as subjectively independent thoughts. Both are first-person dependent for their own existence. However, you might object that whilst I cannot share my toothache with you, what am I currently doing but sharing my thoughts with you? In fact I do not agree that it is possible to share my thoughts with you. Instead, what I am doing is sharing my *ideas* with you, as World Three objects, ones that will become even more permanently[11] part of World Three once they are published.

What I cannot share with you is something William James (1890, 254f) captured very well: the reflexive monitoring that is going on here and now as my thoughts are turned into the complete sentences that you will read at least 12 months hence. Internally, I am engaged in self-monitoring activities that are an inextricable part of my thoughts, such as mundanely checking if a singular subject is accompanied by a singular verb or deciding on the words that seem best to capture an insight. That experience I cannot share with you any more than I can convey to my doctor or dentist what kind of toothache I have, except by metaphors such as sharp and jagged. What I cannot do is take my toothache out and say to the dentist 'Here, you experience it for two seconds please and then you will know with what you have to deal.' So too, thoughts remain intransigently first-person in kind. However, the crucial point is not about sharing or epistemic access – the point is ontological. As Searle (1999, 43) puts it, 'each of my conscious states exists only as the state it is because it is experienced by me, the subject'. That is what makes the ontology of subjectivity distinctive. Most other parts of reality have a third-person mode of existence, sometimes self-sufficient like mountains, sometimes dependent upon people at a prior time like books, but not necessarily dependent upon a knowing subject at this point in time. A thought, however, does require a present-tense subject doing the thinking in the first-person. That is the oddity of subjective ontology.

Irreducibility

If human reflexivity, in the form of Internal Conversations, has the causal power to mediate structural and cultural properties, then it must be irreducible to these emergent social forms. Moreover, reflexivity could not even be a candidate for performing this mediatory role if there was not first-person authority as well as a first-person perspective.[12] Indeed, there are schools of thought that are quite willing to entertain the existence of a first-person perspective but would not accept first-person authority. That would be true of social constructionists in general. In particular, Rom Harré (1983, 61f) maintains that we are merely sites of perception: that is, we are just like the coordinates of Washington, '39N 77W' – a standpoint from which we see things. Today, most social theorists can agree that there is no 'news from nowhere'. However, it is not sufficient simply to argue for the existence of a first-person perspective. First-person authority is needed too if subjectivity is to play a full part in social theorising. Such authority has to be part of a subjective ontology, otherwise utterances about internal mental activities are either reducible or lack causal efficacy because they are merely phenomenological 'froth'.

In other words, a claim has to be sustained that subjects alone have first-person authority to know their own minds about objective social factors better than can anyone else. This claim maintains that we have a special knowledge about ourselves in relation to society that cannot be replaced by a third-person account such as that offered by an investigator. If the two were interchangeable, or the investigator's account was deemed to be superior to the subject's account in all respects (though it can be in some), then our reflexive Internal Conversations would be redundant in social theory. All theory and investigation could be conducted in the third person. In that case, the notion of reflexivity playing any indispensable role, such as is being claimed for it as a mediatory mechanism, would necessarily fall to the ground.

To avoid this I am going to make a claim for the existence of a certain kind of first-person authority whilst avoiding the excessive claims that have been made about first-person epistemic authority. Thus, I am not arguing for first-person infallibility with Descartes, nor for first-person omniscience with Hume, for first-person indubitability with Hamilton or for first-person incorrigibility with Ayer.[13] If there is anything in the psychoanalytic notion that we conceal certain beliefs, desires and so on from ourselves and attribute other beliefs or desires to ourselves, then each of those four claims above is completely undermined. However, psychoanalysis itself does not undermine first-person authority, because recovery of authority by a patient over an attitude is often the only evidence that it was there prior to the therapeutic suggestion.[14]

Instead, it is argued that one can still claim first-person self-warrant. In other words, one can make the claim, 'I enjoy self-warrant whenever I truly believe I am thinking (or feeling) X at the moment; *ipso facto*, I am justified in claiming to know the state of my belief, even if that belief itself turns out to be untrue.'[15] In other words, an agent can be granted self-warranted authority (not infallibility), whose importance is that she bases her public conduct on her own reflexive deliberations. These are known directly to her and only indirectly to a third person (an investigator or interlocutor) through fallible interpretation. If that is the case, it follows that no investigator may properly substitute his or her interpretation for that of the agent. If I tell you 'I am happy to have two children', I know my meaning, its nuances and proper emphases when I produce that utterance – or its opposite. You can only interpret my meaning from my utterance and your notions, connotations and emphases are your interpretations, which may be very different from mine. What warranted first-person authority entails is that an agent may be wrong *in* her beliefs (and often is) but she cannot be wrong *about* her beliefs. This argument maintains that the agent therefore retains an irreducible property – and power – since she acts on her beliefs. Whenever there is acceptance of first-person authority and of its basic asymmetry with third-person accounts, then the contribution of agential subjectivity can never be bypassed in sociological accounts of action and its consequences.

Hence, the admission of first-person authority is a necessary stepping stone for avoiding social 'hydraulics' and asserting instead that it is our deliberations about things structural and cultural, about the contexts and social situations in which we find ourselves, that determine exactly what we do. Certainly, because we are not infallible, it can be maintained that social factors affect agents' outlooks without people actually diagnosing this. That would be the case for ideological influences or for members of a social class overestimating an objective obstacle, such as those working class parents who used to turn down grammar school places on the grounds that 'they are not for the likes of us'. However, the key point is that we cannot know that this is the case without examining agents' subjectivity, their reflexive Internal Conversations. Without that we cannot discover what 'ideology' or 'social class' have encouraged one person to believe but failed to convince another to believe. What cannot be assumed is that every ideological effort will or can be victorious in instilling all people with the desired beliefs. Ideologies, however hegemonic, are not in themselves influences, but rather attempts to influence. They too, as a cultural counterpart of structural factors, involve both impingement upon the subject and reception by the subject. Reception is obviously heterogeneous, or no-one would ever have accepted a grammar school place for their working-class child and no counter-ideology would ever have been formulated.

Sometimes it seems even more tempting, in habitus theory or discourse theorising in general, simply to take reproduction as a passive act on the part of an agent that requires no investigation of his or her reflexive thought. However, reproduction in society rarely means replication and is equally rarely achieved through routine, non-deliberative action. In fact, successful 'reproduction' is usually heavily dependent upon reflexive activity because reproduction is not about staying put, it is about staying ahead. Some of the best examples Bourdieu himself gave depended upon self-conscious subjective ingenuity, such as middle-class parents with non-academic offspring seeking out some form of niche training that could salvage the social status of their not-too-bright child. In sum, it is impossible to explain how agents reproduce or transform the objective social context without examining their subjectivity. This leads directly to the last crucial point, namely the causal powers of agents and the mediatory power of the Internal Conversation.

Reflexivity and its causal powers

It has been maintained that our personal powers are exercised through reflexive internal dialogue and that the Internal Conversation is responsible for the delineation of our concerns, the definition of our projects and, ultimately, the determination of our practices in society. It is agential reflexivity which actively mediates between our structurally shaped circumstances and what we deliberately make of them. There is an obvious caution here: agents cannot make what they please of their circumstances. To maintain otherwise would be to endorse idealism and the epistemic fallacy. Indeed, if people get their objective circumstances badly wrong these subjects pay the objective price whether or not they do so comprehendingly. What the Internal Conversation does do is to mediate by activating structural and cultural powers and in so doing there is no single and predictable outcome. This is because agents can exercise their reflexive powers in different ways according to their very different concerns and considerations.

Thus, a three-stage process of mediation is being put forward, one that gives both objectivity and subjectivity their due and also explicitly incorporates their interplay.

i   Structural and cultural properties *objectively* shape the situations that agents confront involuntarily and possess generative powers of constraint and enablement in relation to them.
ii Agents' own configurations of concerns, as *subjectively* defined in relation to the three orders of natural reality – nature, practice and society.
iii Courses of action are produced through the reflexive deliberations of agents who *subjectively* determine their practical projects in relation to their *objective* circumstances.

162 The ontological status of subjectivity

The first stage deals with the kind of specification that Realists already provide about how 'social forms' impinge and impact on people by moulding their situations. This was summarised as follows in *Realist Social Theory*:

> Given their pre-existence, structural and cultural emergents shape the social environment to be inhabited. These results of past actions are deposited in the form of current situations. They account for what there is (structurally and culturally) to be distributed and also for the shape of such distributions; for the nature of the extant role array, the proportion of positions available at any time and the advantages/disadvantages associated with them; for the institutional configuration present and for those second order emergent properties of compatibility and incompatibility, that is whether the respective operations of institutions are matters of obstruction or assistance to one another. In these ways, situations are objectively defined for their subsequent occupants or incumbents.[16]

However, these become only generative powers, rather than unactivated properties in relationship to agential projects. Stage (ii) examines the interface between the above and agential projects themselves, for, again, it is not the properties of agents that interact directly with structural or cultural properties but their powers as expressed in the pursuit of a project. It is stage (iii) that has been missing in social theorising to date, but which appears essential in order to conceptualise the process of mediation properly and completely. In stage (iii), agents, by virtue of their powers of reflexivity, deliberate about their objective circumstances in relation to their subjective concerns. They consult their projects to see if they can realise them, possibly adapting them, adjusting them, abandoning them or enlarging them in the deliberative process. They alter their practices such that if a course of action is going well subjects may become more ambitious and if it is going badly they may become more circumspect. It is this crucial stage (iii) that enables us to try to do, to be or to become what we care about most in society – by virtue of our reflexivity.

This final stage of mediation is indispensable because without it we have no explanatory purchase upon what exactly agents do. The absence of explanatory purchase means settling for empirical generalisations about what 'most of the people do most of the time'. Sociologists can settle for even less: 'Under circumstances x a statistically significant number of agents do y.' This spells a return to Humean constant conjunctions and a resignation to being unable to adduce a causal mechanism.

Conclusion

Neglect of the subjective contribution to mediation has the consequence that social forms are treated as intransitive, simply as advantages or disadvantages. In effect, the presumption is that no-one looks a gift horse in the mouth and that everybody gets down to cutting their coats to suit their cloth. Yet, 'advantages' are not intransitive because they have to be positively evaluated by the agent for some purpose. This is particularly relevant when the luck of having been dealt better life-chances than others is then presumed to mean that the advantages of 'keeping ahead' will dominate the activities of all who are so placed. This may be a common concern, but, if it is, then it must have been subjectively adopted, for it is not one that can be blandly imputed to everybody. Once again, the conclusion is that if subjectivity is not properly investigated it will be improperly imputed – for it cannot be eliminated.

When a subjective ontology is introduced and agential reflexivity is investigated, three points are acknowledged on the agential side of the equation.

- That our unique personal identities, which derive from our singular constellations of concerns, mean that we are radically heterogeneous as agents. Even though we may share objective social features we may also seek very different ends when in the same social situation.
- That our subjectivity is dynamic, it is not psychologically static nor is it psychologically reducible because we modify our own goals in terms of their contextual feasibility, as we see it. As always, we are fallible, can get it wrong and have to pay the objective price for doing so.
- That as agents we are active, for the most part, rather than passive, because we can adjust our projects to those practices that we believe we can realise.

Unless all of these points are taken on board, what is omitted are agential evaluations of their situations in the light of their concerns and agential re-evaluation of their projects in the light of the situations in which they find themselves – whether voluntarily or involuntarily. In short, a full account of structure and agency and of the process mediating between them entails accepting and examining the interplay between two ontologies – the socially objective and the personally subjective.

Notes

1 If the statement that 'The British electorate now mistrusts Tony Blair' is true, it is only a statement about the views of the majority of people eligible to vote. To attribute a predicate such as 'distrust' to the 'electorate' as such is to reify the latter.
2 See Mouzelis (2000).
3 Archer (1995, Ch. 4).
4 See Archer (1988, Ch. 5).
5 See Archer and Tritter (2001).
6 See Hollis (1989).
7 See Archer (2003).
8 For this distinction, see Hollis (1977).
9 See Frankfurter (1988, Ch. 7).
10 Archer (2000, Ch. 9).
11 The sentence is expressed in this way because this paper was first delivered as a talk to the IACR annual conference, Girton College, Cambridge, 2004.
12 See Shoemaker (1996).
13 See Alston (1971, 225f).
14 See Davidson (1984, 105).
15 See Alston (1971, 236).
16 Archer (1995, 201).

References

Alston, W. 'Varieties of Privileged Access', *American Philosophical Quarterly*, 8(3): 223–41, 1971.
Archer, M. S. *Culture and Agency*, Cambridge University Press, Cambridge, 1988.
Archer, M. S. *Realist Social Theory*, Cambridge University Press, Cambridge, 1995.
Archer, M. S. *Being Human: The Problem of Agency*, Cambridge University Press, Cambridge, 2000.
Archer, M. S. *Structure, Agency and the Internal Conversation*, Cambridge University Press, Cambridge, 2003.
Archer, M. S. and Tritter, J. (eds.). *Rational Choice Theory: Resisting Colonisation*, Routledge/Taylor and Francis, London, 2001.
Bhaskar, R. *The Possibility of Naturalism*, Harvester Wheatsheaf, Hemel Hempstead, 1989a.
Bhaskar, R. *Reclaiming Reality*, Verso, London, 1989b.
Bourdieu, P. *Outline of a Theory of Practice*, Cambridge University Press, Cambridge, 1977.
Bourdieu, P. *The Logic of Practice*, Polity Press, Oxford, 1990.
Davidson, D. 'First-Person Authority', *Dialectica*, 38(2–3): 101–11, 1984.
Frankfurter, H. G. *The Importance of What We Care About*, Cambridge University Press, Cambridge, 1988.
Harré, R. *Personal Being*, Basil Blackwell, Oxford, 1983.
Hollis, M. *Models of Man; Philosophical Thoughts on Social Action*, Cambridge University Press, Cambridge, 1977.
Hollis, M. 'Honour Among Thieves', Proceedings of the British Academy, 75: 163–80, 1989.
Hollis, M. and Smith, S. 'Two Stories about Structure and Agency', *Review of International Studies*, 20(3): 241–51, 1994.
James, W. *The Principles of Psychology* (Vol. 1), Macmillan, London, 1890.
Mouzelis, N. 'The Subjectivist-Objectivist Divide: Against Transcendence', *Sociology*, 34(4): 741–62, 2000.
Searle, J. *Mind, Language and Society*, Weidenfeld and Nicolson, London, 1999.
Shoemaker, S. *The First-Person Perspective and Other Essays*, Cambridge University Press, Cambridge, 1996.

9 Reflexivity as the unacknowledged condition of social life

Reflexivity remains a cipher in social theory. Neither what it is nor what it does has received the attention necessary for producing clear concepts of reflexivity or a clear understanding of reflexivity as a social process. These two absences are closely related and mutually reinforcing. On the one hand, the fact that there is no concept of reflexivity in common currency means that, just as Molière's Monsieur Jourdain spoke prose all his life without knowing it, everyone from the founding fathers through all normal lay people to today's social theorists have constantly been referring to reflexivity or tacitly assuming it or logically implying it under a variety of different terms.

On the other hand, because the terminology that subsumes reflexivity is so varied – from the portmanteaux concepts of academics, such as 'consciousness' or 'subjectivity' through Everyman's quotidian notion of 'mulling things over' to the quaint, but not inaccurate, folkloric expression 'I says to myself says I' – the *process* denoted by reflexivity has been underexplored, undertheorised and, above all, undervalued. Reflexivity is such an inescapable, though vague, presupposition and so tacitly, thus non-discursively, taken for granted that it has rarely been held up for the scrutiny necessary to rectify its undervaluation as a social process. Because reflexivity has been so seriously neglected[1] redressing this state of affairs means making some bold moves. The intent behind the present book is finally to allow this Cinderella to go to the ball, to stay there and to be acknowledged as a partner without whom there would be no social dance.

Our human reflexivity is closely akin to our human embodiment, something so self-evident as not to have merited serious attention from social theorists until 'the body' was 'reclaimed' during the past two or three decades. However, whilst all passengers on the Clapham omnibus would concur that, indeed, they have bodies, most would be stumped by 'reflexivity' if asked whether or not they practise it. In fact, as will be shown in Chapter 2, nearly all subjects agree that they do if the question is rephrased to avoid using the word. Because the term is ill-defined and not in everyday use, let us begin from the ordinary activities to which it refers amongst ordinary people: ones that they do recognise and can discuss if ordinary language is used.

At its most basic, reflexivity rests on the fact that all normal people talk to themselves within their own heads,[2] usually silently and usually from an early age.

166 *Reflexivity and social life*

In the present book this mental activity is called 'internal conversation' but, in the relatively sparse literature available, it is also known *inter alia* as 'self-talk', 'intra-communication', 'musement', 'inner dialogue' and 'rumination'. Indeed, it seems probable that some people engage in more internal dialogue than external conversation at certain times in life and under particular circumstances: those living alone and especially the elderly, those employed in solitary occupations or performing isolated work tasks, and only children without close friends. What are they doing when they engage in self-talk? The activities involved range over a broad terrain which, in plain language, can extend from daydreaming, fantasising and internal vituperation through rehearsing for some forthcoming encounter, reliving past events, planning for future eventualities, clarifying where one stands or what one understands, producing a running commentary on what is taking place and talking oneself through (or into) a practical activity to more pointed actions such as issuing internal warnings and making promises to oneself, reaching concrete decisions or coming to a conclusion about a particular problem.

Two things are clear about this (non-exhaustive) list. Firstly, not all of these activities are fully reflexive, because they lack the crucial feature of the 'object' under consideration being bent back in any serious, deliberative sense, upon the 'subject' doing the considering. For example, a worker tackling a new procedure or someone erecting a wardrobe from a flat-pack asks herself 'What comes next?' and often answers this by consulting an external source such as the manual or instruction leaflet. Of course, this could be viewed as weakly reflexive because their question also stands for 'What do I do next?' But it is weak because the response is to consult the rule-book rather than thrashing it out through internal deliberation about subject in relation to object and vice versa. Hence, the dividing line between reflexive and non-reflexive thought is far from clear-cut because anyone's thoughts can move back and forth between the two.

Secondly, not all of the mental activities listed above concern social matters because the object over which a subject deliberates need not concern people or society. For example, solo climbers talk themselves through handholds and footholds, and riders ask themselves how many strides their horses should fit in before jumping an obstacle. However, it can always be maintained that sporting activities like these are weakly social; they are usually reliant upon manufactured equipment, often entail human artefacts, such as route maps and fences, and frequently presume some social context, such as the existence of mountain rescue or the right to jump some farmer's hedges. Although it is usually possible to invoke some social element of the above type, neither analytically nor practically are such elements primary to the activity. The dividing line can be fuzzy in practice, although the analytical distinction is clear enough.

The present book deals only with strongly reflexive processes and its concern is with reflexive deliberations about matters that are primarily and necessarily social.[3] Reflexivity itself is held to depend upon conscious deliberations that take place through 'internal conversation'. The ability to hold such inner dialogues is an emergent personal power of individuals that has been generally disregarded and is not entailed by routine or habitual action. Myers summarises the unwarranted neglect of this personal property as follows:

> [The importance of] self-dialogue and its role in the acquisition of self-knowledge, I believe, can hardly be exaggerated. That it plays such a role is a consequence of a human characteristic that deserves to be judged remarkable. This is the susceptibility of our mind/body complexes to respond to the questions that we put to ourselves, to create special states of consciousness through merely raising a question. It is only slightly less remarkable that these states provoked into existence by our questions about ourselves quite often supply the materials for accurate answers to those same questions.[4]

Precisely because our reflexive deliberations about social matters take this 'question and answer' format, it is appropriate to consider reflexivity as being exercised through internal conversation.

The following definition is used throughout the present work: *'reflexivity' is the regular exercise of the mental ability, shared by all normal people, to consider themselves in relation to their (social) contexts and vice versa.* Such deliberations are important since they form the basis upon which people determine their future courses of action – always fallibly and always under their own descriptions. Because this book focuses upon people's occupational concerns and patterns of social mobility – in order to have a concrete point of reference for the discussion of reflexivity – the contexts involved are social contexts. However, let us return to the basic question, namely what are people doing when they engage in self-talk?

Some of the subjects interviewed,[5] and also certain social psychologists, respond in a derogatory manner to the idea of 'talking to oneself'. Indeed, this is probably the worst vernacular formulation through which to ascertain anything about their internal conversations from the population at large. At best, it elicits a wary assent, sometimes immediately followed by the qualification: 'But I'm not daft.' Interestingly, in languages as different as English and Romanian the association persists between talking to oneself and 'being simple' or 'off one's head', and it is not eliminated by emphasising that internal dialogue is conducted silently. Resident English speakers are much readier to assent that they engage in inner dialogue and to amplify upon their self-talk if the activity is described to them as 'silently mulling things over' or 'thinking things through in your own head'. The origins of this negative reaction are obvious, but its duration may have been prolonged by psychologists as different as Piaget and Vygotsky, who held that 'speaking out loud' either disappeared or was internalised with age and, thus, its absence in adults represented a sign of mental maturity. Equally, social psychologists often display considerable negativity towards 'rumination', which is seen as interfering with routinised schemes that are regarded as providing quicker and more reliable guides to action.[6]

Folk wisdom can be recruited in praise of routine action, as in the following verse:

> The centipede was happy, quite, until the toad in fun
>
> Said, 'Pray which leg goes after which?'
>
> This worked his mind to such a pitch,
>
> He lay distracted in a ditch, considering how to run.

The book which approvingly reproduced this nursery rhyme expatiates upon reflexivity as 'the curse of the self':

> [T]he capacity to self-reflect distorts our perceptions about the world, leads us to draw inaccurate conclusions about ourselves and other people, and thus prompts us to make bad decisions based on faulty information. The self conjures up a great deal of human suffering in the form of negative emotions . . . by allowing us to ruminate about the past or imagine what might befall us in the future.[7]

Instead, we would do better to stick with tried and trusted routines. However, traditional routines work only in recurrent and predictable circumstances. Certainly, some newly acquired skills may later become embodied and operate as 'second nature', as with driving on 'auto-pilot' – until an emergency occurs. But others remain intransigently discursive, defying routinisation (as in writing a book). Where novel situations are concerned, the more appropriate piece of folk wisdom is 'Look before you leap.'

Contrary to this negativity towards internal conversation, the thesis defended in the present book is that reflexivity is the means by which we make our way through the world. This applies to the social world in particular, which can no longer be approached through embodied knowledge, tacit routines or traditional custom and practice alone – were that ever to have been the case for most, let alone all, people. Although reflexive deliberation is considered to be indispensable to the existence of any society, its scope has also been growing from the advent of modernity onwards. In the third millennium the fast-changing social world makes it incumbent on everyone to exercise more and more reflexivity in increasingly large tracts of their lives. Justifying the decline and fall of routinisation is the theme of the next chapter. The need to incorporate reflexivity more prominently in social theorising is its corollary.

Incorporating reflexivity

The reasons for promoting reflexivity to a central position within social theory are summarised in the following proposition. *The subjective powers of reflexivity mediate the role that objective structural or cultural powers play in influencing social action and are thus indispensable to explaining social outcomes.* This proposition raises three key questions about the nature of human action, which are listed below and will be examined in turn. The argument running through them and serving to justify the proposition is that none of these questions about the nature of human action in society is answerable without serious reference being made to people's reflexivity:

1 Why do people act at all? What motivates them and what are they (fallibly) trying to achieve by endorsing given courses of action? This entails an examination of their personal *concerns* and inner reflexive deliberations about how to go about realising them.
2 How do social properties influence the courses of action that people adopt? This involves a specification of how objective structural or cultural powers are reflexively *mediated*.
3 What exactly do people do? This requires an examination of the *variability* in the actions of those similarly socially situated and the differences in their processes of reflexivity.

The reflexive adoption of projects

'Social hydraulics' is the generic process assumed by those who hold that no recourse need be made to any aspect of human subjectivity in order to explain social action. All necessary components making up the *explanans* refer directly or indirectly to social powers, thus rendering any reference to personal powers irrelevant or redundant. Although few social theorists will go quite as far as that, if only because of the need to acknowledge our biological endowments, the growth of sociological imperialism comes extremely close to doing so. Indeed, the model of agency promoted by social constructionists, which I have characterised elsewhere as 'society's being',[8] subtracts all but our biological properties and powers from us as people and accredits them to the social side of the balance sheet. In consequence, each and every sociological explanation can be arrived at from the third-person perspective because any references to first-person subjectivity have already been reduced to social derivatives and, at most, permutations upon them. In consequence, anything that might count as genuine human reflexivity effectively evaporates. It lacks causal powers and represents only phenomenological froth. 'Hydraulic' theorising, which construes what we do in terms of the pushes and pulls to which we are subjected, is resisted throughout this book, in all its reductionist versions – social, philosophical or neuro-biological.

In contradistinction, internal conversation is presented as the manner in which we reflexively make our way through the world. It is what makes (most of us) 'active agents', people who can exercise some governance in their own lives, as opposed to 'passive agents' to whom things simply happen.[9] Being an 'active agent' hinges on the fact that individuals develop and define their ultimate concerns: those internal goods that they care about most,[10] the precise constellation of which makes for their concrete singularity as persons.[11] No one can have an ultimate concern and fail to do something about it. Instead, each person seeks to develop a concrete course of action to realise that concern by elaborating a 'project', in the (fallible) belief that to accomplish this project is to realise one's concern. Action itself thus depends upon the existence of what are termed 'projects', where a project stands for any course of action intentionally engaged upon by a human being. Thus, the answer to why we act at all is in order to promote our concerns; we form 'projects' to advance or to protect what we care about most.

If projects were optional, in the strong sense that people could live without them, the social would be like the natural world, governed only by the laws of nature. Human beings are distinctive not as the bearer of projects, which is a characteristic people share with every animal, but because of their reflexive ability to design (and redesign) many of the projects they pursue. If we are to survive and thrive, we have to be practitioners, and the definition of a successful practice is the realisation of a particular project in the relevant part of the environment. The ubiquity of human projects has three implications for the relationship between subjects and their natural environment, which includes the social order.

Firstly, the pursuit of any human project entails the attempt to exercise our causal powers as human beings. Since this takes place in the world – that is, in the natural, practical and social orders – then the pursuit of a project necessarily activates the causal powers of entities which belong to one of these three orders. Which powers are activated (beneficially or detrimentally) is contingent upon the nature of the project entertained and, of course, it is always contingent whether or not a particular project is adopted at all. *The key point is that any human attempt to pursue a project entails two sets of causal powers: our own and those pertaining to part of natural reality.* Generically, the outcome is dependent upon the relationship between these two sets.

Secondly, these two kinds of causal powers work in entirely different ways once they are activated. On the one hand, the properties of objects in the natural order, artefacts in the practical order and structural and cultural properties in the social order are very different from one another, but nevertheless the exercise of their causal powers is *automatic*. If and when these emergent properties are activated, then, *ceteris paribus*, they simply work in a specific way in relation to other things. Thus, water has the power to buoy up certain entities and it does so by virtue of its constitution in relation to the specific density of objects – logs float and stones sink. On the other hand, most, though not all, human powers work reflexively rather than automatically.[12] We have the power to lift various objects in our vicinity but also the ability to determine whether we do so or not.

Thirdly, when our causal powers as human beings are interacting with those of different parts of the world, the outcome is rarely just a matter of their primary congruence or incongruence. Certainly, once the causal powers of objects, artefacts or structural and cultural properties are activated they will tendentially obstruct or facilitate our projects to very varying degrees. Conversely, the reflexive nature of human powers means that actual outcomes are matters of secondary determination, governed by our inner deliberations about such obstructions and facilitations, under our own descriptions. We often have the capacity to suspend both: suspending that which would advance our aims by engaging in inappropriate action and suspending that which would impede our aims by circumventory activities. Generically, we

Reflexivity and social life 171

possess the powers of both resistance and subversion or of co-operation and adaptation. Clearly, our degrees of freedom vary in relation to what we confront, but whether or not and how we use them remains contingent upon our reflexivity.

Thus, our physical well-being depends upon establishing successful practices in the natural world; our performative competence relies upon acquiring skilful practices in relation to material artefacts; and our self-worth hinges upon developing rewarding practices in society. It follows that the attempted realisation of any project immediately enmeshes us in the properties and powers of the respective order of natural reality in relation to our own.

Hence, in nature, the project of swimming, whether conceived of by design or through accident, ineluctably entails the interaction of two sets of causal powers. Of course, if *per impossible*, no one had ever sought to swim, then the natural power that enables us to float in water would have been unrealised for humanity. Yet this power is nonetheless real even if it had never been exercised. However, the project of swimming quite literally plunges us into the causal powers of rivers, pools and the sea. We do not instantiate them; rather, we have to interact with them and to discover whether accommodation between their powers and our own can lead to a successful practice – in this case, swimming. Some people never do swim, because reflexively they doubt the water's real powers and also lack sufficient reason for overcoming their frightened incredulity.

Similarly, in the practical world we entertain such projects as throwing a spear, getting through a door or using a computer. But these cannot become skilful practices unless and until we learn how to interact with the causal powers of the objects in question, powers which are usually termed affordances and resistances. A door latch affords a means of opening a door, if used properly, but reflexivity can leave the power of the latch unexercised if our experience has persuaded us that this door, or doors in general, open by being pushed. Improper usage, such as pushing against a latch,[13] will simply meet with resistance. Successful practice depends upon accommodating ourselves to such affordances and resistances, as we do all the time when driving a car.

Matters are no different in the social order, where many of the projects that we pursue necessarily involve us with constraints and enablements. As with the other two orders of natural reality, life in society is impossible without projects; each one of its members has myriads of them every day. Of course we do not usually think of such things as catching buses, going to the pub or taking the dog for a walk in these terms. Nevertheless, a change of circumstances can make us realise that this is precisely what they are: namely, successful social practices which have become taken for granted as embodied knowledge. Yet, any rail strike makes getting from here to there a serious reflexive project. Prohibition had the same effect for acquiring a drink, as did foot-and-mouth regulations for finding somewhere to exercise the dog. As in the other two orders, meeting with serious social constraints incites not only reflexive circumvention by some but also resignation to the abandonment of such projects by many.

To summarise, the pursuit of human projects in the social domain frequently encounters structural properties and activates them as powers. In such cases there are two sets of causal powers involved in any attempt to develop a successful social practice: those of subjects themselves and those of relevant structural or cultural properties. The causal powers of structures are exercised *inter alia* as constraints and enablements which work automatically, even though they are activity dependent in both their origin and exercise, whereas human powers work reflexively. Certainly, it is the case that the perception (or anticipation) of constraints or enablements can serve as a deterrent or an encouragement, but this is the same in both the natural and the practical orders and, in any case, this effect is a result of our (fallible) reflexive judgements. Finally, under all but the most stringent constraints agents have the capacity to suspend the exercise of constraints (and enablements) through their circumventory (or renunciatory) actions. In turn, these actions depend upon our knowledgeability and commitment. The establishment of a successful social practice is dependent upon the adaptive ingenuity of reflexive subjects. They must necessarily take account of the causal powers of social properties, under their own descriptions, but are not determined by them in the conception, the pursuit or the realisation of their projects.

The reflexive mediation of structural and cultural properties

Whilst resisting 'social hydraulics' it is necessary to allow for a milder form of objective 'social conditioning'. Central to an acceptable account of such conditioning is Roy Bhaskar's statement that 'the causal power of social forms is mediated through social agency'.[14] This is surely correct, because unless the properties of structure and culture are held to derive from people and their doings and to exert their causal effects through people and their actions, theorising would be guilty of reification. Nevertheless, the linking process is not complete *because what is meant by that crucial word 'though' has not been unpacked.*

Vague references to the process of 'social conditioning' are insufficient. This is because to condition entails the existence of something that is conditioned and, since conditioning is not determinism, this process necessarily involves the interplay between two different kinds of causal powers: those pertaining to structures and those belonging to subjects. Therefore, an adequate conceptualisation of 'conditioning' must deal explicitly with the interplay between these two powers. Firstly, this involves a specification of *how* structural and cultural powers impinge upon agents, and secondly of *how* agents use their own personal powers to act 'so rather than otherwise' in such situations. Thus, there are two elements involved, the 'impingement upon' (which is objective) and the 'response to it' (which is subjective).

On the whole, social theory appears to have conceptualised the objective side satisfactorily in terms of cultural and structural properties impinging upon people by shaping the social situations they confront. Often this confrontation is involuntary, as with people's natal social context and its associated life chances. Often it is voluntary, like getting married. In either case, these objective conditioning influences are transmitted to agency by shaping the situations that subjects live with, have to confront or would confront if they chose to do x, y or z. Sometimes they impinge as constraints and enablements upon various courses of action and sometimes by distributing different types of vested interests or objective interests to different (groups of) people, which can enhance or reduce their motivation to undertake a given course of action.

However, what this non-deterministic account of 'conditioning' usually omits is why people do not respond in uniform fashion under the same structured circumstances. Subjects who are similarly situated can debate, both internally and externally, about appropriate courses of action and come to different conclusions. This is one of the major reasons why Humean constant conjunctions are not found between structural and cultural influences and action outcomes. At best, what are detected are empirical tendencies in action patterns, which are consonant with objective influences having affected them. These must remain nothing more than trends, partly because external contingencies intervene, given that the social system is open, but partly because a second causal power is *necessarily at play* – namely the personal power to reflect subjectively upon one's circumstances and to decide what to do in them or about them. Such inalienable powers of human reflexivity would generate variations in action responses even if it were possible to achieve conditions of laboratory closure. In short, the conceptualisation of this process of mediation between structure and agency is usually not fully adequate because it does not fully incorporate the role played by human subjectivity in general. In particular, it omits the part reflexivity plays in enabling subjects to design and determine their responses to the structured circumstances in which they find themselves, in the light of what they personally care about most.

Let me now attempt to improve upon this generic account of social conditioning by presenting it as mediated by human reflexivity. The process of 'conditioning' has been seen to entail the exercise of two sets of causal powers: those of the property that 'conditions' and those of the property that is 'conditioned'. This is clearest where constraints and enablements are concerned, the obvious point being that a constraint requires something to constrain and an enablement needs something to enable. These are not intransitive terms because if, *per impossible*, no subject ever conceived of any project, he or she could be neither constrained nor enabled.

For example, the mere existence of a centralised educational system does not constrain curricular variations unless and until somebody advances the policy of, say, introducing geographical or linguistic variants. Only when that project is mooted does centralisation become a constraint, *ceteris paribus*. Equally, in the cultural realm, if there is a contradiction between two beliefs or two theories it remains a purely logical matter, existing out there in the 'Universal Library',[15] but is inert until and unless someone wants to uphold one of those ideas, assert one of those ideas or do something with one of those ideas. In other words, *for an objective structural or cultural property to exercise its causal powers, such powers have to be activated by agents.*

The proper incorporation of personal powers into the conceptualisation of conditioning entails the following three points. Firstly, that social properties or, more exactly, the exercise of their powers are dependent upon the existence of what have been termed 'projects', where a project stands for any course of action intentionally engaged upon by a human being. These projects, *as subjectively conceived of by people*, are necessary for the activation of social properties – that is, their transformation into powers. Secondly, only if there is a relationship of congruence or incongruence between the social property and the project of the person(s) will the latter activate the former. Congruity or incongruity need not be the case. For example, if someone's project was to engage in regular private prayer, no structural power on earth could prevent it though, of course, socio-cultural influences might be at work discouraging the activity of praying. When congruence prevails it represents a structural enablement and where incongruence exists it constitutes a structural constraint. Thirdly, and most importantly, subjects have to respond to these influences by using their own personal powers to deliberate reflexively, always under their own descriptions, about how to act in such situations. What is unique about the reflexivity of human beings is that it can involve anticipation. A constraint or an enablement need not have impinged or impacted, it could just be (fallibly) foreseen. Hence, the efficacy of any social property is at the mercy of the subjects' reflexive activity.

In the case of any such property, outcomes vary enormously with agents' creativity in dreaming up brand new responses, even to situations that may have occurred many times before. Ultimately, the precise outcome varies with subjects' personal concerns, degrees of commitment and with the costs different agents will pay to see their projects through in the face of structural hindrances. Equally, they vary with subjects' readiness to avail themselves of enablements. The one result that is rarely, if ever, found is a complete uniformity of response on the part of every person who encounters the same constraint or the same enablement. The deliberative process involved has nothing in common with cost–benefit analysis. It is emotionally charged, rather than being a simple exercise in instrumental rationality, because it is maintained that our emotions (as distinct from moods) are commentaries on our concerns,[16] which supply the 'shoving power' leading to action (or the resistance resulting in inaction).

To deal adequately with this variation in subjects' responses, when agents are in the same social situation, does indeed mean addressing their subjectivity. It entails acknowledging their *personal powers*, in particular their power of reflexivity to think about themselves in relation to society and to come to different conclusions that lead to variable action outcomes. In short, without knowledge about their internal deliberations we cannot account for exactly what they do. This can be quickly illustrated by considering another potential structural power, namely the differential placement of agents in relation to the distributions of resources and the impossibility of deducing determinate courses of action from such positionings alone. Suppose a collectivity of agents is well placed in terms of remuneration, repute and representation – or 'class', 'status' and 'power'. These positionings cannot in themselves be assumed to engender reproductive projects, despite this group having much to lose objectively if they do not adopt them. To begin with the most obvious reason, not all people are guided by their objective interests; they can choose to marry downwards, to take vows of poverty, to renounce titles or to say a plague on the rat-race. Thus, at best, this leaves a probability statement about the doings of 'most people most of the time', but to what actual courses of action do these probabilities attach?

Since there is no answer to that question we are thrown back upon empirical generalisations such as 'the greater the cost of a project, the less likely are people to entertain it'. Not only is that no explanation whatsoever (merely another quest for Humean constant conjunctions) but also, far from having eliminated human reflexivity, it relies upon a banal and most dubious form of it. Instead, sociologists covertly recognise that subjectivity cannot be ignored. Yet, more often than not, this 'recognition' consists in it being smuggled in by social theorists *imputing subjective motives* to agents rather than examining the subject's own reflexively defined reasons, aims and concerns. Analytically, the result is the 'Two-Stage Model' presented in Figure 9.1. Effectively, this model transforms the first-person subjective ontology [17] of the agent's internal conversation into a third-person 'objectivist' account proffered by the investigator.

Social realists have often been guilty of putting imputed responses to vested interests or objective interests into accounts of action as a kind of dummy for real and efficacious human subjectivity. There are many worse exemplars, and probably the worst is rational choice theory, which imputes instrumental rationality alone[18] to all subjects as they supposedly seek to maximise their preference schedules in order to become 'better off' in terms of some indeterminate future 'utiles'. Subjectively, every agent is reduced to a bargain hunter and the human pursuit of the *Wertrationalität* is discountenanced.[19] Bourdieu, too, frequently endorsed an empty formalism about subjectivity such that people's positions ('semi-consciously' and 'quasi-automatically'[20]) engendered dispositions to reproduce their positions. Such theoretical formulations seem to lose a lot of the rich and variable subjectivity that features prominently in his *La Misère du Monde*. In the cultural counterpart of the above, discourse 'theory' simply holds these ill-defined ideational clusters to have gained unproblematic hegemony over the subjectivity of a given population.

The inadequacies of any version of the 'Two-Stage Model' can be summarised as follows: (1) the failure to investigate anybody's subjectivity; (2) the imputation of

---

The Two-Stage Model

1 Structural and/or cultural properties *objectively* shape the situations that agents confront involuntarily and *exercise powers of constraint and enablement* in relation to –
2 Subjective properties imputed to agents and assumed to govern their actions:

- promotion of vested interests (critical realism)
- instrumental rationality (rational choice theory)
- habitus/induced repertoires (Bourdieu/discourse theory)

Figure 9.1 The Two-Stage Model.

homogeneous concerns and projects to some given group or collectivity; (3) the endorsement of 'passive agents'; and (4) the foundational denial that the personal power of reflexivity needs to be understood. Sociology can neither dispense with reflexivity nor make do with such impoverished acknowledgements of it. If this personal property and power is to be given its due, to do so entails replacing the third-person imputation of subjectivity by its first-person investigation.

It is proposed that 'reflexivity' be incorporated as a personal property of human subjects, which is prior to, relatively autonomous from and possesses causal efficacy in relation to structural or cultural properties. Clearly, this means that only limited tracts of people's subjective lives are pertinent to social theory. For example, I presume no one would suggest that a dislike of spinach has causal powers beyond a capacity to disrupt family tea time. However, I want to defend the much more concrete response, namely that the aspect of 'subjectivity' which should be given its due is our reflexivity. In other words, 'reflexivity' is put forward as the answer to *how* 'the causal power of social forms is mediated *through* human agency'. Our internal conversations perform this mediatory role by virtue of the fact that they are the way in which we deliberate about ourselves in relation to the social situations that we confront, certainly fallibly, always incompletely and necessarily under our own descriptions, because that is the only way we can know or decide anything.

Reflexivity and the endorsement of different courses of action

Reflexivity, exercised through internal conversation, is advanced as the process which not only mediates the impact of social forms upon us but also determines our responses to them. Firstly, reflexive mediation is essential for giving an account of precisely what we do rather than a statement about probable courses of action. And, in relation to constraints and enablements, agential responses can vary greatly: from evasion through compliance to strategic manipulation or subversion. Secondly, if it is held that agential subjectivity has itself been moulded by social influences, such as ideology, 'habitus' or, for argument's sake, 'discourse', it is impossible to ascertain for whom this is and is not the case without examining their inner dialogue. It cannot be the case for all, because 'the sociologist' has seen through these *attempts* at ideational misrepresentation in order to be able to describe them, but cannot claim a monopoly on this ability.

Certainly, because we are not infallible, it can be maintained that social factors affect agents' outlooks without people's awareness. That would be the case for ideological influences or for members of a social class overestimating an objective obstacle, like those working-class parents who used to turn down grammar school places on the grounds that 'they are not for the likes of us'. Again, however, we cannot know that this is the case without examining agents' subjectivity, their reflexive internal conversations. Without that we cannot discover what 'ideology' or 'social class' has encouraged one person to believe but failed to persuade another to accept. What cannot be assumed is that every ideological effort will or can be successful in instilling all people with the beliefs in question. Ideologies, however hegemonic, are not in themselves influences, but rather attempts to influence. They

> **The Three-Stage Model**
>
> 1 Structural and cultural properties *objectively* shape the situations that agents confront involuntarily, and *inter alia* possess generative powers of constraint and enablement in relation to
> 2 Subjects' own constellations of concerns, as *subjectively* defined in relation to the three orders of natural reality: nature, practice and the social.
> 3 Courses of action are produced through the *reflexive deliberations* of subjects who *subjectively* determine their practical projects in relation to their *objective* circumstances.

Figure 9.2 The Three-Stage Model.

too, as a cultural counterpart of structural factors, involve both impingement upon the subject and reception by the subject. Reception is obviously heterogeneous, or no one would ever have accepted a grammar school place for their working-class child and no counter-ideology would ever have been formulated.

In brief, it will be argued that our personal powers are exercised through reflexive inner dialogue and that internal conversation is responsible for the delineation of our concerns, the definition of our projects and, ultimately, the determination of our practices in society. It is agential reflexivity which actively mediates between our structurally shaped circumstances and what we deliberately make of them. There is an important caution here: people cannot make what they please of their circumstances. To maintain otherwise would be to endorse idealism and to commit the epistemic fallacy.[21] Indeed, if people get their objective circumstances badly wrong, these subjects pay the objective price whether or not they do so comprehendingly. To believe incorrectly that one can service a heavy mortgage results in foreclosure, with further objective consequences for obtaining alternative accommodation. What reflexivity does do is to mediate by activating structural and cultural powers, and in so doing there is no single and predictable outcome. This is because subjects can exercise their reflexive powers in different ways according to their very different concerns and considerations.

Thus, an alternative 'Three-Stage Model' is advanced, one that gives both objectivity and subjectivity their due and also explicitly incorporates their interplay through the process of reflexive mediation (Figure 9.2).

Stage 1 deals with the kind of specification already developed about how 'social forms' impinge and impact on people by moulding their situations. This I summarised as follows in an earlier work:

> Given their pre-existence, structural and cultural emergents shape the social environment to be inhabited. These results of past actions are deposited in the form of current situations. They account for what there is (structurally and culturally) to be distributed and also for the shape of such distributions; for the

nature of the extant role array, the proportion of positions available at any time and the advantages/disadvantages associated with them; for the institutional configuration present and for those second order emergent properties of compatibility and incompatibility, that is whether the respective operations of institutions are matters of obstruction or assistance to one another. In these ways, situations are objectively defined for their subsequent occupants or incumbents.[22]

However, these social features become only generative powers, rather than unactivated properties, in relationship to subjects' projects.

Doubtless it will be asked: 'Don't these social factors affect people's motivation and thus the very projects they pursue?' There are indeed structural properties, such as vested interests, and cultural properties, such as ideology, that can motivate by encouraging and discouraging people from particular courses of action without their personal awareness. These are the unacknowledged conditions of action, yet, whilst it may seem paradoxical, it is maintained here that they have first to be found good by a person before they can influence the projects she entertains. How is this seeming paradox resolved? The answer lies in being precise about what a subject needs to be aware of in order to be influenced. Let us first take a structural example. For a person to find a vested interest good does not entail that she has full discursive penetration of that property, as if she were endowed with all the qualities of the best sociologist. Subjects do not and cannot know everything that is going on, or there would be no such things as 'unacknowledged conditions'. There are indeed, but all those conditions need to do in order to shape a subject's motivation is to shape the situation in which she finds herself.

Take a young academic, whose mother tongue is English. What she recognises and takes for granted about her situation are aspects of its ease: books are quickly translated into English, which is also one of the official languages at conferences, is used in the best-known journals and so forth. What she does not need to possess is discursive penetration about *why* her situation is so comparatively easy and rewarding.She does not need to acknowledge that she is a beneficiary of neo-colonialism,which has given English the academic status it has today. In order for her motivation towards her academic career to be enhanced and for her to follow courses of action to this end all she has to recognise consciously and to find good is, for example, the ease and fluency with which she makes interventions at her first international conferences.

Unacknowledged cultural conditions work in exactly the same way, by shaping situations. This same young academic might rapidly be appointed to the editorial board of a journal and regard this as a further indication of her success. However, at successive board meetings she finds her interventions being interrupted, her suggestions ignored and her reservations overridden. What she feels in this situation is unease, and her motivation to participate or even to attend declines accordingly. Her discomfort is all she needs to know in order for her to back out of this potential opening. It is not necessary for her to understand that she had been an instance of female 'tokenism' in order to explain her increasing silence and gradual withdrawal.

Structural factors also operate as deterrents capable of depressing agential motivation and discouraging certain courses of action. They do so by attaching different opportunity costs to the same course of action (such as house purchase) for different parts of the population. This is how 'life chances' exert causal powers, but it must be noted that their outcomes are only empirical tendencies. And what no tendency can explain is why x becomes a home owner and y does not, when both are similarly socially situated. That is a question of the subjects' own concerns and their internal deliberations, which govern whether or not particular people find the cost worth paying. The simple fact that somebody is faced with a deterrent, in the form of an opportunity cost, does not mean that they are necessarily deterred, any more than does the fact that people inherit vested interests mean they are bound to defend them – Tony Benn renounced a title in order to sit in the House of Commons.

In short, there are a number of ways in which both structural and cultural factors can affect people's motivation and, hence, the projects that they will formulate. However, for such social factors to be influential they *do not first have to become internalised as part of a subject's dispositions*. Indeed, some of the ways in which they work – such as giving (situational) encouragement or discouragement – are incompatible with the notion of prior internalisation. Someone's projects cannot be discouraged and thus reduced in the light of their circumstances if their expectations had already been adjusted downwards. In that case, discouragement would never occur.

Certainly, an accumulation of discouraging (or encouraging) experiences *may* become internalised as expectations. Once again, it is impossible to know for whom this is or is not the case without examining the form that their reflexive deliberations have taken during the course of their biographies. And subjects are not uniform in this respect. Thus, we will later meet Billy, an unskilled worker who had been made redundant four times as a victim of the progressive decline in manufacturing industry. On each occasion, his response was to pick himself up and resume the struggle to 'work himself up'. Equally, those who 'accept' discouragement do not simply give up and become 'passive' victims of their circumstances. Instead, they actively use their reflexivity to devise 'second' or 'third' best projects for themselves, as will be seen with Joan in Chapter 3. These are not 'passive agents', dispositionally reconciled to their experiential lot. They are reflexively aware of unfairness and regretful about foreclosed opportunities, but continue to do what they can about what they care about most in circumstances not of their making or choosing.

Stage 2 examines the interface between the above and agential projects themselves for, to repeat, it is not personal properties that interact directly with structural or cultural properties, but subjects' powers as expressed through the pursuit of their projects that activate the powers of social forms. The generic questions posed by a subject over her lifetime and the answers she gives herself during her life course can be distilled into two: 'What do I want?' and 'How do I go about getting it?' The answer to the first question is undoubtedly influenced by what a subject knows or finds out, because such information is not evenly distributed throughout society. Nevertheless, an active subject is still required to actualise such influences, which are not hydraulic determinants. The readiest way of activating these social powers is when a subject can answer the question 'What do I want?' from within her natal context and does so without looking any further. She thus confirms her context by confining her subjective deliberations to it. However, the majority of interviewees could not and did not do so. Some temporised (usually by staying on at school), whilst others actively courted experience and sought information from beyond their social backgrounds.

In other words, the fact that there are indeed socially inegalitarian distributions of information does not generate a uniformity of response from those similarly situated in relation to them. How individual people answer the above two questions involves a dialectical interplay between their 'concerns' – as they reflexively define them – and their 'contexts' – as they reflexively respond to them. The answers that they give to themselves are arrived at through internal conversation. To explain their actions entails understanding their intentions, as arrived at through external 'inspection' and inner dialogue.

In relation to the question, 'What do I want?' I have earlier conceptualised the internal process of answering it as the 'DDD scheme',[23] representing three significant moments that can be distinguished as phases of the life-long internal conversation: discernment, deliberation and dedication.

1 Discernment is fundamentally about the subject putting together reflective, retrospective and prospective considerations about the desiderata to which she is drawn through an inner dialogue that compares and contrasts them. It is an inconclusive moment of review; at most, this self-talk begins to clarify our relationship to our reigning concerns because, as 'strong evaluators',[24] we cannot be lacking in concerns. It does so by clarifying our predominant satisfactions and dissatisfactions with our current way of life. Thus, the moment of discernment serves to highlight our positive concerns without discriminating between them. It is a process of book-marking in which actual and potential items of worth are registered for further consideration. Sifting of a negative kind is involved because, out of the plenitude of possible concerns available to anyone, only those that have been logged in constitute topics for further deliberation.

2 Deliberation is concerned with exploring the implications of endorsing a particular cluster of concerns from those pre-selected as desirable to the subject during the first moment. This is performed by disengaging the demands, the merits and the likely consequences of that constellation of concerns were the subject to embrace them. This phase of the inner dialogue ranges from the one extreme of discarding projects through comparing the worth of contesting concerns to the opposite pole of preliminary determination. Deliberation produces a very provisional ranking of the concerns with which a subject feels that she should and can live. Often, this phase of the process entails a visual projection of scenarios seeking to capture, as best the subject is able, the *modus vivendi* that would be involved, whilst listening to the emotional commentary that is provoked and evoked when imagining that particular way of life. Such musings are still inconclusive, but, as Peirce insisted: 'every man who does

Reflexivity and social life 181

accomplish great things is given to building elaborate castles in the air'.[25] We should be cautious about restricting acts of the imagination to 'great things' or 'golden deeds', because there is nothing necessarily heroic or idealistic about deliberation. What subjects warm to during this dialogical phase might be 'concerns' that are ignoble, associated 'projects' that are illegal and ensuing 'practices' that are illegitimate.

3 Dedication represents the culminating moment of experimentation between thought and feeling that has occupied the preceding phases. In it, the subject has to decide not only whether a *particular modus vivendi* is, in her view, worth living, but also whether or not she is capable of living such a life. Thus, the moment of dedication is also one of prioritisation because the very accentuation of someone's prime concern is simultaneously the relegation or elimination of their others. Within internal conversation, dedication is a phase of inner dialogical struggle because the completion (*pro tem*) of the dialogue has to achieve both prioritisation of and alignment between the concerns endorsed, but also resignation to those relinquished.

It is Stage 3 that has generally been neglected in social theorising, but which appears essential in order to conceptualise the process of mediation properly and completely. In Stage 3, by virtue of their powers of reflexivity, people deliberate about their objective circumstances in relation to their subjective concerns. They consult their projects to see whether they can realise them, including adapting them, adjusting them, abandoning them or enlarging them in the deliberative process. They alter their practices such that, if a course of action is going well, subjects may become more ambitious, and, if it is going badly, they may become more circumspect. It is this crucial Stage 3 that enables us all to try to do, to be or to become what we care about most in society – by virtue of our reflexivity.

This final stage of mediation is indispensable because, without it, we have no explanatory purchase on what exactly agents do. The absence of this purchase means settling for empirical generalisations about what 'most of the people do most of the time'. Sociologists often settle for even less: 'Under circumstance x, a statistically significant number of agents do y.' This spells a return to a quest for Humean constant conjunctions and, in consequence, a resignation to being *unable* to adduce a causal mechanism. Equally wanting is the procedure in which subjectivity is not properly investigated, but is improperly imputed, precisely because it cannot be eliminated.

In contradistinction to both of these unsatisfactory conclusions is an approach which gives the personal power of reflexivity its due. It is to this end that the present book is devoted. To accord reflexivity its due entails fully acknowledging three points about how we make our way through the world.

1 That our unique personal identities, which derive from our singular constellations of concerns, mean that we are radically heterogeneous as subjects. Even though we may share objective social positions, we may also seek very different ends from within them.

2 That our subjectivity is dynamic, not psychologically static or psychologically reducible, because we modify our own goals in terms of their contextual feasibility as we see it. As always, we are fallible, can get it wrong and have to pay the objective price for doing so.
3 That, for the most part, we are active rather than passive subjects because we adjust our projects to those practices that we believe we can realise. Subjects regularly evaluate their social situations in the light of their personal concerns and assess their projects in the light of their situations.

Unless these points are taken on board our way through the world is not a path that we ourselves help to chart and the various trajectories that we describe remain without explanation.

Notes

1 The main exceptions being American pragmatism and social psychology; the former contribution was discussed in my *Structure, Agency and the Internal Conversation*, Cambridge: Cambridge University Press, 2003, ch. 2 and the latter will be examined in the companion volume to this book, *The Reflexive Imperative*.
2 'Human beings have a wholly unique gift in the use of language, and that is that they can talk to themselves. Everybody does it, all the time' (note that the last phrase will receive some refinement in this text). Samuel C. Riccillo, 'Phylogenesis: Understanding the Biological Origins of Intrapersonal Communication', in Donna R. Vocate (ed.), *Intrapersonal Communication: Different Voices, Different Minds*, Hillsdale NJ, Lawrence Erlbaum, 1994, p. 36.
3 The Weberian distinction between 'action' and 'social action' is maintained here. Not all of our personal powers or the actions that we conceive and carry out by virtue of them can legitimately or usefully be considered as social: for example, the lone practice of meditation or of mountaineering. See Colin Campbell, *The Myth of Social Action*, Cambridge: Cambridge University Press, 1996 and also Archer, *Structure, Agency and the Internal Conversation*, ch. 1, 'The Private Life of the Social Subject'.
4 Gerald E. Myers, 'Introspection and Self-Knowledge', *American Philosophical Quarterly*, 23, 2, April 1986, p. 206.
5 Details about the empirical framework on which this study is based are found in Chapter 2 and in the Methodological appendix.
6 See the *Journal of Personality and Social Psychology* from 1970 to date. For example, see Timothy D. Wilson and Jonathan Schooler, 'Thinking Too Much: Introspection Can Reduce the Quality of Preferences and Decisions', *Journal of Personality and Social Psychology*, 60, 2, 1991.
7 Mark R. Leary, *The Curse of the Self*, Oxford, Oxford University Press, 2004, p. 19.
8 Margaret S. Archer, *Being Human: the Problem of Agency*, Cambridge, Cambridge University Press, 2000, ch. 3.
9 For this distinction, see Martin Hollis, *Models of Man: Philosophical Thoughts on Social Action*, Cambridge, Cambridge University Press, 1977.
10 See Harry G. Frankfurt, *The Importance of What We Care About*, Cambridge, Cambridge University Press, 1988, ch. 7 and A. McIntyre, *After Virtue*, London, Duckworth, 1981, pp. 187ff.
11 Archer, *Being Human*, ch. 9.
12 Obviously, there are many of our bodily liabilities, such as their responses to cancer or falling from heights, which are automatic rather than reflexive.
13 For a variety of practical examples see Donald Norman, *The Psychology of Everyday Things*, New York, HarperCollins, 1988.

14 Roy Bhaskar, *The Possibility of Naturalism*, Hemel Hempstead: Harvester, 1989, p. 26.
15 See Margaret S. Archer, *Culture and Agency: the Place of Culture in Social Theory*, Cambridge, Cambridge University Press, 1998, ch. 5. Metaphorically, the Universal Library is where all World Three items of knowledge are lodged.
16 Margaret S. Archer, 'Emotions as Commentaries on Human Concerns', in Jonathan Turner (ed.), *Theory and Research on Human Emotions*, Amsterdam, Elsevier, 2004, pp. 327–56. Thus, I do not follow Max Weber in representing 'affectual action' as a separate form of action.
17 Internal conversations have what John Searle calls a 'first-person ontology' because of their subjective mode of existence: 'each of my conscious states exists only as the state it is because it is experienced by me, the subject'. John Searle, *Mind, Language and Society*, London, Weidenfeld and Nicolson, 1999, p. 43.
18 See Margaret S. Archer and Jonathan Q. Tritter (eds), *Rational Choice Theory: Resisting Colonisation*, London, Routledge/Taylor and Francis, 2001.
19 Martin Hollis, 'Honour among Thieves', *Proceedings of the British Academy*, 75, 1989, pp. 163–80.
20 Pierre Bourdieu, *Outline of a Theory of Practice*, Cambridge, Cambridge University Press, 1977 and *The Logic of Practice*, Oxford, Polity Press, 1990.
21 The 'epistemic fallacy' is the substitution of how matters are taken to be for how they in fact are, even if we cannot or do not know the latter. See Andrew Collier, *Critical Realism*, London, Verso, 1994, pp. 76–85.
22 Margaret S. Archer, *Realist Social Theory*, Cambridge, Cambridge University Press, 1995, p. 201.
23 For a fuller discussion see Archer, *Being Human*, ch. 7.
24 Charles Taylor, 'Self-Interpreting Animals', in his *Human Agency and Language*, Cambridge, Cambridge University Press, 1985, esp. pp. 65–8.
25 Charles Sanders Peirce, cited in William H. Davies, *Peirce's Epistemology*, The Hague, Martinus Nijhoff, 1972, p. 63.

10 A brief history of how reflexivity becomes imperative

Does reflexivity have a history? It seems that, like language, upon which reflexivity depends – without being entirely linguistic – it must have a prehistory. That is, there must have been a time before which *homo erectus* or his kinfolk had learned to speak and to be capable of mentally reflecting about their intentionality. In other words, there was a before and an after. What is not obvious is whether or not 'afterwards' was a long, continuous and unfinished process of constant elaboration, or if reflexivity's biography consisted of distinct and discontinuous periods. Another way of putting the same question is: does human reflexivity show distinct variations in the modes through which it is practised and, if so, were such modalities subject to change over time in response to changing historical circumstances?

A difficulty arises in posing the question in this way: namely, that it would be acknowledged in some disciplines but not in others. On the one hand, in psycholinguistics and as early as 1934 Vygotsky was calling for a 'history of reflexivity'.[1] Certainly, his appeal resulted in very little take-up but not, it seems, because his request was unintelligible or unacceptable. It appears more likely that what accounted for the lack of response was the need for considerable historical probing and bold conjecturing at precisely the time when it was safer for his Russian collaborators to confine themselves to laboratory work and to seek political cover behind 'scientism'. On the other hand, Western social theorists have shared the same reluctance to respond to Vygotsky's call. Instead, their common denominator has been to regard *reflexivity as a homogeneous phenomenon*. Either people exercised it or they didn't, but, when they did, they were engaging in much the same kind of practice and for much the same kinds of reason. At most, they could do so more or less, as in what has recently become known as 'the extended reflexivity thesis'.[2]

Thus, with some oversimplification, the great American pragmatists – who alone took reflexivity seriously at the end of the nineteenth century and at the beginning of the twentieth – generically endorsed the formula that action would follow routine guidelines and resort would be made to reflexive deliberations only when subjects were confronted with unforeseen and problematic situations. Despite the enormous contribution of James, Dewey, Mead and, in particular, Pierce in conceptualizing reflexivity as operating through the 'internal conversation' (rather than as a process of introspection), there is nothing in their works that introduces a historical panorama of changes in relation to the type of reflexivity practised.[3] This was the case despite their willingness to engage boldly with the past and especially the future in other respects. In short, it seems that to them 'problematic situations' would be encountered at all times and the ahistorical response would be a resort to the mental activities and inner dialogue that constituted reflexivity *tout court*.[4]

Conversely, there is the current account proffered by Beck and Giddens which, again with oversimplifications, maintains that for a very long time traditionalism could operate as the guide to action and that only with the arrival of the 'juggernaut' or the 'risk' society did traditional action give way to reflexive action. This makes reflexivity itself a 'newcomer', largely confined by Beck to the onset of what he calls Second Wave modernity. Again, there is no suggestion that reflexivity – when it arrives – is other than a homogeneous mental practice. However, it does arrive on the recent historical scene and with the implication that its advent is for all. This is in contradistinction to Bourdieu's tenacious retention of the *socialized habitus* as the guide to action and his confinement of reflexivity to a practice that could be *collectively developed* only by members of the academic community. The same tenacity is shown by those of his successors who engage in concept-stretching and advance a *flexible habitus* to secure enduring conceptual relevance in the new millennium.[5] Whatever else may be said about this manoeuvre, it contains no suggestion that, if this notion truly seeks to incorporate reflexivity, it will be practised in different ways by different people and differently in different social settings.

These debates will not be re-entered now (their salient elements will be picked up in the next chapter). Instead, two propositions will be advanced here. Firstly, that *reflexivity is not a homogeneous phenomenon but is exercised through distinctive modes*, and that one such modality is dominant for almost every person at any given time. This is an empirical proposition about the present. Secondly, it will be suggested that there *is a historical succession in the dominance of such reflexive modes*. In other words, reflexivity does have a history. Although this is advanced largely in theoretical terms, nothing defies its empirical investigation in principle.

Different ways of being reflexive

The two earlier works in this trilogy outlined four modes of reflexivity *practised by all of us some of the time* through the internal conversations we hold with ourselves: communicative, autonomous, meta- and fractured reflexivity.[6] These are summarized in Figure 10.1.

They can be illustrated by the following everyday example, where someone is pictured using all four modes in relation to a single event. A man with little experience of dentistry begins to suspect that his persistent toothache might require an extraction. He shares these forebodings with friends, thus seeking their confirmation or otherwise by employing the communicative pattern of 'thought and talk'. The same man, now convinced of his need for dental attention, sets out alone, checks the traffic and safely crosses the road to a dentist, practising the self-contained autonomous mode. However, on closer inspection, this dental practice strikes him as appearing expensive and exclusive. He has second thoughts and decides to find a more modest one, thus meta-reflexively revising his first inclination and moving on.

186 *How reflexivity becomes imperative*

Communicative Reflexivity

Internal Conversations need to be confirmed and completed by others before they lead to action

Autonomous Reflexivity

Internal Conversations are self-contained, leading directly to action

Meta-Reflexivity

Internal Conversations critically evaluate previous inner dialogues and are critical about effective action in society

Fractured Reflexivity

Internal Conversations cannot lead to purposeful courses of action, but intensify personal distress and disorientation resulting in expressive action

---

Figure 10.1 Modes of reflexivity.

Finally, an unsympathetic receptionist at his revised choice of dental practice may leave him vacillating between his present pain and his enhanced fear of the extraction procedure she has just described to him; in the fractured mode, unable to decide, he mutters unhappily that he needs to think about it and may come back later.

Although we all do resort to each of the four modes of internal conversation on different occasions and in different situations, the vast majority of the Coventry sample (over 93 per cent) were shown to have a *dominant mode*, with the four being rather evenly distributed across the small, stratified sample.[7] Their dominant modalities were found to be very general in their deployment by subjects, remaining consistent over the following range of mental activities, as interpreted by interviewees: 'mulling over' (a problem, situation or relationship), 'planning' (the day, the week or further ahead), 'imagining' (as in 'what would happen if . . . ?'), 'deciding' (debating what to do or what is for the best), 'rehearsing' (practising what to say or do), 'reliving' (some event, episode or relationship), 'prioritising' (working out what matters to you most), 'imaginary conversations' (with people you know, have known or know about), 'budgeting' (working out if you can afford to do something, in terms of money, time or effort) and 'clarifying' (sorting out what you think about some issue, person or problem).

In other words, reflexivity is not conceptualized here in 'decisionist' or 'rationalist' terms. As can be seen from the above list, a given subject might (and approximately half agreed that they did) engage in self-talk in relation to most, though not all, of the above activities. That is quite compatible with various stock characters: the instrumental rationalist (who would spend most time on 'planning', 'deciding' and 'budgeting'); the archetypal academic (preoccupied with 'mulling over' and 'clarifying'); any kind of day-dreamer (lost in 'imagination', 'reliving' and 'imaginary conversations'); or a scrupulous moralist (preoccupied with 'debating' what is for the best, 'prioritising' and 'clarifying'). These are only lay stereotypes. In their private mental lives real subjects will focus their intra-personal dialogues on any combination or permutation of the above activities because no rules govern what we choose to dwell upon in the privacy of our own heads. Doubtless, at times we have all been enjoined by others to 'wake up', to 'get real' or to 'switch on', but we also know how transitory were our propitiatory responses. Hence, we know too that our internal conversations defy external regulation. As Norbert Wiley puts it, 'we are little gods in the world of inner speech'.[8]

Because we are, it follows that nothing can ultimately prevent us from devoting the vast majority of our internal conversation to anything from contemplation through trivial diversion to vituperation. Equally, nothing stops us from blocking out this self-talk with earphones and a music player. Wiley is also correct when he continues: 'This is our own private little world. It is nobody's business but our own, and it does tasks for us that could not be accomplished in any other way.'[9] Some of these tasks are my concern here, although there are no grounds for asserting that they dominate our inner dialogue to the exclusion of quotidian questions, trivial pursuits or abstract ruminations. Nor do they exclude the days and times when, though we wish to concentrate upon some particular issue or activity, our inner conversations are distracted and flit about like midges or are leadenly unproductive through fatigue.

Nevertheless, internal conversation 'does tasks for us that could not be accomplished in any other way'. Specifically, to have a personal identity is defined by our constellation of concerns and to have a concern is necessarily to be concerned about it.[10] If something matters to us it is nonsense to say that we pay it no attention. The life of our minds is always, to some extent, taken up with the life we want to live. Because it is human life, it will mainly be lived socially and many (though not all) of our concerns will be explicitly social in kind.[11] Thus, the prime social task of our reflexivity is to outline, in broad brush strokes, the kind of *modus vivendi* we would find satisfying and sustainable within society as we know it and know ourselves under our own fallible descriptions. What we are attempting to accomplish is to marry our concerns to a way of life that allows their realization, a way of life about which we can be wholehearted, investing ourselves in it with each personifying its requirements in our own and unique manner.[12] Hence we gain and maintain some governance over our own lives. This is a supremely reflexive task, entailing 'strong evaluation' of our social context in the light of our concerns and adjusting these concerns in the light of our circumstances.[13]

Whilst everybody has to do this for themselves reflexively, through their internal conversations, that does not imply that subjects have to do it alone. To engage in inner dialogue is to activate our personal powers, but that does not make any of us individualistic monads.[14] We all receive and use external information, we all engage in external as well as internal conversation and, above all, being human refers to a quintessentially relational being.[15] Our human relations and the relationality between them form part of both our internal and our external conversations. Finally, it cannot be over-emphasized that this reflexive task does not turn subjects into the humanoids of Rational Choice Theory. To seek 'a life worth living' – which is quite different from Beck's notion of 'a life of one's own' – is in no sense seeking to become 'better off' (unless this is a tautology) or to 'maximize one's preference schedule', precisely because *concerns are not preferences*. Rather, they are commitments that are ends in themselves and constitutive of who we are, for whose sake we will be altruistic, self-sacrificing and sometimes ready to die and always, at least, be trying to live. They are also definitive of our varying forms of social engagement.

Modes of reflexivity and situational logics of action

Drawing upon the findings of my previous two studies, the dominant mode of reflexivity practised by singular subjects did not appear to be psychologically determined because structural and cultural characteristics of subjects' social backgrounds were found to be closely associated with the predominance of different modes of reflexivity.[16] Specifically, those who grew up in a close, harmonious and geo-locally stable family – thus experiencing 'contextual continuity' – showed a strong tendency to be practitioners of communicative reflexivity; those experiencing exactly the opposite – that is, 'contextual discontinuity' – displayed an equally marked proclivity for the practice of autonomous reflexivity. Subjects who had come to endorse concerns at some variance with those contested in their natal backgrounds – thus confronting 'contextual incongruity' – were the adults who tended to practice meta-reflexivity as their dominant mode. Fractured reflexivity was related to the experience of various severely disruptive occurrences, such as acute illness, involuntary redundancy or unexpected marital breakdown, none of which appears amenable to psychological reduction. However, neither is it ruled out that individual psychology may have a part to play here, nor that some subjects might be more psychologically susceptible to 'fractured reflexivity' under these kinds of circumstances, which are not universally associated with this effect. Individual psychology may indeed have an important contribution to make about the sources of these propensities towards a particular dominant mode.[17]

Nevertheless, the importance of contextual factors does raise historical questions about the distribution of the different dominant modes of reflexivity over time because contextual 'continuity', 'discontinuity' and 'incongruity' were respectively the lot of the majority of people during successive historical epochs. The answers must remain speculative, although they can be rendered rather more robust if taken in conjunction with a second question. It has been maintained that the new millennium is already a period of unprecedented morphogenesis and the aim of this book is to ascertain what effects this has had upon young people coming to maturity during it. If such effects are indeed detected in the dominant modes of reflexivity they are now practising or beginning to practise seriously, then it is expected that these would be mediated through prior transformations in their respective contextual backgrounds – which is what will be explored in subsequent chapters. Were this to be so, the case would be strengthened for plotting the historical trajectory of reflexivity retrodictively and coming a step closer to answering Vygotsky's call for a 'history of reflexivity'. At the end of the day, it will not be incontrovertible, but must remain what Weber called a 'peculiarly plausible hypothesis'.[18] Like his own, it would be open to further substantiation, to some extent historical, through use of diaries, 'confessions' and novels, and today through investigation of those vast tracts of the Southern world where morphogenesis has not yet engaged.

In various sections of society – that is, for those associated with particular institutional spheres, organizational activities and role occupancy – the conditions constituting 'contextual continuity', 'contextual discontinuity' and 'contextual incongruity' have doubtless been present to some degree throughout history. However, this is not the case if we consider the lineaments of societies at the most macro level, including the single global society now coming into being. Macroscopically, the structural relationships between parts of the social system and the ideational relationships between components of the cultural system together constitute a generative mechanism productive of one of the three types of context mentioned above, namely contextual 'continuity', 'discontinuity' or 'incongruity'.

However, just as all normal, adult human beings practise elements of all four reflexive modes today, yet nearly all have developed a dominant modality, so all social configurations too, will have shaped contextual pockets where the development of each mode of reflexivity was fostered among some portion of every given population. Nevertheless, specific macro-level configurations of the social system will have been especially favourable to the emergence of a particular mode as the dominant one in the reflexivity of the general population.

Morphostasis, 'contextual continuity' and communicative reflexivity

Although very little time will be devoted here to the morphostatic social formations pre-dating modernity, they will be briefly revisited for three reasons.[19] First, they furnish an important contrast because *early societies, in which structure and culture supplied negative feedback to each other and thus contributed to the restoration and perpetuation of the status quo, were also the ones likely to have fostered communicative reflexivity amongst the large majority of the population*. Second, if this was the case, the processes responsible for it should also be (formally) similar to those continuing to have the same effects *sectionally* (in particular institutions, organizations and roles) across the centuries and up to the present day. Third, they will reveal what generic types of contexts were shaped either for the majority of society's members or for those associated with (enduring sectors) of a similar kind. In turn, this will enable the next stage of the argument to be introduced: namely, how these different types of contexts also give rise to distinctive situational logics of action for the realization of subjects' personal concerns. These three points will be examined in turn.

First, and structurally, early societies were characterized by a low level of social differentiation and correspondingly small distinctions in material interests between people. In parallel, there were few available sources of alternative ideas and correspondingly small distinctions in ideational interests within the population. In these circumstances, where the structural and cultural elites were mutual beneficiaries of each other's activities, they often tended to coalesce into a single hegemonic group (Brahmin, Literati, the Privileged Estates), hence consolidating their control and exercising it to prevent challenge from the less advantaged and to preclude their access to countervailing ideas. Uses of power to contain the differentiation, organization and mobilization of new interest groups were paralleled by ideational containment strategies aimed at cultural unification of the population and the reproduction of a single conspectus of ideas. In short, what was sought by these elite groups served to promote 'contextual continuity' across society and onwards over future generations. This did not last forever, and there are internal reasons why it could not.[20] Nevertheless, 'contextual continuity' could endure and be made to endure for centuries.

Secondly, the maintenance of 'contextual continuity' was obviously not how elites defined their objectives under their own descriptions: chiefs, emperors and kings sought to render their leadership unassailable; witch doctors, high priests and literati sought to make their ideas inviolable. 'Contextual continuity' was, thus, the generative mechanism resulting from their successful and often conjoint implementation of a variety of power strategies. In so far as and for as long as their strategic containment of structural differentiation and ideational diversification proved effective, it worked *because the absence of variety* continued to shape situations for successive cohorts of the population in which neither new interests nor alternative ideas could be consolidated. This is what 'contextual continuity' means, although in 'old and cold' societies it is commonly known as 'traditionalism'.[21]

We can now identify the generic process by which morphostatic scenarios, both societally and sectionally, shape situations for their respective populations that predispose them to develop communicative reflexivity. The necessary condition is that structure and culture are mutually reinforcing through negative feedback, serving to maintain the *status quo* in both over time, as illustrated in Figure 10.2.

The effect of such scenarios is to shape the situations that subjects confront as ones of 'contextual continuity': those encountered by one generation or cohort are much the same as they were for their predecessors. It is through such situational shaping that structural and cultural emergent properties are – as always – transmitted to the agents in question.[22] However, it could very properly be objected that for subjects to find themselves in much the same situation as one another in no way elicits the same response from them. Indeed, that must be correct and it is impossible for any theorist consistently to maintain otherwise *if* subjects are held to possess their own irreducible, emergent properties and powers, both individually and collectively. Therefore, more is required to establish a linkage between morphostasis in the

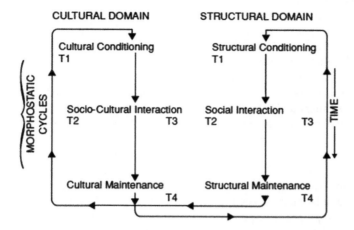

Figure 10.2 Structural and cultural configurations reproducing morphostasis in society and agency.

social order and the dominant practice of a particular mode of personal reflexivity. In other words, the generative mechanism is still incomplete. Two further points are needed to forge the linkage.

On the one hand, we have to note what the maintenance of morphostasis does to the subjects involved as well as to the situations in which they find themselves. Its effect – an intentional one where strategic uses of power are involved – is ultimately to distribute *similarities* throughout the population concerned. This is simply the reverse face of actively sustaining low levels of social differentiation and ideational diversification; subjects develop few different interests or ideas from one another. Clearly, it approximates to Durkheim's characterization of the 'segmented society', whose members are very like one another to the point of constituting 'a jumble of juxtaposed atoms'.[23] As is well known, this led Durkheim to query what, in that case, held them together and to answer this by reference to the 'collective effervescence' generated in religious rituals – a source of solidarity and of normativity. Without denying that shared religious practices can supply both, they seem to be a supplementary rather than a necessary condition of solidarity and of normativity. Instead, similarity and familiarity appear to contain within themselves all that is needed for their development from social interaction.

Given members' common experiential frame of reference (because of 'contextual continuity') and their shared topography and commonwealth of ideas, any issues to be resolved (where to hunt next, which nomadic halt to make and so forth) will find the majority vetoing innovative proposals in favour of established practices. Members increase in solidarity through defending established custom and practice and by repelling idiosyncratic suggestions, which is roughly what Durkheim also says about restitutive law and public punishment producing a return to the *status quo ante*. The interaction between 'similars and familiars' is its own source of normativity, one that endorses conventionalism and whose limited knowledge of alternatives effectively turns 'that's how things are done around here' from being a description of habit into something normatively binding.[24] It is when individuals share their hopes, dreams and aspirations with 'similars and familiars' that these are cut down to size – that is, to the norms of established custom and practice – because when they seek confirmation and completion of their initial thoughts and inclinations, convention is re-endorsed through external conversations.[25] Since 'thought and talk' with 'similars and familiars' is the relational process making for communicative reflexivity – which, in turn, reinforces social solidarity – this is the first part of its linkage with morphostasis via 'contextual continuity'.

At this point, it might be queried why people engage in such 'thought and talk' at all. Whence the need to be reflexive rather than to respond in terms of tacit knowledge and simply 'knowing how to go on'? Precisely the same answer is given both by realists and by pragmatists. Problematic situations can always arise in any open system and appropriate responses to every eventuality cannot be part of traditionalism's coda because unprecedented circumstances cannot be covered by it. Reflexivity is necessary and predisposes towards 'thought and talk' because some have to come up with ideas but also must convince and carry the rest with them in what are collectively binding decisions. In other words, *some reflexivity is indeed universal but in morphostatic social configurations there is no general impetus whatsoever towards the reflexive imperative becoming incumbent on all.*

However, there is the final link to forge and this relates to the guidance supplied by situational logics for action embedded in contexts of different kinds, in this case ones of 'continuity'. At all times and in all places subjects acquire their personal identities through the constellation of concerns that they endorse. This is part of the exercise of their personal powers, the one that makes them unique persons. Those who vest their ultimate concerns within their natal context also seek to project this context forward in time – literally reconstituting it – in order that their concerns may continue to be realized. However, they do more *because*, by virtue of their concerns, they have acquired a vested interest in 'contextual continuity' itself. Undoubtedly, that gives them a generic interest in social reproduction, which is not an unintended consequence of their actions, much less a matter of tacit habituation or of an inarticulate knowing 'how to go on'.

If 'contextual continuity' is threatened, either internally by some accentuating their (minor) differences or selectively stressing some potentially incongruent element in the ideational conspectus, or externally through the importing of attractive differences from elsewhere, the result is the same. Those whose interests are vested in 'contextual continuity' must pursue *a situational logic of 'correction' or 'protection'* in order to defend (the conditions of) what they care about most. Correction and protection are vocal and active exercises against perceived threat. So-called 'mindless' traditionalism is a misnomer; some must be mindful about how generous syncretism needs to be in order to correct and contain 'wrong thinking', and be judicious about boundary maintenance in order to regulate intrusive elements and thus protect a stable environment against 'wrong doing'. In so far as they are successful they perpetuate 'contextual continuity' because it is part and parcel of actualizing their concerns, and thus they preserve the generative mechanism of communicative reflexivity.

Finally, it is important to avoid a possible source of misunderstanding. Namely, what is the exact force of saying that subjects '*must* pursue' a particular situational logic, given that agency is not seen as being socially determined? Any situational logic is of the 'if/then' variety and it is, therefore, the incidence of the 'if' that is primitive to the rest of the logic. In other words, it is our human concerns – especially our ultimate concerns – that are pivotal, not only because they make us what we are as persons but also because they serve to direct what we do with our agency.[26]

Our ultimate concerns are sounding-boards, affecting our (internal) responses to anything we encounter, according to it resonating harmoniously or discordantly with what we care about most. It is these reactions that affect what we do, *not* because we have complete or accurate discursive penetration of the situation. Instead, discordant elements have the capacity to move ordinary people because they are emotionally registered as *offensive*.[27] They are shunned, repudiated or negatively sanctioned since they are antipathetic. This is the spur to action which invokes the 'then' of the 'if/then' logic. Conversely, elements harmonious with the ultimate concern are felt as *congenial*. They are welcomed, encouraged or positively sanctioned because that is what subjects' emotions, as transvalued by their commitments, motivate people to do.[28]

These internal prompts and restraints represent the exercise of personal powers and are what bind agents to following the situational logic of correction and protection. Its manifestations will be quotidian: how children and the young are disciplined or rewarded; what behaviours are positively or negatively sanctioned in a community; which practices are fostered or repressed in a religious group. In this way, the situational logic of correction and protection effectively, though non-teleologically, works to maintain and protract 'contextual continuity' – and with it the conditions propitious to the development and dominance of communicative reflexivity.

Morphostasis/morphogenesis, 'contextual discontinuity' and autonomous reflexivity

The central characteristic of modernity was not simply that differentiation and diversification had engaged in the structural and cultural domains respectively, but that these two domains no longer co-existed in synchrony with one another. Elsewhere, I have argued that it was of no moment whether the structural differentiation of oppositional groups pre-dated the cultural differentiation of ideational adversaries or vice versa.[29] In either case, the emergence of a morphogenetic scenario in the one later induced the same in the other. This is because a new promotive interest group, seeking to challenge the existing hegemonic elite, needed novel ideas to undermine existing legitimacy and to justify its own claims. Alternatively, it is because advocates of novel ideas required sponsorship from amongst the powerful in order to promote their cultural agenda in the face of the dominant ideational conspectus.

However, the lack of synchrony between morphostasis in one domain and morphogenesis in the other meant that both negative feedback (restoring the *status quo*) and positive feedback (amplifying deviations from it) were circulating simultaneously. The effect was twofold. First, a major consequence was to slow down the whole process of transformation. Second, the process was disjunctive, affecting some institutions faster than others, transforming certain bodies of ideas overnight and leaving others virtually unaffected, and reshaping the lives of part of the population whilst those of the remainder continued untouched.

Structurally, the key point about the transition to modernity was its unintended consequence of dichotomizing the peoples of Europe, who became the subjects of European nations, into those experiencing 'contextual discontinuity' and, indeed, seeking to extend it through political and, later, industrial unrest, and those rural populations who, despite the combined impacts of urbanization, politicization and industrialization, appear to have been left in relatively undisturbed 'contextual continuity', whilst the slowness of change allowed the newly urbanized groups to reconstitute community on the basis of class in the towns. After several generations of urban living, everyday life could again take its guidelines from this newly established form of 'contextual continuity'.

The concurrent effects of cultural morphogenesis reinforced those of collective mobilization and vice versa. On the one hand, the organized contenders for power and position necessarily adopted novel ideas to legitimate their aims. On the other hand, those defending their positions elaborated upon their sources of justification in order to buttress their ideological defence and extend its appeal, thus attempting to (re-)establish ideational unification. During the great age of ideological debate the populace did not remain immune in a cocoon of cultural traditionalism because, sooner or later, they became the targets of efforts to mobilize and manipulate them in order to determine the outcomes of issues that were not of their making. As they were dragged into the ideological fray, popular awareness of alternative ideas grew – and to be aware of an alternative to tradition spells the end of traditionalism.

In short, the spread of 'contextual discontinuity' was a sectional phenomenon, growing patchily throughout the course of modernity, even as it gathered momentum. However, only by unpacking the dynamics generating 'contextual discontinuity' it is possible to explain why the latter fostered autonomous reflexivity amongst larger and larger tracts of the population over time, although its practitioners seem likely to have remained in the minority throughout the nineteenth century. This is not simply an instance of 'elective affinity', which is a concept that fails to give an account of the causal powers that link 'interests' to 'ideas'. The concept of 'elective affinity' merely demonstrates their compatibility in principle and leaves the actual forging of the linkage to some kind of magnetic mutual attraction.[30]

Consequently, what is required is a closer specification of the new situations carved out for more primary agents as modernity developed, ones that impacted upon not only their 'contexts' but also their 'concerns', cumulatively resulting in the emergence of newly differentiated forms of collective agency, organized for the promotion of new sectional interests and articulating novel ideas for their advancement or vice versa.[31] Equally, the situational positioning of other groups (who probably constituted the majority of the population) was such that their 'contexts and concerns' induced and enabled newly routinized but non-traditional norms, values and practices to be elaborated and to take root. Without this being taken into account it will not be possible to explain the differential effects of unsynchronized morphogenesis and morphostasis throughout a given population. Without this, it will also remain a puzzle why a seemingly uniform change, which is what the singular term 'modernity' is often used to convey, simultaneously had differential consequences for the emergent social classes. It is this simultaneity that leads me to view the periodization of modernity – into early, high, late, second wave and so forth – as unhelpful because all of these sub-divisions imply homogenous effects within them and consequently downplay or ignore the differential effects, which are quintessential to modernity *because it is based upon a fundamental lack of synchrony between structural and cultural changes.*

In other words, at no stage and during no phase did the complex of institutional and ideational transformations constitutive of the shorthand term modernity ever work to foster a universally dominant mode of reflexivity. During the eighteenth, especially the nineteenth, and most of the twentieth century in Europe collective agents were both the recipients of situations, pre-shaped as ones of 'contextual discontinuity', and also the protagonists of change whose exertions created further 'contextual discontinuities' for others. Simultaneously, primary agents were constrained to relocate geographically, to change their work place and nature of employment and to lose a host of services associated with family life in rural communities. In turn, their urban–industrial life chances represented positive inducements towards redeveloping 'contextual continuity' in towns. Both of these effects, as experienced by different sections of the population, are needed to understand why 'modernity' simultaneously fostered both autonomous reflexivity and the continuation of communicative reflexivity, although not in any stable ratio.

The key distinction between these two influences is that those finding themselves in situations of 'contextual discontinuity' – and through their own exertions often extending such discontinuity to others – also experienced and contributed to the creation and diffusion of new forms of difference throughout society. Thereafter, it was the collective agential interactions between promotive interest groups, both material and ideal, that unleashed the dynamics *leading autonomous reflexivity to become the distinctive mode associated with modernity,* if not the one practised by the majority of people. Conversely, those disrupted and dis-embedded, but remaining primary agents, were responsible for recreating a new and relatively durable form of 'contextual continuity' that accentuated the *novel similarities* of their lived reality out of need, giving rise to the urban community, to intergenerational solidarity and to working-class conviviality, which were propitious to communicative reflexivity.

Whether structurally or culturally, *competitive contradictions* played a central role, without reference to which the eventual hegemony of Autonomous Reflexivity is condemned to remain an 'elective affinity'. Such contradictions are distinctive in that they were completely dependent upon modernist assailants – both materially and ideationally based – asserting themselves against traditional elites and ideas. There was no interdependence between the two that gave these contradictions any salience in society beyond that attained for them by the adversarial parties. The Reformation, the Enlightenment, the French Revolution and the Industrial Revolution were dependent upon their thinkers and leaders continuing their thinking and doing. Only because they did so were traditionalists compelled to reorganize into defensive formations and to overhaul their ideas defensively. Had the challengers somehow faded away there would have been no impetus for existing dominant groups to persist with such manoeuvres. However, since they continued to lock horns, ideational and institutional elaboration continued to result on both sides. From compromise and concession between them emerged those hard-won agencies for participation and governance – representative democracy, unionism and scholarization. In turn, they themselves extended new forms of 'contextual discontinuity' to portions of the population previously untouched by it.

However, the increasing salience of conflict stemming from *competitive contradictions* is quintessentially fissiparous. It promotes competition *beyond* the tendency that Marx rightly identified for capitalism not only to generate conflicts with the working-class movement (which itself displayed the same fissiparousness in ideas and organization) but also the inherent process by which capitalist was set in competition with capitalist, and worker with worker. Equally, competitiveness attached to ideational conflicts, ones that cannot readily be assimilated to class conflict and its super-structural manifestations. Take, for example, the unbridled competition between the established Church of England and the various kinds of dissenting denominations over church- and school-building as the long-term effect of the Reformation having introduced 'private judgement' into religious matters, or the nineteenth-century battle between the Catholic Church and the State over the right to educate the French youth.[32]

This is not the place to enter into the details of any of the above save to note three general consequences. First, that these initial manifestations of *competitive contradictions* spread to affect all social institutions – in state and civil society alike – where the actions of collective agents were a spur to acquire organization and to articulate goals on the part of disgruntled primary agents, as I have analysed at length for education.[33] Second, that this spelt increasing mobilization of greater and greater sections of the population, though far from the majority (see Figure 10.3). Nevertheless, not all of the latter could resist the pressures coming from their own ranks to mobilize them for enfranchisement, for educational provision and for unionization. Finally, the overall result for (European) society was *pluralism* in the realm of ideas and social *cleavage followed by sectionalism* amongst collective agents and their burgeoning and still fissiparous organizations and ideologies. This part of the dynamics of competition is summarized below.

In other words, the mobilization of significant numbers into promotive interest groups effectively divided national populations into those *promoting* further 'contextual discontinuity' – even if for defensive purposes[34] – and a large residuum of others, more preoccupied with everyday concerns, whose practical actions fostered new geo-local forms of 'contextual continuity'. Only the former became subject to

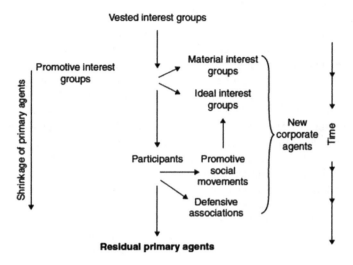

Figure 10.3 From primary to collective agency.

the *situational logic of competition* that accompanies the spread of ideational pluralism and sectional cleavages. That logic strongly induces instrumental rationality, which is the penultimate link to autonomous reflexivity.

Firstly, whatever reasons and values had led particular agents to become involved in sectional struggles also embroiled them in the dynamics of conflicts that were unrestrained by mutual interdependence. That is, competitive conflict involved the attempt to inflict injurious acts, with the ideal aim being the *elimination* of the oppositional party. However, since both sides of each confrontation had the same goal, it was rarely achievable. Instead, more and more strategic thinking had to be devoted to the question of how best to make headway. Thus, for example, the incursion of instrumental rationality into working-class radicalism can be traced throughout nineteenth-century Britain, from the eliminative violence of Luddism through the strategic debates within and between 'moral force' Chartists and 'physical force' Chartism and on to the subsequent disputes about the most effective form in which to develop Unionism – 'grand, national and consolidated' or trades-based. Equally, entrepreneurial interests had to weigh the concessions mooted for industrial quietude – restrictions on child labour, on working hours, on time for elementary education – against their competitive position in the increasingly European market.

Matters were no different for ideal interest groups. If the Church of England sought to defend its hegemony in education, strategically it had to extend instruction beyond its own needs and desires and to teach new material irrelevant to its concerns. On the other hand, some recipients of these strategic ploys were new collective agents who were driven to instrumentally rational considerations about, for instance, their ability to support independent mechanics institutes from their subsistence level wages in order to inculcate oppositional values and alternative skills.

Such examples are commonplace oversimplifications about the effects of competitive conflict upon the collective agents involved. However, the consequences of the situational logic of competition need to be taken down a level, from the promotive interest groups to their members, in order to secure the final linkage with autonomous reflexivity. The very concept of 'mobilization' can too often sound like a hydraulic process in which people are propelled to promote a cause because it is in their objective interests. What this neglects is the ideational and organizational bombardment that 'quasi-group' members are simultaneously receiving from both sides, in addition to the tension experienced between their own 'micro' life world concerns and the demands of larger-scale interests.

In real life, each potential member for 'mobilization' is thrown back upon his or her own resources because they are increasingly badgered to make one of several choices. In Charles Taylor's terms, they are hassled into becoming even 'stronger evaluators'.[35] Each must (fallibly) think through their own concerns in their own currencies: deliberating between jam and justice for tomorrow compared with feeding their families today; determining if violence is being done to the church of their fathers by endorsing innovative practices today in order to defend it; deciding if the Primitive Methodists or Ebenezer Methodists had put matters right where the Methodists had gone wrong; debating if a particular factory should make a local concession to its disgruntled workforce at the risk of reducing its competitive position with rival manufacturers. The key point is that all these examples are of instrumentally rational deliberations. Autonomous reflexivity also expands because *pluralism, sectionalism and competitive conflict have increasingly deprived many people of disinterested 'similars and familiars'* who could act as interlocutors, since most are in the same boat – and are mostly at sea.

This is because competitive situations are 'game-like' with their outcomes approximating to the zero-sum formula. Indeed, it is precisely their zero-sum character that helps to account for why more and more are drawn into competition through 'mobilization'. To be mobilized is not simply a socio-cultural matter of acceding to the persuasive pressure of class, status or party activists. It is also *motivated* by the nature of such games themselves. Either you compete, in the hope of winning (something), or you certainly lose through non-participation, because this allows others to win more easily. In effect, all subjects become part of these institutional 'games', whether or not they chose to play the hands that they had been dealt without choice on their part.

Formally, modernity's 'games' are very similar for all social institutions. Generically, they are about 'having, gaining or retaining a say' in order to obtain or secure benefits for the contending groups. Hence the sameness of competitive conflicts over representative politics, capitalist production and profits, and control of education or religion. For all social groups the zero-sum outcomes serve to place a premium upon strategic thinking of the means–ends variety. Even if, for argument's sake, we credited all members of the embattled churches and warring denominations (in Britain) with the highest other-worldly motives, they were still condemned to

How reflexivity becomes imperative 199

work in terms of instrumental rationality and to ask themselves if they would become *competitively* 'better off' by building a new school, orphanage, hospital or, for that matter, church.[36] Of course, it is important to recall that these institutional dynamics are not necessarily mirrored at the individual level: there are statutory non-players (such as women and Catholics, until the Relief Act of 1829 in Britain), there are half-hearted players (some of those with nothing to sell but their labour power), non-conscripted players (as yet undisturbed in their rural redoubts) and conscientious objectors (various kinds of radicals), which is why autonomous reflexivity remained far from universal.

There were, of course, various agential options: to walk away, to vacillate at length, to give covert support without overt involvement, or to come down decisively on one side or the other. Yet, in any of these cases, this will be a novel – because autonomous – decision for agents who have become caught up in the situational logic of competition. For those who actively assent to mobilization, the initial impetus to develop autonomous reflexivity is then sustained by the constant need to initiate, evaluate and arbitrate between alternative forms of strategic action. Those who decline such personal involvement could remain temporarily untouched by these struggles and their associated situational logic of competition, maintaining their 'contextual continuity' and sustaining their practice of communicative reflexivity – for the time being. Again, *this is why the reflexive imperative does not even begin to become universal during modernity.*

Morphogenesis, 'contextual incongruity' and meta-reflexivity

What is now coming into being is an entirely new phase in the relationship between structure, culture and agency. This is because structure and culture have each become morphogenetic and are coming to stand in a relationship of positive reinforcement towards one another. The new generative mechanism entailed by this is for variety to produce still more variety because, in pure form, nothing restrains it (such as defensive attachment to previous quasi-traditional interests and ideas or adherence to prior forms of routine action). Even more importantly, in pure form it can develop because the very novelty of new variety means that no group has 'commandeered' it and acquired vested interests in it. These had played a significant part in the synchronic account of the maintenance of emergent structures in the morphogenetic approach when applied within modernity (as opposed to the diachronic account of their social origins). Effectively, they divided a population (non-exhaustively) into those with vested interests in prolonging the *status quo* versus those whose interests lay in transformation, and they structured conflict by influencing motivation accordingly, though not deterministically. Indeed, the rapidity of change means that the very notion of vested interests will become outdated if and when morphogenesis becomes truly unbound. Conversely, the objective benefits of opportunity could then represent an open promise to all, but these should not be construed in exclusively material terms.

References to 'pure form' do not signify an ideal type, which may never be actualized or encountered in reality, but simply refer to a process that is currently far

200 *How reflexivity becomes imperative*

from being complete. Indeed, the morphogenetic scenario has yet to come of age and its development is marked and blurred by its co-existence with many structural, cultural and agential properties robustly enduring from late modernity. Nevertheless, the advent of *faster morphogenesis introduces a completely unprecedented influence of structure and culture upon personal reflexivity, which promotes a distinctive mode of reflexive deliberation – meta-reflexivity*. This, of course, is not a completely new modality and evidence from classical writings and especially from the extensive Christian confessional literature bears ample witness to practices of self-examination, self-monitoring, self-critique and resolutions to self-amendment being conducted through the internal conversation.[37] What is new is that meta-reflexivity ceases to be a minority practice (a matter of small pockets of practitioners in all epochs) and, instead, becomes the mode associated with a historical period, in the same way that autonomous reflexivity was related (rather than merely correlated) to developed modernity through the situational logic of competition.

In other words, changes in social and cultural structure are held to be powerful influences (though neither necessary nor sufficient ones for particular subjects) accounting for the growth and dominance of particular modes of reflexivity amongst given populations. Where the developed world is concerned, the recent engagement of the morphogenetic scenario shapes situations for its constitutive members that predispose more of them towards meta-reflexivity. The initial necessary condition for this is that structure and culture are mutually reinforcing through positive feedback, thus serving to *augment deviations from the status quo*, as illustrated in Figure 10.4.

In other words, contrary to the *reflexive modernization* thesis, changed structural and cultural conditions are held here to lie behind today's trend in reflexivity, rather than 'extended' individual reflexivity being the reverse face of structures

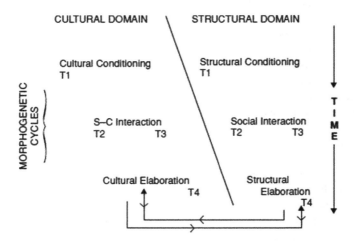

Figure 10.4 Structural and cultural configurations generating morphogenesis in society and agency.

'shrunken' to the dimensions of Beck's 'institutionalized individualism'.[38] It is now necessary to show how these rapid changes generated by the morphogenetic scenario affect many subjects by shaping the situations they ineluctably confront as ones of 'contextual incongruity', and then to specify how this predisposes them towards the practice of meta-reflexivity. Let us proceed by the *via negative* and ask why neither the communicative nor autonomous modes would be appropriate under these changed and quintessentially changing circumstances.

As has been seen, the practice of communicative reflexivity, exercised through 'thought and talk' with interlocutors who are also 'similars and familiars', strongly tends to reinforce normative conventionalism. In other words, it enmeshes the subject in local custom and practice, it drags flights of fancy down to earth, it valorizes the familiar over the novel, it privileges the public over the private, today over tomorrow and certainty over uncertainty.[39] In sum, it encourages conventional, localized responses, even though these would be wrongly construed as routine actions in the contemporary social order. What end or personal concern does communicative reflexivity ultimately serve? It works according to the situational logic of protection and that is exactly its effect. It protects and protracts the micro-life world of, at most, a small community and, increasingly today, a handful of significant others. Such protectiveness towards (usually) the subject's family has been shown to involve objective self-sacrifice, a refusal by subjects to avail themselves of accessible forms of advancement and a willingness to settle for 'living within their means'.[40] This is still possible under the morphogenetic scenario, if some version of 'the family' remains a subject's ultimate concern. However, there are three big snags that make the maintenance of communicative reflexivity increasingly arduous.

First, the price becomes steeper as increasing opportunities are turned down whilst many others 'get ahead' by taking advantage of them. Second, 'staying as we are' is diminishingly possible: new skills must be acquired if jobs are to be kept, new technology mastered if everyday life is to go on and new experiences weathered because they cannot be avoided. Third, and most importantly, there will be a shrinking pool of 'similars and familiars' available as potential and durable interlocutors because many classmates, workmates, children and neighbours will embrace some element of their new opportunities or have novelty thrust upon them (through job retraining, relocation of employment, the difficulty of buying a 'simple' television, the irresistibility of cheap foreign holidays or the son/daughter-in-law from Asia). Communicative reflexivity remains possible, but it has become considerably more costly (in various currencies) and involves a great deal more effort to sustain. Above all, it has become a matter of active choice and bears no resemblance to a default setting. In other words, communicative reflexivity flourishes most easily and appropriately when similarities are continuously distributed throughout the population and similar situations are consistently encountered. This 'likeness' – integral to 'contextual continuity' – also reconfirms the appositeness of conventional responses and, in turn, fosters social reproduction. In return, as it were, communicative reflexivity made a quiet but major contribution to the continuous regeneration of social solidarity throughout modernity. This is now lost in direct proportion to the pronounced shrinkage of this category, augmenting both anomie and isolation during the transitional period.

Conversely, autonomous reflexivity is promoted by situations in which instrumental rationality advances subjects' concerns. These situations are distinctive because they confront subjects with 'contextual discontinuity', which means that conventional responses deriving from their natal repertoire are no longer appropriate guides to action. Because of the intrinsically competitive nature of these situations, subjects must determine where their own best interests lie and deliberate about the best means to achieve these ends – doing both fallibly and under their own descriptions. In other words, extreme practitioners of autonomous reflexivity come closest of all to acting like the 'rational man' of Rational Choice Theory.

Although instrumental rationality cannot flourish in highly stable environments, where traditionalism and conventionalism are the dominant guides to action and promote communicative reflexivity, nevertheless it requires relative predictability from its settings. This is simply an extension of the logical point that means–ends reasoning depends upon a calculability of pay-offs and sufficient knowledge about likely outcomes such that taking risks is a matter of calculated risk-taking. Otherwise it is impossible to act in a goal-seeking, risk-discounting manner with the aim of becoming better off. In other words, Durkheim appears to have been substantially correct that *anomie* – as a serious disjunction between means and ends – will increase the pathologies amongst those most severely affected by profound economic disruption.[41] Thus, instrumental rationality cannot operate in an unpredictable environment where calculability goes out of the window. Yet, quite fundamentally, this is what the beginnings of morphogenesis now represent.

However, this is not the so-called 'risk society', if that really means more than our very real human ability to wipe out our planet. The *situational logic of opportunity is something quite different because it is non-competitive and non-zero sum* in its outcomes. In principle, there is nothing that precludes it from generating 'win–win' outcomes for all. But what the exponential increase in variety rules out are both strategic 'maximizing' or 'satisficing' as well as the more elaborate 'mini–max' or 'maxi–min' strategies of rational choice. What the rapid release of novelty, innovation and synergy is doing is putting paid to calculability, including calculated risks. 'Venture capital' is becoming market betting. Yet, the last thing upon which capitalist competition was ever modelled was roulette. Moreover, morphogenesis cannot be approached in the spirit of the entrepreneurial adventurer or that of the Las Vegas punter because it is hostile to instrumental rationality just as it is inimical to irrational gambling.

If the intensification of morphogenesis spells a precipitous reduction in calculability, and if that, in turn, is inimical to instrumental rationality, should not a sharp and equivalent reduction in the practice of autonomous reflexivity also follow? This would seem to be the logical implication, but in practice the conditions that lead to this conclusion were, until the 2007 financial crisis, fairly effectively contained by the powerful interests involved. Specifically, the multinational corporations and finance capitalists tackled the root cause threatening their activities, namely incalculability. The former moved to an 'assurance game' in order to stabilize key aspects of the environment in which they operate. What this basically entailed was a series of mutual agreements that enabled those whose operations gained them a market advantage to continue to benefit from it for a certain number of years. This is why legal patents became crucially important. They served to 'freeze' uncertainty and, in guaranteeing profitability *ceteris paribus*, thus freed up internal resources to make the next innovative development which, if successful, would then be protected in the same manner. Calculability had been restored and the old game could continue with no more than the old absence of guarantees that new lines of research and development might turn out to be dead ends.[42]

However, the assurance game was not applicable to key areas, the most crucial being the finance market, but the latter had effectively tackled the incalculability of risk, from its own point of view, until the house of cards collapsed in 2007. Up to that date, the insurance game complemented the assurance game. Thus, the complex development of financial 'derivatives' and hedge funds represented forms of insurance by spreading risk over a variety of investments. If the development of 'derivatives' rendered risks calculable for the biggest players, investment supermarkets performed something of the same function for those with surplus capital. Assurance and insurance provided insulation against the quintessential unpredictability of morphogenesis and enabled the old game to continue – *pro tem*.

They were complemented by other devices that manipulate consumption to ensure rising 'demand' and to underwrite increased commodification. The proliferation of the credit card market, with a massive intensification of offers to transfer one's balance (read: 'debts') to a new interest free card for a limited period, was a direct inducement to increased indebtedness, at an exorbitant interest rate, for those who frequently could not pay. An identical role was performed by sub-prime mortgages and unsecured loans. This complete reversal of cautious issuing and lending in the past, on the basis of established 'credit-worthiness' and earnings, artificially stimulated demand over an increasing range of products, from housing to holidays to cosmetic surgery, thus introducing greater stability in market demand and extending this to the tertiary sector.

Market and state collaborated in buttressing finance capitalism, as pictured in Figure 10.5, as the expansion of public services in terms of benefits and employment kept 'demand' buoyant in European countries, which increasingly produced nothing but consumed more and more. Whilst ever the game went on and the devices for concealing the manipulative aspects of marketization became more sophisticated, so too could many continue to work on the basis of instrumental rationality in planning their courses of action in the hope of becoming better off. With its collapse and a few of the most audacious financial players going under, European states were more concerned to re-establish 'business as usual' than to introduce stringent regulation of the finance services, which had replaced the production of goods as the source of national wealth. In other words, there are few grounds for supposing that the associated mode of reflexivity – autonomous reflexivity – would undergo a sudden and sharp decline.

Nevertheless, more and more people and especially the young who, on the whole, have fewer interests in artificially stabilizing the environment for finance capital,

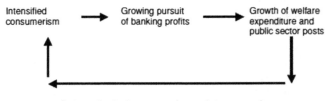

Figure 10.5 How market financialization and state redistribution work together. Adapted from Pierpaolo Donati, 'The Crisis of the World System and the Need for Civil Society', in José T. Raga and Mary A. Glendon (eds.), *Crisis in the Global Economy – Re-planning the Journey*, Vatican City Press, p. 144, 2011.

also have very good reasons to respond positively to *the situational logic of opportunity*. Why should they register the incalculability of rapidly intensifying variety as a threat to be tamed, particularly since they are badly placed to do the taming? Moreover, the positive feedback that spawns unlimited innovations also throws up novelties that appeal to the young and which they are remarkably adept at mastering: electronic games, mobile phones, iPods and the endlessly proliferating uses to be made of the Internet. New technology is 'cool'. The vista of opportunities presented by the Internet should not be underestimated: the chance to extend virtual experience far beyond the confines of the practical ones on offer at home and school, to encounter news and opinions wildly at variance with those of TV and family members, to explore the forbidden and even to extend it and to assume one or many cyber personas: these surely beat the children's encyclopaedias that had been the baby boomers' resort for flat information.

More importantly, an increasing proportion of those growing up after the 1980s found themselves in a situation of 'contextual incongruity', particularly when they came to seeking their first jobs. For growing numbers and for the first time in history their natal social context fitted them for nothing, in total contrast to the simple societies of morphostatic times when the combination of imitation, induction and initiation supplied everything needed for entry to adult life. Because the context was substantially unchanging in the latter, the same skills and the same know-how could be slowly and informally acquired and smoothly applied to unchanged positions by successive generations as they reached adulthood. The name of the game was contextual replication and it depended on the mutual structural and cultural reinforcement of morphostasis continuing to generate 'contextual continuity'.

With the slowness of change characteristic of modernity, it was well known what additional skills or accomplishments were required for offspring to keep their social place or make slight improvements on it. By and large the returns upon these investments were predictable and the only calculation to be made concerned their affordability. Increasingly, as morphogenesis engaged either structurally or culturally, families had to cope with 'contextual discontinuity' by ingenuity or self-sacrifice: new industrialists seeking a practical education for their sons and successors sent them to the (independent) Scottish universities or to study engineering in Germany, whilst radicalized members of the working class scraped pennies together to send them to mechanics institutes – self-run and free from indoctrination by entrepreneurs or the clergy.

Significantly, 'contextual incongruity' was virtually unknown and confined to isolated pockets of society. The clearest historical examples are cultural instances of religious groups whose faiths were incongruous with the established Church, the longest and perhaps hardest case being the small percentage of recusant Catholics practising illegally and sending their sons to Belgium or France for education and potential ordination, often not to see them again. Similarly, Jews and a century of nonconformists were denied a university degree in the UK until the abolition of the Test Acts in 1870. However, such instances implied an intergenerational solidarity of values within the family, which sets them apart from 'contextual incongruity' today.

Equally, three categories of women also experienced 'contextual incongruity': the 'fallen', placed beyond the pale, whatever the respectability of their backgrounds; the necessarily self-subsistent, whom Malthus sought to export abroad as governesses; and the intelligent home-educated who, when novelists, often resorted to male pseudonyms or, as reformers, either married or else found themselves beyond the pale of any reputable context. Yet, at least in the latter cases, the consequences of 'wilful' persistence remained a matter of hard choice and predictable consequences, but it was a choice nonetheless – again, setting such cases apart from today.

Predictability, calculability and thus instrumental rationality continued for most of the twentieth century. The increasing reach of 'contextual discontinuity' certainly acted as a spur to upward social mobility and the fear of its opposite to strenuous exertions on the part of parents to salvage the status of their offspring.[43] Nevertheless, it remained largely a question of what could be afforded, it became a very predictable matter in terms of the growing calibration of qualifications to posts throughout Europe, and its cadence represented slow, calculable and incremental intergenerational moves. The nineteenth-century French saying that it took three generations from the grandfather being an *instituteur* to the grandson becoming a *professeur* had not dramatically shortened.

With the onset of morphogenesis all of that began to change as the situational logic of opportunity engaged because of the proliferation of increasing variety. As far as the young were concerned, especially those transitional cohorts entering the job market in the late 1980s and 1990s, this confronted them with an array of new outlets, of short-term posts – rather than a job for life – whose names and contents were ephemeral, with expectations of postings abroad, with flexi-time, virtual offices and with the first broad hints that if they did not like what was (temporarily) on offer, then why not design what suited them. Why, though, did this represent 'contextual incongruity' for these young people?

It was because this major and unprecedented transformation meant that the parental background no longer possessed any corpus of *cultural capital* whose durable occupational value could be transmitted to their children, as opposed to cultural transmission *tout simple*.[44] Parental culture is rapidly ceasing to be a capital good, negotiable on the job market and counting as a significant element in the patrimony of offspring. *Les Héritiers* are being impoverished by more than death duties. Culture is still their inheritance but is swiftly becoming an internal good – valued at the estimate of its recipients, like the family silver – rather than an external good with a high value on the open market.[45] Consequently, strategies for ensuring the intergenerational transmission of cultural capital started to peter out, partly because it had been devalued almost overnight and partly because rapidly diminishing calculability made old forms of strategic action increasingly inapplicable. Many middle-class and upper-class parents who stuck to past routines, which had served their own parents well, of 'buying advantage' through private schooling began to face offspring who felt they had had an albatross tied round their necks. Confronting the incongruity between their background and their foreground, an increasing number of public school leavers began to blur their accents, abuse their past participles, make out they had never met Latin, refer to their school by its geographical location – all tokens of embarrassment reflecting their subjective recognition of the 'contextual incongruity' in which they were now placed.

Of course, it will be objected that such an education still gained a disproportionate number of entrants to the oldest universities, but some of the sharpest public-school leavers had no desire to go there and, in any case, such establishments were besieged by egalitarian-cum-meritocratic pressures which somewhat undercut their social point. Certain unlikely institutions themselves caught on and the Girls' Public Day School Trust quietly shed 'Public' from the name of its network at this time. Equally, it will be objected that their graduates still have preferential access to careers in the Civil Service, in diplomacy, in the traditional professions. But that is quite compatible with the fact that by the end of the twentieth century some of those from privileged backgrounds began to discount these openings. The fast learners had got the message: the Stock Exchange wanted the 'barrow-boy' mentality on the floor. Effectively, their possession of old-style cultural 'capital' was a disadvantage vis-à-vis new openings and opportunities, although it retains lingering value for the more traditional occupational outlets.

In a very different way, working-class parents found themselves in much the same position of literally having nothing of market value to reproduce among their children. With the rapid decline of manufacturing and frequent joblessness, their previous ability to recommend high wages and to 'speak for' their sons also disappeared. With the computerization of secretarial, reception and much work in retail, mothers found their daughters already more proficient than they were themselves. With involuntary redundancies, make-shift jobs and frequent visits to the job centre, there are fewer and fewer remnants of working-class culture to be reproduced – especially the old attractions of a lasting group of convivial workmates – and decreasing incentives to reproductory practices in employment among both parents and offspring. The latter, in any case, are now mostly 'at college', for varying amounts of time, but long enough for many to come to think that courses such as IT and Design represent a blue yonder of opportunity. Meanwhile, many of their parents retreat into a non-directive goodwill towards their children's futures, usually expressed as: 'We'll support them whatever they want to do.' This passes the burden of decision-making to the next generation and constitutes another dimension of 'contextual incongruity'. The parental generation has thrown up its hands in effective admission that their ways are not congruent with the new ways, which their offspring must navigate for themselves, albeit with diffuse family support.

Whereas the 'past', in the form of one's background, used to be a help in the present towards the future, it increasingly has nothing to give and, at worst, represents a hindrance to be overcome by the young. The old homology between socialized dispositions to accept positions, which the young were then dispositionally suited to occupy and predisposed to reproduce positionally, is coming to an end. As the very notion of *transferable* cultural capital becomes more and more tenuous, simultaneously all those intricate manoeuvres of substituting between different kinds of capital become outdated. Economic capital is always useful, but what can it purchase for the next generation that can be cashed out in terms of cultural advantage? A laptop, a gap year, a well-used passport, graduating debt free; these are certainly financially advantageous but they remain economic because what the offspring derives from them or does with them is at their discretion. Certainly, *social capital* does remain more enduring, but increasingly this is by transmitting a confidence and a lack of trepidation in pursuing the situational logic of opportunity. Nevertheless, *how* and *where* it is pursued is a task to be designed and followed up and often revised or corrected by the young themselves.

Reflexivity and nascent morphogenesis

How do the young launch themselves into the world and what pilots them in one direction rather than another? If past pathways are no guide and if the future speed of change is hostile to the very notion of defined paths to determinate ends, on what basis can they decide how to begin making their way through the world? Certainly, not in terms of instrumental rationality, because this requires strategic thinking about means and ends, which the unpredictability of novelty precludes more and more. Whilst the situational logic of competition was a logic that induced people to make choices, these were between well-defined alternatives. That logic operated through accentuating differences of class, status and power, by insisting upon their salience and pointing to objective gains and losses to make its point, thus undermining both openness and indifference and making the question of alignment inescapable.

By contrast, the situational logic of opportunity is much looser and wider open. It constitutes an invitation to make what anyone will of complementary items in the cultural and social systems, to marry their existing knowledge and skills to some novel development without any certainty about the outcome of this combination, to experiment, to migrate, to innovate and to elaborate. If none of this synergy, syncretism or synthesis works, the reflexive imperative enjoins a return to the drawing board and trying again. In all of this, the burden is placed squarely upon the tyro entrants to chart their own courses of action. There are no fixed alternatives as there were under the logic of competition. Certainly, in these transitional times, the option remains of joining the restyled multi-national corporations, the banking

208 *How reflexivity becomes imperative*

sector or public services, which is why autonomous reflexives are not short of congenial outlets.

Thus, it becomes imperative to deliberate about themselves in relation to the open opportunities they now confront. But in what terms can their deliberations be sensibly conducted? The response is 'in relation to their concerns'. This preserves the active agent without him or her degenerating into the wanton gambler. In the two preceding works the general formula 'contexts + concerns' was presented as the key to what guided the reflexive process, accounted for its outcomes and, indeed, shaped the mode of reflexivity employed. Exactly the same recurs here; the 'context' is changing beyond recognition, 'contextual incongruity' is a newcomer in the sense that it now characterizes a growing tract of the population in the developed world as opposed to the previous small pockets of rather distinctive people. But, given its hallmark features of unpredictability, incalculability and the valorization of novelty, this means that personal 'concerns' play an increasing role in guiding deliberations and the conclusions arrived at. In sum, 'the importance of what we care about' has never been more important.

If subjects' constellations of concerns define their personal identities, then their ultimate concern and its realization will preponderate in their internal conversations.[46] In turn, this means that those (young people) who have committed themselves to a concern or 'cause' have a serious point of orientation from which to approach the situational logic of opportunity. Of course, endorsing such aims and values may well have the effect of intensifying their 'contextual incongruity' with their natal background, because nothing ensures that their values were derived from (consensual) parental socialization or are compatible with family normativity, where that remains. Given the changeable composition and definitions of 'the family', the values endorsed by offspring may represent a selection from what they encountered at home, an accentuation of one strand, or a rejection of all that was on offer in favour of something encountered elsewhere. In all such cases, the young subjects encounter a cultural element of 'contextual incongruity' in addition to those already discussed in structural terms.[47]

Not all have arrived at this point or will necessarily do so, but the fact that most can specify their concerns – as will be seen – gives them a grappling hook on the situational logic of opportunity. It enables them to engage in productive and purposeful internal conversation. This inner dialogue allows them to complete the following sequence: (a) defining and dovetailing their CONCERNS; (b) developing concrete courses of action as their PROJECTS; and (c) establishing satisfying and sustainable PRACTICES. If conducted successfully, this enables subjects to realize their concerns and results in each person constituting his or her *modus vivendi*. What is novel is that its completion is becoming more and more reliant on *the practice of meta-reflexivity*. The defining features of this mode – namely, for subjects to be critically reflexive about their own internal conversations and to be critical about effective action in society – are strongly fostered by nascent morphogenesis and the opportunities it presents. This is the case for three reasons.

To begin with, young subjects are necessarily at an epistemological disadvantage when they first confront the task of making their own match between their concerns and their first form of employment because they know too little about themselves and about swiftly changing opportunities. They have to crystallize both their concerns and to concretize them into a projected course of action in the world of work, yet know they are fallible in these two respects. *Self-critique thus becomes intrinsic to the very formulation and endorsement of a project*, which distinguishes it from the self-monitoring that was always required for the performance of skilled tasks. There are no formal apprenticeships in the morphogenetic society, only a plethora of courses extending dubious promises and always in need of being supplemented by shifting informal networks of proficients working at the cutting edge. During interview, this can appear as indecisiveness or vacillation as students (readily) proffer their lists of future jobs under consideration – lists which often contain seemingly very contrasting contenders: for example, training as a social worker or becoming an antiques dealer. Significantly, they themselves recognize this and, equally significantly, they volunteer that they are sensibly 'keeping their options open' for the time being.

Some can readily define their three main concerns in life but are incapable of prioritizing them; others do so but have revised their priorities a year later; only a few, at the age of eighteen or nineteen, have disengaged an ultimate concern which proves lasting over their undergraduate years.[48] In other words, they are properly tentative or positively distrustful about their first inclinations and the first occupational matches that they suggest to themselves. This means that they rightfully linger long over the first stage of what I have termed the DDD scheme, made up of Discernment, Deliberation and Dedication.[49] That spells prolonged internal conversations in which subjects critically explore and test their self-knowledge and equally critically scrutinize the first 'matches' they have internally suggested to themselves. They do not know enough and are aware of it, but they appear fully cognisant of the fact that only through their own reflexive deliberations can they come to endorse a project, however much information they absorb from careers services and recruitment fairs. In other words, internal self-critique is accepted to be a predicate of safe landings and that is a hallmark of meta-reflexivity.

Secondly, when they feel reasonably – but of course fallibly – satisfied with the concerns they seek to realize, they still have to designate or design a project for future employment that is expressive of their concerns, thus making them prepared to invest themselves in it.[50] Additionally, but crucially, subjects have to deem their projects to be feasible in the outer world. In this they are hampered by their inadequate knowledge: some will temporize by awarding themselves an additional gap year; others will test the waters by taking an internship or placement; and still others will take a job for self-maintenance whilst their project takes shape. In this process, *all are driven to engage to some degree with the second aspect of meta-reflexivity, namely social critique*, even if this constitutes a relatively pain-free assent to the employment route taken – something which tends to be the preserve of autonomous reflexives. For others, the reflexive imperative drives them to further 'deliberation', in which feasible-sounding opportunities are discarded on closer inspection or from experience, and new opportunities are discovered and scrutinized. For still others, their internal critique of the outstanding array of institutionalized outlets is so profound that they recognize the situational logic of opportunity invites 'dedication' to a novel project of their own making, wherever they choose to make it.

Lastly, the growth and diversification of the third, voluntary or social–private sector has increasing attractions because it provides roles that can be personified in terms of the value commitments endorsed by many young subjects. Here, social critique represents profound disenchantment with both market and state and an attempt to locate an institutional base in which they are willing to invest themselves. In this context, Habermas has accentuated the 'colonization' of such new outlets and organizations by the old Leviathans.[51] Yet, as meta-reflexivity increases, it is equally important to emphasize the counter-flow of critique. Some of these young subjects are prepared to enter school teaching, for example, with the aim of encouraging their pupils to thrive in a manner that will clash with governmentally imposed 'performance indicators' and with the professional associations that have currently endorsed them.

As my elder son and his wife happily launched into their tenth season of running mountaineering courses abroad, having skilled and reskilled themselves en route and at their own expense, the comment passed by their nonagenarian grandmother encapsulated what has been argued in this chapter about the newness of the reflexive imperative. 'What a pity', she remarked, 'that they're not using their degrees'. This is an understandable reaction from what had been a bright young girl, born into a numerous family, who was subject to the full brunt of the situational logic of competition in its war-time austerity. Degrees were then a means to an end and her enduring instrumental rationality resulted in ever overvaluing the university place that she was offered only for it to be turned down by her family. That missed degree would have been 'used' to open professional doors; when half of the (British) age cohort was destined to acquire one under New Labour and nearly 40 per cent did so, the only door they were certain to go through was that which opens onto the reflexive imperative.[52]

Conclusion

This chapter has been futuristic in presenting the reflexive imperative as the necessary accompaniment of 'morphogenesis unbound'. Nevertheless, we remain in a transitional period and modernity has not yet breathed its last gasp. Above all, the global world remains a capitalist domain and capitalism has proved remarkably ingenious about developing a civilized ideational face and has adapted successfully towards critique from the better-organized social movements (with green, organic and ecological marketing becoming big business, for example). Hints have been given about how it has sustained its hegemony and hence continued to provide the competitive conditions that foster autonomous reflexivity. Placing the emphasis upon autonomous versus meta-reflexivity as constituting the major divide between educated young people today assumes that the conditions propitious to developing and sustaining communicative reflexivity are becoming consistently harder to maintain (as will be illustrated in Chapter 4). In short, the diminution of communicatives appears to augment the ranks of both autonomous and meta-reflexives.

However, it also increases the proportion of fractured reflexives. This chapter should not be read as a paean of praise to the situational logic of opportunity. Welcome as it may be in terms of enhancing self-determination and of according increased governance over their own life courses for many, it has a negative face that has not yet been examined. The necessity of reflexively defining one's concerns, of deliberatively designating one's own projects and of determining one's own *modus vivendi* also means that responding to the reflexive imperative exposes subjects to the consequences of their own fallibility. It makes them vulnerable to the contingencies of life in an open system – one largely without a safety net, given the loss of community and overall reduction in social integration. The reflexive imperative produces casualties – the fractured reflexives – those who get it wrong and, in their fracturedness, simply cannot work out how to put it right.

Notes

1. Lev S. Vygotsky, *Thought and Language*, Cambridge MA, MIT Press, 1964 (1934). His call was for a 'historical theory of inner speech' (p. 153).
2. For example, the phrase is used repeatedly in Matthew Adams, 'Hybridizing Habitus and Reflexivity', *Sociology*, 40:3, 2006, 511–28.
3. See William Lyons, *The Disappearance of Introspection*, Cambridge MA, MIT Press, 1986.
4. For a more detailed examination of the contributions of James, Peirce and Mead to the theme of reflexivity-as-internal-conversation see Margaret S. Archer, *Structure, Agency and the Internal Conversation*, Cambridge, Cambridge University Press, 2003, chapter 2: 'From introspection to internal conversation', pp. 53–92.
5. Both of these themes and associated thinkers are treated in Margaret S. Archer, *Making our Way through the World: Human Reflexivity and Social Mobility*, Cambridge, Cambridge University Press, 2007, chapter 1: 'Reflexivity's Biographies', pp. 25–61.
6. For discussion in detail see Margaret S. Archer, *Structure, Agency and the Internal Conversation*, chapters 6–9 and *Making our Way*, chapters 4–6.
7. In Archer, *Making our Way*, the following dominant modes of reflexivity were estimated, using ICONI (the Internal Conversation Indicator), for the stratified sample of Coventry inhabitants: communicative reflexives = 21 per cent, autonomous reflexives = 27 per cent, meta-reflexives = 23 per cent and fractured reflexives = 22 per cent (figures rounded up), p. 335. This compares with the following for students at point of entry in the present study: communicative reflexives = 13.5 per cent, autonomous reflexives = 19 per cent, meta-reflexives = 38.6 per cent and fractured reflexives = 17.4 per cent. For further details, especially concerning the development of ICONI, please consult the 'Methodological appendix' of this book.
8. Norbert Wiley, 'The Sociology of Inner Speech: Saussure Meets the Dialogical Self', paper presented at the meeting of the American Sociological Association, August 2004.
9. Ibid., p. 9.
10. For a full discussion of this conclusion see Margaret S. Archer, *Being Human: The Problem of Agency*, Cambridge, Cambridge University Press, 2000, chapter 7: 'Personal identity: the inner conversation and emotional elaboration', pp. 222–52.
11. I do not consider it helpful to make all possible concerns 'implicitly social' by definition. Analytically, people can have primary concerns in the natural, practical or transcendental orders, where social aspects are probably unavoidable but nevertheless remain ancillary.

12 Harry Frankfurt, 'Identification and wholeheartedness', in Frankfurt, *The Importance of What We Care About*, Cambridge, Cambridge University Press, 1988, and see Martin Hollis' consistent defence of our active *personification* of roles, from *Models of Man*, Cambridge, Cambridge University Press, 1977, through *The Cunning of Reason*, Cambridge, Cambridge University Press, 1987, to 'Honour among Thieves', *Proceedings of the British Academy*, LXXV, 1989.
13 Charles Taylor, *Human Agency and Language*, Cambridge, Cambridge University Press, 1985, chapter 1: 'What Is Human Agency?'
14 Granting such emergent personal powers and attaching causal efficacy to their use is wrongly held by some to lead directly to 'monadism'. See Anthony King, 'Against Structure: a Critique of Morphogenetic Social Theory', *Sociological Review*, 47, 1999, 199–227 and *The Structure of Social Theory*, London, Routledge, 2004.
15 Pierpaolo Donati, *Teoria Relazionale della Società*, Milan, Franco Angeli, 1992, chapter 1: 'La relazione sociale come presupposizione prima della sociologia'.
16 This does not mean that individual and social psychology make no contribution. It is only to maintain that modes of reflexivity are not psychologically reducible.
17 For a promising collaborative approach, see Edward. L. Deci and Richard M. Ryan, *Intrinsic Motivation and Self-Determination in Human Behavior*, New York, Plenum Press, 1985.
18 Max Weber, *The Theory of Social and Economic Organization*, New York, Free Press, 1964, pp. 96–7.
19 For a more detailed discussion, see Margaret S. Archer, *Realist Social Theory: the Morphogenetic Approach*, Cambridge, Cambridge University Press, 1995, pp. 213–45.
20 For the socio-cultural dynamics of cultural change see Margaret S. Archer, *Culture and Agency: The Place of Culture in Social Theory*, Cambridge, Cambridge University Press, 1988, chapter 7: 'Socio-cultural Interaction'.
21 Considered as a generative mechanism and one at work throughout modernity, 'contextual continuity', which is often empirically associated with routine action, is more general than traditionalism. This is of importance for instances where it continues to have the same generic consequences *sectorially*, in certain parts of the social order that no one would think of as being traditional and where what is required of those involved are not actions that could properly be called traditionalistic. For example, Kuhn's sociology of science maintains that in normal times only one paradigm enjoys monopoly, leading to the consolidation of new habits in research whose effect 'suppresses fundamental novelties because they are necessarily subversive of its basic commitments'. Thomas Kuhn, *The Structure of Scientific Revolutions*, Chicago IL, Chicago University Press, 1962, p. 5.
22 'Given their pre-existence, structural and cultural emergents shape the social environment to be inhabited. These results of past actions are deposited in the form of current situations. They account for what is there . . . to be distributed and also for the shape of such distributions; for the nature of the extant role array, the proportion of positions available at any time and the advantages/disadvantages associated with them; for the institutional configuration present and for those second order emergent properties of compatibility and incompatibility, that is, whether the respective operations of institutions are matters of obstruction or assistance to one another.' Archer, *Realist Social Theory*, p. 201.
23 Emile Durkheim, *Division of Labour*, New York, Free Press, 1965, p. 130.
24 This is where historically the *proximal* norm circles, the *imagined* and the *actual* circles, distinguished by Dave Elder-Vass, tend to be superimposed. *The Causal Power of Social Structures*, Cambridge, Cambridge University Press, 2010, pp. 122–33.
25 Archer, *Making our Way through the World*, pp. 270–84.
26 Mustafa Emirbayer and Ann Mische, 'What Is Agency?', *American Journal of Sociology*, 103:4, 1998, 962–1023.

How reflexivity becomes imperative   213

27 Archer, *Being Human*, chapter 6 and summarized as 'Emotions as Commentaries on Human Concerns', in Jonathan H. Turner (ed.), *Theory and Research on Human Emotions*, Amsterdam, Elsevier, 2004, pp. 327–56.
28 That there is some such second-ordering process involved for the emotions commands broad agreement. Jon Elster refers to it as 'transmutation' (*Alchemies of the Mind*, Cambridge, Cambridge University Press, 1999, p. 56), John D. Greenwood as 'transformation' (*Realism, Identity and the Emotions*, London, Sage, 1994, p. 156) and Charles Taylor as 'transvaluation' (*Human Agency and Language*, pp. 65–8).
29 Archer, *Realist Social Theory*, pp. 308–24.
30 Indeed, Weber himself, when exploring the specific 'economic ethos' of different world religions, had to abandon his methodological individualism and introduce the interplay between structural and cultural factors to explain the variable nature of rationality in different historical social configurations. In other words, he too became a serious advocate of the notion that the impact of the macro-figurational upon micro-level mental processes was mediated through the combined structural and cultural shaping of the situational contexts of action. This seems to be the central point of his contrast between ancient India and China, on the one hand, and ancient Judaism, on the other.
31 Primary agents are defined as those similarly positioned but deprived of having any say, in contrast with collective or corporate agents who have articulate aims and are organized for their strategic pursuit. See Archer, *Realist Social Theory*, pp. 257–65.
32 The Reformation not only stimulated the Counter-Reformation but immediately unleashed competition within Protestantism: not only the variants contemporaneous with Lutheranism (Pietism, Anabaptism, Zwinglianism), but onwards to Presbyterianism, Methodism, Baptism and so forth, each with its own later clutch of schisms.
33 Margaret S. Archer, *Social Origins of Educational Systems*, London and Beverly Hills CA, Sage, 1979.
34 For example, in the attempt to defend its educational hegemony, the established Church of England had to accept and actively contribute to a large extension of educational provisions – itself contributing to extensions in 'contextual discontinuity' for the newly scholarized – as part and parcel of the competition to retain control over education.
35 Charles Taylor, 'Self-Interpreting Animals', in his *Human Agency and Language*, pp. 65–8.
36 The same was the case for continental struggles between the Church and the State. For example, see Antoine Prost, *L'Enseignement en France 1800–1967*, Paris, Armand Colin, 1968.
37 Religious practices may indeed represent a particular social sector that, of its own kind, tends to foster critical inner dialogue amongst those who are seriously committed. This is a proposition that I endorse but will not explore here. Perhaps it is worth noting, however, that in the morphostatic early medieval period the routinized employment of confessional manuals seems likely to have somewhat depressed meta-reflexivity. Nevertheless, Thomas à Kempis' *Imitation of Christ* (1418) and the anonymous *Cloud of Unknowing* (fourteenth century) cannot, in sociological terms, be seen as anything other than serious exhortations to deeper meta-reflexivity. See Pierpaolo Donati, *La Matrice Teologica della Società*, Soveria Mannelli, Rubbettino, 2010. Much the same point is made by Nicos Mouzelis about the anaphatic mysticism of the Orthodox Churches in 'Self And Self-Other Reflexivity: The Apophatic Dimension', *European Journal of Social Theory*, 13:2, 2010, 271–84.
38 Ulrich Beck and Elizabeth Beck-Gernsheim, *Individualization*, London, Sage, 2002, 'Preface', p. xxi.
39 Archer, *Making our Way*, pp. 270–79.
40 Ibid., chapter 4.
41 Emile Durkheim, *Suicide*, London, Routledge and Kegan Paul, 1968 (1897), chapter 5.
42 For example, Boots the chemists, not noted for their research leadership in pharmaceuticals, were buoyed up by the patented protection of their big winner ibuprofen.

214 How reflexivity becomes imperative

43 These were well documented by Bourdieu and Passeron, which poses the question how such strategic actions could have evaded reflexive deliberation. Pierre Bourdieu and Jean-Claude Passeron, *La Reproduction*, Paris, Ed de Minuit, 1970, chapter 2.
44 One indicator of which (in Britain) was the consistently better performance of Asian girls in state schools, compared with all other categories of pupil, over more than a decade.
45 Alasdair MacIntyre, *After Virtue*, London, Duckworth, 1981, p. 187ff. See also Andrew Sayer, *The Moral Significance of Class*, Cambridge, Cambridge University Press, 2005, pp. 111–26.
46 Archer, *Being Human*, chapter 7.
47 Socialization – in theory and practice – is discussed in Chapter 3.
48 That is during their first of the three-year undergraduate degree, for the majority.
49 For a more detailed discussion see Archer, *Being Human*, pp. 230–41.
50 A 'project' is used as a generic term for any intentional course of action pursued.
51 Jürgen Habermas, *The Theory of Communicative Action*, Cambridge, Polity Press, 1989 (1981).
52 When 'educational inflation' began to develop in the US, Green et al. advanced their thesis that as the educational level of the population approached x the only advantage of attaining x was to avoid penalization because the prizes now went to those with x+1. Thomas F. Green, David P. Ericson and Robert M. Seidman, *Predicting the Behaviour of the Educational System*, Syracuse NY: Syracuse University Press, 1980.

11 Morphogenic society

Self-government and self-organization as misleading metaphors

Introduction

The social is undoubtedly a strange part of reality. Dahrendorf once captured this when he referred to "the vexatious fact of society". It was vexing before he wrote and has remained intransigently so ever since. I once expressed the oddity of its constitution in the following riddle (Archer 1995, 165):

What is it that depends on human intentionality but never conforms to anyone's intentions?

What is it that relies upon people's concepts but which they never fully know?

What is it that depends upon human activity but never corresponds to the actions of even the most powerful?

What is it that has no form without us, yet which forms us as we seek its transformation?

What is it that never satisfies the precise designs of anyone yet because of this always motivates its reconstitution?

It is worth spelling out the challenges set by this riddle. To say that the social order is never ever exactly what anyone wants or wanted, to emphasize that this is the underlying motor of change, to stress that the social origins of any transformation lie in structured struggles between groups, and to underline that the resulting social forms are generated by all of the above is to say two things about it. First, that the process of social structuring is continuously activity-dependent but, second, that action itself is always shaped—though never determined—by the prior structural context in which it takes place. In other words and at any given time the social order is the result of the result of prior social relations conditioned in an antecedent structural (and cultural) context. Such relations between individuals and groups may be in conflict, coalition, or consensus. When interaction leads to change the product of this interaction is "morphogenesis," with "morpho" indicating shape and "genesis" signaling that the shaping results from social relations. Hence, "morphogenesis" refers to "those processes which tend to elaborate or change a system's given form, state or structure" (Buckley 1967, 58). Conversely, "morphostasis" refers to those complex system-environmental exchanges that tend to preserve or maintain a given form, organization, or state of the social order or part of it. As such, the social order is shaped and reshaped but conforms to no mold; it is patterned and repatterned but is confined to no pattern; it is organized and reorganized but its organization needs comply with none of its precedents.

Because of this quintessential ability of the social order to change shape, all traditional analogies and all current uses of the analogical imagination are simply misleading. The social is not a mechanism with fixed, indispensible parts and determinate relations between them, preset preferred states and preprogrammed homeostatic mechanisms that work like the thermostat. The social is not similar to an organism, either phylo-genetically or onto-genetically, whose development can be described in terms of evolutionary adaptation. The social is not a simple cybernetic system, which presupposes a particular (centralized) form capable of carrying out goal-directed error-correction through negative feedback. Finally, nor is the social order the type of self-organizing system required by Chaos and Complexity theories. All the above refer to particular kinds of systems whose common denominator is that they have proved amenable to great explanatory leaps forward within their respective domains. I am assuming that it is unnecessary to belabour the mechanical and organic analogues again for their shortcomings, even though it is necessary to query the continued use of the term *adaptive* in the term "complex adaptive systems," which is only too current.

To talk about the social order at all is to deny that all things social are a matter of contingency. Only given the metaphysical assumption that some relations are necessary ones and are relatively enduring can it be reasonable to study the social, let alone to talk about social science. However, all the analogies mentioned above were bids by social theorists to borrow breakthroughs from other disciplines that were bought at a steep price. Adopting them rightfully spelt a rejection of complete contingency and a commitment to the social being ordered, but buying into them entailed a prior acceptance about *how* the social was ordered. It had to be presumed in advance to be "like x," in the analogue domain. Yet, it seems obvious that no other discipline can presume (or more commonly be presumed) to furnish *a priori* judgments about the nature of social order. Every such attempt at borrowing is misleading for social theorizing because it leads away from examining social reality itself. Each new analogue constitutes a denial of what is ontologically vexatious about the social order. It also usually entails denying the significance of its human and relational constitution.

"Social morphogenesis" necessarily rejects complete contingency, but it makes no presumption that the ordering of the social resembles any other form of reality, nor that the totality is homologous with the form of one of its components (language being the favorite contender) or with some state of it (equilibrium or far-from-equilibrium). The social is only like itself and the task of social theory is to conceptualize and explain how relatively ordered and relatively enduring social forms have their genesis in agential relations, just as social beings have their genesis in social forms.

Reformulating the issue in terms of morphogenesis

I will begin with what seems to be the central proposition at stake: namely, that the form of the social is always and everywhere the product of "structure," "culture," and "agency" in relation with one another.[1] Without being fussy about definitions for a moment, leave out "structure" and the contexts people confront become kaleidoscopically contingent;[2] omit culture and no one has a repertoire of ideas for construing the situations in which they find themselves;[3] without agency we lose activity-dependence as the efficient cause of there being any social order. Then either contingency or determinism would have a clear field—one cleared of social theorizing.

Morphogenesis intensifies throughout modernity but, to become dominant, requires positive feedback to be untrammelled in order to generate ever-accelerating social change. This latter state does not yet characterize the global social order. Nevertheless, the giant steps towards the social being regulated by positive feedback in the last two decades can be used to reframe the issue. That issue is as old as social theorizing: namely, "Where are we going?" It was the main preoccupation of the founding fathers, with their different answers: revolution, rationalization, or reintegration.

Nevertheless "change," "novelty," and "variety" remain imprecise terms. It was mainly the protagonists of (social) cybernetics who first sought to give any *precision* to the notion of "variety," an absence lacking in Luhmann and his followers. Nevertheless, the usefulness of this "precision" was limited because cybernetics continued to bear the marks of its origins in information theory. The reservations that follow are intended as signposts to where reconceptualization is needed.

Difficulties are rooted in the fact that most of the influential pioneers concerned themselves with "variety" alone without giving significant attention to sociological questions about its distribution and diffusion: that is, to "social integration" as distinct from "system integration."[4] Systems theory in general has shown a marked tendency to neglect the conditions necessary for new forms of "social integration" and given almost exclusive attention to "variety" as the main or sole driver and characteristic of social transformation. Taken to its conclusion, preoccupation with increasing differentiation between people ends with "transactional individualism," meaning that "singletons" transact their uniquely specific requirements directly with the system. Fundamentally, this is because the key concepts (borrowed from information theory) to capture morphogenesis[5] are ones that privilege innovation to the detriment of what binds a social order together.

Thus, it seems useful to pinpoint why the increase in "variety" has entirely different connotations and denotations in succeeding generations of cybernetic systems theory. The brief discussion that follows is intended to show that the social sciences cannot simply borrow concepts, propositions, and theories to produce an instant "social cybernetics" or "sociology of complexity." Interdisciplinarity can, at best, stimulate ideas. What it cannot and should not result in is a shuffling and shuttling of concepts between them that is damaging for both.

"Variety" for social science in the first cybernetics

The definition of "variety" in early cybernetics is one where the *quantity of variety* can always be measured. To Ashby, working in terms of information theory, the term "variety" (1956, 126) referred to the number of distinct elements in a set. Hence, the preoccupation of early cybernetics with "codes," very varied in kind but always with a *finite number* of possibilities necessarily capable of enumeration (such as the information given by traffic lights). Hence, too, the operationalization of "variety', such that:

> [I]n a "given set' this is a question "of how many distinguishable elements it contains. Thus, if the order of occurrence is ignored, the set *c, b, c, a, c, c, a, b, c, b, b, a* which contains twelve elements, contains only three *distinct* elements – a, b and c. Such a set will be said to have a variety of three elements.
> (Ashby 1956, 124–25)

In other words, "variety' in the "first' cybernetics is an objective, aggregate concept, best suited to coded information where effort has been given to making distinctions sufficiently clear to exclude subjective interpretation[6] and to reduce any that may nonetheless intrude to the status of human error.

Let us simply note three basic differences between how the term "variety' is used by Ashby and the ways in which it appears useful to incorporate this concept into conceptualizing increasing morphogenesis in the social order.

First, as defined above, "variety' denotes an objective aggregate such that it can be said a set "has a variety of X elements." What is included as "an element" is not problematic within information theory because the purpose of clearly communicating something delineates it in advance (as in the design of traffic lights). However, in society, a crucial distinction has to be made between "variety *per se*" and "novelty" or "new variety," because the effect of novelty is often the displacement of old properties. Thus, in the social order, aggregate variety frequently diminishes with certain innovations,[7] meaning that aggregates of distinguishable elements are not merely unhelpful but can be highly deceptive.[8]

Second, the aggregate approach is atomistic. It is capable of recording only those elements that can be counted in units or on a *per capita* basis. Crucially, this means that "variety" necessarily excludes "relational goods' unless these are reduced to individual terms, yet reducibility is precisely what the concept of "relational goods" excludes. Moreover, disaggregation would entail the erroneous premise that common goods are divisible, that people's "share" of a marriage, a football team, or an orchestra can be portioned out, which is a contradiction in terms because the relational properties making for a great team are not amenable to aggregation, as in an addition sum. Attempts to incorporate relational goods by disaggregation would also imply a fallacious notion of individual substitutability (for example, that any good tennis player can be someone's doubles' partner). The aggregative approach basically deals with individuals and quantifiable things and thus cannot include those forms of variety or novelty that are collective, qualitative, and, above all, relational properties.

Third, the computational approach to defining "variety" is confined to the incidence of "elements" but mute about their distribution. Thus, the same numerical count representing "a variety of three elements" is compatible with the three being distributed amongst different tracts of the population or all being concentrated in the same hands. Although it is usually the case that if incidence has been counted then the distribution can also be calculated, that will only happen if *distributions are considered to be as important as aggregates*. And that will only be the case if social integration is considered to be equivalent in importance: that is, if distributional issues are held to be as important as matters of aggregate variety when social transformation is under discussion.

The second cybernetics and social heterogeneity

In the "Second Cybernetics," as Maruyama termed his approach, positive, deviation-amplifying feedback was allied to some discussion of the *distribution of variety*. Throughout his huge corpus of work (Nyfelt 2011), Maruyama dealt exclusively with "Deviation-Amplifying Mutual Causal Processes" (1963, 164–179)—that is, positive feedback "processes that are loosely termed as 'vicious circles' and 'compound interests'; in short, all processes of mutual causal relationships that amplify an insignificant or accidental initial kick, build up deviation and diverge from the initial condition" (1963, 164). The illustrations he gives are the enlargement of a crack in a rock by water collecting, freezing, and widening the fissure and the "kick start" of a frontier town from the accidental death of a horse or loss of a wheel leading someone to settle in that spot, rather than elsewhere on an otherwise homogeneous plain. From then on, homogeneity gives way to heterogeneity as the first homestead gradually attracted other residents and later prompted the opening of shops, facilities, and transport, as the generative mechanism engaged for variety to stimulate more variety.

Forty years later, Maruyama was to complain that although his emphasis on the quantitative side of change-amplifying causal loops had been well received, most "readers did not even notice the the more important qualitative side: *the necessity, desirability and increase in interactive heterogeneity*" (2003, 607–628; italics added). Over the next four decades he stressed that "interaction among heterogeneous elements can genuinely create new information, not just a new combination of old information, and the way the amount of information can increase" (2003, 618).

Here, *variety* embraces *new variety* or *novelty*, as the product of one kind of *heterogeneity* entering into "symbiosis" with other heterogeneous elements. Symbiosis entails mutual benefits for both parties, meaning by definition that every symbiotic development is positive-sum for those involved. What, however, about those (in any given population) who are not involved? Does a gap widen between a new elite, adept at initiating symbiosis, and benefitting from it and a new mass of "others"? In that case, it is impossible to ignore the plummeting of social integration that would ensue from such a *divided distribution* of morphogenetic variety.

What is of concern is Maruyama's growing preoccupation with *heterogeneity* (differences) alone and his disregard of *homogeneity* (similarities) in a population.

The latter is relegated to the bad old days when theories of "socio-cultural adaptation implied the desirability of sociocultural homogeneity" (2003, 624). Of course "one knows what he means" and I have consistently railed in unison with him against the common equation of "culture" with "shared meanings" (Archer 1985; Archer and Elder-Vass 2012). Nevertheless, an integrated society cannot be based upon *heterogeneity alone*.

Differences are necessary amongst members (as valid expressions of their differing capacities) but so are similarities: the former create the *novelty* resulting in new opportunities, the latter continue to supply a bonding that links together members of a group (community, team, or enterprise), accentuating their human commonalities and making their belongingness something more than rational instrumental opportunism. If similarities are progressively eroded while differences increase (through variety generating more variety amongst a restricted portion of the population) this is a formula for a serious decline in social integration. Such a progressive fall in social integration is not a loss that can be offset by Heterogenistics (Maruyama 1978), the socially engineered symbiosis-for-all that Maruyama advances as the solution:

> Individuals in a culture, or cultures of the world, among which symbiotic combinations can be found, can be hooked up in a network. For example, old people who like to be with children can be housed near families who need babysitters.
>
> (1978, 94)

It is only through the involvement of nearly everyone in the process of generating *new variety* (via social policy interventions) that Maruyama (rightly) believes is capable of intensifying morphogenesis while avoiding a divided social order.

Hence, the part played by social relations and relationality in shaping anything other than a *divided* society largely make their exit. It is precisely when attention is focussed exclusively upon *heterogeneity*, as Maruyama did (1994), because its intensification fosters more and more morphogenesis, that any concern for social integration again disappears. If the consequent distribution of variety is confined to a minority of a given population (those with the appropriate "mindscape") it would result in finer and finer forms of differentiation between them. They could not even be deemed to be an elite because all elites are held to have binding interests in common—however much these are at variance with other sections of the population. The accentuation of *heterogeneity* alone is always a formula for "individualism."

It is so because the differences characterizing each agent so overwhelm any commonalities with others that they increasingly engage in transactions with the system as a whole—detecting, raiding, and exploiting these novelties (Teune and Mlinar 1978).[9] In the process, subjects who can accumulate this new variety are differentiated still further from their peers, prompting a sedulous reduction in what remained of social integration based upon similarities. As these subjects acquire more new variety, their association with other social units becomes less and less rewarding and prompts the multiplication of the number of smaller and smaller social units that follows. For example, the existing number of Political Parties can no longer represent the extent of differentiation in the population.[10] This is why "symbiosis" seems to be a restrictive concept for capturing the dynamics of morphogenetic intensification, because not all can participate and "those among whom no symbiotic combinations can be found need to try different networks" (Maruyama 1992, 94). In other words, let them migrate elsewhere. Social integration decreases proportionately as growing *heterogeneity* deprives the ultra-differentiated of those with sufficient similarities to constitute other than "trading" partners; durable human relations give way to ephemeral transactions.[11]

Complex adaptive systems in sociology

"The modern systems perspective eschews analogizing, and suggests that it is a morphogenetic system, which simply means that it tends to regenerate or change its own structure" (Buckley 1998, 69). Walter Buckley first wrote the above in 1968 as the prelude to answering his own question, "what kind of a system is society?" Despite some important continuities with Maruyama (reaching back to MacIver's welcome clarifications of causality in the social domain), his response signaled a break with "informatics" and a proper introduction of systems theorizing to social theory. In today's context his greatest contribution was to reject the cybernetic *self-governing system* (of explicit goal-seeking controlled by error detecting and correcting feedback), itself an analogue of self-steering missiles in the Second World War. At the same time, he did so while *refusing to endorse* the contrary characterization of the social as a *self-organizing system*. As will be seen, his avoidance of both analogues was deeply rooted in his respect for the distinctive nature of the social order, deriving from the consciousness of its human agents, the tension between its competing interest groups, and the dual role of culture in ideational coordination and ideological manipulation.

As far as I can discover, Buckley never gave a formal definition of "variety" to parallel those discussed above, but contented himself with referring simply to "the continuous introduction of 'variety' into the [morphogenic] system (new ideas, novel ways of doing things)" (1998, 239). He undoubtedly included science and technology, revisions and additions to meanings and symbols, political and economic thought and practical action, but warned that "variety" also included "deviance." In other words, it was not an unalloyed good thing. Through morphogenesis the social system is "continually generating variety by virtue of its normal dynamic interrelations of parts and selectively mapping it against the variety of its external environment and internal milieu" (1998, 69). As he goes on to state, this involves assessing the "sources of variety and change" in a manner different from in the homeostatic systems (of functionalism) that view variation as abnormal, external, and potentially disruptive and hence always counteracted by a system whose viability hinges on maintenance of a given structure (1998, 71).

Which of these sources of variety come to prove relatively enduring, where and how? Significantly, Buckley talks of a selection process through which "new behaviours, ideas, meanings, and definitions of the situation act as the bases for new structures." In other words, the structuring and restructuring of society are the means of institutionalizing new variety, which becomes the socio-cultural framework from where the next process of change or recursiveness is generated. He is equally clear that these processes are continuously activity-dependent but the actions involved always emanate from prior structural and cultural contexts: "all the sources of sociocultural change work through the choices and decisions of some groups of people, working within their various social structural and cultural environments" (1998, 74). Note that this sketch of a "structure, culture, and agency" excludes reductionist "agent-based modelling," where the state of the macro-system derives directly from agential characteristics and the combinations of individuals. The second respect in which it dissociates itself from any affinity with *self-organization* is that "social selection has an at least partially reasoned *and directed* quality to it, although often there are opposing or parallel forces directing it in different directions" (1998, 73).

The social order is recognized for itself and of its own kind and thus is equally unlike the "completely opportunistic process" of biological selection as it is unlike goal-seeking missiles and thermostats. Social systems are purposeful rather than goal-seeking because conscious agents, especially working in groups, can form, articulate, and pursue purposes even though they will usually encounter the active promotion of aims contrary to their own. Modeling such group interaction (which does not exclude individual contributions) is social theory's own task and borrowing from other disciplines will not avail. One way of seeing the task set is that its accomplishment would be a fit response to the riddle set at the start of this paper.

One way of going awry would be to endorse the *self-government* model advanced from within cybernetics. "A simple, cybernetic feedback model of explicit group goal-seeking does not fit most societies of the past and present because of a lack in those societies of informed, centralized direction and widespread, promotively interdependent goal behaviors of individuals and subgroups" (Buckley 1967, 206). Another way of putting this is that *self-government* is a form of social organization that requires a centralized structure—one greatly more efficient than any of our historical exemplars—and the active support of those affected by its regulation. Buckley immediately supplies an economical five-point critique (1967, 172–176) of why such a system will not be encountered. At this point in his argument, he clearly anticipates a parting of the ways (not a bifurcation point, as will be seen) and asks, "To what extent, and in what senses, are the existing social and cultural structures the results of the purposeful, goal-seeking actions of men, and to what extent are they the 'blind' consequences of the confluence of sociocultural 'forces'?" (1967, 177).

"Blind" consequences stand for *self-organization* and he no more endorses this than the version of *self-government* examined. Instead, he turns to the struggles between groups, interest-based and ideational, and the bearing of power, authority, and legitimacy upon them.

> [T]he goal-seeking actions of men enter in at every point, except that: 1) these actions are not coherent or "congruent," but interact to produce the

accommodations, compromises, and "side effects" producing the overall "blind" configuration; and 2) the goal-seeking actions of some individuals and subgroups ramify but little into the social fabric, while those of others – whether playing official or nonofficial roles – account for important seams and patterns in that fabric.

(1967, 177)

The development of my own "morphogenetic approach" has followed the path Buckley laid out by disengaging three analytical phases of <structural conditioning → group interaction → structural elaboration>, as discussed in the Introduction to this book. What was advocated there is a conception of the social order as what I term a *Relationally Contested Organization*, one in which different material interest groups and cultural interest groups struggle for institutional hegemony, with the outcome at any given time being the product of their power play, their coalitions, compromises, concessions, and unintended consequences.

From systems theory to complexity theory

Our one global social system is now coming much closer to a social order that works through social morphogenesis. This means putting temporary brackets around discussing how it came about, which was by the self-same process underpinning globalization. However, social theorists appear collectively stumped by "globalization"—their favored way of characterizing the rapid changes taking place in the last two decades—such that they are not even in agreement about whether they are talking about cause or effect when using the term. The best-known theories of globalization[12] simply seized upon one element of SAC as the leading component. Thus, "culture" led for those who branded the changing social order as "Information (or Knowledge) Society"; "structure" for others calling it "Globalized Capitalism" or even capitalism's "Empire"; and "agency" for the third group, stressing the "de-structuration and individualization" of the risky, uncontrollable juggernaut—Reflexive Modernization.

Perhaps this disarray among social scientists goes some way towards explaining the attractions of Chaos and Complexity theory to them. In what follows I have nothing at all to say about the merits of these theoretical developments within their own fields of natural science but only about "Complexity" as another misleading metaphor applied to the social. If some renowned natural scientists have played at being Red Riding Hood's granny, let us stick with the behavior of the granddaughter.

When his theories began to have influence beyond physics, Prigogine (writing with Allen) defined the system characteristics that were to be taken up by social theorists:

[T]he systems that interest us are large, nonlinear systems operating far from thermodynamic equilibrium. It is precisely in such systems that coherent self-organization phenomena can occur, characterized by some macroscopic organization or pattern, on a scale much larger than that of the individual elements in interaction. It is a structure whose characteristics are a property of the collectivity and cannot be inferred from a study of the individual elements in isolation.

(1982, 7)

Let us focus on the notion of a *self-organizing system*, upon which all the other concepts depend: those of a system in a state far-from-equilibrium, of change not being linear, being irreducible and generating emergent features that are held to be "evolutionary." In fact, there is no generally accepted and cross-disciplinary definition of "self-organization" and various authors have supplied informal stopgaps:

> a self-organizing system is one in which there is no central locus of information and control. Information and control are both thoroughly distributed, and collective behavior is emergent from the individualistic dynamics of components in a manner that produces the illusion of coordinated effort.
>
> (Ismael 2011, 332)

Termite colonies—yes, ants—are the best-known animate example, along with schools of fish, turbulent fluids, traffic systems, and economic markets. I will return to this last "exemplar."

Its appeal amongst certain social theorists was because such a self-organizing system appeared able to deal with rapid social morphogenesis. The following statement is typical of those who enthusiastically adopted it.

> In the last decades, self-organization theory has emerged as a transdisciplinary theory that allows describing reality as permanently moving and producing novelty ("emergence"). The concept of self-organization grasps the dynamic, complex, evolving nature of systems in nature and society. The main motivation for taking up this notion is that contemporary society seems to be inherently complex, networked, and dynamic and that an explanation of its phenomena with this concept is manifest.
>
> (Fuchs 2008, p. 8)

In their haste to establish a new orthodoxy about the rapidity of change and evolutionary character of new novelty, the same authors also sought to distinguish millennial society from any tinge of morphostasis. In twentieth-century theory, that could only mean theories that were soft on homeostatis, since morphogenesis had already engaged. Hence, a new round of hostilities towards functionalism ensued, as the only candidate within living memory. This was ironic because some of those now pillorying it (Byrne 1998; Reed and Harvey 1992; Urry 2003; Walby 2009) had never shown the slightest affinity with functionalist thought. There is a double irony, because these theorists made no mention of the simultaneous enthusiasm for "habit" and "habitual action" amongst those keeping Bourdieu's memory green, and yet having major problems with the rapidity of *fin de siècle* change (Archer 2010).

What is a self-organizing system?

According to Fuchs,

> Self-organization is a process where a system reproduces itself with the help of its own logic and by the synergistic activities of its components, that is, the system produces itself based on an internal logic. Self-organizing systems are their own reason and cause; they produce themselves (*causa sui*).
>
> (2008, 32)

Only a decade earlier this statement would have won an Oscar for reification. Let us try to get a proper handle on the concept since it is a matter of dispute if there is any formal definition at all or even characterization that covers each and every intuitive instance of a self-organizing system. As the philosopher J.T. Ismael states:

> There is no generally accepted definition of self-organization. The mechanisms that underpin the emergent behavior of self-organizing systems are complex and in many cases not well understood . . . It is contested whether there is a general characterization of self-organization, whether there is some dynamical essence that can be distilled out of these examples, or just a cluster of cases, exhibiting a syndrome of properties, remains to be seen.
>
> (2011, 332 n.5)

Moreover, *how and when* is it claimed that the social order became *self-organizing*? After all, from the political perspective, the long history of modernity was one of irregular movements towards *self-government*: the establishment of nation states, the accountability of monarchy, parliamentarianism, representative democracy and universal franchise, political parties and trades unions, the League of Nations, the United Nations, and the mooting of global governance. Equivalent points could be made for economics and for all other social institutions, since institutionalization is an attempt to exercise governance in a particular social domain. My claim is not that such historical developments were efficient or effective in societal guidance—Etzioni's *Active Society* (1968) repays rereading for why they were not. Instead, they are better viewed as part of society's *contested organization*—that is, as the relational products—most relatively enduring— of unfinished historical struggles between structured social groups. What developed at any point bore the trademark of compromise and concession, fuelled further struggles for re-elaboration, and generally conformed to the riddle in never being exactly what anyone wanted—that is, fit for their purposes.

The point is simply that *contested relational organizations* did not and have not yet disappeared. In most parts of the world groups are still contesting elections, still writing constitutions, still mobilizing in social movements, and still overturning governments. Even more importantly, global capitalism organizes new markets and its structured competition produces new winners and losers. What the ongoing financial crisis revealed is the highly structured nature of finance capitalism. That it is in huge need of overhaul is not the point here. What is indisputably the case is that every attempt to return to "business as usual" is an effort to reinforce and protract this form of economic governance. Similarly, other institutions, education (and health) being at the forefront, seek to govern the market in credentials, the International Baccalaureate, MBA, and IMBA being remarkably successful in extending the governance of Western universities. In other words, all that is structurally solid has not melted into air. The social order struggles on as *contested organizations* do, thanks to the exertions of those with vested interests in its institutions—or their transformation. These are anything but exemplary forms of *self-government*, but they are battling on and incorporating greater tracts of the global population. How, then, is it credible to announce that the social is a *self-organizing system*?

Social change always comes from somewhere and that somewhere is the preceding structural context in which, for whatever reasons and by dramatic or less arresting means, interaction generates change. From the point of view of the historic durability of the *relationally contested organization*, as the generic model of modernity's social order, the proponents of or converts to Complexity theory owe us an account of the changes bringing about *self-organization*. It is not forthcoming. They have adopted a paradigm shift and what we are asked to endorse is an instance of the epistemic fallacy in which their change of theoretical framework is taken for social reality itself.

Various forms of social theory are averse to social structures, or more precisely to crediting them with properties that can be exercised as causal powers. Some such theorists unwittingly prepared the ground for conceptualizing the social as *self-organized* by replacing structures with flows, waves, and liquidity. This proved helpful to the take-up of Complexity theory for two reasons. First, this replacement entailed the endorsement of "destructuration" in late or Second Wave modernity, along with the disappearance of "zombie categories" such as social classes, until "institutionalized individualism" was presented as the main "unit" of the social order.[13] Second, Giddens' earlier work (1979) had already broken up the ground: structures had only a "virtual" ontology until "instantiated" by agents, with the two clamped together in what I termed the vice of "central conflation" (Archer 1982). It is small wonder that Giddens is having something of a revival amongst those advocating Complexity theory for analyzing the social order. With the middle ground now cleared of structures, diagrams such as the one reproduced here became common in complexity circles (Fig. 11.1).

Giddens' indefiniteness and indeterminacy about who is responsible for social change, how, why and what they do in relational opposition to others in order to attain transformation, was the main criticism of structuration theory. But it is currently re-presented as its strength.

Although theorists who endorse *self-organization* are rarely explicit, they effectively marry Holism and Individualism: holism (respectable again) for the social system and individualism for social agents. The space between the two is occupied exclusively by "networks," in the absence of structures. What then flourishes is "actor-based modelling" using large data sets and powerful software. Why? Because, in Epstein's words: "Agent-based models allow us to study the micro-to-macro mapping" (1999). Even more directly, "Agent-based models provide computational demonstrations that a given micro-specification is in fact

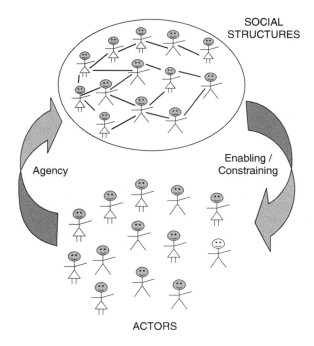

Figure 11.1 The self-organization of social systems.
Source: Fuchs (2008, 52).

sufficient to generate a macrostructure of interest . . . the generativist wants an account of the configuration's *attainment by a decentralized system of heterogeneous autonomous agents*" (1999, 42–43). Not surprisingly, this author has difficulty in maintaining that such accounts are not Methodologically Individualist. Thus, complexity theorists "expect" to be dealing with decentralized systems as part and parcel of *self-organization*. The trouble is that the social order does not always oblige. Structures matter and it is therefore time to get back to those traffic flows and economic markets as supposed exemplars of *self-organization*.

How to turn a heap into a whole

Many kinds of statistical regularities, about both social order and disorder, are presented as exemplifications of *self-organization* by Complexity theorists. For illustration let us briefly examine how they deal with "market trading."[14] As with many different topics, the empirical regularities detected mathematically are greeted with a "Humean Wow!" Yet, this goes much further because great expectations for social theory are also extended by followers of the Santa Fe school: namely, the capacity to solve the micro–macro issue and the problem of structure and agency (Byrne 1998, 37). Let us see how they go about doing so.

The recipe for generating a systemic whole (the finance market) out of a human heap (individual market traders) is very easy to follow. It consists in, first, simply *removing the structural (and cultural) contexts in which action takes place*. Second, *relations and relationality* are carefully excised because "each trader is modeled as an autonomous, interactive agent and the aggregation of their behavior results in market behavior" (Neuberg and Bertels 2003, 28). The remaining ingredients are now ready for placing in a powerful computer for cooking.

These two "preliminary operations" are essential. When the structural and cultural contexts are stripped away what remains is nothing but the *collective behavior* of collections of traders on the stock markets. Once more, the object of sociological study has become the crowd![15] Interestingly, this manoeuvre of eliminating structure by *fiat* in order to address current behavior has considerable similarities to Searle's method (1996, 127–147) of consigning it to the "Background," although he acknowledges that it has to be wheeled in and out to make sense of what is going on. The removing of human, interpersonal, and group relations is equally necessary because "actor-based modelling" deals in terms of monads who are busy trying to out-guess their fellows and are never motivated by relational considerations. Formally, there are similarities here with Rational Choice theory, except that crowd behavior is not instrumentally rational.

The monadic trading agents make transactions based upon individual risk-aversion and their expectations about future prices together with market information influencing the decisions of each trader (Arthur et al. 1997, 15–44). Traders compete freely on the basis of the common market information with their next decisions determining the next market prices (whether in New York or Shanghai) in a cyclical process where price movements feed back continually and influence traders' future decisions about whether to buy or sell. In the diagram reproduced here, all that is involved is "information" and "aggregation" (Fig. 11.2).

The excitement arises because instead of market movements around the world showing a random pattern (where the value of a would be 0.5), regardless of market location, many show a typical value for a of approximately 0.7, thanks to the feedback effect, which "provides a wonderful example of how emergent phenomena from a Complex System can have universal properties" (Johnson 2007, 113–127)—that is, until the current crisis, strangely not mentioned in the 2010 edition of the book just quoted, when the above fractals "died" and banks went in quest of bail-outs.

I will leave the details of how the house of finance capital came down to those better qualified but, in the spirit of Mandelbaum discussing the referents necessary to understand cashing a cheque, these include unsecured credit, the housing market and its packages of sub-prime mortgages, inter-bank trade in loans, hedge funds, derivatives, and so forth. The point is not that these suddenly appeared on the scene (or the Background was wheeled back in) but, rather, that they were active factors throughout, which produced the stock markets that produced the fractals that produced the universals—while ever they got away with these doings. In fact, we are dealing not with a so-called social "power law" but with power play between groups of economic agents in a *relationally contested organization*, one whose structures became more clearly visible as the house of cards crashed.

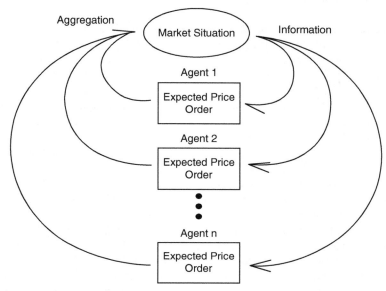

Figure 11.2 Market Trading explained by 'information + aggregation'.
Source: Neuberg and Bertels (2003).

Why agents are not ants

Human persons and the social agents and actors they become (Archer 2000) show a variety of responses to their environments that are mediated through their internal properties and powers, the most important of which is their conscious mental "reflexivity." Reflexivity enables them actively to internalize, employ, and elaborate the cultural representations (beliefs, theories, practical knowledge, etc.) created by their forebears. Thus, they can add new or modified items of their own (new theories, new knowledge, etc.) to the Cultural System, extending the range of "intelligibilia"[16] at any given time. Socio-culturally, the ideas of agents (dead or alive) can be used to encourage or discourage courses of action amongst fellow agents, ones that cannot be reduced to *collective behavior* (for instance "voting," "church going," "house buying," "consulting a dictionary," or "undertaking research"). Culture and agency thus work together in creating representational loops between themselves and their social environment. In this lies the difference between action and behavior. Human action is more varied and complex than the informational input received from the environment. This is not the case for the ant's response to environmental stimuli, which cannot exceed the pieces of information received. Ants' responses, unlike those of agents, are incapable of much flexibility, of fast innovation, of envisaging changes in their habitats or collectively planning to change them.

In an ant colony, as a *self-organizing system*,

> the link between stimulus and response is not mediated by anything that has the form of a deliberative process involving explicit representation of goals and means-ends reasoning about how to achieve them. To refuse to recognize this difference is to refuse to recognize a distinction that has practical as well as theoretical significance. Self-organizing systems do not exhibit the flexibility of deliberators, they do not adapt spontaneously to changes in circumstances, they do not have goals of their own, they cannot form temporally extended plans.
>
> (Ismael 2011, 346)

Conversely, persons with their cultural representations of their social settings *and of themselves within them* deliberate reflexively about their social environment. They act as what Charles Taylor calls "strong evaluators" (1985), and exert some governance over their own lives by forming "projects" for making their way through the social world (Archer 2007). In short, human agents both individually and collectively aspire to *self-governance* and they succeed to some—always limited—degree.

There are those, such as Dennett, who wish to deny any distinction between colonies of ants and competing chess players (2009) and try to do so by demoting human intentions to "as-if" intentionality. This is complete demotion because an "as-if" intention does not really exist and thus cannot have causal power. When we treat one another as intentional systems—as friends do—attributing "beliefs" and "desires" to them and to ourselves in our interactions, to Dennett we are merely "finessing our ignorance of the details of the processes going on in each other's skulls (and our own!) (1987, 5). Dennett wants to annul the properties and powers of human consciousness in order to remove the dividing line between agents and ants. In this, he relies on the fact that examination of the human brain discovers no equivalent to a Commander in Chief directing activities. Yet there is nothing in his arguments or in neurological evidence to exclude the conscious mind being emergent from the brain's hardware.

In my trilogy of books on reflexivity, although I have indeed talked a lot about "people exercising some governance in their own lives," this is far from considering agents to be paradigms of *self-government*. Granted that the majority of agents do have unimpaired powers of reflexivity, used in mental activities (such as planning, decision-making, budgeting, clarifying, self-monitoring), this does not make them *self-governing*. They are not because their autobiographies (singular or collective) are never made in circumstances of their own choosing. Structures constrain and enable, and what constraints and enablements work upon are agential "projects" (Archer 2003). But structures also motivate, with subjects enlarging or contracting their projects in the light of the circumstances they confront. When balked by them, they do not behave like an ant which discovers its hole has been blocked. Human agents reflexively deliberate about circumvention and subversion (which significant numbers pursue) or they think out a second or third-best project that they believe can be carried out. Yet, the circumstances will never be of their choosing.

In exactly the same way as was argued for the social system at the end of the third section above, "'Variety' for social science in the first cybernetics," where agency is concerned we are also dealing with a *relationally contested organization*. Persons and groups can neither be reduced to *träger* of social forces or cultural discourses that work from the "top down," nor be portrayed as free-wheeling monads who combine and recombine from the "bottom up." All human agents are born into social relations and live in and through relationships. Nevertheless, this is a fundamentally *contested* way of life: socialization is not simple internalization but the receipt of "mixed messages" (Archer 2012); subjects have to make conscious decisions about which relationships to prioritize and which to subordinate or eliminate; and agents have to deliberate about what relational goods matter sufficiently for them to invest something of themselves in them. All of these reflexive activities are internal to human agents but without them the social order cannot be understood or explained.

Conclusion

If "structure," "culture," and "agency" are involved in every instance of social change it is futile to set up a two-cornered fight between whether the social order is *self-governing* or *self-organizing*. (In any case, the more sophisticated commentators conclude it to be a "mixed type.") In the physical sciences the changing nature of far-from-equilibrium systems is held to derive from "external perturbations." However, as Reed and Harvey openly agree, the "questions of agency raised by the symbolic production of humans is quite another matter, for in human societies we confront the possibility that the locus of perturbations in certain instances maybe internal to society itself" (1992, 370). Let the last word go to Nicolis and Prigogine, who do allow that "internal perturbations" deriving from human values and actions mean that social systems may differ radically from the analogue of natural systems. The social order

> [I]s an interplay between the behaviour of its actors and impinging constraints from the environment. It is here that the human system finds its unique specificity. Contrary to the moleclues, the actors in a physico-chemical system, or even the ants or the members of other animal societies, human beings develop individual *projects and desires* . . . The difference between desired and actual behaviour therefore acts as a constraint of a new type which, together with the environment, shapes the dynamics. A basic question that can be raised is whether, under those circumstances, the overall evolution is capable of leading to some kind of global optimum or, on the contrary, whether each human system constitutes a unique realization . . . In other words, is past experience sufficient for predicting the future, or is a high degree of unpredictability of the future the essence of human adventure, be it at the individual level of learning or at the collective level of history making?
>
> (1989, 238)

The two authors suggest that they lean towards the second alternative. My own conclusion is that the more morphogenetic the social becomes, the more we will need to examine social morphogenesis on its own social terms—of increasingly complicated interplays between structure, culture, and agency, their emergent properties and causal powers. Analogues from natural science would only prove more and more misleading.

It is by coming to terms with these complicated interplays—ones that cannot be assimilated to a mindless and aimless complexity—that the outcomes of social morphogenesis do not becomes matters of complete contingency. Simultaneously, however, we have to forfeit the consolations of an equally automatic and non-conscious "adaptation." In our structural, cultural, and human relations we—as agents and actors—still have to take responsibility for both the proximate and the distant effects of our doings and deal with their unintended consequences.

Notes

1. Even if other factors are involved (e.g. natural disasters), their *social reception* is mediated through the above.
2. The reason for not imposing definitions (yet) is that this statement applies equally to those Individualists for whom "structure" is generically no more than an aggregate as it does to strong "Emgergentists" such as Critical Realists.
3. Again this statement is impartial between those who define culture in one way or another as "shared meanings" and those who, like me, do not.
4. Lockwood (1964).
5. To characterize the social order, as opposed to the analytical "morphogenetic approach" that provides an explanatory framework for examining when, whether and why structural, cultural, and agential elaboration versus replication will result from a given period of social interaction.
6. Ashby does admit that "a set's variety is not an intrinsic property of the set: the observer and his powers of discrimination may have to be specified if the variety is to be well defined" (1956, 125). However, the insight is not followed up.
7. Although this is also the case in industrial technology, displacements are less susceptible to changes in fashion or manipulated consumption.
8. This is without entering the methodological and evaluative issues surrounding the designation of "an element" itself, let alone when it acquires the above adjectival prefixes, all of which are challenges to or for the supposed "objectivity."
9. In Teune and Mlinar (1978) a chapter is devoted to precisely this issue (pp. 127–146).
10. A "transaction" on the part of the super-differentiated subject may involve no one else and entails no human relationship. Already this can be seen in the development of investment supermarkets, where individuals no longer follow their hunches about the likely success of specific products, or in the erection of apartment buildings with no particular inhabitants in mind and no consultation of their particularistic preferences. In such cases, the investor already transacts with systemic "market trends" rather than with a market made up of human buyers.
11. The suggested use of "Heterogenistics" as the basis for a Social Policy bringing about marriages of symbiotic convenience (such as the lone old ladies as baby sitters) is to take a systemic view of human relations and to neglect the human characteristics precluding or potentially stymying such relationships; some old ladies wish to retire early, detest the children's music and feel threatened by bands of teenagers hanging out on the streets. Such manipulated and dehumanizing fixes are no solution to the deficit in social integration.
12. In the vast literature on "globalization," a clear distinction is not usually made between how it came about and how it works, the diachronic and the synchronic.

13 "Individualization is becoming the social structure of second modern society itself." Beck (1992 [1986]), p. 135.
14 Neil Johnson, a reputable scientist, produced a popular book, *Simply Complexity*, packed with examples from forecasting finanical markets, war-time casualties, marital partnering, avoiding flu and curing cancer. They are examples that give away the game I describe above.
15 Johnson (2007): "Complexity Science can be seen as the *study of the phenpmena which emerge from a collection of interacting objects*—and a crowd is a perfect example of such" (pp. 3–4).
16 Intelligibilia refer to all items possessing the dispositional capacity to be understood, whether or not they are at any given time. The corpus of intelligibilia is lodged in the Universal Library or Archive (see Archer 1988).

References

Archer, M. S. (1982) Morphogenesis versus structuration. *Br J Sociol* 33(4):455–483.
Archer, M. S. (1985) The myth of cultural integration. *Br J Sociol* 36(3):333–353.
Archer, M. S. (1988) *Culture and agency*. Cambridge University Press, Cambridge.
Archer, M. S. (1995) *Realist social theory: the morphogenetic approach*. Cambridge University Press, Cambridge.
Archer, M. S. (2000) *Being human: the problem of agency 2000*. Cambridge University Press, Cambridge.
Archer, M. S. (2003) *Structure, Agency and the Internal Conversation*. Cambridge University Press, Cambridge.
Archer, M. S. (2007) *Making our way through the world: human reflexivity and social mobility*. Cambridge University Press, Cambridge.
Archer, M. S. (2010) Routine, reflexivity, and realism. *Sociol Theor* 28(3):272–303.
Archer, M. S. (2012) *The reflexive imperative in late modernity*. Cambridge University Press, Cambridge.
Archer, M. S., and Elder-Vass, D. (2012) Cultural system or norm circles? An exchange. *Eur J Soc Theor* 15(1):93–115.
Arthur, W. B., Holland, J. H., LeBaron, B., Palmer, R., Tayler, P. (1997) Asset pricing under endogenous expectations in an artificial stock market. In: Arthur, W. B., Durlauf, S. N., Lane, D. N. (eds) *The economy as an evolving complex system ii*, vol 27. Addison-Wesley, Reading.
Ashby, R. (1956) *An introduction to cybernetics*. Wiley, New York.
Beck, U. (1992) *Towards a New Modernity*. Sage, London.
Buckley, W. (1967) *Sociology and modern systems theory*. Prentice-Hall, Englewood Cliffs, NJ.
Buckley, W. (1998) *Society—a complex adaptive system: essays in social theory*. Gordon and Breach, Amsterdam.
Byrne, D. (1998) *Complexity theory and the social sciences*. Routledge, Abingdon.
Dennett, D. C. (1987) *The intentional stance*. MIT Press, Cambridge MA.
Dennett, D. C. (2009) Intentional systems theory. In: McLaughlin A., Beckerman, Walter S. (eds) *Oxford handbook of the philosophy of mind*, Oxford University Press, Oxford.
Epstein, J. M. (1999) Agent-based computational models and generative social science. *Complexity* 4(5):41–56.
Etzioni, A. (1968) *The active society*. The Free Press, New York.
Fuchs, C. (2008) *Internet and society: social theory in the information age*. Routledge, New York and Abingdon.
Giddens, A. (1979) *Central problems in social theory*. Macmillan, London.

Ismael, J. T. (2011) Self-organization and self-governance. *Philos Soc Sci* 41(3):327–351.
Johnson, N. F. (2007) *Simply Complexity: A clear guide to Complexity Theory*. Oneworld, Oxford.
Lockwood, D. (1964) Social integration and system integration. In: Zollschan, G. K., Hirsch, W. (eds) *Explorations in social change*. Houghton Mifflin, Boston.
Maruyama, M. (1963) The second cybernetics: deviation-amplifying causal processes. *Am Sci* 5(2):164–179.
Maruyama, M. (1978) Heterogenistics and morphogenetics: toward a new concept of the scientific. *Theor Soc* 5(1):75–96.
Maruyama, M. (1992) Interrelations among science, politics, aesthetics, business management, and economics. In: Maruyama, M. (ed) *Context and complexity: cultivating contextural understanding*. Springer, New York.
Maruyama, M. (1994) Interwoven and interactive heterogeneity in the 21st century. *Technol Forecast Soc change* 45(1):93–102.
Maruyama, M. (2003) Causal loops, interaction, and creativity. *Int Rev Soc* 13(3):607–628.
Neuberg, L., Bertels, K. (2003) Heterogeneous trading agents. *Complexity* 8(5):28–35.
Nicolis, G. Prigogine I (1989) *Exploring complexity: an introduction*. Freeman, New York.
Nyfelt, P. (2011) *Professor Maruyama's writings*. http://heterogenistics.org/maruyama/bibliography/bibliography.html [accessed 14 July 2016].
Prigogine, I., Allen, P. M. (1982) The challenge of complexity. In: Schieve, W.C., Allen, P.M. (eds) *Self-organization and dissipative structures: applications is the physical and social sciences*. University of Texas Press, Austin, TX.
Reed, M., Harvey David, L. (1992) The new science and the old: complexity and realism in the social sciences. *J Theor Soc Behav* 22(4):353–380.
Searle, J. R. (1996) *The construction of social reality*. Penguin, London.
Taylor, C. (1985) Self-interpreting animals. In: his *Human agency and language*. Cambridge University Press, Cambridge.
Teune, H., Mlinar, Z. (1978) *The developmental logic of social systems*. Sage, Beverly Hills CA and London.
Urry, J. (2003) *Global complexity*. Polity, Cambridge.
Walby, S. (2009) *Globalization and inequalities: complextity and contested modernities*. Sage, London.

12 The generative mechanism reconfiguring Late Modernity

Introduction

Accounts of 'industrialization' and of 'globalization' were responses to unprecedented social novelty and both attempted – in very divergent ways – to answer the question of the day: 'What's going on and where is it leading?' The biggest difference between them is, that 250 years later, there are no redoubts providing shelter from the brunt of change even in the less developed parts of the world. Today, there is general unease that things are in a mess, such a complicated mess that critique has quavered and utopianism withered. In their place are facile and conflicting proclamations of New Ages by social scientists. If 'humankind cannot bear very much reality' (T. S. Eliot), perhaps the most unbearable aspect is the long-drawn-out state of 'transition', without any assurance of eventual 'transformation'.

This is not a reassuring chapter, but rather an attempt to disentangle the generative mechanisms at work, their interplay and their inevitable interweaving with contingency in the open system that is global society. That the present state of affairs is indeed complicated does not mean that it becomes more comprehensible or tractable by borrowing 'complexity theory' from the natural sciences (any more than the 'organic analogy' helped to explain the lineaments of industrial society). Nor can its complications be understood or explained by sweeping them under a portmanteau term such as 'detraditionalization', which falsely homogenises past diversity by calling it all 'tradition' (see Heelas et al. 1996). Nor can it be explained by grasping at some overt empirical patterning of events and holding one factor responsible for it, be that Structural (global capitalism), Agential (institutionalized individualism) or Cultural (information society) (Archer 2013a).

It is only by drawing upon a stratified social ontology and advancing generative mechanisms that causality is no longer wrongly seen as an empirical relation between events, even a complicated series of events. Instead, when Critical Realism 'speaks of causal mechanisms, then it speaks of what makes things work. Generally, that involves a reference to some kind of causal structure' (Porpora 2011). Gorski offers a succinct definition of generative mechanisms 'as emergent causal powers of related entities within a system' (2009). In turn, 'related entities' are defined as *'entities and relationships that are necessary to the recurring effects of the mechanism in question'*.[1]

He rightly insists that *'relational* entities' may also be non-observables, but 'they must have a physical substrate'. In other words, to describe capitalism as relationally 'competitive' is anchored in the substrata of relationships between the positions of owner and worker and other owners and workers (their relations of production). Porpora (1989) had already furnished the general concept of 'structure' as referring to relationships between (pre-established) social positions, such as manager/worker; teacher/pupil or landlord/tenant. In parallel, I have maintained (Archer 1988) that 'Culture' refers to relationships between (pre-established) ideational positions (beliefs, theories, ideologies, propositions), whose substratum is ultimately the universal archive in which they are lodged and from which they can be accessed.[2]

Were a generative mechanism to be correctly identified, were other processes found to be at play that deflected, distorted or suspended the causal powers of the first, and could the intervention of unrelated contingencies be specified, we would possess the basic elements needed to answer the key questions.

1   What underlies and unifies ordinary people's experiences of different disjunctions in their lives (new jobs, skills, locations; novel practices; the loss of taken-for-granted normativity and routine action; and the unprecedented extension of the 'reflexive imperative' to all). These may be encountered and understood as discrete occurrences. But the objective of an account couched in terms of generative mechanisms is to reveal how they are interconnected.
2   Is the generative mechanism held principally responsible for recent rapid social change one whose tendency is to produce a social order that heralds a new social formation; one where Morphogenic society supersedes Modernity?
3   'Social morphogenesis' may indeed be increasing exponentially. Yet, if the social order is generically neither 'self-governing' nor 'self-organizing' but is rather a 'relationally contested system', what if anything prevents contestation from merely prolonging 'modernity's mess' without promise of finalism or reintegration – systemic or social?

Social morphogenesis' is an umbrella concept, *whereas any generative mechanism is a particular that needs identifying, describing and explaining* – by its own analytical history of emergence. If we want to talk seriously about 'Morphogenic Society' this can only be in terms of specific mechanisms that are potentially important enough to have a global societal impact. Otherwise, it could rightly be objected that positive feedback and morphogenesis have always been with us, even before the first spark ignited the first fire. The amplification of an effect by its own influence on the process that gave rise to it is hardly the preserve of trans-modernity. Equally, it could also be countered that morphostasis is still with us or, in Maccarini's words, that everything 'was not lost in the fire' of recent change (Ch. 3 in this volume). Such enduring negative feedback would or could be held to offset the results of the positive feedback, which introduces new variety and encourages still greater variety because of the growing pool of complementary entities that can be combined – to morphogenetic effect.

The generative mechanism in Late Modernity 237

To focus upon 'social morphogenesis' as a general process of change is very different from examining its particular results over the last quarter of a century. Instead, explaining where we are right now means concentrating upon the outcomes of morphogenesis; upon the specific changes produced; and upon whether or not the new social forms elaborated do gel with one another and have some directionality. These are its knock-on effects. Yet, equally important are its knock-out effects, of eliminating those morphostatic processes that previously 'counterbalanced' morphogenetic changes by continuing to preserve a degree of contextual continuity for agents and actors in their everyday social lives.

To explain both these 'arrivals' and these 'departures' it is necessary to draw upon three orders of emergent properties that exert causal influence through conditioning social action and its outcomes at different levels. There is nothing sacrosanct about this number because new strata can be added whenever the emergent powers pertaining to a given stratum can be substantiated on the causal criterion. The three coincide with what are conventionally known as the micro-, meso- and macro-levels: dealing respectively with the situated action of persons or small groups, because there is no such thing as 'contextless' action; with 'social institutions', the conventional label for organizations with a particular remit, such as government, health, education etc. at the meso-level; and with the relation between structure and culture at the most macroscopic level.

This stratified ontology of the social order, despite being ever revisable, is unacceptable to many social theorists. Particular resistance is encountered from those who claim to have 'transcended' the 'micro–macro problem' by one form of conflation or another (Archer 1995: 4–13; Porpora, Ch. 4 in this volume). Currently it is popular to clear the middle ground and then to use some variant on 'actor-based modelling' that supposedly reveals the macroscopic to be the aggregate product of the microscopic.[3] I have criticised this manoeuvre by 'flat ontologists' before (Archer 2013a; 2013b) and will not repeat it because the rest of this chapter is my critique.[4] The tentative propositions advanced in it do depend on using all three strata. The argument starts at the macro-level, but with the reminder that each stratum is activity-dependent on that or those beneath it and that downwards causation (Lawson 2013) and upwards causation are continuous and intertwined.

Relations between structure and culture (macro-level)

In Fig. 12.1, the magnified section shows culture and structure in a mutually morphogenetic relationship. Changes in culture amplify those in structure and vice versa through positive feedback. This contrasts with the archetypical picture of early societies, where the morphostatic stability of the one reinforced that of the other. Modernity stands between the two. The question is, where does Late Modernity take its place? More specifically, has rapid change over the last quarter of a century brought the social order to resemble Fig. 12.1 more closely? Because Fig. 12.1 represents the most macro-societal level, it does not deny that there may well be many negative feedback loops working for morphostasis at lower strata. *Nevertheless, the diagram does presume that they are overridden in the societal outcome.*

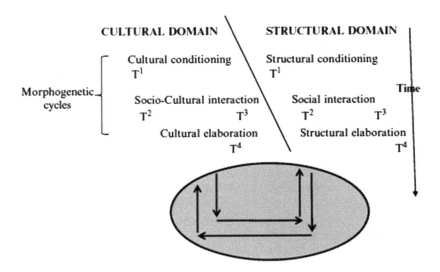

Figure 12.1 Morphogenesis: culture and structure are mutually reinforcing.
Source: Archer (1988: 304).

One implication is that I do not regard 'society' as anything other than (or more than or additional to) the relations between 'structure' and 'culture'. It is the resultant of relations between relations, all of which are constantly activity-dependent. What particular kind of resultant this is depends upon the dominant relationship forged between the cultural and the structural orders. Since both components are necessarily heterogeneous, various relations are possible and would remain so even supposing untramelled morphogenesis on both 'sides'. That is why the question of the 'good society' never disappears.

A great deal clearly turns upon how these two macro-components are conceptualized. In an earlier work 'culture as a whole is taken to refer to all intelligibilia, that is, to any item that has the dispositional capacity of being understood by someone' (Archer 1988: xvi). This means, for example, that the Rosetta Stone, when lost, buried and used as building material, retained this capacity (to act as a translation manual). In other words, intelligibilia do not depend upon a current knowing subject. All such items are lodged in what I used to call the Universal Library but now have to rename the Universal Archive. Cultural components are differentiated from the structural by their primarily ideational constitution, whereas structures are primarily materially based.

Cultures are made up of entia such as beliefs, theories, value systems, mathematical theorems and novels. There are different *logical* relations between these constituents themselves, each of which *causally* influences socio-cultural action and its outcomes. This is because by taking up a given body of ideas and asserting them, a group defines its ideal interests. These, as Weber's 'switchman' simile underlined, are not *reducible* to that group's material interests, although related to them.[5] In other words, structural factors play a significant role in what is adopted from the cultural system and the ends to which it is put.

To uphold a body of ideas is to become involved with the logical relations between them and with others. This embroils those who assert or assent to any ideational corpus in a particular *situational logic of action*. Where there is high coherence amongst the ideas available, as in early and Ancient societies, the situational logic is that of *protection*, meaning ideational innovations are repulsed and cultural morphostasis is reinforced – altering mainly to increase in density. In early Modernity this logic was one of *correction*, namely reconciling logical inconsistencies through syncretic refinement in order to enhance the coherence and viability of the ideas supported (as in the historically elaborated doctrines of liberal economic philosophy). Throughout later Modernity different materially based interest groups drew selectively upon the cultural system to legitimate and advance their ends, unleashing the *situational logic of elimination* between their ideas and those of subordinate groups (as in 'the great age of Ideology' that intensified subsequent class conflict).

Finally, during Late Modernity the rarest historical form of situational logic comes to prevail because of the exponential addition of new items and novel sources of ideational variety, vastly exceeding the pool of ideas available in any of the three preceding forms.[6] Precisely because of the newness of these ideas, existing material interest groups have no (defensive or promotive) *positions prises* towards them. This results in the loosest *situational logic of opportunity* where socio-cultural action is concerned and, for the first time in history, it is becoming predominant. The prizes go to those who will explore and can manipulate novel contingent 'cultural compatibilities' to their advantage. Which agents and actors do so, the interests they seek to serve and their relations with other groups that are similarly involved are what shapes the precise nature of the outcome. Thus, *the 'contingent complementarity' alone is the form of cultural system uncompromisingly related to morphogenesis*.

'Contingent complementarities' came to prominence in the late twentieth century. During the last 25 years the incidence of new cultural items has been unprecedented and raises the following questions:

- Where did they come from – that is, what accounted for this flurry of innovation?
- How did they gel with the existing structural array of vested interests?
- Who seized upon (some of) this cultural novelty and to what ends?
- Was the resulting state of affairs conducive to nascent Morphogenic Society?

Cultural and structural relations in Late Modernity

I will work through this list in a sketchy manner, but I hope in sufficient detail to establish the basic argument, namely that a considerable transfer and fusion of ideas took place between Culture and Structure, representing the inception of a novel synergy between the ideas and the interest groups first involved. However, the divergent interests of these groups meant that, although both were intensively

240 *The generative mechanism in Late Modernity*

morphogenetic, they pulled in different directions. Whilst the one sought to appropriate ideational novelty to reinforce their prior material interests, the other tried to induce the new social relations inherent in the synergy to promote universal interests. In turn, the fact that entrenched structural vested interests – although themselves morphing – have prevailed to date accounts for the 'mess we are in', especially in the developed world. Finally, such intense morphogenesis does not yet constitute a Morphogenic Society, but neither does it nullify this potential form of societal transformation.

The cultural provenance of novelty

The contributory cultural components were themselves intertwined but space precludes their proper analysis. Instead of presenting the analytical histories of their emergence, six factors will simply be listed historically. First was the proven military utility during the Second World War of what had previously been 'pure' science. This continued to prove itself as applied science during the Cold War and the Space Race. Second was educational expansion, which entrenched more science courses at universities, although the growth in university enrollment was more closely associated with boosting economic growth in Europe. Third came the related proliferation of new 'hybrid' disciplines and specialisms (such as biochemistry, astrophysics, genetic engineering). Fourth was the allied growth of international professional associations of academic specialists and unenforced academic migration (from Visiting Professorships to the later Erasmus and Junior Year abroad programmes). Fifth were effects upon the media, especially publishing, in terms of not only academic journals but also the arrival of paperback books, alongside the domestic spread of TV in the 1950s. Significantly, television was given an 'educational mission' at the beginning, but became more populist by the decade. Sixth were the proliferating social movements (for nuclear disarmament, anti-apartheid, feminism, green environmentalism and sustainable development), ones that drew upon other available cultural items – often encountered at university – producing different contributions that augmented counter-culture and were to fuel the ongoing 'relational contestation' reshaping the global social order.

All six processes of growth (some of them morphogenetic) pre-dated 1980, at least in their inception. Some were mutually compatible, but others involved forms of contestation. Very broadly, culture can be viewed as a novel source of 'contingent complementarities', intensifying as such from the end of the war but peaking from the 1980s onwards. If that is the case, the crucial questions posed at the end of the last section concern the relationship between the cluster of institutions that made up 'social structure' during the same period – and which of them drew what from the enlarging cultural pool of ideas.

The structural precursors of synergy

After the Second World War the developed democracies in the European nation states, their institutional configurations and particularly their economies were manifestations of enduring contestation based upon 'constraining contradictions' and dating back to the (French) political revolution and the (British) industrial revolution. After centuries of conflict, with elites attempting to limit political participation in order to be able to regulate the people and the popular classes seeking to extend their democratic access in order to regulate the elites, the post-war formula of social democracy, citizenship and variants upon the welfare state was a compromise in which mutual regulation took the revolutionary edge off enduring class divisions.

In the post-war economies, after two centuries of struggle between entrepreneurs trying to control wages, hours and conditions and workers responding with Luddism, syndicalism, unionization, strikes and lock-outs, there was still unfinished business on both sides. Capitalism remained unwaveringly and necessarily competitive, holding itself threatened as national unionized workforces flexed their organized muscles. After various showdowns, the progressive incorporation of the unions into political parties and industrial management itself was the compromise that inserted the 'neo' into capitalism.

This compromise derived from their mutual regulation, because in both the polity and the economy the state of opposition mattered to the governing elites and vice versa, just as the state of managerial control mattered to organized labour and vice versa. That was the case whilst ever the nation state remained the 'outer skin' bounding – at least to a significant extent – a 'society'. It diminished as this boundary reduced in importance with increasing 'globalization'. However, 'globalization' is merely a portmanteau term for a great variety of interrelated changes and is not itself a causal generative mechanism. Instead, and in quest of a real generative mechanism, it seems important to begin with how pursuit of the situational *logic of competition* increasingly promoted multinational corporations (for production rather than trade) as a means of sloughing off the compromises inherent in the 'constraining contradiction'[7] in which the market was embedded.[8]

The delinking of the economy from the confines of the nation state is vital because, with it, the source of mutual regulation based on the state of the national workforce mattering to corporate economic leadership and vice versa largely disappeared. Because the managerial elite no longer depended upon one (mainly) national workforce, their concern vanished about whether or not multinational practices were endorsed without resistance in any particular country, which in the past had meant accepting conciliatory regulation. Instead, enterprises moved parts of their operations to employ personnel throughout the world. Thus, corporate management loosed itself from the constraint that the need for legitimacy had previously imposed, now that there was no determinate population of indispensable employees who were also its national legitimators. Correspondingly, economic power had less and less need to transform itself into authority. If the local workforce resisted, this was not met by durable concessions but by relocating operations.

Towards the synergy that intensified morphogenesis

In other words, corporate *multinationals* had freed themselves to pursue the *situational logic of competition* intrinsic to capitalism. However, simultaneously, such enterprises also had new requirements: for the speediest communication, for comparative cost/benefit data analysis on productivity and for administrative logistics. The same requirements were redoubled in the burgeoning finance market, especially after the Bretton Woods restrictions on foreign exchange dealing were abandoned. Both developments paved the way for a new synergy between Structure and Culture.

A culture that is independently generating an enlarged pool of 'contingent complementarities' also opens up innumerable new opportunities – such is its situational logic – that may be seized upon by external parties to enhance their practices. That Information Technology was the source of the transfer of knowledge between the economy and the universities[9] is in line with my argument elsewhere that technology acts as the indispensable bridge between pure science and concrete practice (Archer 2000: 154–190). The synergy that developed accentuated only those cultural items that seemed profitable and were congruent with gaining profit in the market. All the same, it worked to redouble morphogenesis in both the structural and cultural domains. To understand and explain how this came about, it is necessary to examine the institutions involved.

Institutional synergy (meso-level)

The key institutions in question are the neo-capitalist market and university science, constituting elements of structure and of culture respectively. Historical accounts are plentiful but space precludes developing them into two analytical histories of emergence that would fully account for their symbiosis in the last quarter of a century. Synergy, deriving directly from the Greek 'synergia', is generally defined as things working together to produce a result not independently obtainable. However, in the present argument it does not carry the frequent connotation of the results being 'co-operative effects'; most of the relevant actors and agents were too self-interested for that. Nevertheless, the two became increasingly symbiotic. This is novel because their interrelationship was the exception rather than the rule until the last decades of the twentieth century.

In general, the state (or public) educational systems emerging in the developed world (Archer 1979 [2013]) were inhospitable to vocal industrial demands for technical training. For example, the highly centralized French system consistently privileged State requirements, confining science to certain *Grandes Ecoles*. It sought to restrict any vocational instruction to the primary level, and later intellectualized 'special education', then 'modern studies' and again the technical *baccalauréat*, after its creation in 1946. As Antoine Prost epitomised the situation in 1967: 'French schooling disdains to train the producer. Its rationalism turns into intellectualism' (1968: 340; my trans.). In Bourdieu's words, students were regarded 'as apprentice professors and not as professional apprentices' (Bourdieu & Passeron 1964; my trans.).

Similarly, in the decentralized English system, burgeoning forms of technical instruction were accommodated by confining them to lower, inferior and generally terminal levels of schooling. The 1918 Act, which confirmed the hegemony of the academic Grammar School, restricted technical schools to the elementary level, an inferior status that the 1944 Act confirmed. Consequently, historians have maintained that the science upon which the industrial revolution was based was available 100 years earlier but its application waited upon self-trained inventors with practical experience (such as Watt, Crompton and Arkwright) to translate it into the technology of the mill and factory (Jewkes et al. 1969). Eiffel and Brunel were the exceptions, both being civil engineers who were personally intrigued by technical challenges.

Thus, neither in France nor England did a strong practical, real or technical definition of instruction develop because it was never a priority of the most powerful interest groups contesting educational control, as was also the case in most of Europe. Pure science attained a place in universities towards the end of the nineteenth century, but applied science gained no foothold in higher education from which it could act as its practical translator by demonstrating its practical advantages through introducing new industrial technology.

The significant exceptions were Federal states (Germany, whose *Technische Hochschule* formed part of the university sector, and Switzerland's two Polytechniques, later to contribute in CERN's development of the World Wide Web). The biggest exception of all was obviously the US. Some latter-day systems theorists have associated Federalism with subsidiarity as a mode of institutional governance 'between anarchy and Leviathan', benefiting 'functioning social units' by avoiding both the lack of coordination promoted by decentralization and the over-control of centralization (Wilke 2003). Leaving aside the question of its equation with subsidiarity, the relative autonomy that federalism gave to university development and the readier incorporation of the sciences into universities undoubtedly played a part in the 'social digitalization'[10] that eventually advanced societal morphogenesis. What distinguished this recent 25-year development from the 250-year 'slow movement' (Forbes 1958: 148) of the Industrial Revolution?

How (morphogenetic) synergy came about

By definition, synergy involves at least two parties and their contributions. In turn, this entails accounting for the participants, their motives and their interactions as well as their outcomes. Castells' summary stands as a valid generalization: 'What characterizes the current technological revolution is not the centrality of knowledge and information, but the *application* of such knowledge and information . . . in a *cumulative feedback loop between innovation and the uses of innovation*' (2010 [2000]: 31; my emphasis). However, his actualist account is a painstaking empirical description of the process and its results rather than an identification of its generative mechanism.

My argument hinges on the fact that, in the beginning, *industry was not a key player*. The foundations of the 'digital revolution' – micro-electronics, computers and telecommunications – were first laid in the US between the military and university science, with the Second World War as their midwife and the Cold War as nanny. The serious kick-start was the Russian launch of the Sputnik in 1957, prompting the US Defense Department's ARPA (Advanced Research Projects

244 The generative mechanism in Late Modernity

Agency) to enter the communications field and the development of the first computer network in 1969 (Abbate 1999). Significantly, its first four nodes were established at universities, three of them in California. In turn, this enabled 'establishment science' and 'countercultural innovation' (Himannen 2001) to vaunt the relative autonomy of scientific culture for different reasons: what it had delivered for national security and what it could supply to civil society. Significantly, when CERN produced the World Wide Web (1990), it was based not on ARPA's military funding and specifications but on the 'hacker's model' of horizontal informational links, although again its first sites were in scientific research centres.[11]

The Silicon Valley story (sub-titled 'Where new industry married new science') does not need retelling (Rogers and Larsen 1984; Malone 1985). The locale owed its origins to Stanford University's Industrial Park (1951), to which micro-electronics firms were attracted by the growing pool of technical skills available and by the ready collaboration of those such as Steve Jobs, Steve Wozniak, Bill Gates and other drop-outs inventing in garages owing to a lack of capital to form companies. However, the narrative of the 1970s needs supplementing by an analytical account of silicon synergy that involves more than happenstance and magnetism. Castells may be descriptively correct in concluding that it was

> by this interface between macro-research programs and large markets developed by the state, on the one hand, and decentralized innovation stimulated by a culture of technological creativity and role models of fast personal success, on the other hand, that new information technologies came to blossom.
>
> (2010: 69)

but the generative mechanism is still missing.

'Working together' as a definition of synergy is not sufficiently precise. People and organizations can do so for wildly different reasons. Because doing so freely is not entailed, even colonization could qualify. So too could alliances of convenience against a third party (e.g. electoral coalitions), the division of labour (e.g. Adam Smith's pin-makers) or the market exchange of equivalents, because all conform to producing a result independently unobtainable by the parties involved. Corning's 'Synergism Hypothesis' suffers from being even broader, because synergistic effects (largely in the animal world) may 'arise from linear or additive phenomena. Larger size, frequently the result of an aggregation of similar units, may provide a collective advantage' (Corning 1998: 4).

To adduce a generative mechanism is to narrow down synergy to that subsection of 'working together' that gives rise to relatively durable *relational emergent properties*. It is only if these are real emergents, yielding objective benefits to both parties (not necessarily equally or symmetrically) and which are believed by both to be unattainable in any other way (or less advantageously under their current circumstances), that the relations involved have some durability rather than being ephemeral matters of convenience. It is not essential that the parties have mutual respect or forge good collective relations. What is essential is that both parties *orient themselves to the relational properties (goods or evils) that they generate together.* The division of labour is a good illustration: work became more monotonous and stultifying (as Adam Smith was aware),[12] but the increased productivity and profits benefited factory owners and enabled those with 'only their labour power to sell' to at least be able to sell it – and to start thinking about how to negotiate wage increases as profitability grew. In other words, there are both ontological and epistemological conditions attaching to relational generative mechanisms in the social order.

Thus, more is involved here than a simple universal formula such as 'scientific innovation requires capitalization and industry needs new marketable ideas'. Firstly, neither may be met (most of the inventions advancing the industrial revolution were bought cheap, leaving their inventors to die poor) and secondly, neither may be true (in the 1960s and early 1970s industry was extending its multinational markets, cutting its unit labour costs and gaining cheaper raw materials in a boom period, none of which depended upon new scientific ideas) (Centre d'Etudes Prospectives et d'Informations Internationales 1992).

The relations constituting generative mechanisms must be internal or necessary ones. In the present case of 'working together', no necessity attaches to the contingencies of 'garage geeks seeking big bucks' and 'voracious corporate bosses spotting winners'. In any case, many of the former failed, as did many of the latter (recall the dot.com boom and then doom). In fact, the necessary relations in question are so simple in this case that they are easy to miss and tempting to obfuscate: internal relations turned upon the need for market enterprises to be *competitive* and for 'digital science' to gain *diffusion*. This way of putting it also allows the two 'parties' to have divergent interests and goals whilst still working in synergy, just like the pin-makers and the owner of the pin factory.

The divergent interests involved in synergy

Collaboration, rather than co-operation or co-ordination, is required if the two parties pursue their own agendas; their endorsement of collective goals is far from essential for synergy and was not the case here. On the one hand, for-profit enterprises are by definition in zero-sum competition with one another and their global expansion was a competitive manoeuvre, one aided by the business-led move for financial deregulation that succeeded in the early 1970s. There is nothing novel in market history about maintaining, for instance, that if one old-established electronics corporation decided to invest heavily in micro-electronics, others are induced to do so in order not to be overtaken (and many who held back did go under). With corporate amalgamation attaining global proportions, when IT began to develop its civilian potential its adoption or non-adoption was no longer a competitive option.

Conversely, new hardware and software developments by engineers and scientists had not only made access to communication and information unimaginably faster but had pulled off the trick of turning something abundant, whose value does not diminish with use, into a temporarily scarce commodity. This form of scarcity vanished as firms equipped and re-equipped their new computing departments and pioneered ingenious ways in which they could be profitably used in 'information mining' itself. However, digital science and the fast turnover in software had its own requirement – diffusion. Otherwise, there would be no next funding grant or venture capital, meaning the innovation could stay in the garage and the parental loan remain unpaid. The important point is not about geeks rushing to found small companies without a qualm about joining neo-capitalism, which plenty did. It is rather that the need for diffusion was general, and equally strong amongst opponents of the for-profit market.

Diffusion costs: it has overheads and these become very large if the proponent, for example, rejects advertising revenue, and frighteningly large the more successful it becomes. Here is Jimmy Wales today (21 November 2012), trying to raise €10 per capita user per year, sufficient to maintain Wikipedia. That represents €540 million of overheads last year on the figures given. For those seeking to advance the cybercommons against the for-profit sector and to foster a civil economy based on crowdsourcing, collaboration with 'the enemy' was inevitable. For example, on the P2P (peer to peer) web site, most videos and audios have to be accessed via Google and its YouTube subsidiary. Here is Michel Bauwens, who has battled with diffusion's overheads from the start, counselling:

Use the existing infrastructures for immaterial exchange for personal and social autonomy

We started by creating an infrastructure that allowed for peer to peer communication. Out of this striving came the internet and its end to end principle, web 2.0 and its possibilities for participation, and social media allowing for intense relational interaction, and tools such as wikis which allow for the collaborative construction of knowledge.

The creation of this infrastructure was a combination of efforts of civil society forces, governments and public funding, and private R&D and commercial deployments. It's an imperfect world full of governmental control, corporate platforms, but also many capabilities for p2p interaction that did not exist before. . . . They have become civilisational achievements that are just as necessary for p2p-commoners [as for] for the powers that be. (https://blog.p2pfoundation.net/the-new-years-message-of-the-p2p-foundation-what-digital-commoners-need-to-do/2011/01/01 [accessed 21 November 2012]).

The generative mechanism of Late Modernity is thus constituted by market competition and the diffusion of applied science needing to 'work together'. The internal effects were profoundly morphogenetic for both elements, fostering further synergy. Their collaboration transformed the market itself in the developed world, facilitating further multinational advances. As their target sites quickly adopted and became highly proficient in using the same digital science, international market competition accelerated with India, China and Brazil and other countries that caught up fast. These countries turned the game plan of multinational trade through 180°, given their lower production costs.

In turn, this precipitated the surge of finance capitalism in the West, which was even more dependent upon information technology. After all, London had been a

The generative mechanism in Late Modernity 247

'financial capital' since the end of the nineteenth century but grew more in the last decade than during the rest of the twentieth century. The 'Roaring nineties' (Stiglitz 2005) not only witnessed the desertion of the real economy (epitomized by the rust belt of Detroit and the wasteland of the British West Midlands), but the intensification of entirely speculative investment.

The generative mechanism continued to be robustly supported by further 'digital science' for harvesting and analyzing informational abundance. The development of social interaction sites was probably the least technically demanding but was hugely consequential because of its fast and democratic appeal. Effectively, it harnessed 'free' global communication to form a virtual *gesellschaft* for 'all those lonely people', who came from everywhere, were going anywhere or getting nowhere. Yet, without the advertising revenue, these might have remained the 'boys' toys' of Harvard students. One key point is that the 'entrepreneurial spirit' of Mark Zuckerberg and his ilk was not nurtured by the market but in university. The other is the inflated price at which Facebook was floated on the stock exchange. Although this immediately slumped, it was not another dot.com disaster because it did offer an asset – if only targeted advertising space – to economic competitors. Diffusion was ensured when corporate competitors became convinced that it would be damaging *not* to be 'seen on f' and, to some, that here were billions of volunteers freely offering themselves for commercial 'data mining'. Undoubtedly, many young people with small businesses were playing his own game back at its founder – but this is one way that synergy spreads.

Certainly, those highly proficient in IT were and remain divided, but that does not prevent the take-up of an opportunity by others when it is out in the open. Opposition grew from protagonists of the cyber-Commons, of General Licensing, of Openflows etc. who operate their own sites. However, the point is that they were also part and parcel of the *same* synergistic and morphogenetic changes, assuming a relationship similar to that of the early socialists to factory production. Indeed, the co-operative movement has been recreated in virtual reality.

I have restricted myself to a perfunctory account of the rapid progress of this form of synergy and its internal transformations, all of which depended upon the swift succession of positive feedback cycles and all of which led to new variety fostering further variety. Yet, it is necessary to secure the generative mechanism itself, because several have suggested that an accelerated pace of change alone, 'driven by the logic of acceleration', is all that is needed to account for the above (Rosa 2003). Hartmut Rosa maintains that 'we should apply the term "acceleration society" to a society if, and only if, technological acceleration and the growing scarcity of time (i.e. an acceleration of the "pace of life") occur simultaneously, i.e. if growth rates outgrow acceleration rates' (Rosa 2003: 10). However, first, talking about growth should strictly refer to the output of more of the same, for growth is not morphogenesis. Yet, the two are elided: 'technological acceleration is prone to go hand in hand with the acceleration of change in the form of changing social structures or patterns' (Rosa 2003: 10). However, these latter changes are not matters of growth.

Furthermore, if acceleration in one domain is associated with acceleration in another, it does not follow from this correlation that (a) acceleration is an independent variable, or (b) that we do not need to ask for the causes of acceleration itself. However,

248 *The generative mechanism in Late Modernity*

when Rosa does the latter, and looks for the 'driving forces of acceleration beyond the feedback cycle itself', he finds 'three (analytically independent) primary factors that can be identified as the external "key-accelerators"'(Rosa 2003: 11). These are detailed as the 'economic motor' (capitalism's need to increase production (growth) as well as productivity (output per unit time); the 'cultural motor' (more of the options on offer can be experienced the faster we live); and the 'structural motor' (intensified functional differentiation increases both complexity and contingency, so selecting between options spells accelerated processing). Hence, three 'variables' are held responsible for 'acceleration', raising the question about the *relationship* between the three factors held responsible for it. We need to know *how* they work together, not *that* they work simultaneously.

Instead, Rosa concludes with the statement that 'social acceleration reveals the unitary logic underlying all four dimensions of modernization' (Rosa 2003: 27). Because I disagree that there is a 'unitary logic' – maintaining exactly the opposite – I want to examine further the consequences of the generative mechanism I am advancing. Because of regarding the social order as a *relationally contested organization* rather than a self-governing or self-organizing one, the process responsible for current social morphogenesis needs to accentuate *relationality* rather than multivariate analysis; contestation rather than co-variance; and *malintegration* rather than functional differentiation in the organization of Late Modernity.

Effects on other social institutions

The pre-eminence of politics was a dominant feature of Modernity, whereas, in Late Modernity, 'the nation-state may have crossed the zenith of its power to define the rules of the game – in relation not only to the economic subsystem but to every subsystem in society' (Wilke 2013: 207). The reason is the development of transnational decision-making bodies such as the EU, one consequence being that turnout in national elections plummets as voters recognize that the nation state is not the prime seat of policy making. However, although national governments have indeed lost power, they retain more than enough to influence subsystems and to have had an impact on the global economy.

The macro-level synergy discussed in the last section represented two different logics of action (of *structural competition and of cultural opportunity*) that pulled in two different directions. In theory, governments could have fulfilled their Hobbesian role of providing public protection by different responses to the two. They could have behaved morphostatically towards one, thus dampening it, and morphogenetically towards the other, thus amplifying it. They had a choice of siding with either competition or opportunity, so why did polities throughout the developed world consistently throw in their lot with the economy and generalize *competition* to every social institution accessible to their control? Moreover, if governments did so, why did opposition parties not do the opposite?

On the one hand, the promise of plenty, when translated into national affluence, also solves plenty of political problems, particularly when European manufacturing had already lost its global hegemony. States in the developed world buttressed the banking sector, positively through accepting rising national debt and negatively by non-intervention. They boosted the retail market by expanding employment in public administration and services, thus increasing consumer spending, especially as public services became the main employers in geographical areas whose real economies had declined fastest. They also began dismantling the Welfare State, with public–private 'partnerships' subtracting from the costs to central government.

On the other hand, to have endorsed the *logic of opportunity* would have entailed an innovative coordination of flexible openings (new forms of training, sponsorship of novel endeavours, investment in community projects, encouraging experimentation with alternative currencies etc.) all without precedent, rule book or guarantee of practical or political success. Seeking the political authority to balance encouragement and openness with revision and correction in what Merton (1973) termed a framework of 'organized skepticism' is not that on which most career politicians would stake their futures or see as an electoral clarion call. Yet there was no returning to government based on Luhmann's (1982) formula where normatively institutionalized structures secure the complementarity of expectations.

The collusion between the state and the market throughout the developed world spelt political centrism since the main priority of governments became securing their countries within the global economy. Political centrism displaced the previous oscillation between 'lib'/'lab' politics (Donati 1983; 1991; Donati and Colozzi 2006): in part because of 'the internalization of a prevalent, neo-liberal, "logic of no alternative", by social democratic actors themselves' (Bailey 2009: 16), given the transition to a service-based economy, following shrinkage of the traditional working class and leaving insufficient voters seeking to challenge market operations (Kitschelt 1994). In equal part, it was because the centre-right had gained its main economic point and now had to try to establish its electoral base amongst the service classes, dubbed with names such as 'middle England'. Politics was now about daily tactics rather than strategic differences and governments were more responsive to scandals than to the pursuit of policy.

Yet politics without normativity is in trouble. There is neither the 'complementarity of expectations' (i.e. a general cultural consensus on core values) nor the institutionalization of opposed expectations, making 'who governs' of concern to national populations and stimulating their political participation. It is in this context that formal democracies concluded their unholy alliance with the press and mass media. Not as in the post-war period, with particular newspapers overtly supporting one party or another, but by consorting with the popular press, which was more than willing to play at the 'politics of personalities'; and such personalization distracted from broader socio-economic issues.

Distraction became the media's mission, with its creation of 'celebrities' and its collusion with them about disclosures of their 'private' lives. As per capita viewing hours for television came close to equalling those of the statutory working week, there was no need for George Orwell's picture in *1984* of the coercive dispensing of 'trank' (tranquillizer): it was consumed voluntarily. With media-made 'icons' came their life styles, representing a normalization of practices that would have affronted the post-war electorate. The message was that normatively anything goes so long as it is verbalized with political correctitude. Distraction is a huge political bonus, enabling parties to get on with 'business as usual', despite a shrinking electoral mandate.[13]

Simultaneously, political centrism transferred the 'logic of competition' to those social institutions remaining most dependent upon government funding: education, health, welfare, public transport and even sport, through the blanket imposition of performance indicators, League Tables, Evaluation and ranked Assessment criteria.[14] Government became governance by bureaucratic regulation with the proliferation of Regulators for public utilities, educational inspection, energy and so forth. Each new scandal provoked the same response: re-regulate the failing Regulators, but don't blame us.

The diffusion of opportunity (micro-level)

In all of this, what has happened to the potential for Morphogenic society and its situational logic of opportunity? The above paragraphs, accentuating the increased influence and scope of the neo-liberal *situational logic of competition*, also contain the most common representation of the current state of affairs and reinforce the message that 'there is no alternative' for the social order. Yet, there is another side to the story precisely because the generative mechanism continues to promote synergy, despite it serving two ultimately incongruent ends. It is the part that TINA's supporters would prefer to edit out.

This concerns the other face of the generative mechanism: the quest for diffusion by innovators, who continue to come from the universities, and some of whom are decidedly counter-cultural. The TINA story is a 'top-down' narrative dealing with (often incomprehensible) doings in high places. Conversely, the dynamics of 'diffusion' require a 'bottom-up' account. This resonates with our quotidian experiences – ones shared with ordinary lay agents – that the contexts of action are shifting daily under our feet and their taken-for-grantedness has been made obsolete, along with habitual or routine action.

It is this that accounts for the 'Reflexive Imperative', namely that agency in general has to think (individually and collectively) about its 'concerns' in relation to its shifting social contexts and vice versa in order to deliberate reflexively about courses of action likely to result in a satisfying *modus vivendi* (Archer 2012). Their own concerns are the only compass agents have.

The positive role of meta-reflexivity and countervailing restraints

Without reference to reflexivity we cannot account for what different people do when faced with contextual constraints and enablements, because all those in the same position do not do the same thing (Archer 2003: Ch. 4). Micro-level reflexivity forms the crucial agential link with the macroscopic and meso-level changes in structure and culture examined above as constituting the generative mechanism of change in Late Modernity. The results of this mechanism also reshape the context for the formation of reflexivity in young subjects, the environment in which they will live and work, and try variously to evade, to extend or to subvert. It is a context that now precludes 'socialization' being a process of 'internalization' (given the demise of consensual normativity and its replacement by 'mixed messages') or of acquiring a dispositional *habitus* that fosters positional reproduction (given the proliferation of novel positions newly becoming available) (Archer 2012: Ch. 3).

In terms of the generative mechanism put forward here, the importance attached to reflexivity contrasts with 'acceleration theory' whose advocates presume 'rapid change' is antipathetic to its exercise, leading instead to agential impotence, disorientation and an inability to make life plans. The readiest way of explaining this disaccord is that in the phrase 'the rapidity of change' those such as Rosa attend to its *speed alone*, whereas I accentuate not only its rapidity but also the new *variety* constitutive of social change in Late Modernity. *Rapidity plus variety* represents an entirely new agential context: the morphogenesis of neo-capitalism does not. Even in its most speculative excesses, the finance market both encourages and rewards the same 'Autonomous reflexive' mode in which agents approximate to competitive Rational Actors pursing their individual preference schedules. The internships through which they are recruited represent 'speculation' as a courageous adventure that is rewarded accordingly; unpredictability certainly means you can lose more, but also gain much more, and no recruitment crisis hangs over the banking sector.

However, new *variety* (novel jobs, skills, openings) – especially those opportunities now introduced through the synergy of the generative mechanism advanced – present choices for which neither natal backgrounds nor formal education (struggling to keep up) can prepare. The young confront 'contextual incongruity' between their background and their foreground, and that invites critical scrutiny of both. For subjects already disengaged from their families (in response to the tensions and mixed messages experienced) the same scrutiny is turned on the opportunities available. This is the cradle of Meta-reflexivity; of the practice by young subjects of surveying all accessible openings in the light of their nascent concerns and considering the things that matter to them in relation to what they can do about them. This makes them both self-critics and socially critical.

In other words, the dominant mode of reflexivity practised has a history (Archer 2007: Ch. 1). The Reflexive Imperative entails a change in modality, not simply an extension or intensification of reflexive practice. One key feature of the rise of Meta-reflexivity is that its young educated practitioners are critics of both market and state, preferring to make use of the new occupational opportunities becoming increasingly available in civil society, the civil economy and the Third Sector in general. As such, they provide aggregate reinforcement for the initiatives of the 'diffusionists', driving them forward through positive reinforcement. Moreover, this reinforcement does not derive from the aggregation of individual actions alone. Meta-reflexives are also those most drawn into social movements – for justice, peace, environmental issues, regeneration of local areas and global support for migrant humanity – in which collective reflexivity can develop through orientation to the relational goods already generated but having a long way to go to attain the Common Good. Conversely, it is the Autonomous reflexives who are 'minimalist citizens' (Archer 2007: Ch. 5), individualists with little political involvement, non-participants in social movements and people trusting in corporate enterprise to exercise corporate social responsibility.

252 *The generative mechanism in Late Modernity*

If this were all there was to the picture – and given that Autonomous and Meta-reflexives seem to be proportionately at parity[15] – it would appear that the two parties to the generative mechanism attract roughly similar support and therefore that societal transition will take time and is not guaranteed. Yet, the canvas is even more complicated in two respects. First, 'Communicative reflexivity', in which decision-making is shared with 'similars and familiars', gives every indication of shrinking as mobility of all kinds reduces the 'contextual continuity' necessary for its development and practice. In turn, the substantial contribution it made to social integration in the relatively recent past diminishes, thus augmenting one of the major problems of Late Modernity. Second, 'Fractured reflexivity', disabling subjects from devising purposeful courses of action, augments the ranks of 'passive agents', suffering only distress and disorientation in their internal conversations.

Passive agency – those to whom things happen rather than their exercising any governance in their own lives – would, if its proportions increase, be a major countervailing influence against fast and decisive social transformation. Indeed, the proliferation of marketized social media and apps for mobiles seem to infiltrate the time/space available for the uninhibited practice of reflexivity. In that case, a growing tract of the population would become expressive rather than reflexive, and self-preoccupied without possessing self-identity. If this phenomenon is increasing, it re-poses one of the problems generic to the advent of a Morphogenic social formation: namely, how to integrate variety as inclusive diversity.

The diffusionists' achievements and the crisis of market and state

The interplay between Meta-reflexives and the opportunities becoming available in organizations at the meso-level are mutually reinforcing, hence the need for a quick overview of the latter, or what Hofkirchner calls the 'Commons'. The 'diffusionists'' best-known achievement is *Wikipedia*, launched as an open source in 2001 and based upon revisable voluntary contributions. Its policy has been to refuse advertising because it is contradictory to impartiality. It has therefore successfully withstood the for-profit market (although the Wikidata Project is partly funded by Google). Wikipedia is run on a 'bottom-up self-direction' policy and offers 23 million articles in 285 languages that are freely useable. In 2005 *Nature* conducted a comparative peer review of test articles appearing in Wikipedia and the *Encyclopedia Britannica*, concluding that they were of comparable accuracy. In support of the 'commons' movement, there was a 24-hour shutdown protesting against two pieces of US legislation in 2012: the 'Stop Online Piracy Act' and the 'Protect IP Act'. The cultural 'wing' of the generative mechanism was becoming more oppositional towards the barriers impeding open Opportunity.

One barrier that could not be imposed concerned the global diffusion, imitation and adaptation of projects that successfully implemented the situational logic of opportunity and turned their backs upon competition. Specifically, these are ones that valorise alternative currencies and operate in terms of socially useful value rather than exchange value. For example, food banks (as well as solidarity and time banks) were significant in Italy, where legislation – the 'Good Samaritan Act' – was

The generative mechanism in Late Modernity 253

passed in their support (Vittadini 2008), as it had been in the USA. There are now more than 300 in Britain and they are making progress in Eastern Europe and Latin America. Free-Cycle, mainly involving domestic goods, clothing and tools, has spread to the small towns of Europe. Charity shops take advantage of reduced rents on high streets where commercial enterprises have failed. Micro-credit, pioneered by the Grameen Bank, has migrated to the developed world, enabling the poorer to avoid commercial banking and 'loan sharks' alike. There are many other examples, but all share a second common denominator: that of rebuilding social integration and reanimating local neighbourhoods (Donati and Colozzi 2007).

Lest these instances appear small scale, the Ecoislands project, starting from the Isle of Wight in Britain, is global. The Isle of Wight plans to become self-sustainable in renewable energy by 2020 and fully sustainable by 2030 through signing the Ecoislands Accord (2012). In 2012 it held its first global summit under the banner of 'saving our world one island at a time' (2012). Undeniably, the project is dependent on pump-priming support from the market and state, which raises problems about its independence. However, *what has changed here is that the protagonists of Opportunity have led and the old Leviathans have followed*, without being able to insert competition with its winners and losers.

More ambitiously, new agencies in numerous countries such as Brazil are attempting to create financial markets for social enterprise as initiatives in horizontal subsidiarity. Such alternative investment markets envisage a stock exchange for non-profit social enterprises and community interest companies using shares and debt bonds as their financial instruments. In principle, these are not competing as high yield investments. On the contrary, they are an opportunity for gratuitousness where the shareholder, unlike the regular contributor to a charity, retains a say, a vote and a real involvement. However, whilst adopted in theory, these are not even the aims of the proposed British Social Stock Exchange, which seeks to sign up for-profit enterprises and overtly has an eye to the pension funds as investors.[16]

Such 'colonization' by market and state is indisputable. The market turns many activities that have been successfully pioneered by voluntary initiative into business ventures (as in chains of care homes) floated on the stock market. This makes them party to the 'logic of competition'. Similarly, 'green' and 'organic' have been profitably assimilated into marketing strategies. Attempts to create the 'cyber commons' through Peer2Peer exchanges were promptly appropriated by Wikinomics (Tapscott and Williams 2008) as a method for corporations to harvest technical solutions *for free* – euphemistically called 'dispersed production'. The trick consists in taking over voluntary innovations (micro-credit, for example) and simply turning them into for-profit. In direct parallel, the state absorbs voluntary initiatives (in schooling, health, mental care or palliative medicine), not only passing on some of the bill to them, at least for start-up costs, but also then throttling voluntary action with bureaucratic regulation.[17]

As a response, counter-institutionalization is understandable. It consists in performing the trick the other way round. Charities become charitable enterprises, losing their relational character in the process. This was already presaged several decades ago by the commercialized 'plate dinner', where the self-promotional photo-call became the chief motive. More recently, employing commercial fundraisers.com has become standard (competitive) practice, as has media promotion, the employment of lobbyists and 'celebrity' representation.

Conclusion

Where does this leave the three questions that were posed at the start of this chapter? The generative mechanism discussed seems sufficiently robust to account for the experience of disjunctions in daily life and the absence of shared normative guidelines for action. The interplay between economic competition and technological diffusion has fuelled intensified morphogenesis throughout the gamut of social institutions. Simultaneously it augmented the cultural system by the rapid addition of new items, thus extending the range of 'contingent complementarities' available for exploration. Hence, the two constituents of the generative mechanism have themselves undergone morphogenesis and their synergy has extended this to the rest of the social order through its knock-on and knock-out effects.

Although these do potentially contain the seeds of a new social formation, they do not yet announce the advent of Morphogenic society. This is because, despite these two crucial parts of 'structure' and of 'culture' both being forces promoting morphogenetic change, nevertheless, the difference between their situational logics of action means that they pull or steer in different societal directions. The for-profit market sector would basically extend the logic of competition throughout the social order and neo-liberalism has introduced the principles of marketization, commodification and productivity in such incongruent domains as hospitals, schools or universities. Performance indicators are generic bureaucratic expressions of the situational logic of competition. Conversely, the scientific community's logic of opportunity is hostile to bureaucratic regulation and restricted access; it fosters spin-off groups pursuing their own agendas and does not evaluate breakthroughs by reference to economic profitability. Some also feel driven to engage in cyber whistle-blowing as an effective form of opposition, including its institutionalization in Wikileaks.

At this point it would be possible to conclude that there are two sources of morphogenesis whose *aggregate effect* is to make the social order more morphogenetic. However, this would be to drift into a version of the multivariate 'acceleration' theory already examined. Moreover, Morphogenic society, which is a qualitative notion, cannot simply be defined by the quantitative sum of occurrent changes deriving from positive feedback – always supposing that these could be measured.

Instead, it is crucial to accentuate that the two situational logics of action are in mutual opposition. If either had supreme hegemony over the state of social affairs the two would result in very different social orders. In fact, neither is in that position; rather, they co-exist, as do the forms of morphogenetic change they introduce. This is the contemporary manifestation of the social as a *relationally contested order*.

However, the generative mechanism of '(structured) competition' in synergy with '(cultural) diffusion' does not result in the chaos of uncontrolled contingency. It is empiricism that cannot resist the temptation of interpreting Modernity's 'mess' in that way. In fact, the generative mechanism of 'competition-diffusion' is extremely morphogenetic, but what it does is to moderate the effects of both situational logics of action.

On the one hand, unbridled economic competition is hampered by the 'diffusionists' steady breaching of intellectual property rights, on which the former depends, by their expansion of the cyber-commons, by their facilitating new social movements promoting socially useful value over exchange value, and by their articulating the values for harnessing new opportunities to the common good rather than embroiling them in the zero-sum logic of competition. On the other hand, 'diffusionism' is restrained by the equally steady colonization of the initiatives it has promoted and their incorporation into the for-profit sector. The latter currently blocks the way towards Morphogenic society; simultaneously, the former makes a return to 'business as usual' increasingly difficult after the economic crisis provoked by competitive excess.

The internal relations of dependency between the two parties do not indicate imminent social transformation. The most likely scenario in the immediate future is that we will have to live with gradualism and even encourage it. Terms and practices such as 'corporate social responsibility' and 'social enterprise' have been placed on the agenda of competitive and for-profit enterprises, which are now aware they will be held to account. Cyber-diffusion is adding new variety to the Third, voluntary or social–private sector and fostering its expansion, diversification and new aspirations for effecting global transformation. Although it is undoubtedly subject to colonization and incorporation, it can nevertheless exert some influence from within and respond with further new initiatives from without. This conclusion seems in broad agreement with Donati's (Ch. 7 in this volume), namely that what he terms the 'state/market binomial' is already giving way to a triadic relationship between state-market-and-Third sector, transforming both the dynamics between them and their social outcomes.

Perhaps we should look at 'diffusionist' agencies as the research and development department for a future civil society and civil economy. Their interim task is to make the 'logic of opportunity' more wide-reaching within economic activity and to demonstrate that incremental increases in socially useful value and augmentation of the commons are contributions to the common good that are genuinely beneficial to all – thus illustrating that win–win outcomes are realistic goals for the social order. That alone grounds optimism about gradualism leading to the transformation of global society.

Notes

1 To talk about 'entities' entails neither physicalism nor substantialism: 'entia' in Latin refers simply to what exists, thus including non-observables such as 'beliefs', 'preferences' or 'theories'. Importantly, for the argument I am going to advance, this entails that 'culture', though 'insubstantial', stands alongside 'structure' as a real social entity.
2 For a recent defence of this position against my co-author, see Archer and Dave Elder-Vass (2011).
3 This is the case for Actor-Network theory and most versions of Complexity theory in the social sciences and it reaches its climacteric in a work such as that of Elliott and

Lemert (2006), who leave no room between 'global forces' out there and psychic life 'in here'. I owe this last example to Mark Carrigan.
4 It should be noted that, although working in terms of strata and the relations between them is, in principle, uncontroversial for Critical Realists, it is nonetheless the case that most realist social theorists have remained preoccupied with the question of how structural or cultural emergent properties can exert a causal influence upon agents full stop.
5 Max Weber, 'Not ideas, but material and ideal interests, directly govern men's conduct. Yet very frequently the 'world images' that have been created by 'ideas' have, like switchmen, determined the tracks along which action has been pushed by the dynamic of interest.' Cited in Gerth and Wright Mills (1967: 280).
6 Consider this, for example, in relation to our own discipline.
7 I have maintained that structural and cultural formations can be described and analysed in the same terms because the same four types of second-order emergent property obtain in culture as in structure, despite their substantive differences ('necessary complementarities', 'necessary incompatibilities', 'contingent incompatibilities' and 'contingent complementarities'). Moreover, these 'generate parallel forms of situational logics' (Archer 1995: 217–18).
8 It should be noted that I date the rise of multinational enterprises from the late 1960s and 1970s, which is rather earlier than does Tony Lawson (Chap. 2 in this volume). In consequence, I attach more importance to their combination with other (cultural) developments in the 1980s.
9 Michael J. Mulkay (1972) recounts the growth of scientific knowledge exclusively in terms of developments within the universities.
10 A term I use to avoid committing to the Information Age or Knowledge society.
11 Castells writes: 'In fact, it seems that the emergence of a new technological system in the 1970s must be traced to the autonomous dynamics of technological discovery and diffusion, including synergistic effects between various key technologies' (2010: 59–60).
12 Adam Smith (1904): 'The man whose whole life is spent in performing a few simple operations, of which the effects are, perhaps, always the same, or very nearly the same . . . generally becomes as stupid and ignorant as it is possible for a human creature to become' (vol. 2, bk 5, ch. 1, p. 267).
13 Note the disproportionate attention given to *individual* murders and abductions by 'respectable' media channels (BBC Radio 4 News), serving much the same purpose of public distraction as the first gruesome news-sheets in the nineteenth century.
14 The irony is that those least dependent upon state funding were so because they had embraced the market.
15 This statements is based upon such a small and non-representative sample (Archer 2012) that it requires replication.
16 The proposed Social Stock Exchange UK is defined as for-profit and indicates 'colonization' from the time of its conception: 'The Big Society Investment Fund was set up by the Big Lottery Fund under the Dormant Accounts Act to make early investments prior to the establishment of Big Society Capital (previously known as the Big Society Bank)' (Social Stock Exchange UK 2012).
17 Trivial but telling: my younger son and his wife had to undergo a 'home inspection' before being allowed to rescue a mature cat with three legs.

References

Abbate, J. (1999). *Inventing the internet*. Cambridge, MA: MIT Press.
Archer, M. S. (1979 [2013]). *Social origins of educational systems*. London/Beverly Hills, CA: Sage.
Archer, M. S. (1988). *Culture and agency: The place of culture in social theory*. Cambridge: Cambridge University Press.

Archer, M. S. (1995). *Realist social theory: The morphogenetic approach.* Cambridge: Cambridge University Press.
Archer, M. S. (2000). *Being human: The problem of agency.* Cambridge: Cambridge University Press.
Archer, M. S. (2003). *Structure, agency and the internal conversation.* Cambridge: Cambridge University Press.
Archer, M. S. (2007). *Making our way through the world: Human reflexivity and social mobility.* Cambridge: Cambridge University Press.
Archer, M. S. (2012). *The reflexive imperative in late modernity.* Cambridge: Cambridge University Press.
Archer, M. S. (2013a). Introduction. In M. S. Archer (ed.), *Social morphogenesis* (Vol. I, pp. 1–22). New York: Springer.
Archer, M. S. (2013b). Morphogenetic society: Self-government and self-organization as misleading metaphors. In M. S. Archer (ed.), *Social morphogenesis* (Vol. I). New York: Springer.
Archer, M. S., & Elder-Vass, D. (2011). Cultural system or norm circles? An exchange. *European Journal of Social Theory,* 15(1), 93–115.
Bailey, D. J. (2009). *The political economy of European social democracy.* Abingdon: Routledge.
Bourdieu, P., & Passeron, J.-C. P. (1964). *Les Héritiers, les étudiants et la culture.* Paris: Minuit.
Castells, M. (2010 [2000]). *The information age: Economy, society and culture* (The rise of the network society, Vol. 1). Malden/Oxford: Wiley-Blackwell.
Centre d'Etudes Prospectives et d'Informations Internationales. (1992). *L'Economie Mondiale 1990–2000: l'impératif de la croissance.* Paris: Economica.
Corning, P. A. (1998). The synergism hypothesis: On the concept of synergy and it's role in the evolution of complex systems. *Journal of Social and Evolutionary Systems,* 21(2), 133–172.
Donati, P. (1983). *Introduzione alla sociologia relazionale.* Milan: Franco Angeli.
Donati, P. (1991). *Teoria relazionale della società.* Milan: Franco Angeli.
Donati, P., & Colozzi, I. (eds). (2006). *Il Paradigma Relazionale nelle Scienze Sociali: le prospettive sociologiche.* Bologna: Mulino.
Donati, P., & Colozzi, I. (eds). (2007). *Terzo settore, mondi vitali e capital sociale in Italia.* Milan: Franco Angeli.
Ecoislands Accord. (2012). www.ecoislands.org/about-us/our-vision/. Accessed Nov 2012.
Elliott, A., & Lemert, C. (2006). *The new individualism: The emotional costs of globalization.* Abingdon: Routledge.
Forbes, R. J. (1958). Power to 1850. In C. Singer et al. (eds), *A history of technology* (The industrial revolution, c. 1750 to c. 1850, Vol. 4). Oxford: Clarendon.
Gerth, H. H., & Wright Mills, C. (1967). *From Max Weber.* London: Routledge & Kegan Paul.
Gorski, P. (2009). Social "mechanisms" and comparative-historical sociology: a critical realist proposal. In P. Hedström & B. Wittrock (eds), *Frontiers of sociology* (pp. 160–162). Leiden: Brill.
Heelas, P., Lash, S., & Morris, P. (eds). (1996). *Detraditionalization.* Oxford: Blackwell-Wiley.
Himannen, P. (2001). *The hackers' ethic and the spirit of informationalism.* New Haven: Yale University Press.
Jewkes, J., Sawers, D., & Stillerman, R. (1969). *The sources of invention.* New York: W.W. Norton.

Kitschelt, H. (1994). *The transformation of European social democracy*. Cambridge: Cambridge University Press.

Lawson, T. (2013). Emergence and morphogenesis: Causal reduction and downward causation. In M. S. Archer (ed.), *Social morphogenesis* (Vol. I). New York: Springer.

Luhmann, N. (1982). *The differentiation of society*. New York: Colombia University Press.

Malone, M. S. (1985). *The big score: The billion-dollar story of silicon valley*. Garden City: Doubleday.

Merton, R. K. (1973). The normative structure of science. In R. K. Merton (ed.), *The sociology of science: Theoretical and empirical investigations*. Chicago, IL: University of Chicago Press.

Mulkay, M. J. (1972). *The social process of innovation*. London: Macmillan.

Porpora, D. V. (1989). Four concepts of social structure. *Journal for the Theory of Social Behaviour*, 19(2): 195–211.

Porpora, D. V. (2011). Recovering causality. In A. Maccarini, E. Morandi, & R. Prandini (eds), *Sociological realism*. Abingdon: Routledge.

Prost, A. (1968). *L'Enseignement en France, 1800–1967*. Paris: Armand Colin.

Rogers, E. M., & Larsen, J. K. (1984). *Silicon valley fever: Growth of high technology culture*. New York: Basic Books.

Rosa, H. (2003). Social acceleration: Ethical and political consequences of a desynchronized high-speed society. *Constellations*, 10(1), 1–33.

Smith, A. (1904). *An inquiry into the nature and causes of the wealth of nations* (Cannan edition). London: Methuen.

Social Stock Exchange UK. (2012). www.socialenterpriselive.com/section/social-investment/money/20111228/uk. Accessed Nov 2012.

Stiglitz, J. (2005). *The roaring nineties*. New York/London: W.W. Norton.

Tapscott, D., & Williams, A. (2008). *Wikinomics: How mass collaboration changes everything*. London: Atlantic Books.

Vittadini, G. (2008). Organizations acting in a subsidiary way in civil society (the case of the 'Food Bank'). In M. S. Archer & P. Donati (eds), *Pursuing the common good: How solidarity and subsidiarity can work together*. Vatican City: Vatican Press.

Wilke, H. (2003). *Heterotopia. Studien zur Krisis der Ordnung moderner Gesellschaft*. Frankfurt am Main: Suhrkamp.

Wilke, H. (2013). Complex governance and Europe's model of subsidiarity. In M. S. Archer & A. Maccarini (eds), *Engaging with the world: Agency, institutions, historical formations*. Abingdon: Routledge.

13 How agency is transformed in the course of social transformation

Don't forget the double morphogenesis

Introduction

I have already ventured a specific generative mechanism whose potential could be the transformation of late modernity into a Morphogenic society (Archer 2014, Ch. 5). This is not a prediction; Social Realism always acknowledges that such potentials may remain unrealized because of (a) countervailing mechanisms and (b) unforeseen contingencies – neither of which can be excluded from the open system that is society.

In brief, the generative mechanism advanced was grounded in the existence of 'contingent complementarities' between structural and cultural elements of late modernity that were explored and exploited by two different groups working in synergy. On the one hand, it resulted from an exponential addition of new items and novel sources of ideational variety that vastly exceeded the pool of ideas available in previous historical periods. These originated from positive feedback between digital scientists working in universities. On the other hand, the linkages established between compatible items are always reliant upon agents who see advantages in making them. In this case, the new variety of ideas had technological applications that readily translated them into practice, thus encouraging their take-up by enterprises in the nascent global economy. In other words, this is an important instance of the interplay between 'structure' and 'culture', whose properties and powers are irreducible to one another.

At the meso-level this morphogenetic potential was amplified by the synergy that developed between digital science and neo-capitalism, its multinational enterprises and financial institutions. Since the primary concern of the digital scientists was with the *diffusion* of their innovations and that of the economic vanguard was in their *profitability*, they worked together, but their synergy pulled social morphogenesis in two different directions: a reinforcement of *competition* on the part of the economy and the introduction of new *opportunities* on the part of digital innovators. This makes for a more complex story than the usual empiricist accounts of the 'rise of information society'.

In this chapter I will focus upon the recent effects of the changes in Structure and Culture introduced by Agency (the protagonists respectively of digital science and contemporary capitalism). However, any major change in the social order also has

260 *Agency and social transformation*

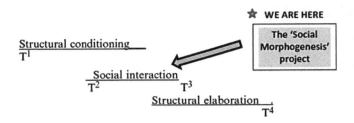

Figure 13.1 The basic M/M diagram of one morphogenetic cycle.

repercussions upon agency through being differentially beneficial or prejudicial (objectively and subjectively) to existing social groups. In the broadest terms, this prompts the reorganization of certain social groupings, including the degrouping of others. This secondary impact of the generative mechanism is the 'double morphogenesis' that is the subject of this chapter.

The Morphogenetic/Morphostatic (M/M) approach seeks to make the components of SAC methodologically tractable. The M/M framework had been used in a variety of different settings to deal with problems at all levels of sociological analysis. However, this book series is the first time when the M/M approach has *not* been used to give an account of morphogenetic changes that have already taken place.

Instead, in examining whether or not the emergence of a 'morphogenic social formation' from late modernity is not only conceivable but realistic, we break into an unfinished cycle in the middle (that is, in its T^2–T^3 phase). The basic M/M diagram is reproduced below, for those unfamiliar with it (Archer 1995). It also helps to situate the discussion taking place in the present volume (Fig. 13.1).

Some have suggested that there is a 'clean break' between the morphogenetic origins of any social form (such as the Internet) and the morphostatic processes that then maintain such a form in being. To such theorists, the diachronic causes for the existence of a phenomenon are firmly separated from the subsequent synchronic account of what sustains it in that form. Whilst those such as Sawyer (2005) and Elder-Vass (2010) are obviously philosophically correct in distinguishing between the causes of origin and the causes of continuation of given phenomena, my empirical conviction is that large-scale social change is rarely (if ever) a matter of 'clean breaks' and that they can be neither understood nor explained in such terms – even in the case of revolutions.

At the end of a morphogenetic cycle T^4 will be different in form, organization and state from at T^1, but T^4 is not a switch occurring overnight. This is important because were our one global social order to become a Morphogenic Society, this new social formation would not be a 'clean break' that suddenly greets us one morning.

Although the diagram is extremely simple (Archer 1995, 192–4), it is also very precise, but only three points need to be signalled here:

- Why the top line representing prior structural (in this case) conditioning does not have a definite temporal ending, having ceased to be *a conditional influence* when the bottom line representing 'Structural elaboration' gets underway. Traces of historic structures can linger on in the same way as other relics without their exercising any conditional influence at all (such as the now meaningless European titles that can be bought, shorn of their past legal privileges and obligations). Please note, however, that the top and bottom lines are always temporally continuous; there is never a moment without 'structural conditioning'.

- Next, 'social interaction' on the middle line at T^2–T^3 is the only temporally determinate phase, whose implication is that the relations between groups *cease to take that particular form* once 'structural elaboration' has fully engaged (bottom line). Prior to that, the *double morphogenesis* of agency, in which groups and group relations are themselves transformed when social transformation *starts to get underway, also intensifies as structural elaboration makes headway.*
- Finally, 'Social Interaction' is shorthand; it summarizes intergroup relations: $< R^1 \leftrightarrow R^2 : R^2 \leftrightarrow R^3 : R^3 \leftrightarrow R^4 : R^3 \leftrightarrow R^1 : R^2 \leftrightarrow R^4 : (R^1, R^2, R^3, R^4) >$ and does so iteratively for however many groups happen to be involved, as Donati has frequently pointed out.

This sounds exigent, but it is essential to the arguments I will advance in the next sections. These, in order of appearance, are that there are no 'clean breaks' between morphogenesis and morphostasis; if preferred, it is extremely difficult and I believe impossible in practice to sever causes of origin cleanly from causes of continuation, at least in the social domain. As far as I am aware, neither of the authors who hold this view has ever conducted a sociological study over time and, as such, clean hands account for thinking in terms of 'clean breaks', rather than the inescapable messiness of macroscopic social processes.

The absence of 'clean breaks' also illustrates (it is not a necessary condition) how the M/M approach deals with the synchronic question about causes of continuation, which empirically are not simply about maintenance but concern *successful maintenance* involving varying degrees of agential contestation. Unlike Elder-Vass, who always wants to separate the '*morphogenetic causes* that bring each type [of emergent entity] into existence' from 'the *morphostatic causes* that sustain their [emergent powers'] existence' (Elder-Vass 2010, 69), I hold that there is no point at which nothing but morphogenesis gives way to nothing but morphostasis or exclusively positive feedback to exclusively negative feedback.

This is because during any social contestation that generated some given social form those who lost out do not quietly fade away; on the contrary, they may retain their organisation and their objectives, fight on and later win concessions. Thus, morphostatic analysis cannot suffice alone and neither can the analysis of any institution or organization concentrate exclusively upon negative feedback. The explanation of why a new structure endures is often in part because it accommodates changes in its form pursued by rear-guard action – changes that 'punctuate' morphostasis synchronically. In other words, an emergent entity (such as an educational system) can retain its key relational organization of parts (those making it, say, a centralised system) without it remaining *exactly* the same entity or able to exhibit identical properties and exert identical powers as at the point of its emergence.[1] Simultaneously, an emergent organization also defines new groups of losers. Such groups have no interest in contributing to the current organization's morphostasis, although their actions and aims will differ from those of old contestants who still battle on.

To my knowledge, neither Sawyer nor Elder-Vass has ever mentioned, let alone given attention to, '*the double morphogenesis*', to how groups themselves and group relations are transformed in important respects in the course of pursuing and introducing social transformations (Archer 1995, Ch. 8). In fact, I don't know of a single commentator or critic who has ever referred to the 'double morphogenesis'. Yet, in this chapter I will argue that the agential regrouping and degrouping involved is one of the most crucial features taking place in late modernity as nascent structural and cultural morphogenesis engage, and it explains why globally we still remain in the prolonged T^2–T^3 phase.

In fact, any generative mechanism that is transforming the social order also ineluctably sustains or transforms the prior groupings of Primary and Corporate Agents. 'Primary Agents' are collectivities of people who share the same life-chances. They are aggregates, but these can have important social consequences. However, they are different from 'Corporate Agents', who are never aggregates because they have organized themselves in pursuit of certain goals and have articulated the changes they seek.

The examination of the 'double morphogenesis' is about what is *already* happening to social pre-grouping and regrouping in late modernity as social morphogenesis does begin to engage. The effects of the generative mechanism are still unfolding during T^2–T^3 and have been doing so for approximately 30 years. Therefore, it should be possible to pinpoint some of the changes already registering on the bottom line, which constitute both 'social morphogenesis' and *the double morphogenesis* (well before we get to T^4). This chapter will examine the two processes together, showing how, as the generative mechanism engages, Corporate Agency, 'in its attempt to sustain or transform the social system, is ineluctably drawn into sustaining or transforming the categories of Corporate and Primary Agents themselves' (Archer 1995, 260–1). Generically, the two together will be decisive for whether or not T^4 is eventually reached and whether or not it merits being called a Morphogenic society.

The generative mechanism of late modernity and the double morphogenesis

To account for the engagement of a generative mechanism propitious to intensified morphogenesis, it is necessary to backtrack briefly to the context that allowed the 'contingent compatibility' between structure and culture to be explored and led to the emergence of new variety that, in turn, fostered further variety (Archer 2014). In doing so, importance is always attached in the M/M approach to the relation between 'system' and 'social' integration and to Lockwood's insight that the conditions for substantial social change are found in the relations between the two (Archer 1996). This chapter concentrates upon the systemic changes introduced by the generative mechanism and how the low social integration entailed in the 'double morphogenesis' both reflects the dual directions in which the social order is being pulled and works to delay resolution between them and the imminent arrival at T^4.

The plummeting of system and social integration in late modernity

In the quarter of a century following the Second World War the developed democracies achieved *mutual regulation* between their institutional orders and their social orders. This is usually summarized in the formula 'social democracy + the neo-liberal economy + the welfare state'. Mutual regulation derived from mutual dependence – particularly of national industry upon its national labour force. Without that, industrial interests would have pursued the *situational logic of competition*, inherent in the liberal market economy, and the unionized workforce would have responded with industrial militancy.

The necessary but not sufficient conditions for mutual regulation were rooted in the nation-state itself. Whilst ever the state's boundaries also largely defined national societies, then the necessary interplay between the systemic and the social within the same territorial confines ineluctably meant that the state of the one mattered to the state of the other, prompting compromise between them.

Such mutual regulation was largely *morphostatic*,[2] representing a balance between the existing institutional and social orders that stabilized relations between them by virtue of the compromise formula. During these 'golden years' the two-way regulation established between system and society was better than it had been throughout modernity, even though developed societies remained far from egalitarian and their institutions far from fully participatory. What had been gained represented conciliation and concession within a *relationally contested* social order rather than the outworkings of social solidarity. Any promise of further mutual regulation, such that fairer societies might be progressively and peacefully negotiated, began to disintegrate in the 1980s. It did so as two *morphogenetic* processes came into synergy with one another and fostered one another's intensification (as spelt out in Archer 2014, Ch. 5 of Vol. II).

On the one hand, the growth of multinational corporations became unfettered by one national pool of organized labour as they freed themselves to pursue the *situational logic of competition*, intrinsic to capitalism, but on a new global scale. Yet, to do so globally simultaneously increased their reliance upon digital science (developed in the universities thanks to serious military backing at the start) for communication, cost/benefit analyses and logistics. As such, this is the well-known phenomenon of the rise of multinational Corporate Agency, whose members articulated the longer and more complex supply chains involved in production without reference to the social integration of their geographically dispersed workers. Indeed, there is evidence from the International Labour Organization (ILO) (2012) that the human trafficking of 'forced labour' increased apace (estimated at over 20 million), especially in East Asia.

However, multinational enterprises were neither all of one kind nor were their operations consensual in practice. Large banks, too, are multinationals, as are the (relatively) smaller pension funds of developed countries. After 1980 it became increasingly fallacious to conflate multinationalism with economic financialization as the gulf widened between the real economy and novel financial processes such as the sale of derivatives or huge growth of hedge-fund activities. Although the latter were even more dependent upon digital science and computerization, these played the market as a whole rather than having interests vested in any given enterprise within it. Hedge funds, for example, were estimated to account for half of the trading on the London and New York Stock exchanges by 2006 (Stulz 2007, 175), profiting from statistical arbitrage (exploiting short-run anomalies in share prices, rather than investment being based upon evaluation of equities themselves) and promoting high-frequency computerized trading. As such, their complex operations are supremely dependent upon vanguard digital science[3] and indifferent to the disruptions induced in corporate environments within the real economy.

Thus, the finance marketeers represent a new and growing Corporate Agent alongside that of the global productive enterprises, and most often with divergent interests from them and their workforces alike. As Morgan (2013, 15) concludes:

> if we resist thinking of corporations as financialized entities and think of them as productive units that carry the economic obligations of societies expressed through labour, then from this perspective hedge funds have proved on balance more of a problem than a benefit. Hedge funds are active elements of a pathologically dysfunctional finance system.

For, in turn, the corporate response to instability in the credit markets created by banks prompted limitations in company investment, with negative knock-on effects for employment rates, for occupationally based pension funds with their growing deficits and, ultimately, for social integration itself.

On the other hand, turning to digital science and its innovators, the forward thrust of informatics depended above all upon *diffusion* of its achievements in the pursuit of the *situational logic of opportunity*: that is, exploiting 'cultural compatibilities' to practical technological effect, whose visible successes were followed by further funding or venture capital. The relations between globalized capitalism (productive and financial) and digital science were internal and necessary ones, despite the pursuit of their different structural and cultural agendas. As with the two types of multinational enterprise differentiated above, it is necessary to distinguish two emerging forms of digital Corporate Agency. Whilst the stories of successful software entrepreneurs ('digital collaborators') are well rehearsed in paperbacks (and briefly reviewed in Ch. 5, Archer 2014) the diametrically opposed agenda of the 'digital diffusionists' constituted a distinct form of Corporate Agency. In important ways their objectives became even more distinctive, with 'diffusionists' promoting the 'cyber-commons'. My argument will be that the contestation between these four new Corporate Agents, each with their own (morphogenetic) aims, made them jointly and severally responsible for the ensuing economic crisis and systemic mal-integration.

Conversely, the *overall synergy* between the new forms of globalized capitalism and the generic innovations of digital science became increasingly interdependent and collaborative: the overlap between them grew in terms of personnel, further innovation and ever-newer applications. In short, in the last volume I advanced *the generative mechanism of late modernity as constituted by market competition and the diffusion of digital science needing to work in synergy*.

However, collaboration is not co-operation and, as synergy undoubtedly grew in scope and intensified in impact, the bulk of the literature on the *Roaring Nineties* (Stiglitz 2003) and the crisis that followed was monopolized by economics. There is no dispute with heterodox economists who accentuated the growth in 'systemic mal-integration' that accompanied the crisis and the fallacious attempts to prop up the status quo with international and intranational austerity measures. Nevertheless, there is a sociological theme running alongside and constantly obtruding itself. This is such that 'the crisis' cannot be presented in terms of rebalancing the books, of austerity as the harbinger of new economic growth, of future transparency of economies being introduced by business leaders coming to adopt virtue ethics. What is missing is the plummeting of 'social integration', because it affected both the possibility of 'economic recovery' and *also* the adoption of opportunities to re-envisage economic activity that are inherent in digital technology. In short, the two forms of mal-integration – social and systemic – grew in parallel.

Secondly, those sociological accounts that interpret the development of 'networked connectivity' as synonymous with growing social integration seem erroneous as, for example, in Wellman's argument that the triple revolution of social networks, the rise of the Internet and the advent of mobile connectivity served to *build trust*, 'the primary currency of social networks', for husbanding resources that provide support (Rainie and Wellman 2012, 19), as will be argued in the last section of this Chapter.

Synergy and its tensions: the contestation of intellectual property

Simply because two parties 'work together' (the meaning of synergy), it does not follow that they do so harmoniously and certainly not with any regard to the particular interests of each other. That was why, in outlining the generative mechanism, I maintained that the two main parties – economic and scientific – were pulling society in different directions through the very forms of morphogenesis promoted within each (Archer 2014). Digital science needs diffusion – that is its requirement for developing – while market enterprises need informatics – that is their requirement for profitability. In part these needs are compatible; the more competitively successful a corporation is, the more it diffuses the hardware and software it uses. Equally, the more popular a digital advance proves to be, the harder it becomes for any enterprise to ignore its existence because, for example, *not being seen on Facebook* constitutes a commercial penalty.

As already seen, their synergy works in tension and, with over-simplification, this is epitomized in one form of contestation that grew in importance. Its usual name is 'intellectual property', but the radical *diffusionists* contested this nomenclature from the start as it implies that cultural goods are subject to the same scarcity, loss of value through sharing and proprietary monopolization that characterizes most material goods. Contestation goes much further, into challenging intellectual copyright, circumventing patents, substitution of pharmaceuticals, products and trade secrets – all of which will be discussed further. The reason for doing so is that 'intellectual property' is the battleground upon which *the form of morphogenesis* that will most likely predominate in the reshaping of late modernity is being played out. Should there be an outright 'winner' then the form of Morphogenic society would be very different, as would its beneficiaries.

Intellectual property: opportunism versus opportunity

That we are indeed on cultural terrain is acknowledged by all who have supported the proclamation of the 'Knowledge Society', the 'Information Age' or 'Technological Society', and these are the most common characterizations of late modernity. What is glaring by its absence is the general failure to recognize that the nature of culture itself means that its social dynamics are entirely different from those attaching to material scarcity, be it in land, military strength or means of production. As Thomas Jefferson expressed the difference on 13 August 1813:

> If nature has made any one thing less susceptible than all others of exclusive property, it is the action of the thinking power called an idea, which an individual may exclusively possess as long as he keeps it to himself; but the moment it is divulged, it forces itself into the possession of everybody . . . Its peculiar character, too, is that no one possesses the less, because every other possesses the whole of it. He who receives an idea from me, receives instruction himself without lessening mine; as he who lights his taper at mine, receives light without darkening me.

In other words, cultural items are strangers to the workings of scarcity, which can only be imposed artificially. Containment strategies (edicts of seclusion, the burning of books, censorship) require coercion in order to be even temporarily effective (Archer 1988, 188–98). The situation becomes much more precarious once morphogenesis engages because the rapid release of cultural novelty, innovation and new variety all spell a precipitous reduction in future calculability. To protect market investment, the multinational enterprises responded by extending and reinforcing legal patents and copyright law to ensure a calculable market by temporarily 'freezing' uncertainty (Fig. 13.2). *Ceteris paribus*, this assured short-term profitability and freed up corporate resources to make the next innovative development that would then be protected in the same manner (Morgan 2013). In the finance market, the development of complex derivatives and hedge funds rendered risks more calculable and provided insurance for the biggest players, whilst the popular 'demand' for financial services was manipulated by the proliferation of credit facilities, sub-prime mortgages and payment protection

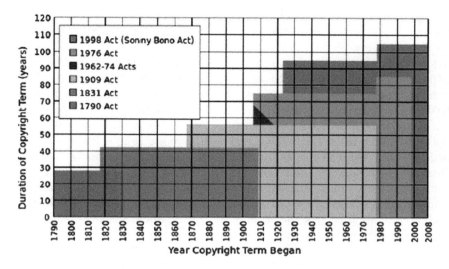

Figure 13.2 Growth in copyright.
Source: Wikipedia (undated a).

schemes, all the way down to payday loans, with their 6,000 per cent annual interest rates.

The economic importance of intellectual property grew in the second half of the twentieth century, being featuring in the Universal Declaration of Human Rights[4] and protected by the World Intellectual Property Organization (WIPO), a UN agency after 1967. By 2013 the US Patent and Trademark Office claimed that the worth of intellectual property to the national economy exceeded $5 trillion and was estimated to underwrite the jobs of 18 million people, with similar values being registered in the EU. Two-thirds of the worth of large US corporations can be traced to intangible (intellectual) assets and 'IP-intensive industries' are estimated to generate 72 per cent more value added (price minus material cost) per employee than 'non-IP-intensive industries'. Penalties for copyright infringement became more stringently criminalized under the ACTA trade agreement (2011), whilst trade in counterfeited works traducing copyright represented a worldwide $600 billion industry by that date (Bitton 2012). Meanwhile, the concept of intellectual property enlarged, thanks to the influential Motion Picture Association of America (Wharton 1992), and also came to include CDs, DVDs and computer games (Fisher 1999). It invaded the Internet with, for example, Mark Zuckerberg succeeding in upholding his property rights to all material posted on *Facebook*.

This proliferation of intellectual property rights represented commercial *opportunism*. In every case, such rights allowed companies to charge higher than marginal costs of production, supposedly to recoup their research and development investment, but usually (especially in medicine) at prices prohibitive to the poor (Sonderholm 2010). However, it is salutary to note how competitive strategy can temporarily work both ways in relation to intellectual property rights. For example, Tesla Motors recently released its patents for the electric cars it produces 'in order to advance the production of more electric cars'[5] and doubtless increased profit from their sales (Fig. 13.2).

Moving over to the other party working in synergy, Richard Stallman, a graduate of the original hackers, questioned the use of 'property' in a cultural context, where 'intellectual protectionism', 'monopoly' or 'digital restrictions management' were held to be more appropriate terms. His 'Free Software Foundation' (1985) launched the *diffusionists'* offensive with 'copyleft', which was quickly followed by Linus Torvalds' release of the Linux kernel, the modifiable source code that was placed under General Licensing in 1992. In turn, this led on to the Open Source and later the Open Access movements. In all instances, 'Opening the source code enabled a self-enhancing diversity of production models, communication paths and interactive communities' (Wikipedia undated b). Many anti-copyright organizations followed, such as the Swedish think-tank Piratbyrån, one of whose founders (Fleischer) argued that copyright law is obsolete since it cannot cope with Internet diffusion, particularly with the advent of Web 2.0. Many focused on peer-to-peer file sharing, digital freedom and freedom of information, to be shared in solidarity. Others pioneered the distributed search engine, directly challenging copyright policy (for example, Kazaa and Gnutella).

The details of this cut and thrust are complex, but in every case they exemplify a commitment to *opportunity in opposition to opportunism*: to groups working co-operatively to make what they would of the digital resources now culturally available, but first needing to be publicly accessible.

The group formation and reformation involved in this contestation are a crucial part of the *double morphogenesis*; it is responsible for many of the technical developments that came into existence over the last 20 years, responses to which have, in turn, resulted in further agential regrouping. What I have termed the *opportunists versus protagonists of opportunity* is what journalists called 'the copyright wars', and these are matters of global contestation. Although the *opportunists* have the forces of the economy, the state (e.g., the Chinese censorship of computer servers) and the law (the Digital Millennial Copyright Act and its European equivalents) on their side they are nevertheless on the defensive. WIPO has acknowledged the conflict between the current protection of intellectual property and human rights (World Intellectual Property Organization 2002). The UN Committee on Economic, Social and Cultural rights maintained in 2001 that such 'property' was governed by economic goals, whilst it should be recognized as a social product (Chapman 2002).

In short, contestation promoted further morphogenesis, which consequentially reduced the artificial scarcity that had been placed upon cultural goods, thus opening up new *opportunities* for the exploration and exploitation of 'contingent complementarities'. However, as far as the 'double morphogenesis' of agency is concerned, the newly defined Corporate Agents promoting the cyber-commons were small and highly educated groups in relation to the population at large, even in the developed world.

The generative mechanism's divergent consequences for the 'double morphogenesis'

The double morphogenesis: the top-down effects of the economic crisis

To recapitulate, the 'double morphogenesis' results from agents succeeding in introducing structural and/or cultural transformation but being transformed themselves and transforming other agents in the self-same process. In other words, it entails agential re-formation in terms of personal motivation and also a regrouping of alliances. The reason for dwelling initially upon the *economic crisis* is because it changed the social context affecting the actions of all agents through its systemic mal-integration. The effects of digital science on the 'double morphogenesis' are 'bottom-up' and were entirely different in kind. But they had to confront an agential environment where social integration and trust had slumped even lower.

In the welter of literature on the current crisis, few commentators have picked up on the importance of the mal-integration of the financial system in exacerbating social mal-integration, probably through according exclusive significance to economic considerations. Yet integration and trust cohere closely because, as Colledge et al. (2014) emphasize, 'trust seems to be no more or less than a generalizable term for a situational social glue in the form of *how* relations are engaged', but one that lost its adhesive quality within the financialized economy. Certainly, Bachman had written about 'a tremendous global trust crisis' (Bachmann 2011), but did so from within Giddens' structuration approach, whose central conflation does not permit any analysis of the interplay between the SAC components.

Trust involves uncertainty, otherwise it would be redundant, and it is relatively resilient to booms, bubbles or slumps, *provided* that public investors (financial advisors, bank managers, mortgage granters) appear to be winning or losing alongside their clients. Oversimplifying considerably, the global crisis provided many indicators of a growing divide between the concerns and practices of public investors and those of their clientele, all with *repercussions for denting trust and fuelling the slump in social integration.*

Jamie Morgan and Ioana Negru have detailed these briefly and clearly for the finance industry as follows (2012):

a   A pervasive sales culture in both investment and commercial banking that took an adversarial attitude to the customer, as though the interests of the organization and client were opposed.
b   A general standard of service that led the finance industry to have the highest rate of (retail) customer complaints amongst any recognized major industry (including construction).
c   The specific mis-selling of payment protection insurance (PPI) on a multi-billion-pound scale.
d   The specific mis-selling of unsuitable interest-rate hedging products to small firms.

e The specific mis-selling of investment products to investors who were unaware of the 'risk' of the ultimate destination of their capital (e.g., transmitted through Ponzi schemes, such as the Madoff investment vehicle).
f The specific sale of investment products in which the bank also had a proprietary and sometimes a counter interest.
g The general operation of transnational payment and capital transfer systems that facilitated the activities of organized crime and pariah states.
h The long-term manipulation of key benchmark rates used in multiple ways in finance markets: Libor, Euribor etc.
i A compensation system for senior executives that has seemed divorced from the context of the rest of the economy and from the actual performance of the individual banks and which has served to create a sense of alienation and indignation amongst the ordinary populous.

The effects of crisis were augmented by those of 'curative' austerity measures. Objectively, these impacted hardest upon the poor because of increased unemployment and further reductions in welfare benefits, leaving even the full-time working poor worse off. However, their residual class consciousness had never made this increasingly heterogeneous group a 'trusting' collectivity; even during the 'golden interlude' they had effectively been bought off by new-found 'affluence' – and its extrapolation into the future. Subjectively, those whose trust was most savagely dented were precisely those 'middle Englanders' and French *fonctionnaries* (52 per cent of the active population) to whom centrist political parties all now appealed as their support base. Their new inability to afford mortgages, to feel securely pensionable, to count on annual salary increments and to depend upon free health care provisions undercut trust and precipitated many into scapegoating by supporting the ultra-right (UKIP or the Front National of the Le Pens). Those who did not immediately blame 'migrants' or 'Europe' personalized matters by fastening upon bankers' bonuses or politicians' fiddling of their expenses.

Incorrect as all these individualistic diagnoses were, they indicated a negative form of 'double morphogenesis' in which the previous mainstay of support for the econo-political system (small shareholders and members of political parties) was effectively regrouped into a suspicious and fearful collectivity of Primary Agents. That its members had no revolutionary heritage whatsoever did not mean that they were immune to other morphogenetic changes and the new forms of Corporate Agency they were fostering. Latter-day capitalism continued its zero-sum production of winners and losers, but what had altered was the growing proportion of the latter – many of whom had an inchoate awareness that they had been betrayed by the old competitive ways. However, did this spell their greater openness to new opportunities?

The double morphogenesis: the bottom-up effects of digital diffusion

Digital science originated in the universities and, from the beginning, not all research scientists embraced big business, despite their reliance upon capitalization

Agency and social transformation 271

for the diffusion of their innovations (Archer 2014). From the original group of 'hackers' can be traced the origins of new Corporate Agents who very quickly articulated alternative aims (the cyber-Commons, open-sourcing of knowledge, peer-to-peer production and subsidiarity) and implemented them in new organizational forms (General Licensing, Wikipedia and, eventually, social networking media). All of these were predicated upon 'win–win' scenarios; that the cultural sharing of digital resources enhanced everybody and impoverished no-one. As they advanced and diversified, these too introduced their own 'double morphogenesis', with its dual aspects of regrouping tracts of the global population into novel types of alliance formation (some to become Corporate Agents) and transmuting the personal motivation of a significant proportion of Primary Agents.

The double morphogenesis of Corporate Agency

There are four elements it is particularly important to highlight because each of them intensifies morphogenesis whilst simultaneously holding the potential to increase social integration. Firstly, the **Open Source Movement** (Tiemann 2006) is literally based upon software source codes being publicly available (via free licensing), making them accessible to all and enabling their adaptation to specific ends as defined by users themselves. It is based upon collaborative production and its products are open for further elaboration and sharing. As a result – only possible because of the Internet – the marginal costs of appropriating digital innovations are reduced to near zero. Since the movement coincided with a huge growth in personal computer ownership its thrust was towards social inclusion, which grew incrementally as more agents came to appreciate the *variety* of new applications possible, and then to appropriate these themselves. Moreover, because rooted 'in the open-source ARPAnet, its hacker culture, its decentralized, scattered architecture made it difficult for big, established candidates, companies and media to gain control of it' (Trippi 2004).

The Open Source Initiative supplies many practical examples of how morphogenetic variety encourages further variety. By the time of the Open Source Summit (1998), the movement was working as a consumers' co-operative, aiming to reduce the restrictions imposed by copyright in order to stimulate creativity outside the proprietary model, and spawning organizations such as 'Creative Commons' that stressed voluntary collaboration rather than 'crowd-sourcing' that benefits the market. Free co-operation proved a gratuitous source for the relational production of goods and is both the exemplar and foundation of how the 'win–win' scenario is a realistic alternative to the 'win–lose' model of competition.

There is no space here to detail the novel applications and the developments that followed, but their range covers the following: in scientific research, 'The Science Commons (Open Source Summit 1998); in publishing, Project Gutenberg (2014) and Wikisource; in pharmaceuticals, the 'Tropical Disease initiative' (2014) and the 'Open Source Drug discovery for Malaria Consortium' (Openwetware 2014); in technology, sensitive to environmental implications, 'Open-source-appropriate technology' (Buitenhuis et al. 2010); in teaching, providing open-source courseware, forging the connection between science and social benefit; and, in retailing, producing coca cola taste-alikes!

At the same time, it is proper to signal that inclusive creative autonomy can also generate relational evils. The development (2012) of 'Defense Distributed', with the aim of designing 'a working plastic gun that could be downloaded and reproduced by anybody with a 3D printer' (Poeter 2012), highlights the dangers (that appear to have been realized in Britain during September 2013). If Open Source seeks to thrive through beneficent Corporate Agents, then it needs to work out a binding form of normative self-regulation along the lines that Wikipedia has done 'in-house', but is much more difficult to achieve in the open ether.

Secondly, **Commons-based peer production** is differentiated from the centralized decision-making process typical of most for-profit enterprises and market-based production, where performing different tasks for differential pay is regarded as a necessary incentive and the centralized co-ordination of tasks to be indispensable. The operability of commons production depends upon the modularization (of tasks), granularity of modules (allowing those with variable levels of skill and motivation to contribute) and low-cost integration for combining contributions into finished products (Benkler 2006). Its advantages include 'customization' and 'specialization' in line with specific needs, 'cross-fertilization' – often between surprisingly disparate fields – and the accommodation of variations in human creativity and commitment. It results in information diffusion and contributes to the integration of variety as diversity within the population, thus countering the potential monopolization of new variety by elites or the fissiparous tendency of increased heterogeneity (Benkler and Nussbaum 2006). Thus, it is not simply pro-social but pro-social integration.

Although often criticized for downplaying the need for supervisory co-ordination, Michel Bauwens' 'peer2peer' organization has already addressed some of the problems of 'open manufacturing' (2009).[6] Whether or not peer production can build a nuclear reactor is not the issue. Commons-based production is not intended to be analogous to the existing real economy (though there is nothing to prevent it entering areas such as building design or the clothing trade). However, authors such as Tapscott and Williams immediately seized upon what peer production, under the new name of 'dispersed production', could do to assist firms in acquiring technical solutions for free, thus lowering costs and raising profits (Tapscott and Williams 2007). The 'Wealth of Networks' *is* digital and playing to its strengths, rather than mimicking highly capitalized production, is precisely what ensures that commons-based production remains both morphogenetic and socially integrative.

Thirdly, **Virtual Communities** in the form of networking sites may indeed perform an integrative role through furnishing friendship, acceptance and understanding of distant others, in contra-distinction to the strong tendencies towards trivialization, stereotyped self-presentation and the devalued meaning of friendship encouraged by the commercial social networking sites. More important here is the contribution of virtual communities in fostering new Corporate Agents that emphasise reciprocity among members and perform the novel task of countering the individualism inherent in growing heterogeneity without endorsing the authoritarian bent of Maruyama's heterogenistics (1978). These new Corporate Agents work by combining dispersed forms of specialist concerns into interactive support groups that are morphogenetic in influencing mainstream practices. In other words, they transform the isolated members of aggregates into agencies for mutual assistance at the micro-level and at the meso- and macro-levels can assume the form of Corporate 'single-issue groups'.

In health issues, for example, and especially ones involving relatively rare or embarrassing conditions, sometimes rebuffed by general medical practitioners and sometimes simply not recognized, the virtual community becomes the store of specialized knowledge, advice, assistance and personal encouragement.[7] Such initiatives have led healthcare providers to initiate their own sites for patients, who can direct their questions online to doctors.

Substantively different, but formally similar, are virtual communities that facilitate the coalescing of isolates and the articulation of new identities (for example, 'asexuals') (Carrigan 2011). If this illustration seems to be one confined to mutual assistance, there are plenty of cases where sites promote digital altruism by helping people to connect with voluntary associations, with civic engagement, to support 'concealed causes' such as the victims of human trafficking, which is where virtual communities interface with political pressure group activity and their acquired and shared knowledge is used to combat the ultra-right's false homogenization of those trafficked with 'illegal migrants'.

Obviously, this is where the virtual community impacts upon the politics of reform movements, speeding their mobilization,[8] and on International Relations through well-known sites such as Wikileaks and OpenLeaks, whose impact Colin Wight discusses in Chapter 3. What has been accentuated here is *the digital proclivity to spawn new Corporate Agents*, who are spearheading direct democracy and generically counteracting the 'individualism' proclaimed by several decades of sociologists by relationally integrating the heterogeneity that intensified morphogenesis undoubtedly promotes and replacing lost sources of building trust and rebuilding social integration. Far from the meso-level becoming progressively evacuated, it is densely populated by these novel forms of Corporate Agency – the agential outcomes of the 'double morphogenesis' induced by the diffusion of digital science. Nevertheless, while the Corporate Agents involved may be numerous, they remain small in scale.

The double morphogenesis of Primary Agency

Collectivities of Primary Agents (those sharing the same life chances) have undoubtedly become more heterogeneous, to the point where 'the poor' is now a disparate aggregate of those in such varied situations that 'poverty' is their highest common denominator. Add to this the falling membership of trades unions, of political parties, of voter turnout – especially amongst the under 35s – and of newspaper readership, plus the 30 hours on average per week spent watching TV throughout Europe, and it seems this adds up to the 'passive agent' in late modernity, those to whom things happen rather than those making things happen. Of course, there are counter-indicators, the most important being the growth of voluntary associations and the Third Sector in general.

Although far from free of their own motivational ambiguities, those responsible for the growth of the **blogosphere** in the 1990s cannot be deemed 'passive' and are largely interactive. In spring 2011 more than 156 million public blogs existed[9] and the numbers have kept increasing exponentially because they help fuel one another. As an aggregate phenomenon, they have driven some respectable newspapers out of business and the other kind to illegal excesses (phone-hacking) to sustain readership. They challenge copyright, engage in political commentary in close to real time, raise inconvenient social issues and monitor the workings of public services as well as undertaking a host of self-serving purposes. There is no doubt that their existence enhances information diffusion and there is little that they have increased the public accountability of elected politicians, given that these now rely upon Twitter for making their personal and policy announcements. In other words, it is equally indubitable that the blogosphere is the home of certain Primary Agents who are taking advantage of the *situational logic of opportunity* and together are exerting significant aggregate effects. However, although they have changed the environment in which all Corporate Agents operate, the question remains as to whether or not their 'direct action' is cumulative in its aggregate effects.

In short, the conjoint result for the double morphogenesis of the 'top down' effects of finance capitalism's attempted 'recovery' has done nothing to remedy the absence of trust. Equally, the efforts of *digital diffusionists* to promote trust, co-operation, reciprocity and subsidiarity have produced green shoots, but not ones with vigorous growth. The public at large has been bombarded by mixed messages, which probably dampened the impact of both, preventing a radical *double morphogenesis*. However, I want to introduce a final synergistic consequence in conclusion.

Why Primary Agents predominate

Unbridled opportunism has indeed induced a *double morphogenesis* because the continuing economic crisis has regrouped the population of the developed world. Fifty per cent of those in southern Europe are unemployed, most Europeans fear for their job security, occupational pensions are of diminishing value, some have had their houses repossessed, the young cannot get a mortgage to put them on the housing ladder, social security has been rolled further back, the costs of utilities rise and the burden of austerity measures leaves the poor worse off, though professional incomes have also deteriorated in real terms.

All of these people have lost their previous vested interests; namely, those embedded in holding a given post with reasonable expectations of promotion and incremental salary increases or negotiated pay rises, and in supporting a particular political party or coalition because it represents their interests. Market and State have undermined both. The general public has lost its trust in public institutions as governance is increasingly dependent on so-called 'performance indicators' and 'regulators', in health, education and social services. Apart from the 20 per cent or so who scapegoat migrants for their woes, the majority now form a mistrustful bunch who do not even recognize themselves as stakeholders. Given this simultaneous breakdown of both system and social integration, why would they not pursue their *concerns* through the *situational logic of opportunity*?

To answer this, I want to stress the greatest 'success' of digital science and ironically the perverse triumph of *diffusionism*. It is not any of the four factors examined as the 'bottom-up' effects of digital diffusion, nor the indisputable achievements of Wikipedia, nor the macroscopic influence upon international politics exerted by WikiLeaks in general or Edward Snowden in particular. Instead, I want to suggest that it is something that (just) predated the economic crisis but also neutralized its potential for outrage producing change; something that was fundamentally parasitic upon the general loss of social integration, of trust and of meaningful relationality; and something that *infiltrated the life-world* of the majority, rendering them increasingly passive and inflating the ranks of Primary Agents.

This was the direct effect of the synergy constituting the generative mechanism that I have advanced, but that also 'pulled the social order in two directions'. It is another warning against 'clean breaks' and, if there is anything in this thesis, it illustrates how the parties to the synergy may produce overall morphogenesis, but their components can operate morphostatically *vis-à-vis* one another, as Porpora maintains in his chapter. 'Bread and circuses' was the classic recipe for quietism, so let's bring on the clowns in the guise of today's great distraction.

Emailing introduced *selective* connectivity, based on free-giving and reciprocity that made new ways of life possible. Prior to it, I could not have lived between three countries, edited this book from the foothills of the French Alps or maintained close friendships all over the world. Similarly, the mobile phone linked people together over distances and did/does good service for African agriculture and development in general. To begin with, the advent of social networking services (SNS) also promised to build communities of shared interests, as opposed to shared geography, and to offset the loneliness that is the scourge of the developed world.

The prototypes of social networking services were up and running on the Web more than a decade before the economic crisis, with some, such as 'Classmates.com', simply supplying e-addresses to those who had lost contact. The second generation became much more pro-active: SixDegrees.com (1997), Makeoutclub (2000), Hubculture and Friendster (2002). They were characterized by three new elements: some shed the dot.com self-avowal; the *quest* for new 'friends' was a novel thrust; and the accompanying presentation of 'personal profiles' became a central feature by the late 1990s. The latter was later described as 'type yourself into being' (Boyd and Ellison 2007) – with as 'cool' a self-presentation as possible – and did not come with the warning 'what you read is not what you share' (Byrne 2012) when compiling lists of 'friends'. By 2005 MySpace was gaining more views than Google, and Facebook, launched in 2004, had become the world's largest networking site by 2009. A national US survey by the Pew Centre in 2011 found 73 per cent of online teenagers were using SNS sites, an increase on the 55 per cent of three years earlier (Lenhart et al. 2010), and 47 per cent of adult Americans were users.

What accounts for this amazing rise as captured in recent user figures? By 2012 Facebook announced it had passed 1 billion monthly active users and 600 million active mobile users (73 per cent of the total user base). Last quarter it exceeded 700 million daily users. It is estimated to own 100 billion photos that have been posted by individuals. The key seems to open a lock with three tumblers: that this service, like most SNSs, charges no fee for joining or use, that it is inter-operative with mobile phones and that it gains its revenue from advertising. It is the latter upon which I will focus first, because it is not self-evident why Swiss Air, for example, would choose to advertise there – on the face of it.

Normalising commercial enterprises

The answer goes beyond crude commercialization, as in pay up to be visible where the people are found, such as renting digital display boards in airports. This is the scatter-shot approach; one that can be seen, for instance, on 'The Weather Channel', a quite accurate site providing free forecasts covering the globe. However, it is obvious as I type 'Evian-les-Bains' into this US service that its adverts simply aim at the lowest common denominators of those wanting to know whether to carry an umbrella or a sunhat: weight loss, dating and package holidays. Conversely, the synergy of our generative mechanism outdates simple targeted advertising by the development of 'network analysis software' for data-mining. Most supermarkets and retailers such as Amazon already use it: buy two pairs of shoes online and be surprised at what you are next offered. However, Facebook offers to dig deeper through its 'Social Ads' that tailor and sell the demographics and interests of its voluntary users to enable 'bulls-eye' advertising. It will also offer the results of its own programme, 'Facebook Beacon', to track the websites users have visited outside Zuckerberg's domain.

That these activities continued to expand during the economic crisis itself is hugely important. Companies built 'brand image sites', merging business interests with digital advances, such as cloud computing, and the SNSs became online 'reputation management tools'. In other words, they normalize and naturalize their presence, even if they happen to be selling financial derivatives. They also engage in some free interactive crowd-sourcing and herd the traffic onto their own online sites to these ends.

Returning to the contestation of intellectual property, paralleling all of the above has been the growth of US patents covering SNS technologies. There are now 3,500 published applications, representing a huge growth from 2003 to 2010, as shown in Fig. 13.3. Only about 400 of these have as yet been issued as patents, owing to the backlog accumulated. Undoubtedly, social networking is big business. What Fig. 13.3 brings home is that its growth was not in the least diminished – on the contrary – as the economic crisis unfurled.

Thus, morphogenesis continued through the crisis, but in a manner that harnessed digital developments and their diffusion to *competition*. Although it has often been noted that the SNSs can catalyze public demonstrations, they work through disaggregation and reaggregation for commercial purposes rather than fostering the development of new Corporate Agents spearheading the *opportunity* for oppositional regrouping. The *Occupy* groups were hardly durable beneficiaries of their

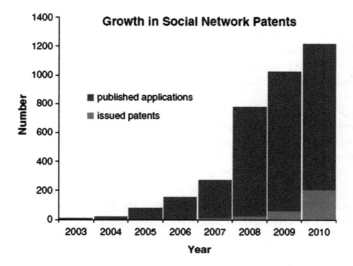

Figure 13.3 Number of US social network patent applications published per year and patents issued per year.

Source: Wikipedia (undated c).

capacity for mobilization or for collectively articulating new aims and objectives, despite Castells' (2012) peon to them.

Reinforcing the passivity of Primary Agents

I have accentuated how the economic crisis undermined a variety of Corporate Agents and how this 'double morphogenesis' was assisted by the SNSs, but the influence of the latter went further because it not only militated against regrouping into new Corporate Agents but constituted a morphostatic influence on agency in general by inducing passivity. This exceeded their impact as sources of pre-occupation and distraction (that have to be added to the time spent with the mobile phone and the homage still given to television, even if now streamed), all subtracting from time available for reflexive internal conversation. Increasingly, the most successful SNSs fostered a new form of intense 'presentism' among users. This is something I began to explore in *The Reflexive Imperative* (2012), terming it *événementalisme*, those whose temporal horizon was limited to today's events, with their responses reliant upon 'gut feelings', thus precluding the subject from designing a course of action; one that necessarily entails future time and the (fallible) understanding of how events and actions are linked (Archer 2012, 277–91).

For Expressive Reflexives such as these, 'their method of "reducing variety", by attending to the pressing and the proximate is a response . . . governed by situational immediacy and intensity alone' (Archer 2012, 281). The implication is that these subjects accept 'shapeless lives' because, in effect, they have rescinded the agential power to become (something of) their own 'sovereign artificers' (Hollis 1987, 1–14). Another way of putting this is that, rather than making their way through the world, they ad hoc their way through it.

Although the media in general foster this tendency to view the social order as a succession of contingencies, as does centrist politics and public broadcasting, by remorselessly dwelling on today's 'scandal' – with the news becoming reminiscent of the first gruesome nineteenth-century broadsheets – the SNSs have moved this tendency into top gear. Twitter, now number two in terms of users, introduced 'real time' services (in words), Clixtr followed (in pictures by streaming photos from an ongoing event) and Facebook joined in with 'Live Feed'. This fixation on 'presentism' is at the expense of mentally contextualising causes and attempting to project consequences; in terms of (in)action, it generalizes the 'bystander effect' that Porpora discusses in Chapter 9. Reductions in thought and action increase agential passivity. Conversely, to seize upon *opportunity* always requires a thoughtful and active agent; to do so with societal effect requires not merely active Primary Agents but those ready to coalesce relationally into Corporate Agents, with effective organization and articulated aims that contest *événementalisme*. Last year, I took consolation from two young lads on the Lausanne métro whose T-shirts read, 'You won't find me on Facebook: I have a Life'.

Conclusion

In the Introduction I maintained that we remained in the T^2–T^3 phase, where morphogenesis and morphostasis still worked together and implied that this phase will be long-lasting. I also argued against 'clean breaks' in which morphogenesis introduces some significant change and 'immediately' analysis shifts to the forms of morphostasis reproducing it. One lesson from this excursion into popular digital diffusion and its colonized perversion is that the two processes intertwine, because I do not see the intensification of passive Primary Agency as an unintended consequence or perverse effect; it is too convenient to be merely contingent. The result is to protract late modernity and to delay T^4 at which a Morphogenic social formation could conceivably be reached. The challenge as far as the generative mechanism advanced is concerned is whether or not conditions can be specified under which 'synergy' would not buttress the status quo. These would need to be such that the prevailing form of 'double morphogenesis' is reversed and ceases to generate an ever-growing pool of passive Primary Agents, lacking the social integration to coalesce into Corporate Agents and engage in relational contestation.

Notes

1 As in the French Loi Falloux (1850), under which the Church regained the freedom to open schools after almost half a century of prohibition.
2 Walter Buckley defines 'morphogenesis' as 'those processes which tend to elaborate or change a system's given form, structure or state,' as contrasted with morphostatic processes 'that tend to preserve or maintain a system's form, organization, or state' (1967, 58).

Agency and social transformation 279

3 'It is nearly impossible for human portfolio managers and traders to implement a strategy involving so many securities and trading so frequently without making use of quantitative methods and technological tools such as automated trading platforms, electronic communications networks, and mathematical optimization algorithms' (Khandani and Lo 2007, 7). The authors conclude that 'It is no wonder that the most successful funds in this discipline have been founded by computer scientists, mathematicians, and engineers not by economists or fundamental stock pickers' (p. 12).
4 Article 27 reads: 'everyone has the right to the protection of the moral and material interests resulting from any scientific, literary or artistic production of which he is the author'.
5 See http://guardiananlv.com/2014/06/tesla-motors-releases-its-patent-to-the-public.
6 In the first semester of 2014, Michel Bauwens was research director of the floksociety.org research group, which produced the first integrated Commons Transition Plan for the government of Ecuador in order to create a 'social knowledge economy', with 15 associated policy papers. One version of the plan is available at http://en.wiki.floksociety.org/w/Research_Plan.
7 One of my PhD students, Pamela Higham, has explored this by e-interviewing for the female condition PCOS and for Psoriasis, where some of those meeting on the forum also graduate to holidaying together. When a woman with PCOS has an appointment upcoming with a new specialist, members send encouraging messages and want to know the outcome.
8 'The Internet is tailor made for a populist, insurgent movement', wrote Joe Trippi (2004).
9 Archived from the original www.blogpulse.com/ on 4 June 2012.

References

Archer, M. S. (1988). *Culture and agency*. Cambridge: Cambridge University Press.
Archer, M. S. (1995). *Realist social theory: The morphogenetic approach*. Cambridge: Cambridge University Press.
Archer, M. S. (1996). Social integration and system integration: Developing the distinction. *Sociology*, 30(4), 679–699.
Archer, M. S. (2012). *The reflexive imperative in late modernity*. Cambridge: Cambridge University Press.
Archer, M. S. (2014). The generative mechanism re-configuring late modernity in her (ed.) *Social morphogenesis*, Vol. II, Chap. 5, Late modernity: Trajectories towards Morphogenic Society. New York: Springer.
Bachmann, R. (2011). At the crossroads: Future directions in trust research. *Journal of Trust Research*, 1(2), 203–213.
Bauwens, M. (2009). The emergence of open design and open manufacturing. www.wemagazine.net/we-volume-02/the-emergence-of-open-design-and-open-manufacturing/#.V4k2fDW1ynM [accessed 15 July 2016].
Benkler, Y. (2006). *Wealth of networks*. New Haven: Yale University Press.
Benkler, Y., & Nussbaum, M. (2006). Commons-based peer production and virtue. *The Journal of Political Philosophy*, 4(14), 394–419.
Bitton, M. (2012). Re-thinking the anti-counterfeiting trade agreement's criminal copyright enforcement measures. *Journal of Criminal Law and Criminology*, 102(1), 67–117.
BlogPulse. (2011). http://archive.is/XHRF, 16 February 2011.
Boyd, D. M., & Ellison, N. B. (2007). Social network sites: Definition, history, and scholarship. *Journal of Computer-Mediated Communication*, 13(1), 210–230.
Buckley, W. (1967). *Sociology and modern systems theory*. Englewood Cliffs NJ: Prentice-Hall.

Buitenhuis, A. J., Zelenika, I., & Pierce, J. M. (2010). Open design-based strategies to enhance appropriate technology development. http://nciia.org/sites/default/files/pearce.pdf [accessed 15 July 2016].
Byrne, C. (2012). What you read is not what you share. http://venturebeat.com/2012/08/23/bitly-realtime-hilary-mason/ [accessed 15 July 2016].
Carrigan, M. (2011). There's more to life than sex? Difference and commonality within the asexual community. In *Sexualities*, http://sex.sagepub.com/content/14/4/462 [accessed 15 July 2016].
Castells, M. (2012). *Networks of outrage and hope*. Cambridge: Polity.
Chapman, A. R. (2002). The human rights implications of intellectual property protection. *Journal of International Economic Law*, 5(4), 861–882.
Colledge, B., Morgan, J., & Tench, R. (2014). The concept(s) of trust in late modernity, the relevance of realist social theory. *Journal for the Theory of Social Behaviour*, 44(4), 481–503.
Elder-Vass, D. (2010). *The causal power of social structures*. Cambridge: Cambridge University Press.
Fisher, W. W. (1999). *The growth of intellectual property: A history of the ownership of ideas in the United States*. Göttingen: Vanderhoeck and Ruprecht.
Hollis, M. (1987). *The cunning of reason*. Cambridge: Cambridge University Press.
International Labour Organization. (2012). *Global estimate of forced labour: Results and methodology*. Geneva: ILO.
Jefferson, T. (1813). Letter to Isaac McPherson. http://presspubs.uchicago.edu/founders/documents/a1_8_8s12.html, 13 August 1813.
Khandani, A., & Lo, A. (2007). What happened to the Quants in August 2007? http://papers.ssrn.com/sol3/papers.cfm?abstract-id=1015987 [accessed 15 July 2016].
Lenhart, A., Purcell, K., Smith, A., & Zickuhr, K. (2010). Social media and young adults. http://pewinternet.org/Reports/2010/Social-Media-and-Young-Adults.aspx [accessed 15 July 2016].
Maruyama, M. (1978). Heterogenistics and morphogenetics: Toward a new concept of the scientific. *Theory and Society*, 5(1), 75–96.
Morgan, J. (2013). Hedge funds: Statistical arbitrage, high frequency trading and their consequences for the environment of businesses. *Critical Perspectives on International Business*, 9(4), 377–397.
Morgan, J., & Negru, I. (2012). The Austrian perspective on the global financial crisis: A critique. *Economic Issues*, 17(2), 22–55.
Open Source Summit. (1998). http://linuxgazette.net/issue 28/rossum.html [accessed 25 October 2012]
Openwetware. (2014). OpenSourceMalaria, http://openwetware.org/wiki/OSDDMalaria [accessed 15 July 2016].
Poeter, D. (2012). Could a 'Printable Gun' change the world? http://forbes.com/sites/andy-greenberg/ [accessed 27 August 2012].
Project Gutenberg – free ebooks. (2014). www.gutenberg.org/ [accessed 25 October 2012].
Rainie, L., & Wellman, B. (2012). *Networked: The New Social Operating System*. Cambridge, MA: MIT Press.
Sawyer, K. (2005). *Social emergence: Societies as complex systems*. Cambridge: Cambridge University Press.
Sonderholm, J. (2010). Ethical issues surrounding intellectual property rights. *Philosophy Compass*, 5(12), 1107–1115.
Stiglitz, J. (2003). *The roaring nineties*. New York: Norton.

Stulz, R. (2007). Hedge funds: Past, present and future. *Journal of Economic Perspectives*, 21(2), 175–194.
Tapscott, D., & Williams, A. D. (2007). *Wikinomics: How mass collaboration changes everything*. London: Atlantic Books.
The Tropical Disease Initiative (2014). www.tropicaldisease.org [accessed 25 October 2012].
Tiemann, M. (2006). 'History of the OSI', open source initiative. www.opensource.org/history [accessed 15 July 2016].
Trippi, J. (2004). *The revolution will not be televised*. New York: William Morrow/HarperCollins.
Wharton, D. (1992). MPAA's rebel with cause fights for copyright coin. *Variety*, 348(2).
Wikipedia. (undated a). 'Intellectual property', p. 8. http://en.Wikipedia.org/wiki/Intellectual_property [accessed 19 November 2013].
Wikipedia. (undated b). 'Open Source', p. 1. http://en.wickipedia.org/wiki/Open_source [accessed 13 November 2013].
Wikipedia. (undated c). http://en.wikipedia.org/wiki/Social_networking-service. [accessed 20 November 2013].
World Intellectual Property Organization. (2002). *Human rights and intellectual property*. www.wipo.int/tk/en/hr/ [accessed 15 July 2016].

The trajectory of the morphogenetic approach

An account in the first person

As a philosophy of social science Critical Realism (Archer et al. 1998) holds that reasons are causes for action and that is as true of writing books and developing a theory as it is for any other intentional human activity. Thus, following the lecture I was honoured to deliver at ISCTE (March 2007), I was very pleased to be invited to present this overview of the reasons that initially prompted the 'morphogenetic approach' to be advanced, the rationale linking the six key books (and associated articles) through which it has been elaborated, and to explain what the next three works hope to accomplish in order to complete this project. However, for every social theorist the elaboration of a theoretical framework is always 'work in progress' and never a *fait accompli*.

In this short piece, I have been given the rare licence to explain the trajectory taken, though still to be completed, by my own theoretical work. This is a license that some would withhold as part of their withdrawal of *authorial authority*. Although the respect due to one's readers necessarily means that each book one publishes should be self-standing, that does not (and cannot) mean it is self-contained. Each should be self-standing – that is, worth reading by itself, because it would be futile arrogance to presume that readers already had a familiarity with one's collected works or intended to become conversant with them.

However, in the last two decades of the twentieth century and most markedly in the Humanities, the balance shifted dramatically from assigning excessive authority to the author to according the reader exclusive interpretative authority. This can be epitomised as placing the author in the Derridian *hors texte* which, for all his later equivocations, never involved a restoration of authorial privileges. From this perspective, authors were seen as loosing texts on the public and, in so doing, their personal intentionality was transformed into a conduit for social forces. That is, authorial intentions were subordinated to expressions of their class position, symptomatic of their engendered standpoint, or subsumed into that ill-defined but capacious portmanteau, the hegemonic discourse. If what the writer intended could not be crammed into that suitcase, there was no baggage limit and such intentions could be packed in a smaller hold-all, labelled subversive discourses. With the author now 'shut up' and 'shut out', the text itself supposedly became the property of the *demos* (let a thousand interpretations bloom without questions about their legitimacy arising because 'fairness', 'accuracy' and 'substantiation' were the tainted currency of Modernism/ity). Yet, as we well know, proceedings were far from being democratic, let alone approaching the Habermasian 'ideal speech situation' or the Gadamerian 'fusion of horizons'. Instead, rhetorical persuasion ruled where the rules of the game were Feyerarbend's 'anything goes'. However, most goes – in a manner distinctly non-postmodernist – to those best hierarchically placed to make their interpretations count.

Undoubtedly, in the past, excessive claims had been made for first-person epistemic authority, including that of the author – infallibility (Descartes), omniscience (Hume), indubitability (Hamilton) and incorrigibility (Ayer). Nevertheless, it is possible to defend authorial authority without making such claims and thus to prevent textual understanding from becoming an exercise conducted wholly in the third person. The defence is a matter of ontology, which is prior to any epistemological question of sharing or of third-person interpretation.

Conscious states, such as those involved in an author developing a theory, can only exist from the point of view of the subject who is experiencing those thoughts. In other words, the intention to write a book has what John Searle (1999) terms a first-person ontology. This means intentions have a subjective mode of existence, which is also the case for desires, feelings, fantasies and beliefs. That is, only as experienced by a particular subject does a particular thought exist. Just as there are no such things as disembodied pains, there are no such things as thoughts that are independent of subjectivity. Both pains and thoughts are first-person dependent for their existence.

However, you might object that whilst I cannot share my toothache with you, what am I currently doing (in writing) but sharing my thoughts with you? In fact I do not agree that it is possible to share my thoughts with you. Instead, what I am doing is sharing my *ideas* with you, as Popperian World Three objects (Popper 1972), ones that will become even more permanently part of World Three once they are published. What I cannot share with you is something William James captured very well, the reflexive monitoring that is going on here and now as my thoughts are turned into the complete sentences that you will read several months hence. Internally, I am engaged in self-monitoring activities, which are an inextricable part of my thoughts, such as mundanely checking that a singular subject is accompanied by a singular verb or distilling an insight into words that seem to capture it adequately. This ontological point has far-reaching implications. Quite simply and very radically, it means that we cannot have a sociology exclusively in the third person: one in which the subject's first-person subjectivity is ignored. That is as true for any author as it is for any respondent in a sociological inquiry.

The subjective ontology of thought(s) has epistemological consequences, one of which concerns the nature of epistemic sharing possible between an author and his or her readers. Without making any of the excessive claims mentioned above, I can still claim self-warranted authority in the first person because my thoughts are known directly to me and only indirectly, through fallible interpretation, to a third-person commentator. Following Patrick Alston (1971, 235–6), 'I enjoy self-warrant whenever I truly believe I am thinking x; *ipso facto*, I am justified in claiming to know my state of belief, even if that state of belief turns out to be untrue.' Thus, I may be wrong *in* my beliefs concerning my authorial intentions but not *about* them. Moreover, those are the beliefs upon which I acted in conceiving of the theory (Morphogenetic Approach), reflectively deliberating on how best to explore it and determining the form and sequence of books in which to present it.

Being human – and therefore fallible – I admit to irritation when reviewers exercise a dictatorship of the third person. In the first person I have warrant to know and say what I was trying to do in proceeding from (a) to (b) to (c) and only I can know that I still have (d) in mind. Of course, that trajectory (sequence of books) may be ill-conceived or misguided, as each and every reader has the right to judge it, but that is not the same thing as claiming to know my thoughts better than I do or substituting their interpretations for my intentions. Since self-warrant is something I claim and defend for every (normal) human subject in his or her intentional acts, it is 'only human' that I do object when a reviewer asserts that I have 'been blind to the interpersonal' (in early works), have 'forgotten about structure and culture' (in later works) or have now 'become absorbed in the intrapersonal' (as if this will be the case in future works).

None of the above deprives (third-person) critics and commentators of a generous role *within* the context of discovery and not merely one confined to the context of justification. For example, they *may* know more about the formation of my intentions (and particularly their context) than I was aware of myself, they might accurately fault the (sociological) beliefs that grounded my project, and it is highly probable that they would be able to design a more economical trajectory for its development. That is one of the points and benefits of third-person critique. All I am seeking is acceptance of my self-warrant to explain the 'how' and the 'why' of the actual trajectory taken. This the author alone can give, because the development of an explanatory programme is not pre-defined from the start. Rather, each book sets the problems to be tackled in its successor and thus defines the next section of the pathway, without one having any clear idea about how many more sections will be required before reaching that rather indefinite goal, the 'finished project'. Of course, the account furnished is a reflexive personal judgement, which is necessarily fallible.

All social theorising takes off from a springboard that is itself theoretical. That springboard is akin to what Gouldner called the 'domain assumptions' we make and to Merton's image of our clambering on the shoulders of giants. Rather than labouring all of this in personal terms, I think it suffices to say that the philosophical under-labouring supplied by Critical Realism provides the backcloth for all my works, except for the first – whose aporias the Realist philosophy of social science filled in. These commonalities between Critical Realism and the Morphogenetic Approach can be summarised as: (i) promoting *relationality* (namely, that sociology's very claim to existence derives from the fact that its key concepts are relational in kind, often referring to emergent yet irreducible properties capable of exercising causal powers); (ii) that the historical configurations and courses taken by social structures are *morphogenetic* in nature (conforming to none of the traditional analogies – mechanical, organic or cybernetic – but being shaped and reshaped by the interplay between their constituents, parts and persons, meaning that society is open-ended and not 'finalistic' in its elaboration); (iii) that the *Wertrationalität* is crucial to the sociological enterprise if it is to serve a humanising 'mission'. This exceeds an abstracted defence of *humanism* (which reduces to ideology) and advances a 'vision' of the social commensurate with human thriving. It is central to society's members, who should never be seen as mere exponents of instrumental rationality, as is the case for *homo oeconomicus* and his siblings; to social institutions, which are both sources and bearers of value orientations; and to social theorists themselves, who, far from celebrating the death of man, the decentring of the subject or the dissolution of the human person into uncommitted and socially non-committal acts of playful self reinvention, should uphold the needs and potentials of human beings. Indeed, such human concerns define value relevance for sociology itself.

In the *Social Origins of Educational Systems*, published in 1979, the morphogenetic approach can be found – by anyone willing to tackle its 815 pages – not only outlined but already put to work, the work of disengaging where state educational systems came from and what new causal powers they exerted after their elaboration. These powers work as underlying generative mechanisms, producing empirical tendencies in relation to *who* gained access to education, *what* constituted the definition of instruction, *which* processes became responsible for subsequent educational change, and *how* those ensuing changes were patterned. Crucially, the answers to all of these questions differed according to the *centralised or decentralised* structuring of the new educational systems. This raised a major philosophical problem. It was being claimed that educational systems possessed properties emergent from the relations between their parts – summarised as centralisation and decentralisation – that exercised causal powers. However, these two properties could not be attributes of people, who cannot be centralised or decentralised, just as no system can possess the reflexivity, intentionality and commitment of the agents whose actions first produced and then continuously sustained these forms of state education.

The issue can be restated as 'the problem of structure and agency', although this is only part of a broader problem about whether or not sociology needs to endorse a stratified social ontology. This kind of ontology entails that the properties and powers pertaining to a 'higher' stratum are dependent upon relations at a 'lower' stratum, whilst the former are irreducible to the latter. Its direct implication is that the 'problem of structure and agency' cannot be solved (or, as some put it, 'be transcended') by eliding the two into an amalgam, through holding them to be mutually constitutive. It is also why the 'problem of structure and agency', *as part* of a broader ontological issue, cannot be dismissed as 'tiresome' or 'old fashioned'. This problem consists in what Dahrendorf rightly called 'the vexatious fact of society': we the people shape it, whilst it reshapes us as we go about changing it or maintaining it, individually and collectively. The problem does not vanish because we become vexed by it, tire of it or try to turn our backs upon it. Yet, its intransigence does explain why many social theorists were indeed experiencing vexation at the end of the 1970s. They did so precisely because existing philosophies of social science *could not articulate a stratified ontology* of society. Instead, they proffered only reductionist approaches – methodological individualism and methodological holism/collectivism – as unsatisfactory in principle as they were unhelpful in practice.

Hence my next pair of books, on culture and structure respectively (*Culture and Agency* (1988) and *Realist Social Theory* (1995)), which had two aims: to develop a stratified social ontology along the lines of transcendental realism (ironically, Bhaskar's seminal *Possibility of Naturalism* had also been published in 1979) and then to advance this in the form of a framework that was of practical use to those working on substantive sociological problems. Hence, the morphogenetic approach acquired its full philosophical underpinnings. These account for the mature morphogenetic framework standing in *contradistinction* to any form of social theory that endorsed the conflation of structure and agency: 'upward conflation' (methodological individualism), 'downward conflation' (methodological holism, whether Marxist or functionalist in orientation), and 'central conflation' (the then fashionable Structuration theory).

However, even very generous philosophical 'under-labouring', as Bhaskar called his realist philosophy of social science, cannot provide an instant fix for all the problems besetting social theory. Realism and its three pillars – ontological stratification, epistemological relativism (better, 'relationalism') and judgemental rationality – made an effective case for distinguishing between structures and agents in terms of their distinctive and irreducible properties and powers (as it did for mind in relation to matter). Nevertheless, it was better at conceptualising 'structure' than 'agency'. In short, realism concentrated upon 'agency' only as responsible for introducing social transformation or perpetuating social reproduction – all structures being continuously activity-dependent. Realism had too little to say about 'persons': about who they were, in their rich but concrete singularity, and about what moved them to act, be this action individual or collective. This aporia in realism proved particularly dangerous at a time when social theory welcomed that vacuum. Sociological imperialism had gathered strength and, especially in the form of social constructionism, presented the 'person' exclusively as society's gift. In Rom Harré's words, persons were 'cultural artefacts' (1982, 20). Hence *Being Human* (2000) was not a turn away from structure and culture. It was a turn towards the reconceptualisation of human beings, people who were inescapably born into a social context 'not of their making or choosing' and who ineluctably confronted social and cultural structures in most of their doings – two different kinds of structures that *Culture and Agency* argued should not be taken to be homologous, much less homogeneous, throughout the course of history.

Being Human could fairly be called a polemical book. It seeks to resist sociological imperialism and its representation of persons as remorselessly and exhaustively social. Instead, it begins by emphasising that constituted as human beings are, the world being the way it is, interaction between the two is a matter of necessity. This means that each and every one of us has to develop a (working) relationship with every order of natural reality: nature, practice and the social. Distinctions between the natural, practical and social orders are real, although it is usually the case that they can only be grasped analytically because they are subject to considerable empirical superimposition. Nevertheless, that does not preclude the fact that human subjects confront dilemmas that are different in kind when encountering each of the three orders. Neither does it diminish the fact that it is imperative for human survival to establish sustainable and sustaining relations with each. Nor is it incompatible with the fact that human beings, characterised by what Charles Taylor (1982, 50) calls the 'significance feature', invest more of themselves in one order than others – even though this must mean the subordination rather than the exclusion of the remaining orders.

In other words, we all have concerns in every sphere of natural reality *but* we prioritise our concerns – loving 'in due order', to use St Augustine's words. Indeed, it is precisely our particular constellation of concerns that defines each of us as a particular person, with strict personal identity. In short, who we are is what we care about (Frankfurt 1988). And the greatest of these concerns in relation to our personal thriving and for explaining the social roles in which we invest ourselves – thus acquiring social identities – are our 'ultimate concerns'.

However, even our 'ultimate concerns', which we care about most, do not automatically define courses of action for us. Each person has to deliberate about 'what is to be done to achieve the good', in order that his or her life promotes their 'ultimate concern' but also accommodates their other concerns, which cannot be repudiated. In short, they have to work out a *modus vivendi*, commensurate with their values but also sustainable as a lived reality. As social beings we have to try to find a place for ourselves in society – one which is expressive of who we are by virtue of the roles we actively personify (Hollis 1977), rather than executing their requirements robotically. In trying to find such a place, persons necessarily confront structural (and cultural) properties as constraints and enablements, as vested or objective interests, as motivating or discouraging influences – 'thrown' as they are into their natal contexts and venturing as they do (and have to) into further contexts beyond family bounds.

That is the link between *Being Human* and the next book, *Structure, Agency and the Internal Conversation* (2003). *Being Human* is the pivotal work. It 'descends' to the personal level in order to conceptualise unique human persons – the ultimate moving agents of all that is social, though not the only constituents of society. Thereafter, the theoretical trajectory begins its 're-ascent' into the social world of positions, roles, organisations, institutions and, eventually, the global social system. But, as in mountaineering, one proceeds in short pitches and, in fact, by securing even smaller handholds and footholds.

Society is different in kind from its component members. On that we can all agree, even if it is conceptualised as being no more than the aggregate effect of people's conceptions and doings. The crucial difference is that no society or social organisation truly possesses self-awareness, whereas every single (normal) member of society is a self-conscious being. Thus, however differently the social may be conceptualised in various schools of thought – from an objective and emergent stratum of reality to a negotiated and objectified social construct – the social remains different from its component members in this crucial respect of lacking self-consciousness. It follows that a central problem for social theorists must be to provide an answer to the question: 'What difference does the self-awareness of its members make to the nature of the social?'

Historically, the answers given have varied from 'all the difference', as the response shared by idealists, to 'no difference at all', as the reply of hard-line materialists. Today, the variety of answers has increased but the question remains because it cannot be evaded. For example, social constructionists cannot dodge the issue by regarding all societal features as products of 'objectification' by its members. This is because each and every individual can mentally deliberate about what is currently objectified in relation to himself or herself (in principle, they can ask the reflexive question: 'Should I take this for granted?'). Conversely, no objectified 'entity' can be reflexive about itself in relation to individuals (it can never, as it were, ask: 'Could this construct be presented more convincingly?'). The unavoidability of this issue means that the argument about 'objectivity and subjectivity' is as fundamental as the argument about 'collectivism and individualism'. Not only are these two issues of equal importance but they are also closely intertwined.

The 'problem of structure and agency' has a great deal in common with the 'problem of objectivity and subjectivity'. Both raise the same issue about the relationship between their component terms, which entails questioning their respective causal powers. Once we have started talking about causal powers, it is impossible to avoid talking about the ontological status of those things to which causal powers are attributed or from which they are withheld.

However, a popular response to these two recalcitrant problems is the suggestion that we should *transcend* both of them by the simple manoeuvre of treating them as the two faces of a single coin. Transcending the divide rests upon conceptualising 'structures' and 'agents' as ontologically inseparable because each enters into the other's constitution. Therefore, they should be conceptualised as one mutually constitutive amalgam. In a single leap-frog move, all the previous difficulties can be left behind. This manoeuvre has direct implications for the question of 'objectivity and subjectivity'. If 'structure' and 'agency' are conceptualised as being inseparable because they are held to be mutually constitutive, then this blurring of subject and object necessarily challenges the very possibility of reflexivity itself. If the two are an amalgam, it is difficult to see how a person or a group is able to reflect critically or creatively upon their social conditions or context.

Conversely, by upholding the distinction between objectivism and subjectivism we can acknowledge that agents do indeed reflexively examine their personal concerns in the light of their social circumstances and evaluate their circumstances in the light of their concerns. Only if agents are sufficiently distinct from their social contexts can they reflect upon them as subject to object. As Mouzelis (n.d.) puts it:

> It is only when the objective–subjective distinction is maintained that it is possible to deal in a theoretically congruent manner with cases where situated actors distance themselves from social structures relatively external to them in order to assess, more or less rationally, the degree of constraint and enablement these structures offer, the pros and cons, the chances of success or failure of different strategies etc.

They do so by deliberating subjectively, under their own descriptions, about what courses of action to take in the face of constraints and enablements; about the value to them of defending or promoting vested interests; about their willingness to pay the opportunity costs entailed in aspiring to various goals; and about whether or not circumstances allow them to become more ambitious in their life-politics, or induce them to be more circumspect.

This is what *Structure, Agency and the Internal Conversation* is about, namely conceptualising the *interplay* between subjective personal properties and powers and objective social properties and powers. Specifically, it is argued that personal reflexivity mediates the effects of objective social forms upon us. It gives an answer to the question: '*How* does structure influence agency?' Reflexivity performs this mediatory role by virtue of the fact that we deliberate about ourselves in relation to the social situations that we confront, certainly fallibly, certainly incompletely and necessarily under our own descriptions, because that is the only way we can know anything. To consider human reflexivity playing that role of mediation also means entertaining the fact that we are dealing with two ontologies: the objective pertaining to social emergent properties and the subjective pertaining to agential emergent properties. What is entailed by the above is that subjectivity is not only (a) real but also (b) irreducible and (c) possessed of causal efficacy (Archer 2007a).

It is probably helpful to specify what kinds of subjective properties and powers are presented as constitutive of this mediatory process. I have termed it the Internal Conversation, which designates the manner in which we reflexively make our way through the world. This inner dialogue about ourselves in relation to society and vice versa is what makes (most of us) 'active agents', people who can exercise some governance in their own lives, as opposed to 'passive agents' to whom things merely happen.

Being an 'active agent' hinges on the fact that individuals develop and define their ultimate concerns, those internal goods that they care about most and whose precise constellation makes for their concrete singularity as persons. No one can have an ultimate concern and fail to do something about it. Instead, each seeks to develop a course(s) of action to realise that concern by elaborating a project in the (fallible) belief that to accomplish the project is to realise one's concern. If such courses of action are successful, which can never be taken for granted, each person's constellation of concerns, when dovetailed together, becomes translated into a set of established practices. This constitutes their personal *modus vivendi*. Through this *modus vivendi*, subjects live out their personal concerns within society as best they can. In shorthand, these components can be summarised in the formula <Concerns → Projects → Practices>. There is nothing idealistic here, because 'concerns' can be ignoble, 'projects' illegal and 'practices' illegitimate.

These are the kinds of mental activity that make up the strange reality of reflexivity, as part of broader human subjectivity. To accept reflexive activities as real and influential entails the endorsement of plural ontologies. This should not, in principle, be a problem. The reality of what I have called the 'Internal Conversation' (also known as 'self talk', 'rumination', 'musement', 'inner dialogue', 'internal speech', 'intra-personal communication' and so on) does not mean that when we deliberate, when we formulate our intentions, when we design our courses of action or when we dedicate ourselves to concerns such mental activities are like stones or trees – they are not. Yet, this has nothing to do with whether or not they are real because reality itself is not homogeneous. The whole of reality cannot be confined to and defined in terms of the Enlightenment notion of 'matter in motion'. Indeed, in post-positivistic science, physical reality is made up as much by quarks and genomes as it is by magnetism and gravity or by rocks and plants.

Abandonment of that Enlightenment assumption paves the way to the acceptance of plural ontologies. It is now more than thirty years since Popper (1972) distinguished his Three Worlds as ontologically distinct sub-worlds: the world of physical states, the world of mental states and the world of objective ideas. What is important about this for the present argument is that Popper had put his finger on the genuine oddity about World Two, the world of mental states: namely, that it is objectively real and yet it has a subjective ontology.

What the *Internal Conversation* describes is how and why each and every person deliberates reflexively, in their own fallible terms, about their personal concerns in relation to their social context and about their contexts in the light of their concerns. In the process, they are shaping themselves and contributing to (re)shaping the social world. The process of reflexivity is not seen as one homogeneous mode of inner deliberation but as exercised through different modalities – 'Communicative', 'Autonomous' and 'Meta-Reflexivity' – whose dominance for particular persons derives from their relationship to their natal context in conjunction with their personal concerns.

This is traced in the following volume, *Making Our Way Through the World: Human Reflexivity and Social Mobility* (2007b). As generative mechanisms, different dominant modes of reflexivity have internal consequences for their practitioners and distinctive external consequences for society. Internally, the connections are tracked between practice of these different modalities and individual patterns of social mobility by interviewing subjects about their life histories: Communicative reflexivity is associated with social immobility, Autonomous reflexivity with upward social mobility, and Meta-Reflexivity with social volatility.

Externally, the effects are that the communicatives make a huge contribution to social stability and integration through their *evasion* of constraints and enablements, through endorsing their natal contexts and through actively forging a dense micro-world that reconstitutes their 'contextual continuity' and projects it forward in time. Conversely, Autonomous subjects act *strategically*, seeking to avoid society's 'snakes' and to ride up its 'ladders', thus augmenting the 'contextual discontinuity' that went into their own making and increasing social productivity through their energetic exertions. Meta-reflexives are society's *subversive* agents, immune to both the bonuses associated with enablements and the penalties linked to constraints, thus resisting the main engines of social guidance/control through their willingness to pay the price of subversion themselves. In turn, their consistent pursuit of value rationality in living out the 'contextual incongruity' that formed them as they endorsed a 'vocation' (in Max Weber's terms) means that their main contribution is to ensure that the *Wertrationalität* retains its salience in society. It represents a source of counter-cultural values challenging the commodification of human relations, which stems from the market, and their bureaucratisation, which emanates from the state.

The Reflexive Imperative (currently in progress) goes further to maintain that millennial changes are increasingly reshaping and distancing the social from the parameters of Modernity. The creation and geographical redistribution of new *opportunities* at the global level (almost occluded by the current unilateral preoccupation with risk), coupled with migration, increasing education and the proliferation of novel skills rebound upon the nature of reflexivity itself. They prompt a shift away from the 'communicative' mode, which used to buttress traditionalism, because social reproduction becomes just as reflexive an enterprise as those that promote yet further transformations. These changes swell the ranks of those practising the 'autonomous' mode, propitious to the new global Leviathans: transnational bureaucracy and multinational enterprises. Most important of all, 'meta-reflexivity' increases disproportionately during nascent globalisation and its practitioners can be seen as patrons of a new civil society expressive of humanistic values.

However, the shift towards the 'socio-logic of opportunity', which prompts this intensification of reflexivity and shift in its dominant modalities, also claims an increased proportion of victims – those experiencing the distress and disorientation of 'fractured' reflexivity. This is because the new logic of opportunity demands the continuous revision of personal projects, involving the successful monitoring of self, society and relations between them, and denies the establishment of an unchanging *modus vivendi*. In other words, the imperative *to be reflexive* intensifies with the demise of routine action – a decline that becomes precipitous once (partial) morphostasis gives way to the unremitting morphogenesis which underlies the shift towards one global system in the new millennium. Or so it will be argued in *The Reflexive Imperative* (forthcoming).

However, this trio of books on intrapersonal deliberations about society will still leave the morphogenetic project unfinished. They will have dealt with the *aggregate effects* alone of the dialectic between changing human subjectivity and the objective transformation of society – as modernity gives way to untrammelled morphogenesis and its generative tendency for variety to produce yet more variety. *Pace* those who think I have 'forgotten interpersonal relations', have 'privileged the internal conversation at the expense of the external conversation' or, above all, have given 'primacy to the primary agency of persons over the collective action of groups'. I have not.

All of the above need to be linked together precisely because, unlike Beck and Beck-Gernsheim (2002, xxi), I do not consider that the social structure of the future diminishes to 'institutionalised individualism'. Neither do I accept, unlike Zygmunt Bauman, that 'liquidity' is displacing structuring, much less can pretend to represent the form of trans-modern society. There never is an unstructured social world and there never is a (normal) human person without reflexively defined projects. Nevertheless, it is equally true that there is never a hope of explaining the 'vexatious fact of society' by addressing its two poles without examining the conduit between them – how subjective reflexivity promotes new objective structures. This means that the examination of social movements, of communal experiments, and of new forms of collective reciprocity is needed to complete the morphogenetic framework.

As Frédéric Vandenberghe (2005) noted, in the most perspicacious review of the corpus of books published to date, a further instalment is required to link up with collective agency and to incorporate the intriguing potential for collective subjectivities and representations in the new world order now coming into being.

Yet even that is not quite 'The End'. Globalisation is undoubtedly part and parcel of the millennial transformation of the social, but it is not its generative mechanism. It is the effect rather than the cause. The *leitmotif* of contemporary commentators is to accentuate that 'flows' have replaced 'structures'. In so doing, Critical Realists would regard this as an observation (and extrapolation) confined to the empirical level. What it crucially omits are the new structures that generate these detectable flows at a deeper ontological level. If the new millennium has truly begun to sever its links with Modernity, including all those adjectives (post-, late-, high-, second-wave, as well as the ubiquitous 'beyond') that merely signal adherence to it, then we need to identify what is generating a true disjunction. This I will examine in *Morphogenesis Unbound*, as a new and unique époque in which morphostatic and morphogenetic cycles no longer circulate simultaneously, with the former restraining the latter and protracting variants upon the themes of Modernity. Perhaps that will indeed be the end of the trajectory whose course I have described and have been describing here.

References

Alston, Patrick (1971), 'Varieties of privileged access', *American Philosophical Quarterly*, 8(3): 223–41.
Archer, Margaret S. (2007a), 'The ontological status of subjectivity: the missing link between structure and agency', in Clive Lawson, John Latsis and Nuno Martins, *Contributions to Social Ontology*, Abingdon, Routledge.
Archer, Margaret S. (2007b), *Making Our Way Through the World. Human Reflexivity and Social Mobility*, Cambridge, Cambridge University Press.
Archer, Margaret, Roy Bhaskar, Andrew Collier, Tony Lawson and Alan Norrie (eds) (1998), *Critical Realism. Essential Readings*, London, Routledge.
Beck, Ulrich, and Elizabeth Beck-Gernsheim (2002), *Individualization*, London, Sage.
Bhaskar, Roy (1979), *The Possibility of Naturalism*, Hemel Hempstead, Harvester Wheatsheaf.
Frankfurt, Harry (1988), 'The importance of what we care about', in *The Importance of What We Care About*, Cambridge, Cambridge University Press.
Harré, Rom (1982), *Personal Being*, Oxford, Basil Blackwell.
Hollis, Martin (1977), *Models of Man. Philosophical Thoughts on Social Action*, Cambridge, Cambridge University Press.
Mouzelis, Nicos (n.d.), Habitus and Reflexivity (unpublished manuscript courtesy of the author).
Popper, Karl (1972), 'On the theory of the objective mind', in *Objective Knowledge*, Oxford, Clarendon Press.
Searle, John (1999), *Mind, Language and Society*, London, Weidenfeld and Nicolson.
Taylor, Charles (1982), 'Consciousness', in Paul F. Secord (ed.), *Explaining Human Behaviour. Human Action and Social Structure*, London, Sage.
Vandenberghe, Frédéric (2005), 'The Archers: final episode?' *European Journal of Social Theory*, 8(2): 227–37.

Interview with Maggie

Part 1: The London School of Economics

MARK CARRIGAN: What was the experience of graduate school like? How did it shape you intellectually?

MAGGIE ARCHER: It was a huge disappointment. The whole process, how I ended up with the supervisors, which was a matter of allocation at LSE. I turned down the first one allocated to me. Then it was made perfectly clear that this is an exception; that people could not refuse what was graciously offered to them. I was told I was being given the great honor of having David Glass. This was a sort of cognitive disruption for me. Because the paradox of LSE was that it was so authoritarian about this issuing of supervisors. You didn't even have the option of naming preferences or anything. Or, you could name an area, but not your topic within the area.

The incongruity was between this sort of virtually dictatorial process and the freedom we'd had on the curriculum. For example, the second year you had almost total freedom. It was the ultimate cafeteria. I spent the entirety of my second year doing lots of philosophy of science, philosophy of social science. Brilliant experience with people like Karl Popper, Imre Lakatos – who obviously was a lifelong influence – John Wisdom, John Watkins. It was the last of the really quality star-studded LSE and it was great.

I kept that mindset that disciplines with boundaries are totally unimportant. You can't do sociology without also doing implicit or explicit philosophy of social science. There was a huge amount of social science that hadn't actually penetrated to some of the philosophers, whereas others like Watkins – the classic example – had nailed his place unassailably as the doyen of methodological individualism and its philosophical underpinnings. With that background, it was rather hard to confront one of Britain's leading empiricist demographers whose hinge linking him to sociology was social mobility.

Already I was interested in – I call it reflexivity now though I'm not sure I'd even met the term then – in parents' subjective wishes for their children. I'd not seen these as determined by anything in particular. Probably more by their own life courses and happenstance events than anything else. But compared to sociology education at the time . . . I once spent an incredibly boring two weeks on my father's long carriage imperial typewriter typing up the factors. That was the approach, factorial not multivariate. Just factorial. Reaching the dizzy heights of the partial correlation coefficient. A list of the factors that had been established as having some correlation or relationship to any indicator of kids' school achievement, which could go from their results to the class teacher's assessments, et cetera, et cetera.

This was very much David Glass's approach to things. It was the beginning of a real introduction to empiricism at work. If it moved, measure it. If it spoke, scale it. Graduate seminars, yes, I resisted them, though we had to do them. They taught us a variety of scaling techniques and things you could do with maths to clean up your data.

All of which just intensified my hostility towards empiricism. This growing unease that this was missing out on whole tracts of life that were important, as well as statistically mashing the ones they did include into a simple list of variables. It was all a search for the golden dream, which was never ever reached, of finding the factor. I think it is, I thought this within the next 10 years, that this was the overwhelming appeal of Bourdieu and the concept of habitus. I'm not saying this critically at the moment. I have many criticisms of it, as you well know. But it was such a broad and let's face it, diffuse, concept that it could provide an umbrella under which all these factorial theorists could dwell and from which they could draw. It looked as though progress was being made.

It was an extraordinarily dissatisfying time doing the PhD. Its title tells you everything about me giving into the pressures that were bigger than I was: The educational aspirations of working-class mothers for their children's school attainment and future careers. It's the only piece of work I've been entirely ashamed of. I've never published a word from it. On empiricist terms, I don't know there's much wrong with it. In every other respect, there was everything wrong with it.

It all came down to one interview in Leytonstone with a young woman, clearly living under considerable stress with four children and, as far as I could tell or guess, an absentee father. It was clearly the centre of the house, the only room that physically accommodated them. With damp stains running down the wall, wallpaper hanging off, the kids' main idea of entertainment being running with coloured chalks all the way around the room making stripes on the wall. In the middle of this was the mother, who was kind to the kids. She was not shouting, she was not doing anything the least bit abusive to them. But when we got on to talking about aspirations, 'Well, I would like this one to be a doctor, and if that one could be a lawyer or maybe an engineer, a really big engineer who'll build bridges and QE2s and that sort of thing, that's what I'd really like for them.'

This discontinuity between her private dreams, the reality in front of me, and the general pretty low performance of working-class kids in Leytonstone. It was just so great, I wanted to go down the track of, in some polite way, asking where the dreams had come from. What sustained them in the face of pretty obvious difficulties, financial and care-taking, that she was facing? How had she sustained this and did she have any network of friends who were also living in some kind of educational dream world?

MC: But the influence of your supervisors left you feeling unable to pursue these questions?

MA: They were never dissatisfied. As long as I went on cross-tabbing. We then reached the wonderful day, that was supposed to make me overwhelmed with joy, when the first computer was installed in LSE. If I could get the data punched in, how many cross-tabs could we run? That took another three months and you had to walk in with your shoe box of punched cards. Again, you weren't allowed to have the lateral thought of what on earth is the life of a card code puncher like?

That was the thesis. Any robot could have done it. It was so formulaic. Provided you didn't stray from the straight and narrow and your partial correlations did check out, you couldn't go very wrong with it. Basically: get that out and work out a scale. Which I did.

Again, I've never been more ashamed of anything in my life, particularly when it was taken up by various educational research institutions and used because it simply asked them to record, 'I want my son to be a doctor.' No supplementaries, no nothing. You just had to write down the answer. Out came this metric. Then, I was told to cross-correlate it with anything I could think of that was objective. These are the days where we're into things like Chapin's Living Room Scale.

MC: Were you thinking about what would come next after your PhD?

MA: I systematically evaded answering the question. There were plenty of vocation jobs, night jobs, weekend jobs. One of them, Glass himself put me on to, which was rather nice of him. It was sitting at the library of the Department of Health, manually calculating for each borough what the take-up had been on the government's free offer of installation of a toilet and running water in your kitchen.

I didn't want to stay around LSE because I had no qualification to go on with the philosophy of social science. I'd always had a love of France. Nothing to lose. Just go.

MC: It sounds like the philosophy of social science at LSE was a more important intellectual influence than your PhD in some ways.

MA: In terms of critique, yes. In terms of how to do something else, that wasn't methodologically individualist, no. It was Lakatos, a huge influence still to this day, who introduced me to the idea there is no ultimate proof or disproof. There are only progressive and denigrating research programmes. The sign of a degenerating, deteriorating one was the more it shifted over into ad hoc hypotheses to prop up the central proposition. This idea that there was an inner core to a theory which was protected by concentric circles of greater and greater specificity. The idea of theory as something growing rather than just being additive in the ways that these positivist indicators were additive.

Part 2: Educational systems

MC: Did Paris prove to be a more intellectually stimulating environment than London?

MA: I was very lucky in having godparents in Paris. It didn't cost me anything to stay. It didn't cost me anything to eat. My godfather was professor in administrative law at the Sorbonne. I started attending classes and there structure arrived. It was almost like one of those gestalt experiences. It arrived in the form of an accumulation of experiences over a very short period of time.

So, for example, it was now 1966, Raymond Aron and his 18 lessons on industry in society. He was a huge name and he was writing a little box every day that was on the front page of Le Figaro, about some social question of the moment. He was giving a series of lectures and obviously I went, I'd never set eyes on him. I went into a small amphitheater that was three-quarters empty. I thought this was bizarre, as he's even better known in Paris. Maybe they've all done it before?

I asked some fellow students, 'Where are all the others? Why such a small turnout?' It's actually typical for lecturers in Paris. Why would you come to the lecture when you go around the corner to Press Universite de France and you can buy the course booklet? The course booklet even contained student answers to particular questions. You could get the content and you could get the form and you could splice the two together. Most students, according to my companion, decided why bother getting out of bed when you can do it the easy way?

These experiences just accumulated. Yes, you can call it selective perception and that came into it. Aron was about to retire, so I set off asking fellow students very benign questions such as, 'Will his replacement go on teaching to the same booklet? How free are they to change the course, change the reading, change the arguments?' They said, 'Well, you know, it's not as bad as school.'

It's a national curriculum. Mid-60s. It's the same everywhere. Haven't you heard about this apocryphal Minister of Education who looked at his watch and said, 'Ah, it's 10:45, every pupil in a French Lycée throughout the country will be looking at page 94 of Virgil.' I laughed and they said, 'Yeah, we laughed too but it's really rather a sick joke.' It means no teacher, school teacher certainly, could come across a novel that impressed them greatly and say let's give a couple of lessons to reading a chapter of this and discussing it. No space for that whatsoever. It was all regulated.

On the ground, I began to learn what centralization felt like. Very different from my year two of freedom at LSE, pick what you like and do what you like with it. It was following up on that which gave me the central idea for Social Origins because the difference between a decentralized structure and a centralized structure was obvious phenomenologically, it was obvious experientially over a tract of time, and it was obvious in some of its effects on who got in, what happened to them when they were inside, what they came out and did, or were directed to do at any rate. In other words, the main questions that the first book actually sought to try and answer.

MC: What happened next? Was the idea just in a nascent stage? Or was it in a nascent form at this stage?

MA: It was. But it was more and more directing my reading. I actually did find administration interesting. The reason I found it interesting was because you got exactly the same picture there. Highly centralized administrative structures, with a whole raft of bureaucratic regulations for how anything was done from sewage to hospital injections. Compared with – and the timing is very important here – this is probably the heyday in Britain of the Local Education Authority. So we've got places like Leicester, which went Comprehensive without asking any permission from the Ministry of Education. The Ministry of Education was rather like an accountancy office, whereas in France it was directed, dirigiste. How that had come about was what I was reading on. I was actually enrolled by that stage for a French doctorate. One I was awarded but could never collect because I never succeeded in fulfilling their residential requirements.

MC: Did you get funding for this?

MA: I did eventually, but in a sort of perverse way. I always seem to have had two jobs. Ernest Gellner had asked me to teach in Cambridge. At the time, there was no sociology degree at all, but there was a sociology module under the economics Tripos. That was how I was actually supporting myself again, night work. Or, in this case, weekend work, because Christ College took me on. I tutored all the Christ men, they were all men in those days, who had opted to take the sociology module.

They did extraordinarily well. I suppose most of the other supervisors, who were the lowest form of life at Cambridge, paid two pence an hour, wouldn't have been sociologists at all. Just needed the cash and so on. They didn't only keep me on, they increased my rate of pay, which was rather nice. That plus continuing to live with my godparents in Paris, enabled me to go as a post-doc and be admitted to Bourdieu's équipe.

MC: What was that like, as a working environment?

MA: Hilarious. Quite hilarious. For instance, we would break for coffee at about 11 o'clock in the morning, and we'd go across the road to the Lutetia Café, which is huge. Clearly they'd been doing this for ages. There was actually a nearly complete circle, a horseshoe of chairs that were acknowledged to be where the équipe came in to take coffee in the morning. There was also a seating plan. Bourdieu was at the head of the table. There was also a conversational plan. Today, we will discuss . . . we were only staying there 20 minutes, 30 at most.

To his eternal credit, he was a theorist who always did an *empirical*, not an empiricist, back up to whatever he was writing on. He had a wealth of interests that all came off this central concept of habitus, which I saw as the inviolable theoretical core in the Lakatosian sense, but the concentric circles were up for grabs.

MC: Did you have a sense then of an unwarranted generalization from the social condition of Bourdieu's France to the capitalist world at large?

MA: Yes, I did. I tried to do something about it. I had a flat and then a house in Notting Hill Gate. He and Luc Boltanski used to come over on the train and stay for a couple of days. We would have seminars in Reading about allied topics.

I was very cautious. He wasn't the kind of guy you met head on. Certainly I wasn't feeling secure enough in developing this thesis to engage with him, but I was secure enough in my incipient critique to try and expose him when he came to England to the equivalent of my first experiences in France. He didn't know England at all. So it was as strange for him wandering into a British university or school as it had been for me walking into the amphitheater and finding no one wanted to listen to Raymond Aron.

I tried to make it live for him without making it into a verbalized critique. It wasn't cowardly. Again, it was one of those things that's very hard to communicate these days because the practice has ceased. This huge gap between the full professor and the post-doc researcher, even though he was an incredibly kind man, and occasionally we would start a discussion that was so interesting he'd say, 'Oh, come on, let's go out for lunch or for dinner.' He would always pay. Personally, he was as kind as anybody could have possibly been, and to be fair, he tried to minimize the distance, this huge gap.

I could have gone further, but I didn't want to damage this relationship because I was just getting so much out of working with him and his people. They were really giving me French education, French sociology on a plate. It was like being at the most glorious buffet where you didn't have to go out looking and searching and making connections. You just sort of took a bit of this and a bit of that.

MC: But you were also working at Reading during this time?

MA: I got a lectureship at Reading. No good reason except it was close to London and very close to Heathrow. It made a bizarre life of three days a week in Paris and three days a week in London possible. Total cost of air round trip: £14. I suppose these days it would be absolutely outrageous for anybody to do that even if their workload allowed them to do it, which it wouldn't with all these add-ons and extras and expectations.

That was the next three years, which were mainly devoted to clarifying this project. *Social Origins of Educational Systems* became clearer and clearer, at least in its theory. There was still the enormous historical slog through its various histories.

MC: Did you work on other projects while you were doing this?

MA: I published on the growth of public administration in France. We did a lot of work at Reading editing volumes on European things. Then came May 68. I re-read it about six months ago for some purpose or other. It's not bad. Certainly, the ideas are more than half-formed by then.

MC: Did those events then feed into the bigger projects, as well?

MA: In order to get this mob off the streets all kinds of verbal promises were made. All of them were about autonomy, decentralization, specialization. Participation, reduction, dilution of central control. It was a perfect spontaneously given critique by the agents themselves of what was wrong with the structure.

Then what happened during the next year? Everything that had been given was clawed back. Centralization was back, assured and reassured. Then the concessions that had been made to get them off the streets and back behind their desks were simply ratted on.

Part 3: The International Sociological Association

MC: How did you first come to be involved in the International Sociological Association?

MA: How did it come about? In the strangest of ways. I have to back-track a bit to LSE, to my second great friend, who I mentioned, Tom Bottomore, who I'd met via CND. We had always been very friendly and he had taught sociological theory.

I was quite surprised when Tom said to me, 'I'd like to talk to you about a proposition because you've been in France. You know French. You clearly like travel. How about a drink tonight?' I said, 'Absolutely fine.' He came straight out with it and it struck me as wonderful. He said, 'We have this journal covering sociology. How do you feel about editing it?'

Absolutely gobsmacked. I just couldn't imagine that this offer was there. He said, well, 'It's not such a wonderful deal as it maybe sounds to you. Let me tell you the downside. It's nine issues behind and we're in danger.' It came under the United Nations social science framework, it was in great danger of getting its funding cut if we didn't get it quickly up to date. I said, 'Yeah, I'll take it on gladly. You say the current editor is in Paris?' He told me where to go. I said, 'Do ask him for me, the back documentation, because it could be that he's sitting on nine issues that the writers have delivered but he hasn't got around to editing.' He went to a drawer and he brought out two cardboard folders, which had precisely one piece of paper in them each. I tentatively said, 'No manuscripts in course of editing?' On one of these pieces of paper turned out to be the list of planned and future issues.

MC: Did taking over the editorship lead inevitably to further involvement in the ISA?

MA: In the course of doing all this editing, and then these additional projects that I started floating, they said 'You must come to our meetings.' I went to a meeting every year for about eight years, saw the world, which was nice, and had a real feel for how decisions are made and so on. There was no vice chairman in charge of publications, and by then I had quite a raft of publications that I was responsible for: *Current Sociology*, a book series with Sage, we had other plans. We ought to have had a fourth vice president for publications, which was obviously designated for me. I've always enjoyed editing. I mean, in general. It's a way of keeping up. You really do have to read it very carefully, indeed, to be able to edit it. Simple as that.

I went to Delhi with the mindset that if they made a fourth VP for publications then, yes, I would be delighted to do that and continue with pushing forward these two projects. That was the expectation when I went off to India, which came crashing down on about day three when the committee reported back that the frontrunner for President was ineligible for reasons which are a long and technical story.

MC: What was the experience of being president like from 1986 to 1990?

MA: The experience was great. One year we went to Varna in Bulgaria and ended up bringing back clandestine articles that we published. We met regularly in Poland, both in Krakow and Warsaw, which even then was outstanding. I'd like to write a chapter on why Poland was ahead of the rest of Europe. Ljubljana in Slovenia. Intellectually, it was extraordinarily bright. There are endless funny stories I could tell you. Funny and sad. But you don't want this to be a kind of rambling travelogue do you?

MC: How did this intersect with your work at Warwick?

MA: Perfectly well. Nobody much cared. If anything, this was a feather in their cap that they had the president of the ISA on their teaching staff.

MC: Were you working on *Culture and Agency* at the time?

MA: Yes. That was my salvation in a way, as far as work was concerned. I was looking the other day down the list you've done on our website of my bibliographical items. I thought that was really interesting because you cannot spot the years 1986 to 1990, when I was very heavily involved in working for the ISA. You can't spot it in terms of publications because I'd written all but the last chapter of *Culture and Agency*. Before that summer meeting in 1986, I'd only done two things. I wrote the last chapter and sent it off to Cambridge University Press and I took my intensive Spanish course.

MC: And it was in your early years at Warwick that you finished *Social Origins of Educational Systems*?

MA: Yes. I was pregnant with Kingsley in 1975 and I had never encountered a baby in my life. Had some totally unreal expectations that they slept all the time and you just worked on. The reason, quite honestly, why that book became so long was because I was writing it in hand at the side of his cradle and I had no idea it was growing so much.

MC: But it was always going to be a massive undertaking though, right? To not only write analytical histories of emergence for such complex systems but to then compare them?

MA: Yes. I couldn't do two countries because what did that say? They were different, so I had to find another centralized system, which was Russia, and another decentralized system, which was Denmark. I played with the States, but with it being a Federal system, you would have had to have done a history of each one of the states and you'd have needed a research team for that.

MC: And the morphogenetic approach was developed in the course of this undertaking?

MA: The theory was born in the course of explaining how these systems got the structural characteristics that they did and how they kept them and what difference it made to action in and around education. If you look at the book – you don't have to read it – but if you look at it, there's actually a table that says 'this table summarizes the chapters in the book' and it names the cycles on the bottom line.

Part 4: Structure and culture

MC: How did *Culture and Agency*, your next big project, emerge from *Social Origins of Educational Systems*?

MA: From what are simple questions, particularly in the centralized system. If culture is the football, what appears in schools and universities on the curriculum is a golf ball inside the football. So the football is a cultural system and so is the golf ball, but how does that boundary get defined? You can ask the same question about a decentralized system. All these forms of knowledge are out there. Some of them particular to a specific area or activity and so on.

How do they actually get into schools? In the schools or in the night schools in a particular area?

MC: So it's the selection of a particular range of elements from the whole cultural system and how that happened socio-culturally? That's substantively the question that came straight out of your earlier work.

MA: It was a very substantive question. The moment you start digging into that question, that question almost . . . It doesn't recede, but it becomes very retractable. The bigger problem is, what the hell is culture? I read and read and read, it was just like throwing books over the left shoulder. All these people had something to say on it and nothing to be gained from having said it. I don't mean to sound arrogant or pretentious or anything like that. You've got to go back to square one and get a working definition of culture to answer your football to golf ball question because what is the football?

There are no units of culture. There still aren't. That's how that book starts. I think the first paragraph says something like 'culture's always been the poor relation of structure'. For example, we have no units. We have no equivalents of roles, of institutions, et cetera, et cetera. What are its boundaries? Is mythology part of culture? Is a scientific theory? Is a painting? Where do you stop? It seemed to be quite pointless to have a concept which is coterminous with everything because all you're doing is putting a name or label on everything.

Since I wanted to talk about processes and action and saw these as being structured, the differentiation between culture and structure seemed to me to be imperative. As it had done to everybody, particularly from Marx onward, talking about the difference between the material mode of production and the ideological devices used to try and buttress it or change it. That's what that book was all about and that's why, quite rightly, people like Dave Elder-Vass jumped on my use of Popper's World 3 as a stepping stone towards performing this delineation exercise.

MC: So was that something you drew upon as you were solving the problem? So the notions developed as you went along?

MA: Yes. They're always the residual problems left by the preceding book.

MC: The theme underlying them is objectivity and subjectivity?

MA: I wasn't aware of that, at the time. It's easy to pretend that you're all-knowing in old age and looking back, 'yes, it was obvious it was this trajectory'. I wouldn't object to someone looking back and concluding that this was the line, the theme, although obscured by going off to teach this or that, or have another baby.

MC: It's kind of an animating thread? Part of the process of doing this work is that your understanding of what you're doing becomes clearer as it goes on?

MA: Yes. Exactly. It's just like going back to standing on, I think it was Pont Neuf, or one of the bridges over the Seine, and thinking reflexively and subjectively, my goodness, universities are different here. The learning process is different. The books, assimilation process, the career building. Everything is different. Yes, that was the whole initial impetus. I can almost see my feet standing on that bridge now.

MC: It's been a while since I've read the book, but it occurs to me the language you use in it is more systems theoretical. I think you say, at one point, it's a general theory of cultural dynamics.

MA: Yeah. Because there wasn't one. I'm not saying this is the greatest and the terminus. But it was better than anything that was there before. Which is why I picked out that part of it and published it, long before the book was finished, in the *British Journal of Sociology*, called the 'Myth of Social Cultural Integration', which I hold true to this day. Cultures are seen to be things you can share, they are naturally delineated and if you say I'm a Muslim and you say you're a Muslim, we mean the same thing and share the same beliefs from it.

I thought it was absolutely wrong, inane, and didn't match anything I'd ever encountered in my travels. Countries are as varied as parts of England are varied. I suppose this is the Marxist thread, as well as the resistance to Foucault, because some particular faction or class faction or whatever you want to call them, took up a particular ideology; a term I still like and still regret because it maintains the nexus between interest and ideas. They're two different things, but they certainly play a very interesting role in relation to one another, whereas narrative and discourse just assume power.

MC: And David Lockwood's distinction between social integration and system integration was crucial to developing your argument?

MA: If I had to do Desert Island Discs those 14 pages would probably be number one. I've got more and more out of that article the longer I've lived.

MC: How did your work develop in relation to critical realism? It was around the time you were writing *Culture and Agency* that there was the latent CR community in the UK.

MA: Well, there was, but I wasn't part of it, precisely because of what we've been talking about. The ISA and two babies.

It was only when the ISA was over. I've always taken the view that when you stop being president of something, the kindest thing you can do for all concerned, if you care about the organization, is just walk away, so I did. I walked away into the Centre for Critical Realism. Though it wasn't called that in those days.

MC: Had you been reading CR work before that? My sense was that *Realist Social Theory* is explicitly framed as a contribution to CR and *Culture and Agency* isn't.

MA: That's right. I think when I wrote *Culture and Agency* I didn't know the first thing about CR.
MC: But there does seem to be a compatibility?
MA: Loads of compatibility. I thought afterwards, after I'd become part of CR organizations, that I could have written *Culture and Agency* slightly differently. It wouldn't have taken any doing, really, to make it a directly CR book. In a way, it's a pity I didn't, because somebody will come along and talk about epistemic breaks and the way they love handling dead authors.
MC: When did you first encounter CR?
MA: If you're asking me when did I first read *The Possibility of Naturalism*, which was the first CR book I read, I really cannot remember. Very, very shortly after *Culture and Agency* was published.
MC: I'm rather intrigued by that in particular because one of the concerns in *Culture and Agency* is about how you theorize cultural compatibility. But the relationship between that book and CR is a great example of such a compatibility.
MA: Yes. I loved *Possibility of Naturalism*. I think I'm unique in not having read *A Realist Theory of Science* first. I should have done. I probably at the time didn't know it existed. I just went on from it to reading out around everything I could find on that.

I made great friends with Roy from the beginning and that was a lovely, long friendship. We never had a cross word, ever, even though I think he was sometimes a little bit bemused by things like reflexivity. But he was very open minded, he had a very generous disposition. He was ready to entertain anything and see if he could fit it in or accommodate it. I was amazed but in reading his posthumous book, there are any number of references to reflexivity in it.

I know I gave him the books. But I had no confidence he ever read them. Sometimes, it's obvious from footnotes in later ones of his that he had, but he always said, I think it's footnote 54 or page 54 of the *Dialectic*, that I saved him from getting sucked into Giddens and structuration theory.
MC: How did this feed into *Realist Social Theory*?
MA: I always saw *Realist Social Theory* as a pot boiler. Going back to it, it's not as easy reading as I thought it was at the time I wrote it. The intention in writing it was not to say one original thing. It was just to bring my own thoughts together with the CR that I had been busy assimilating and mentally playing with.
MC: It's just a continuation in a way, then?
MA: A continuation. A clarification for self and others.
MC: Were there particular reasons why you chose the targets you did in *Realist Social Theory*? Was it the prominence of Giddens in British sociology?
MA: Well, you see 1979, retrospectively, it was such a key year. *Social Origins of Educational Systems*, which contains every element of the morphogenetic approach and uses it for two cycles. *The Possibility of Naturalism. The Central Problems of Social Theory.* That was historically pretty important. It distanced me from Giddens, made morphogenesis and structuration two entirely different approaches. The fact that they were concurrent in 1979 didn't make an impact at

the time. In other words, I'm sure none of the three of us read all three books that year, but cumulatively it did. That was one of the things *Realist Social Theory* really wanted to lay on with a shovel.

Part 5: Human agency

MC: How did your books on reflexivity follow on from your earlier work? Some people have seen it as a radical break.

MA: Well, I'd written a book on culture, another that really concentrated on structure, then I surveyed the field of CR. At the time, it was bloody weak on agency. It doesn't say a thing about people.

MC: Was it intellectually challenging to do that kind of move because you're going from the big, historical sweep to the individual and everyday.

MA: They were all challenging and daunting. I think if you start writing a book and you don't feel as if you're drowning, it's not worth doing. It's always been the same. One thing that's become easier is purely the knowledge that 'I've been here before and this is what the process involves.' All you've got to do is sit tight, wait for one of those wonderful times when you went to sleep with a problem and you wake up, and there it is all clear before you.

So, yes, challenging. Not so much at the level of things like oppositional social movements, because that flowed on from how to change a structure and what legitimation devices you drew upon from the pool available to you to try and advance your end.

But very challenging when it came down to the 'what is a person' level. I don't believe in disciplinary boundaries. I never have done and I've always broken them. The one I've always maintained, not out of principle but out of practice, is the sociology–psychology one: resist all attempts at reductionism because the *being in a context* is quite different from the *being pushing buttons in a laboratory*.

MC: *Realist Social Theory* raises the question of the variability of how subjects respond to their contexts. So was the subsequent work an exploration of what that variability entailed?

MA: It was a question I'd often pose: how does structure influence agency? There has to be an answer to that because we don't want hydraulic pressures or determinants or pushes and pulls. It was a totally mechanical model of the human agent. That was all out. But what was going to get rid of it? Then, the internal conversation just hit me. It's not my name, it's from Charles Peirce. Then, we're back to putting objectivity and subjectivity together again. We're back to structure and agency and the two have completely distinct emergent properties and powers. How does it work for particular people?

MC: And how that plays out over the lifecourse?

MA: Yes, well, that part of the lifecourse that I was able to reconstruct with them in *Making Our Way Through The World*. Mature subjects on the whole, from Coventry. Then the Reflexive Imperative, apart from the theoretical argument about reflexivity having overtaken habit, what it's like when you *begin* to do this? Taking students, it's an easy way out. They're available. But they are at that crucial age of entering to university. To do what and why. Crucial questions they have to answer. How do they find it? That's very much Andrew Sayer territory. Discovering what matters to them. It's a lovely book, *Why Things Matter To People*. It's an act of exploration for each and every person. Many things, unless you've done them, you can't understand. It's society's catch 22. You can't know whether you'd be a surgeon unless you've been repeatedly into an operating theatre, by which time of course you are changed and so is your view on what you prioritize and what you want to pursue.

MC: At what point did you decide you needed to study this empirically?

MA: It began in *Structure, Agency and the Internal Conversation*. The sheer realization that, yes, you can mine yourself, your friends and your family. That's a closed world. But there was the surprising discovery, which you've experienced too, how ready and generous interviewees and subjects actually are. I was gobsmacked, at first, the things that they will tell you and even more gory detail if you wanted to know.

I think I was a very good interviewer and I've got no idea why. Other than being very interested, which is probably the most important thing. Good on supplementary questions, good on picking up cues, good on not pushing people too far when you're manifestly getting into emotional depths. You have to give the whole time. If they want to talk about their childbirth experiences, you trade with them, you swap yours, but all the time, you keep saying, 'Only tell me what you're comfortable to.' You know this as well as I do. There is a lot of trade in it.

MC: You were very influenced by Doug Porpora's book and the approach he took to it.

MA: Yes, yes! Get rid of the bloody clipboard and stop treating yourself like a white-coated lab technician or medical person or psychiatrist or whatever. If you disagree with them, say so. I loved it in *Landscapes of the Soul*. If some subjects said something Doug disagreed with, he'd say 'Well, I don't think that, what makes you think that?' They'd end up having a wonderful interchange. There is a footnote that says something about treat them as real, don't dehumanize them. What you ask of them, be prepared that they have every right to ask of you.

Structure, Culture and Agency: selected papers of Margaret Archer
Annotated bibliography

Margaret S. Archer (2013 [1979]), 'Thinking and Theorizing About Educational Systems', in Archer, M.S. (2013 [1979]), *Social Origins of Educational Systems*. Routledge: London, pp. 1–53.

Archer is a systematic theorist who has carefully developed a series of fundamental concepts over the past thirty years, e.g., the morphogenetic sequence, analytical dualism, the internal conversation. In this revised introductory chapter to her first book the *Social Origins of Educational Systems* (1979) Archer revisits the arguments that led her to develop a unified morphogenetic social theory – the 'Morphogenetic Approach': a theoretical synthesis that tightly integrates the concomitant complementarities of the morphogenetic systems theory of Walter Buckley, the neo-Weberian analysis of Lockwood and (later) the critical realism of Roy Bhaskar to properly analyse the emergence, reproduction and transformation of cultural systems and social structures. Borrowing insights from Buckley's cybernetic study of positive and negative feedback mechanisms, Archer composes an explanatory framework of systemic change through the analysis of 'morphogenetic cycles' over time. A morphogenetic cycle helps explain the dynamics (positive/negative feedback) between the system and socio-cultural interaction through a process of systemic conditioning, whereby the particular configuration of the system (at T1) conditions the practices of the life-world (at T2), which aim to reproduce or transform the system and lead eventually (at T3) to a new elaboration of the system, which will be contested and modified in a second cycle, and so forth. Thus, in examining the social origins of educational systems in France, England, Russia and Denmark, Archer produces an 800-page comparative analysis of the process through which educational policies (as structural configurations) effect pedagogical practices and how variability within and between systems emerge.

Margaret S. Archer (1981), 'On Predicting the Behaviour of the Educational System', *British Journal of Sociology of Education*, 2:2, pp. 211–219.

Archer further examines the so-called 'logic' of educational systems in this extended review of Green, Ericson and Seidman's (1980) *Predicting the Behaviour of the Educational System*. Building on her own work, she critiques the claim that the educational system is predicated on a singular internal logic, which can be explained in reference to the patterned regularities that result from the rational interests of external groups. Archer disagrees, and suggests that the educational system does not embody a singular logic; how can it when the system appears to emerge from often competing interests between policy, professionals and parents? Archer (p. 216) is clear: 'the growth of the educational system is what nobody wanted'. Rather, what we come to understand about the nature of systems is that they are *open* to the irrational and unintended consequences of different interests and divergent values. Importantly, this complexity does not preclude us from generating social scientific knowledge about the educational system. Archer is interested in explaining how such a system appears to take on a 'life of its own'; but what is needed is a theoretical account of how agency is structured, and how such structures may be the heritage of unintended consequences of past actions. In other words, what Archer offers in this review is a clear rejection of a functionalist account of causality in favour of emergence and an explanation of the educational system in terms of how individual interests are structured and, in turn, elaborated upon over time.

Margaret S. Archer (1985), 'The Myth of Cultural Integration', *British Journal of Sociology*, 36:3, pp. 333–353.

Sociological discussion of cultural phenomena has been plagued by 'the myth of cultural integration', according to which all societies that are considered to be viable are normatively integrated with culture performing the major function in this regard. In this article, Archer's primary concern is to distinguish culture as an objective, ideational phenomena – possessing considerable autonomy in terms of its own inner 'logic' (but not necessarily consistency) from agents, who, in specific circumstances, seek to comprehend, invoke, manipulate and act in reference to systems of ideas. The analysts who consider culture to be almost exclusively of significance in terms of its capacity to constrain action (and social structure) are classified by Archer as 'downward' conflationists. The basic myth of cultural integration derives mainly from the latter, particularly the anthropological functionalists of the 1930s, whose ideas, in Archer's view, were incorporated into sociological structural–functionalism in the 1940s and 1950s. We've also witnessed another form of the myth, arising from Marxist and neo-Marxist schools of thought. Deeply concerned about the problem of the persistence of capitalism, a considerable number of Marxist social scientists have created their own version of the 'myth'. Archer classifies this as 'upwards conflation', on the grounds that, in contrast to downwards conflation, it involves the notion of culture deriving from being imposed by one set of agents upon members of a collectivity and pays little attention to the idea of culture having some kind of objective inner logic. Archer also deals with the third approach – 'central' conflation. Anthony Giddens' structuration theory is provided as the prime example; it leaves neither room for action in relative independence of culture or for the objective status of the latter.

Margaret S. Archer (1995), 'The vexatious fact of society', in Archer, M.S. (1995), *Realist Social Theory: The Morphogenetic Approach*. Cambridge: Cambridge University Press, pp. 2–30.

In the behavioural sciences, the analytical connection between individual and social processes is often understood as the big problem of bridging the 'micro' and 'macro' levels. The diversity with which this problem has been approached within social theory points to the complexity of the underlying issue, which Archer (1995) dubs the 'vexatious fact of society': how do we make sense of the relationship between actors and the wider social order that appears to influence and, yet, is influenced by their actions? In this chapter, Archer suggests that it is the failure to resolve this underlying question that has resulted in the proliferation of various dualisms in social theory, the worst offenders of which give explanatory power to *either* 'micro' *or* 'macro' accounts of social reality. Archer questions the assumption that we should accept this as the only way of characterizing the problem. Rather, what is offered is the suggestion that these terms are *relational* and what characterises their relationship(s) are emergent properties that cannot be reduced to either level. Importantly, this position is not endorsing 'duality' – the suggestion that individual and social processes are co-constitutive of one another *in the moment*. On the contrary, Archer's position is that of 'analytical dualism' – that structure and agency (and culture and agency) are interdependent but analytically distinct phenomena that operate on different timescales.

Margaret S. Archer (1996), 'Morphogenesis versus structuration: on combining structure and action', in Bryant, Christopher G.A. & Jary, David (eds), *Anthony Giddens: Critical Assessments*. London: Routledge, Vol. 2, pp. 25–52.

This chapter details the major theoretical differences between Giddens' Structuration Theory and Archer's Morphogenetic Approach. Archer argues that central to Giddens' theory is his attempt to overcome three dichotomies that he sees as problematic in social theory: (i) voluntarism–determinism, (ii) subject–object and (iii) synchrony–diachrony. Archer suggests that it is in Giddens' attempt to overcome these dichotomies, most notably through his notion of the 'duality of structure', that he substitutes an analysis of the relations that pertain between these dualisms, and thus obscures the emergent properties and the discontinuity that characterises complex systems. In other words, Archer suggests that Structuration Theory overlooks both the sequential and dialectical interplay between structure and agency, and that the Morphogenetic Approach was designed to account for both without privileging the causal efficacy of either. In this chapter, Archer sets out to question the capacity of Structuration Theory and whether it can transcend such dichotomies in a way that is sociologically useful. Archer is critical of the ways in which Giddens' insistence on the 'duality of structure' inhibits any theoretical formulation of the variability of the conditions under which social change and reproduction occurs. Archer defends the theoretical utility of analytical dualism here, and argues that the analytical separation of structure and agency (interaction) over time permits theorising about the *degrees of freedom* and *stringency* of constraints as part of a wider temporal (re-)structuring of any given system (or context). To this end, the Morphogenetic Approach renders the transformative capacity of agency in terms of its logical relations to structure, rather than an appeal to the (semiotic) notion of 'instantiations'.

Margaret S. Archer (2000), 'For structure: its reality, properties and powers: A reply to Anthony King', *The Sociological Review*, 48:3, pp. 464–472.

Despite the systematic approach that Archer has taken to the problem of structure and agency, her Morphogenetic Approach has been the subject of critique, particularly from theorists of the interpretive tradition, who reject the concept of structure as 'metaphysical' and 'reified'. In this chapter, Archer responds to this claim by reasserting the importance of an understanding of (social) structures as relatively autonomous, logically prior, relational and emergent, and which have the generative capacity to modify the powers of its constituents in fundamental ways by potentially enabling or constraining social action *sui generis*. Archer suggests that this realist-informed perspective is better suited to an explanatory – that is, causal – account of social action, rather than the 'descriptive individualism' offered by King's interpretive sociology. Archer links King's misrepresentation of her position, and his account of intersubjectivity, to what Roy Bhaskar calls the 'epistemic fallacy' – to confuse knowledge *about* reality with how reality *is*. Knowledge about our affairs can never be taken for that state of affairs, much like our biographies cannot be taken as the basis for ontological statements about how reality is.

Archer contends that King's interpretive sociology attempts to explain social reality by reference only to the episodic accounts of meaning that result from intersubjectivity. Not only is this atemporal and ahistorical, but Archer suggests that it obscures the ways in which agency is shaped by socio-cultural constraints and enablements, such as the distribution of wealth, which mark the ways in which agents can elaborate on their socio-cultural contexts through morphogenetic processes.

Margaret S. Archer (2003), 'The private life of the social agent: what difference does it make?', in Cruickshank, J. (ed.), *Critical Realism: The Difference it Makes*. London: Routledge, pp. 17–29.

Having recovered the notion of structure from interpretive sociology and critics of realist social theory, Archer turns her attention to agency, and attempts to recuperate it from another longstanding dualism between 'Modernity's Man' and 'Society's Being'. The former refers to an account of agency grounded in Enlightenment thinking, which strips down the agent to an instrumentally rational actor, e.g., *Homo economicus*. The latter is social constructionism's contribution to the debate: an account of agency as the 'gift of society' or as a 'cultural artifact'. In this chapter, Archer questions these interpretations of agency and attempts to reclaim a sense of the human agent that is active and reflexive, rather than passive and instrumental. Archer argues that critical realism offers the tools to conceptualise agency as the emergent properties of people who have the power to monitor their own lives and, as such, mediate structural and cultural conditions, thereby contributing to the elaboration of social reproduction or change. Importantly, this process is always ongoing and is reflexive: we are all 'strong evaluators' (Charles Taylor), meaning that we establish, biographically, interests that may lead us to make certain choices in any given circumstance, and yet these circumstances may influence what choices we make. Understanding the inner conversations that people have with themselves is crucial to making sense of this process, though the decisions we make may never be reduced to them for the private life of the social agent is always stratified and relational.

Margaret S. Archer (2007), 'The Ontological Status of subjectivity: the missing link between structure and agency', in Lawson, Clive, Latsis, John & Martins, Nuno (eds), *Contributions to Social Ontology*. London: Routledge/Taylor and Francis, pp. 17–31.

Archer uses this chapter to extend her analysis (and defence) of subjective ontology and agential reflexivity. In particular, she revisits 'the problem of structure and agency' and 'the problem of subjectivity and objectivity' and is critical of attempts to *transcend* the issue by treating the two as ontologically inseparable. Archer once again forwards the importance of analytical dualism and the morphogenetic sequence, but more pertinently focuses on how human agents reflexively deliberate on the properties and powers exercised by structures in their attempt to condition behaviour. Sociologists (and Realists), Archer suggests, are often guilty of imputing *their* subjectivity, vested interests and objective concerns onto agents, which act as a kind of dummy for real and efficacious human subjectivity. To avoid this, we can embrace analytical dualism and take reflexivity seriously, as the 'missing link' between structure and agency. This means recognizing that the capacity of human agents to consider themselves in relation to their (social) contexts and vice versa has real emergent properties and powers that cannot be reduced to reflexive deliberations (or internal conversations) but nevertheless are causally efficacious in the reproduction or transformation of social contexts and their power to condition behaviour. In other words, without an adequate account of an agents' own configurations of concerns, as subjectively in relation to 'others' (nature, practice and society), then sociologists (and Realists) will obscure the mechanism – reflexivity – and the biographical processes through which agents come to subjectively determine their practical projects in relation to their objective circumstances.

Margaret S. Archer (2007), 'Introduction: reflexivity as the unacknowledged condition of social life', in Archer, M.S (2007), *Making our Way through the World: Human Reflexivity and Social Mobility*. Cambridge: Cambridge University Press, pp. 1–23.

In this chapter, Archer (p. 1) argues that 'Reflexivity remains a cipher in social theory . . . neither what it is nor what it does has received the attention necessary for producing clear concepts of reflexivity or a clear understanding of reflexivity as a social process.' Archer (p. 4) defines reflexivity as 'the regular exercise of the mental ability, shared by all normal people, to consider themselves in relation to their (social) contexts and vice versa'. This definition is reached through a careful analysis of the ways through which one *comes to make choices in everyday life*, and the necessary psychological processes and biographical contexts that structure these deliberations. This is best captured in her 'DDD scheme' – discernment -> deliberation -> dedication – three stages that help decrypt the concept of reflexivity, to show the processes through which one attempts to evaluate choice(s) in reference to their biographical concerns or life-long projects. Importantly, Archer's contribution here means that we are all radically heterogeneous as subjects; even when we share similar objective social positions or our 'concerns' appear to be singular in nature, we may seek very different ends from within them. This means that our subjectivity is dynamic, and not reducible psychologically, as we will modify our own goals in terms of their contextual feasibility. Finally, we are, for the most part, active agents, because we adjust our projects to those practices that we believe we can realize, however fallible, the goals we seek in terms of our wider circumstances.

Margaret S. Archer (2012), 'A brief history of how reflexivity becomes imperative', in Archer, M.S. (2012), *The Reflexive Imperative*. Cambridge: Cambridge University Press, pp. 10–47.

In this chapter, Archer questions the tendency in social theory to treat reflexivity as a standardized phenomenon, such that people either exercise reflexivity or do not. Rather, Archer (p. 10) asks: 'does human reflexivity have a history?' and explores the possibility that reflexivity has distinct variations in the *modes* through which it is practised. In the prevailing view, any variation in reflexivity is only conceivable in the following terms: that it is either practised more or less (as suggested by Beck, Giddens and other proponents of the 'individualization thesis'). Archer offers an alternative perspective. She suggests that variations in reflexivity are subject to change over time, particularly as we respond to the changing historical circumstances brought about by the increasing rapidity of social change in late modernity. In other words, Archer provides a brief history of how reflexivity *becomes* an imperative, but in such a way that she resists uniform macro-sociological statements in favour of examining how such changes are always mediated biographically. Indeed, the 'imperative' for 'reflexivity' may differ from person to person and Archer seeks to elaborate on the distinctive modes of reflexivity through an analysis of the biographies of those who practise such modes. Importantly, these modes are theorized as distinctive configurations of structural and cultural factors that will tend to produce actors of each mode, though one should always be aware of 'conflating' these factors without an adequate biography of the person.

Margaret S. Archer (2013), 'Morphogenic Society: Self-Government and Self-Organization as Misleading Metaphors', in Archer, M.S. (ed.), *Social Morphogenesis*. New York: Springer, pp. 145–164.

Nearly two decades later and Archer returns, in this chapter, to 'the vexatious fact of society' – the 'riddle' about how human intentionality is shaped by but also influences social processes. This time, however, the focus is very different, as Archer sets to tackle the question: is the social order *self-governing* or *self-organizing*? In doing so, she engages with arguments from the biological and social sciences to consider whether the possibility of social transformation comes from *outside* or *within* social systems. With the trilogy on reflexivity completed, Archer (p. 162) is clear about the possibility of self-governing social systems: 'They are not because their autobiographies (singular or collective) are never made in circumstances of their own choosing'. Structures always enable and constrain upon what agential 'projects' may be, and agents will always find alternative courses of action should these projects be blocked. But what about self-organization? Do social systems simply reproduce themselves based on some kind of internal logic? Archer is critical of such reification and suggests that one must return to the terms of morphogenesis if one is to avoid it – structure is always logically prior to agency – that is, reflexive deliberation – and this leads to structural elaboration over time. To talk of self-organization, then, is misleading. It obscures the *relationally contested* nature of how people interact with parts of the system, often reflexively, and always with unintended consequences that cannot simply be 'co-opted' back into the (often functional) logic of the system. Let the last word go to Archer (p. 163): '. . . the more morphogenetic the social becomes, the more we will need to examine social morphogenesis on its own social terms . . . to take responsibility for both the proximate and distant effects of our doings and deal with their unintended consequences'.

Archer, M. S. (2014), 'The generative mechanism re-configuring late modernity', in Archer (ed.), *Late Modernity*. Dordrecht: Springer International Publishing, pp. 93–117.

In this chapter, Archer examines social morphogenesis on its own terms to identify the pivotal situational logics of the present, in particular, the generative mechanism (s) of *structural competition* and *cultural diffusion*, and how these mechanisms operate causally to shape the present era of financial capitalism (post-1970s). Archer considers how, on the one hand, unbridled economic competition may be hampered by the activities of 'diffusionists' – digital scientists and activists – whose attempt to expand the cyber-commons has facilitated new social movements that promote useful value over exchange value, and whom articulate values oriented towards the common good rather than the zero-sum logic of competition. On the other hand, 'diffusionism' is restrained by the equally steady colonization of its innovations, leaving organizations to contest, relationally, how such initiatives may be either incorporated into the for-profit sector or kept open-source. Archer suggests that the former blocks the way towards a Morphogenetic society, encouraging a return to 'business as usual' despite the crises provoked by competitive excess, whilst the latter seeks to reinvigorate civil society through opportunities like 'corporate social responsibility' and 'social enterprise'. What Archer offers, then, is not a manifesto or concrete prediction of the future but rather a gradual view of the future scenario that may be possible: one where organisations *relationally contest* the logics of late modernity. Archer suggests that this is why the question of the 'good society' will never disappear, because during any social contestation that generates some given social form, those who lose out do not quietly fade away; on the contrary, as people, *they have changed*, and so may retain their organization and their objectives, fight on and later win concessions. Archer refers to this process as 'the double morphogenesis'.

Archer, M. S. (2015), 'How Agency is Transformed in the Course of Social Transformation: Don't Forget the Double Morphogenesis', in Archer, M. S. (ed.), *Generative Mechanisms Transforming Late Modernity.* Dordrecht: Springer, pp. 135–58.

The double morphogenesis refers to how groups themselves and group relations are transformed in the course of pursuing and introducing social transformations. In this chapter, Archer argues that the agential regrouping and degrouping involved in pursuing and introducing social transformation is one of the most crucial features taking place in late modernity. In particular, Archer suggests that we live at a time when nascent structural and cultural morphogenesis prolongs our uncertainty about the future and protracts the possibility of structural transformation. To support this, Archer distinguishes between Primacy and Corporate Agents: the former a collectivity of people who share the same life chances, and the latter those who have organized themselves in pursuit of certain goals and have articulated the changes they seek. This enables Archer to concentrate upon the systemic changes introduced by the generative mechanism of late modernity to show how structural and cultural morphogenesis operate to prompt low system and social integration, leading Primary Agents to largely pursue their concerns through the situational logic of opportunity. On the one hand, this leads to what Archer calls the 'perverse triumph' of diffusionism and ongoing debates concerning intellectual property rights – a key battleground for the future. On the other, it also reinforces the 'passivity' of Primary Agents. Archer suggests that social networking sites are not only broadly orientated towards competition, but foster a new form of intense 'presentism' among *some* users (notably 'Expressive reflexives'), precluding them from designing courses of action that entail long-term planning or cognisance of their consequences.

Index

acceleration theory 247–8, 251
accumulation 73–4
actions: context and 40–1, 115–16, 215; goal-seeking 222–3; structuration and 105–7; structure and 88, 103; variability of 169, 174–5
active agents 146, 163, 169–70, 289
activity dependence 45, 215, 221–2
actors 23, 27–32, 62
agency: Archer's work on 304–5; cultural changes and 20–1; morphogenetic basis 24; problem of 138, 147; reshaping itself see double morphogenesis; social forms and 7, 13, 152, 216; theories of 22–3
agency and structure see structure and agency
agent-based models 226–8
agential regrouping 262
agents: active 146, 163, 169–70, 289; as human 138; and powers 157, 172; and projects 154, 230; and reflexivity 148, 155–6, 161, 163; and relationality 22, 172–3, 231; social 24–7
aggregation 147–8, 218, 228–9
analytical dualism: Archer's approach xvi–xviii; and culture 11–12, 75; and duality of structure 122; and morphogenetic approach 39, 105; and philosophical dualism 129; and social realism 88–9
anti-copyright movements 268
Archer, Margaret: graduate school 293–5; and International Sociological Association 299–300; work on educational systems 296–9; work on human agency 304–5; work on structure and culture 301–4
assurance game 202–3
austerity measures 270

authority: of authors and readers 282–3; first-person 147, 159–60, 283–4
autonomous reflexivity xviii, 185–6, 194–5, 198–9, 251–2, 290–1
Azande culture 64–5

Being Human xvi–xvii, 286–7
Bhaskar, Roy 1, 37, 38, 92, 152
Blau, Peter 121
blogs 274
Blumer, H. 135–6
Bourdieu, Pierre 41, 157
Brodbeck, May 96–8
Buckley, Walter 2, 38, 103, 220–1

calculability 203–5, 267
capitalism 148, 210–11, 236, 241–2
'Castro's example' 114–17, 130–1
causal consensus 12, 61–3
The Causal Power of Social Structures (Elder-Vass) 46
causal powers: and agents 155, 169–70; detecting 4–5; of educational systems xiv–xv, 152, 285; and projects 169–70; and reflexivity 157, 161–2; resistance to 36; of structure and agency 2, 151–2, 172; and temporality 3
causality 5, 12, 235
central conflation 37, 148
Central Problems in Social Theory (Giddens) 37, 103–4
central value system 60–1, 62
centralised/decentralised systems 2–3, 5, 7, 9–10, 43
civil society 251
coherence 60–1, 64–5, 239
collaboration 245–6
collective agency 194–5, 292
collective behavior 228, 229

collective subjectivities 292
Collectivism 93–4, 95, 97
commercialisation 276–7
'commons' movement 252, 264, 272
communicative reflexivity xviii–xix, 185–6, 188–92, 195, 201–2, 252
competition: alternatives to 245, 248–9, 271; and diffusion 254–5, 259, 264–5, 276
competitive contradiction 19–20, 195–9
complexity theory 223, 226–8
concerns: and internal conversation 31, 187; and opportunity 208, 275; projects and practices 157, 162; types of 29, 31; *see also* ultimate concerns
concomitant compatibility 15–16, 18, 21
conditioning: causal powers 154; cultural 14–17; social 152, 172–3; structural xvi, 6–7, 11, 115, 260–1 conflation xv–xvi, 36, 74–5, 79, 81–6, 147–8
conflict 6, 109–10, 197–8
consistency: within culture 61–2; between ontology and method 90; questions around 65
constraining contradictions 15, 18, 241
constraints: and freedoms 77–8; and objectivity/subjectivity 154; on professionalisation 54; and projects 171–2; responses to 155, 174; stringency of 108–10, 122, 148
contestation 261
contested relational organisations 46–7, 225–6, 228, 231, 254
context: of actions 40–1, 115, 121, 215; concerns and 180, 208; reflexivity and 188, 250; sytemic properties as 85; variety and 222
contextual continuity xviii, 188–93, 194–5, 199, 212n21, 290
contextual discontinuity xviii, 188–9, 194–5, 290
contextual incongruity xviii, 188–9, 204–5, 207–8, 251, 290
contingency 216–17, 278
contingent compatibility 262–3
contingent complementarities 20, 239, 240, 241–2, 255, 268
continuation 261
contradictions 70, 109
contradictions and complementarities 11, 13, 14–16
conversations 191–2; *see also* internal conversation
copyright 266–9

corporate agents 25–6, 32, *197*, 262–4, 268, 272–3
correction 15, 18
counter-cultural values xviii, 290
counter-institutionalisation 253–4
creativity 20, 32, 146
Critical Realism xv, 3, 302–4
critical situations 111, 117
critics 284
cultural accumulation 73–4
cultural capital, intergenerational 206–7
cultural coherence 12, 70–1
cultural conditioning 14–17
cultural dynamics 301–2
cultural elaboration 14, 19–21, 72
cultural emergent properties (CEPs) 23, 153, 155
cultural integration: anthropological background 60, 63, 74; as myth 12, 59–61, 63–5, 69–74
cultural manipulation 70
cultural patterns 60, 61
cultural pluralism 65–6
cultural properties 171–3
cultural stability 16, 71
Cultural System (C.S.) xv, 11–12, 14, 16–18, 229
cultural system integration *21*, 63–71, 73–5
cultural variety 21
culture: conceptualisation of 59–61; definition 11, 75n2, 236, 238–9; and novelty 240; parental 205–6; social dynamics of 266
Culture and Agency xv, 135, 286
culture as praxis 68
cybernetics 122–3, 218–21

DDD scheme 180–1, 209
decentralisation xiv–xv
dedication 181
degrees of freedom 77–8, 110–12, 148, 170–1
deliberation 180–1
Dennett, D. C. 230
deroutinization 110–11
description and explanation 90–2, 95
diachronic analysis 3, 45–6
diachrony/synchrony 104, 112–14, 117, 260
differentiation 71–2, 190, 220
diffusion 245–6, 250–5, 263–4, 270–1, 274
digital revolution 243
digital science 263–4, 270–2
dimensional approach 118

discernment 180
disorder 18
distraction 249–50, 275, 277
distribution 218
divergent interests 245
domain assumptions 284
dominant modes of reflexivity xviii, 186, 188–9, 190, 211n7, 251
double morphogenesis 9, 10, 26, 46, 259–62, 269–74
downwards conflation 79, 147
dualism vs duality 125n11
duality of structure 104, 105–7, 118–20, 122
Durkheim, Emile 72, 78–9, 191

economic competition 254
economic crisis 269–70, 274
economy 240–1
educational systems: and agents 45–6; and Archer's work xiv–xv, 296–9; causal powers of xiv–xv, 152, 285; definition 58n5; emergence of 9–10, 36–7, 42–4; expansion of 54–5; logic of 50–7; and morphogenesis 6–8, 46–7; structure of 41–2; and technical training 242–3
Elder-Vass, Dave 3, 8, 12–13, 45–7
elective affinity 194
elimination of opposition 21, 239
elites 62
emergence 3, 36–7, 44–5, 87–8, 120–1, 130
emergent properties: activation 170; causal powers and 6, 130; discontinuity and 105; orders of xix, 131–2; as relational xiv–xv, 83–4, 120–1, 129–30, 136n7, 244–5; unintended consequences and 4–5, 109
emotions 29, 141–3, 174
empiricism: critiqued 99–100; in social theory 82
enablements 148, 154–5, 171–2
endurance of social entities/structures 8, 9–10
entrepreneurship 247
epiphenomenalism 81
epistemic fallacy 22, 133–6, 161, 183n21
equality in education 57
Ericson, David P. 50–7
Evans-Pritchard 64, 65
événementalisme 277–8
evolutionary adaptation 47
existence, causal criteria of 95
explanation and description 90–2, 95
explanatory emergence 96, 97

explanatory framework: and morphogenetic approach 1–3, 37–8, 80–1; and social ontology 89–90
expressive reflexivity 277–8
expressivity 252

feedback 85, 121–2, 217, 219
financial crisis 202–4, 269–70
first-person authority 147, 159–60, 283–4
first-person epistemic privilege 146–7, 159–60
first-person ontologies 158, 283
flows and structure 292
fractured reflexivity xix, 185–6, 188, 211, 252, 291
freedom, degrees of 77–8, 110–12, 148, 170–1

Gellner, Ernest 65–7, 68, 95
general systems theory 121
generative mechanisms xix–xx, 235–6, 245
Giddens, Anthony 37, 103–4, 105–7, 122–4, 226
globalisation 223, 241, 263–4, 291, 292
goal-seeking actions 222–3
gradualism xx
Green, Thomas F. 50–7
groups: and individualism/collectivism 91; interaction *24, 27*, 222–3; interest 19–20, 197–8, 239–40, 272–3; and re/formation 268; and social agency *24, 27*

habitual action 110–11
habitus 148
heterogeneity 219–21, 273–4
Holism 78–9, 80, 81
homogeneity 219–20
human beings in social context xvi–xvii, 286–7
hydraulic theorising 169
hyperactivity 106

ideas 14–16, 20–1, 158, 238–9, 266, 283
ideational diversification 21
ideational positions 236
ideologies 21, 160–1, 176–7, 194
incoherence within culture 61
inconsistencies: significance of 67; at systemic level 70
Individualism 79, 81, 93–4, 95–6, 97
individualism: and collectivism 81–2, 86; and heterogeneity 220; within traditional societies 72

individual/society dichotomy: difficulties of 128–9; Giddens' approach 117–22
individuation 31, 70, 72
information technology 243–4, 245–7, 254
information theory 71, 218–19
infrastructure 246
innovation: constraints on 16, 111; feedback and 204, 243; in traditional societies 73; variety and 218–22, 251
innovative amalgamation 19
institutional analysis 112–13
institutionalisation 20–1
institutions 242–3
instrumental rationality 202, 205, 207
intellectual property 265–8, 276
intelligibilia 12–13, 238
intentionality 230, 282–3
interdisciplinarity 217
interest groups 19–20, 197–8, 272–3
interests, abstract *see* vested interests 52–3
internal conversation: and active agents 146–7, 157–8, 289–90; and concerns 142–6; and identity 30–2; and objectivity/subjectivity 159, 175–6; and reflexivity xvii–xviii, 167–8, 186–7; types of 165–6; and young people 208
International Sociological Association 296–9
interpretations: of texts 282–3; by third persons 160
interpretive sociology 128–9, 134–5
irreducibility 87, 159

job market 205–7, 208–9, 240–1
judgemental rationality 286

King, Anthony 128–36
knowledge 11, 12–13, 134–6

Late Modernity: macro-components 237–9; structure and culture xx, 239–42
literacy rates 114–17, *115*, 130–1
Locke, J. 140, 149n2
Lockwood, David 2, 37–8, 63
logic, types of *see* situational logic
logic of educational systems 50–7
logical consistency 12, 15–16
London School of Economics 293–5

Making Our Way Through the World xviii, 290
mal-integration 265, 269
Manicas, Peter 11, 44

marginals 19
market competition 246
market trading 227–9
markets 53, 248–9, 253
Maruyama, M. 109–10, 219–21
media 249–50
mediation: and culture 13; process of 161, 162; questioning of 11; of structural/cultural powers 169, 177; and subjectivity 153, 157, 289
mediums of exchange 52, 57
meso-level changes 242–3
meta-reflexivity xviii, 185–6, 200–1, 208–9, 251–2, 290–1
methodological bracketing 112–13
Methodological Collectivism 38, 90, 96
Methodological Holism 36
Methodological Individualism 6, 36, 90, 96, 128–9
methodology and ontology 78–81, 96–7
micro-macro problem 81–6, 117, 121, 237
Mill, J.S. 79
mobilization of populations 196–9
modalities of structuration 118, 119–20
modernity: late 199–207, 291–2; and morphogenetic society 236; transition to 193–9
Modernity's Man 22–3, 30, 32, 138–40
modes of existence 158–9
modus vivendi: completion of 181; and concerns 142–3, 157, 187, 287, 289; development of 29–31; and meta-reflexivity 208; and practices xvii–xviii
morality 138–9, 146
Morgan, Jamie 269–70
morphogenesis: definition 2, 38, 124n3, 215–16, 278n2; double 9, 10, 26, 46, 259–62, 269–74; intensification of 200, 216–21; and reflexivity 207–10; social xix, 216, 231, 236–7, 260; and structuration 104–5; and variety 291
Morphogenesis Unbound 292
morphogenetic approach: Critical Realism and 3, 284; as explanatory framework 1–3, 37–8, 80–1; future work 291–2; introduction of xiv, 37; origins of 39–40, 103, 123, 282, 286; and realist social ontology 89; temporality 114
morphogenetic 'breaks' 8, 39, 46, 260–1
morphogenetic cycles 8–11, 39, 44–5, 89, 105, 116–17

318 *Index*

morphogenetic sequences xvi, 4–8, 39, 105, 114–17
morphogenetic society xviii–xx, 236, 254
morphogenetic/morphostatic framework 46, 88–9, 260
morphostasis: changes within 10; conditions 26; definition 2, 38, 124n3, 215–16, 278n2; in early societies 189–93; and morphogenesis 193–5; and morphogenetic 'breaks' 46, 260–1
motivation 6–7, 56–7, 155–6, 178–9, 269
multinational corporations 241–2, 263–4
myth of cultural integration 12, 59–61, 63–5, 69–74

nation states 241, 248, 263
natural order 29–30, 141, 171
natural reality: causal powers and 170; nature, practice and social order 29–30, 32
negotiation 43
Negru, Ioana 269–70
non-conflationary theories 81, 86, 88–9
novelty 20, 218–19, 220, 240

objectification 288
objectivity/subjectivity 103–4, 151–2, 177, 288–9
ontology: as conceptual regulation 92–4; and explanatory method 89–90; first-person 158, 283; and methodology 78–81, 86, 88, 98–9, 128–9; pluralism 158; of social realism 87–8; stratified social 36–7, 83, 138, 237, 285–6; and subjectivity 158, 159, 163
Open Source Movement 271–2
opportunism 266–8, 274
opportunities xviii, 20, 241–2, 253, 291
opportunity costs 156, 179

parental culture 205–7
'parts-whole' relationship 117–18, 120–2
passive agents 176, 179, 252, 277
peer production 272
performative skill/competence 29, 141, 171
personal emergent properties (PEPs) 23, 138, 147, 166–7
personal identity 29–31, 72, 138, 141–5, 163, 181
personal powers 152–3, 154–5, 169, 172, 177, 193
personal reflexivity 200, 289
philosophy of social science 1–2, 36

physical well-being 29, 141
pluralism 20, 73, 196–7
politics 248–50
Popper, Karl 10, 158, 283, 290
Possibility of Naturalism (Bhaskar) 37, 38
power 17, 19, 125n12
power relations 62, 111–12
practical order 29–30, 141, 171
practical rationality 52, 54
practical social theory 78–81
Predicting the Behavior of the Educational System (Green, Ericson & Seidman) 50–7
pre-grouping 27
presentism 278
Prigogine, I. 223–4
primary agents 23–6, 32, 213n32, 270, 273–4, 278
primary principles 118–19, 126n19
'primitive mind' 64–5, 66–7
professionalisation 53–4
projects: and agents 162; and constraints 154, 173; definition 214n50; and internal conversation 208; and reflexivity 169–72, 230; and social factors 173–4, 179–80
promotive social movements 196–7
psychology 188, 212n16

qualifications 52, 54

Rational Choice Theory 156–7, 175, 187–8, 228
realism 1, 286
Realist Social Theory xv, 135, 162, 286
reality 77–9, 158–9
recursiveness 106–7, 112, 122
reductionism 96, 128–9
The Reflexive Imperative xviii, 277, 290
reflexive imperative 192, 199, 207–11, 250
reflexivity: and agents 155, 230; and Archer's work 304–5; and causal powers 161–3; as concept 165–7; history of 184–5, 189, 251; and identity 30, 141–6; mediatory role xvii, 157, 159, 172–7, 229; modalities of xviii, 185–9, 200, 290; reality of 289–90; and responses 176–82, 207–10; and social theory 165–9
regulation 93–5, 98, 263
relational contestation 41, 42
relational entities 236
relational power 131
relational properties 218, 244–5
relationality 228, 248, 284
reproduction 160–1, 201–2

Index 319

responses 176–7, 190, 193, 229
roles 132–3, 144–5
Rosa, Hartmut 247–8
routine action 106, 167–8
routinisation 110–11

'savage mind' 64–5, 66–7
Sawyer, Keith 44–5
scarcity in culture 266, 268
science education 242–3
Searle, John 11, 158–9
sectional struggles 197
segmented society 191
Seidman, Robert 50–7
self-awareness xvii, 151, 287–8
self-critique 208–9, 251
self-governance 230
self-governing/self-organising systems 221–2, 224–30, 231
selfhood 23–4, 29, 31–2, 138, 140–1
self-monitoring 158–9, 283
self-regulating properties 109
self-talk *see* internal conversation
self-warrant 147, 160, 283–4
self-worth 29, 141, 145, 171
semiotics and structuration 123–4
sequences of educational systems 51, 53
situated practices 40
situational logic: of action 17, 191–3, 239, 254; of competition 197–9, 241–2, 248–50, 263; of correction 17, 239; of elimination 239; of opportunity 202–5, 207–8, 239, 249, 264, 274; of protection 16, 201, 239
size of societal units 82–6
small-scale systems 57
social actors 23, 27–32
social agency 24–7
social backgrounds 188, 205–7
social change: generative mechanisms 235–6; structural context 226; structure culture and agency 231
social class 160–1
social cleavage 20, 197
social conditioning 152, 172–3
social constructionism 139–40, 286
social critique 209, 251
social disorder 18
social emergent properties xvii, 154
social enterprise initiatives 253
social forms 13, 162, 172, 216, 261–2
social identity 30–2, 138, 143–6
social institutions xix, 7, 41, 105–6, 108–9

social integration 62–3, 68, 219–21, 252–3, 263–4, 278
social interaction xvi, 52–3, 57, 260–1
social mal-integration 265
social morphogenesis 216, 231, 236–7, *260*
social movements 26–7, 210, 251, 273
social networking services 275–7
social order 29–30, 141, 171, 215–16, 222, 254
Social Origins of Educational Systems xiv–xv, 36, 44–5, 285
social positions 236
social powers 169
social practices 108–9, 171–2
social realism 86–8, 148
social reality 77–9, 83–4, 89–95, 133–4
social selves 22–3, 143–4
social structure 133–4, 215
social systems 109–10, 222, 231
social theory xiii–xv, 1–2, 82–3, 216
social uniformity 62
social websites 247
society xix–xx, 77–8, 151
Society's Being 22–3, 30, 32, 138–40, 169
socio-cultural integration 17–19, 67–8, 71–3
socio-cultural interaction xv, 12, 14, 16–19
sociological imperialism xvi, 286
sociology of culture 59, 63–4
specialisation 20–1
stability and change 63, 109–12
states and markets 248–9
strata 87, 88, 237
strategic action 7, 112–13
stratified nature of social reality 83–4
stratified social ontology 36–7, 83, 138, 237, 285–6
structural change: conditions 63; morphogenetic approach 7–8, 39
structural conditioning/contextualisation xvi, 6–7, 11, 115, 260–1
structural elaboration xvi, 88, 105, 111–14, 116–17, 133
structural emergent properties (SEPs) 23, 132–3, 153, 155
structural properties 106, 108–9, 115, 171–3
structuration 37, 103, 105, 112–14, 117–20, 123–4
structure 2, 38, 194, 236
Structure, Agency and the Internal Conversation xvii–xviii, 287, 289
structure and agency: and Archer's work xiv; and causal powers 2, 37–8; debates around 81–2, 85–6; distinction between

xvii, 4, 39, 88; interdependence between xvi, 27, 128, 152–7; and morphogenesis 200; problem of 37, 102–3, 138, 285–6, 288; social selves and 22–3, 143–4; temporality 4, 39, 113
structure and culture: interplay between xix–xx, 19, 190, 193–5, 237–40; and reflexivity 172, 200
structures: accommodating change 261–2; antecedent effects of 46; identification of 122–3; self-organisation and 226–7
'study of wo/man' 78, 79
subjective ontology *see* first-person ontologies
subjectivity xvii, 157–8, 161, 163, 172–3, 181
subjectivity of agents 148, 155
subject/object distinction 148
symbiosis 220–1, 242
synchronic relations 3, 8, 9–10, 193–5
synchrony/diachrony 104, 112–14, 260
syncretism 15, 18
synergy 242–6
system contradictions 109
system integration 62–3, 263–5
systematisation 16, 18–19, 21
systemic mal-integration 265
systemic properties 85, 112
systems theory 221–3
systems vs the system 51–2

technology 243–4, 245–7, 254
temporality 104, 112–14, 122, 260
third sector 210, 251, 255, 273
third-person sociologies 147, 283
thoughts 158, 283–4
'Three-Stage Model' 177
time xvi, xix, 104–5; *see also* temporality

traditional societies 64–5, 70–1
traditionalism 67–9, 190, 194
transcendence 152
transformation 112, 114–17, 122, 131
transition 235
trust 269–70, 274
'Two-Stage Model' 175–6
typicality 147

ultimate concerns: and identity 23, 142–3, 191–3; *Modernity's Man* and 139; prioritising 30–1, 209, 289; and projects 169–70
ultimate constituents of social reality 93
unacknowledged conditions 155–6, 178
under-labouring 1, 37–8
unintended consequences 4–5, 103, 109
upwards conflation 79, 147

values xviii, 210, 252–3
variety 20–1, 71, 73, 199, 217–22, 251
vested interests: definition 49n36; professionalisation and 54; projects and 155–6; in reproduction or transformation 5, 9–10, 115, 133; variety and 199
virtual communities 272–3, 275
vocational training 242–3
voluntarism/determinism 30, 103–5, 108–9, 122, 143

Watkins, J.W.N. 93, 130
Weber, Max xviii, 79
Wikipedia 252
Wiley, Norbert 187

young people 203–10, 250–1

Zuni concepts of self 140–1